Sir George Cornewall Lewis

Letters of the Right Hon. Sir George Cornewall Lewis, Bart.

To Various Friends

Sir George Cornewall Lewis

Letters of the Right Hon. Sir George Cornewall Lewis, Bart.
To Various Friends

ISBN/EAN: 9783337031473

Printed in Europe, USA, Canada, Australia, Japan

Cover: Foto ©ninafisch / pixelio.de

More available books at **www.hansebooks.com**

LETTERS

OF

SIR GEORGE CORNEWALL LEWIS, BART.

LONDON: PRINTED BY
SPOTTISWOODE AND CO., NEW-STREET SQUARE
AND PARLIAMENT STREET

G C Lewis

LETTERS

OF

THE RIGHT HON.

SIR GEORGE CORNEWALL LEWIS, BART.

TO VARIOUS FRIENDS.

EDITED BY HIS BROTHER, THE

REV. SIR GILBERT FRANKLAND LEWIS, BART.

CANON OF WORCESTER.

LONDON:
LONGMANS, GREEN, AND CO.
1870.

PREFACE.

The Letters collected in this volume were written by Sir George Cornewall Lewis to some of the most intimate and valued of his friends. They form no series, nor are they devoted to any particular subject or class of subjects; they are merely unconnected private letters, written in various years without the slightest expectation of their being published.

It may then be enquired, why are they printed? Why are they not suffered to remain in that privacy for which no doubt they were intended? I would answer that three reasons have mainly contributed to their publication. The first, because they forcibly illustrate the character, the intellect and learning, and the wisdom of their remarkable writer. The second, because they contain many facts, and relate to many subjects in which the public cannot but take interest, and respecting which, I believe, they will be glad to know the opinions of the author. The third, because some of Sir George Lewis's friends—and especially two of them, to whom he was deeply attached and who were equally attached to him—were earnestly desirous that they should be printed.

Sir George Lewis's was no ordinary character: there was mixed with his clear intelligence and capacity for profound and distinct thought a peculiar singleness and simplicity with which such qualities are rarely found in union. A part of this simplicity was his entire freedom from vanity. Aware of his own superiority he could hardly fail to be, but on no occasion was he ever tempted to make a display of it, either in order to obtain praise or gain an advantage. Neither did he on any occasion take offence: he never felt animosity towards persons who misunderstood and disparaged him, nor dislike to those who treated him slightingly because in some common-place matters they were more efficient than himself. He was gentle and unassuming, calm, dispassionate, and just, and was consequently beloved in private and respected in public life. An anonymous writer has well described him as 'peculiarly devoid of fuss;' he might have gone further, and said that circumstances which almost invariably vex and excite other men disturbed him but little. A contested election, for example, neither made him angry nor anxious; a parliamentary attack scarcely annoyed him. When under disadvantageous conditions, one candidate against three, he contested the county of Hereford, I well remember his calmness, and power to cast from his thoughts all the petty vexations of his tedious work. One morning he corrected in the carriage the sheets of a book that he was carrying through the press; he then canvassed in a town for many hours. Afterwards, on our return home, before we had left the streets in which he had been thus occupied, fresh sheets were spread on the cushions, electioneering passed out of his mind, and he was again busy preparing for the printer. On another day, when a political attack had been made on him, no sooner had he resumed his journey homewards than he began conversing on indifferent subjects, so little had the proceedings of the day affected him. He has likewise told me that his rest was but seldom broken when there had been vehement struggles and hostile debates in the House of Commons—that he could sleep as well on the nights on which they occurred as he could on any other nights. Such was his equanimity on occasions when most other men would have been excited.

The love of letters was, in Sir George Lewis's mind, the dominant passion, and that for its own sake. It was this quality which rendered his commerce so delightful to his learned associates. Ever ready to plunge into discussions of grave questions, bringing to them stores of heaped-up knowledge, with a candid appreciation of opinions at variance with his own, no man was more sought after as a converser by the distinguished members of the literary republic. The stores of his knowledge were indeed wonderfully large. The fact that his intellect was powerful never offered to him in his early life, as it might have done to other young men, a temptation to be contented with its existing strength: his anxiety and assiduity to improve and to extend it were uninterrupted. Very few scholars have, I believe, permitted so small a portion of their time to remain unemployed—very few devoted so large a portion of it to careful study. To many among them, idleness is in itself a pleasure, whilst common conversation and amusement occupy a more or less large portion of their day. It was not so with Sir George Lewis: he was always employed, and for the most part with occupation of a severe kind. So earnest was his desire to elucidate, to remember, and to record, that from his youth he thought that to be doing nothing amounted to a crime. '*Read*,' he has often advised me, 'when you have plenty of time at command; *write* in the shorter spaces when your time is broken up: this is the way to employ yourself to the best advantage: you will forget what you read in fragments of time—what you write in them will not be lost.' And this was the practice that he followed. He also in his younger days provided against the waste of any fragments which circumstances might cause to be lost to him, by either learning by heart or repeating in these intervals. I think that I remember my father telling me that once in Italy, when travelling after dark with George, he repeated to him a great part of the third book of the Æneid; and I well recollect, when on one occasion I was waiting with him in the ante-room of a physician, he took a Horace or Virgil from his pocket, and gave it to me, that I might hear him say a portion of its contents by heart, and he had repeated a large number of lines before he was summoned to his interview.

With his mind and his memory thus carefully cultivated, his learning soon became varied and extensive. Before he was five-and-twenty years of age, being, as I have stated, an advanced classical scholar, Lewis frequently employed himself in writing critical papers relating to the history, the literature, and the philosophy of the ancients. He had read with a conveyancer and special pleader, and had been called to the bar.* At that age he also read and spoke French,

* He was called to the bar in 1831.

German, and Italian, and had gained a considerable acquaintance with the principal authors in each language. He had likewise made some progress in the study of Spanish and Anglo-Saxon. Nor was his attention engrossed by these studies to the exclusion of English literature, or of his interest in the current topics of the day. His practice, steadily adhered to, of losing no time, always enabled him to find hours which he could devote to them. Thus he became, as his valued friend Dean Milman has written, 'a man who not only might have aspired to the highest dignity in the State,' but a man 'who might also have done honour, as professor of Greek, to the most learned University in Europe.' This is an estimate of Sir George Lewis's learning and character set forth by a friend than whom no one was better capable of forming one. And if the worthy and learned Dean had added, that there were several other subjects, besides the Greek language and literature, in respect to which Sir George Lewis was well fitted to become a professor in an University, I believe that he need not have feared contradiction.

Sir George Lewis had indeed a peculiar fitness for such a sphere, and would, I feel sure, have held a high rank among professors, had he formed one of their body; for if his knowledge was varied, so was it accurate and clear, and he had besides a patience in and love of teaching which made it a sort of recreation to him. I remember his taking pleasure for many months in giving instruction regularly to a young scholar of promising abilities.

It is sufficient to refer to Sir George Lewis's published

works to prove the wide scope of his learning, together with his remarkable assiduity. They exhibit accuracy, research, and a terseness of reasoning which few writers have attained and employed. After a clear statement of his subject, an exhaustive treatment of it follows, in which all that is extraneous and superfluous is set aside, and whatever can be adduced is brought together for the development and establishment of his views.

It must not be supposed that even an approach to a complete portraiture of a writer can be gained from reading a single volume of his miscellaneous letters. The materials are in this and every similar instance too scant for the forming a detailed judgment of the author: but scant though they be, I think that the contents of this volume serve in some degree to illustrate Sir George Lewis's character, intellect, learning, and cast of mind, and it is in this view that I publish them, believing that they will be acceptable to many readers.

To turn to the second reason which induces me to publish these Letters. The respect was so high in which Sir George Lewis's opinions were held whilst he was living, that he was continually consulted by speakers, writers, and reasoners of all classes and of all parties. Scholars and politicians were alike glad to seek the benefit of his wisdom and to listen to his mature, dispassioned, and well-disciplined judgment. In the House of Commons he was no orator, and seldom took a share in party debates; but on other occasions he often spoke, labouring, with few references to persons, to give information on the subject which was before the House, striving to sweep away whatever was irrelevant to it, and to cause it to be better understood. And the members of the House had a peculiar confidence in his word and in his statements; partly through his quiet, veracious, honest manner of speaking; partly through his occasionally avowing his ignorance of a subject, as he now and then did, and could indeed well afford to do; and partly from the knowledge that he never spoke with any secondary object, for the sake of his own aggrandisement or promotion, or any other personal or selfish motive. It was known to all his friends, and to many members of the House of Commons likewise, that he preferred literary to political occupation, and cared nothing for office and not much for a seat in the House of Commons. He has several times told me, during the time that he was a Cabinet minister, that he should before long give up official and parliamentary life. He had, however, so unusual a fitness for it that it may well be doubted whether he would have been permitted to do so; and could he have been persuaded that the public required his services, I feel sure that he would have continued them, setting all personal considerations aside.

If the estimate of the weight and value of Sir George Lewis's opinions was high during life, it has certainly not diminished since his lamented death. The void which that death left is still recognised as wide. Many a time since it took place has it been said that confusions would have been avoided, difficulties been simplified, and events and decisions guided into better channels, had his calm and wise counsel been still permitted to prevail among us. Again and again, since his death, with an unusual frequency which does honour to his memory, has his authority been invoked—in

Parliament and out of Parliament, by politicians on both sides of the House, by scholars, philosophers, and critics. Such, then, being the respect in which his opinions have been and still are held, I venture to think that the Letters which I now publish, containing as they do a great variety of statements, commentary, views, and thought, will be cordially welcomed by the reading public.

A third reason why I have felt desirous to print these Letters is, because many friends of my brother who valued him, and whom he likewise valued, have strongly urged their publication. For the judgment of two of these friends especially (I say this, of course, without a thought of disparaging the judgment of the others), namely, that of the Right Hon. Sir Edmund Head (Sir George Lewis's companion at college, and throughout life his most intimate friend), and that of Mrs. Austin, with whose powerful, refined, and highly cultivated intellect the public has long been well acquainted, I have always felt deference. Qualified in every respect to decide what is suitable for publication, they urged that these letters deserved to be given to the world. Both these friends have, alas! within the short space of a few months from each other, been taken from the society which they enlivened and adorned, and in whose memory they will long and deservedly live. Their opinions, however, with respect to this publication, still weigh with me, as do also the opinions of others whom I likewise respect; and hence the third reason for which I consign this volume to the printer's hands.

I add a short introduction, which is necessary, with a few occasional explanations, to enable the reader to understand the circumstances in which Sir George Lewis was placed, as well as various allusions in his letters.

It remains for me to express to my brother's friends, and to my own whom I have consulted in this matter, my gratitude for the large share of kindness which they have shown me; and especially to Earl Stanhope, Mrs. Edward Villiers, Mr. Twisleton, Mr. and Mrs. Grote, Mr. Freeman, Mr. Hayward, Mr. Reeve, and other contributors, who have been so obliging as to allow letters addressed to them to be included in this collection, I beg to offer my sincere thanks.

GILBERT FRANKLAND LEWIS.

HARPTON COURT, RADNORSHIRE:
February, 1870.

LETTERS.

George Cornewall, the eldest son of Thomas Frankland Lewis, of Harpton Court, in Radnorshire, and Harriet, daughter of Sir George Cornewall, Bart., of Moccas Court, Herefordshire, the writer of the following letters, was born in London on April 21, 1806. His boyhood was spent chiefly in London and Radnorshire; his frame was strong, and, at this period of his life, his health was good, with this single exception, that he frequently suffered from severe headache. I can recollect only one point which marked a distinction between him and other boys—the eager pleasure which he had in reading. The 'Arabian Nights,' two translations of Portuguese romances, 'Amadis de Gaul,' and 'Palmerin of England,' were among the books that gave him especial entertainment, and were in continual requisition. The usual boyish lessons were done with facility; and, when he left home and took his place among the forty boys at the school of Monsieur Clement, at Chelsea (who contrived by some means to make his pupils talk French and to work at their school-business whether they liked it or not), he was found to be forward of his age, as well as inclined to be studious. In January 1819, at about twelve years of age, he was moved from this private school in Chelsea to Eton College, where, after being examined by his tutor, Mr. Hawtrey, he was at once placed in the Remove. The first letter that I print, written in the following year, is chiefly descriptive of a sad calamity which occurred in the school, but is likewise indicative of the writer's feelings, and the subjects in which he took an interest :—

Eton : Sunday (1820).

Dear Mamma,—Since I wrote to you last a poor fellow of the name of Angerstein has been drowned here. He took a skiff after twelve and sculled himself up as far as Boveney, where there is a most furious stream, but not deep; unluckily, he dropped one of the sculls, and, in reaching over to get it, the boat, which was a very light one, toppled over, and he fell in. He rose three times and cried out, 'Help! help! Make haste!' When he sank for the third and last time, there were some fellows in a boat not more than twenty yards off, but they could not save him. His boat drifted to the land directly, but, unluckily, the other scull fell out, so that it prevented a fellow who was standing on the bank from going to his help; otherwise he might perhaps have been saved. The moment he was drowned some fellows ran down with all their might, and gave the alarm, and in a very short time the whole river near the place where he fell in was filled with punts and people dragging all around. Keate and all the masters, and I should think very near the whole school, were there. He fell in about one o'clock. However, although they went on dragging the whole of that and the next day, they were unsuccessful; but, about eight o'clock in the morning of

Wednesday, they dragged out his body about a quarter of a mile down the river, in a deep hole of dead water close to the bank. The hooks caught round his leg below the knee. When he was first brought out, his face was quite red, so that it is supposed that from having pulled up against a strong stream and being very hot, being suddenly plunged in very cold water drove all the blood into his head and caused an apoplexy; so that if they could have dragged his body out sooner it would have been of no avail. He was then immediately brought on a hurdle to his tutor's house, where, I believe, his body now is, but he is not to be buried here. It is a horrid thing, and has completely stopped the boats for this half, which Keate could not have done with all his slang. I do not believe that a single Eton fellow has been out on the water since.

I am very glad the holidays are so near, for this has been the most stupid time I ever passed: the only thing that it is possible to do is to play at fives, but that is entirely prevented by the rain—there are hardly ever two hours together but what some falls. The fellow's name, who was nearly drowned by the boat being upset when he was sailing, is Hylton. I know nothing more about him as he boards at the other end of college. My cousin Fitzharris had a most dreadful battle the other day with Buccleugh; I do not believe that either of them were the worse for it, as the only claret that was spilled was by one of them slipping and falling on his nose, which made it bleed. Our subject last week for verses was *Avarice*, which, of all subjects, is the worst. Yonge does not think proper to ascend from tolerable to good, but makes a grand bathos, and goes from middling to horribly bad. It is a miserable, narrow, cramped, and confined subject; it admits of no poetical idea, and the verses are consequently as niggardly as the subject. I have not been looked over a single exercise in school for more than a fortnight, and since I have been read over by Knapp, he has only looked [over] one copy of lyrics and a theme of mine, so that I have no chance of being sent up this time. Pray read this letter to Gilbert, for I have nothing to tell him which I have not said in this letter, and it is not the slightest use to copy this out for his inspection. I have read 'King Lear' and 'Hamlet,' and have begun 'As you Like it.' 'King Lear' is a most wonderful thing, it leaves such a striking remembrance on one's mind. The fool and the king are such a good contrast; the scene on the heath is a most surprising effort of genius. 'Hamlet' is not so striking; I must own that altogether I was rather disappointed with it, the plot flags so much after the two first acts; but there are some beautiful passages in it. However, one does not look back to it with so much wonder and admiration as the other. I shall most likely go to town in a post-chaise, and, if the roads are tolerable, shall very likely be in time for breakfast.

I remain, dear mamma, your affectionate son,

G. C. Lewis.

Sir George Lewis wrote Latin verses when he was at Eton not only with great facility, but with elegance and correctness. Many copies that he showed up in school are collected in a MSS. book, which is in the Library at Harpton; and should any lover of Latin verse desire to continue the volumes of the 'Musæ Etonenses,' he will find a number among them that are well worthy of being included in his collection. He was sent up for good, as the Eton phrase is, many times for verses, and for play. A letter written by his tutor, Mr. Hawtrey, to George Lewis's father at the time of his leaving Eton, shows that his love for classical literature was already felt, and the foundation of the scholarship laid which was afterwards so laboriously and successfully built upon:—

The Rev. Edward Craven Hawtrey to T. F. Lewis, Esq.

Eton College: Dec. 10, 1823.

My dear Sir,—I have great pleasure in assuring you that your son has left Eton with great credit to himself as a scholar, and that in all other respects he stands deservedly high in the good opinion of all who know him.

The distinction of being twice sent up for play in three weeks is not only unusual under any circumstances, but has been obtained by him at a time when there was no want of boys of talent in the sixth form, and the difficulty has been rather which to reject than which to choose.

In Latin he has certainly read much more than most boys of talent have done at his age; in Greek, I think, as much. And his taste and habit of observation in both are such as give every reason to expect that his success at Oxford will be as gratifying as it has been at Eton.

His good sense and right feeling appear to others, as well as myself, to have corrected those defects in manner which were the only impediments to his progress. His success during the last six months is a convincing proof that this has been the case.

I have only to add, that I have parted with him

with very sincere regret, and shall ever feel the warmest interest in his welfare.

I am, my dear sir, your most obedient and faithful servant,

E. C. HAWTREY.

The friendship between Dr. Hawtrey and the pupil in whom he took 'the warmest interest' continued during the remainder of their lives.

Soon after his leaving Eton, Sir George Lewis travelled for a few months in Switzerland and the north of Italy; he writes thus to his father from Lausanne:—

Lausanne: Sept. 13 (1824).

My dear Father,—We have now been staying some time at a country house half-way between Lausanne and the lake, with a very steep hill to climb every day to go up to the town, which of course is the regular walk. Friday last was the great fast and holiday of the Swiss, both Catholic and Protestant, and everything was shut up as close as Edinburgh on a Sunday: the three following days are celebrated by a fair, in which there is nothing pretty to buy—nothing but large tubs, gingerbread, and thin, bad silk handkerchiefs. Lausanne is a dirty, steep, irregular town, famous for nothing—one can hardly spin out a day of real sight-seeing; for now that we have been in the German part of Switzerland, we despise any common lions: 'La gloire m'est fade,' as Buonaparte said; we must have something super-excellent in that line. I went the other day with Mr. Fazakerley to see the public library here; there is nothing worth seeing in it, except the Duchess of Devonshire's 'Virgil,' Annibal Caro's translation of the 'Æneid' only, illustrated with copperplate engravings from drawings by modern artists of the places mentioned in the poem; it begins with a view of Carthage from the sea.

* * * * * *

There is an English church both at Geneva and Lausanne, and a regular clergyman who is paid by subscription. The service here is read in a Roman Catholic church, and the altar, and candlesticks, and images, and pictures, are separated by a low curtain. What a good example for the Irish—I think that you had better mention it to Sir Abraham Bradley King. The Catholics are earlier risers than we are, and they have their prayers in the morning, and leave clear room for us at half-past eleven. 'Galignani' gave the other day an article out of the 'Courier' about your last report on the leather and paper [duties] and quit rents.*

The censure has been re-established in France, and the newspapers all bear evident marks of it: sometimes whole columns and pages are left blank. I have been reading lately a very well written book by a Mr. Cramer, who was a tutor at Christ Church, on 'Hannibal's Passage over the Alps;' it proves beyond a shadow of a doubt a long-contested point—it is a book well worth having. 'Galignani' informs us that there is a new Quarterly Review, and somebody said there was a new Edinburgh, but I know nothing about them whether they are amusing or not. This is not at all a bad place for books, particularly old ones. There are a number of old classics printed at Basle; there is a very good library at Berne, with a number of manuscripts and old books, and a museum of stuffed birds and animals. Mr. Vaughan came here the other

* Mr. Frankland Lewis was on a Commission of Inquiry into the collection and management of the revenue in Ireland.

day and went on to Geneva, where he spent Saturday, and went back to Berne this morning. Mr. and Mrs. Henley Eden came back from Geneva on Saturday, having staid a day at Chamounix—raining the whole time. Like us, they never saw Mont Blanc. There is a steamboat of ten-horse power that performs its journey from here to Geneva, thirty-six miles in six hours, set up by a Mr. Church, an American; the engineer used to work in the Liverpool packets. The Geneva people have just launched an opposition boat of greater power; the same Mr. Church has just set up one in the lake of Constance. We go to-morrow to Vevey and see the Castle of Chillon, and if it is fine I shall go on with Mr. Fox to the Great St. Bernard, and make a second attempt at seeing Mont Blanc. * *

Your affectionate son,

G. C. Lewis.

Soon after the last letter was written, in the Michaelmas term in 1824, Sir George Lewis commenced his residence at Christ Church, and his wish was first to obtain the highest university honours within his reach, and afterwards to follow the law as a profession. With these views he read with his usual assiduity, liking thoroughly the work in which he was engaged. A first class in classics, taken in 1828, was the earliest reward of his labours; he was confident of gaining also a first class in mathematics; but in this hope was disappointed—his name appeared only in the second class. No lack of will, no lack of intellect interfered; but an unhappy failure of health. One morning when he awoke his pillow was stained with blood; a vessel in his lungs was ruptured; care and rest were prescribed as necessary. But as the bleeding from the lungs continued, by the advice of his physician he lived for a year on a vegetable diet; and spent winters in the south of France and in Italy. We find from the following letter of Dr. Smith, then Dean, that he was elected a student of Christ Church in 1828:—

Christ Church: June 18, 1828.

Dear Sir,—I am happy to have it in my power to express my approbation of your diligence and good conduct during your residence at Christ Church, and the sense I entertain of the distinction you have obtained in the university, by nominating you to a studentship.

It will be necessary that you should come to Oxford on Tuesday or Wednesday next, as I shall propose you for election to the chapter on the 25th or 26th, and you will be admitted on the day following.

I am, dear sir, very faithfully yours,

S. Smith.

As soon as Sir George Lewis had honourably finished his university career, he commenced the study of law, with a view, if his health should permit, to practise at the Common Law bar. He entered at the Middle Temple in June 1828, and was called to the bar in November 1831.

The following letter, dated at York, was, I believe, written in the summer of 1831, when he was travelling the Northern Circuit as marshal to Baron Vaughan:—

York: July 14.

My dear Father,—We have got through three of the public dinners of the judges; that of yesterday was given to a select party of forty-five barristers; the remaining forty-five dine to-day. People are very venisonivorous, as I have experienced by carving a haunch of venison one day and a neck another.

There are about 120 causes on the cause-list at this place, which is considered a small number. Pollock has the most business here; it is said that he sometimes makes 1,000*l.* at York alone. John Williams is the second fiddle, and he does his business extremely well. He is a better speaker than Pollock, though he is not, I suppose, so good a lawyer. My brother marshal informs me that the marshal's fees sometimes amount to more than 200*l.* on this circuit; this time, however, they will not be so much. All the building part of the Minster is completed; the inside woodwork alone remains, which has been done very cheaply by some foreign workmen who came over to carve wood for the interior of Buckingham House, and were dismissed when the works were stopped.

I rejoice that ministers succeeded on the wine duties, and Sir Abraham Bradley King.

Your affectionate son,

GEO. C. LEWIS.

Sir George Lewis decided on joining the Oxford Circuit, and on December 19 we find him attending the Worcester Quarter Sessions. His letter is addressed to Mr. Head,* then Fellow of Merton College, whose acquaintance he made at Oxford, and who, as will be seen from subsequent letters, continued until the time of his death to be one of his most intimate and highly valued friends.

* The Right Honourable Sir Edmund Walker Head, a Poor Law Commissioner, and Governor of New Brunswick and afterwards of Canada, died January 1867.

17, Henrietta Street: Dec. 19 [probably 1831*].

My dear Head,—I am sorry that I did not at once send you my copy of 'Buttman,' as it would have saved you much trouble; but I have carefully looked over your article, and found nothing to correct except clerical errors. There are, however, several points on which I still entertain considerable doubt; so much so, that if you think that you are not likely to write an article† in the spring number, I would ask you to keep it back for a time, that I might have an opportunity of looking into some of the points with you; for to discuss it on paper would be endless.

* * * *

I am going out of London for a short distance on Saturday, the 24th; on the following Monday I shall be at Worcester for the sessions; and shall probably pass through Oxford on my return to London about the 7th or 8th. It would be time then to send your article to the press, if there was no delay, as Hare writes me word that he has matter for 160 pages at Cambridge, which is the reason why I have not sent your article to him. Till I hear from you, I will do nothing; but if a letter does not arrive by the 24th, I will leave the parcel under sailing orders, so that it may be despatched whenever I write. Direct to *me* if the letter will not be in London by the 24th; if it will, you may enclose to my father.

Ever yours truly,

GEO. C. LEWIS.

* From many of Sir George Lewis's letters the date of the year is omitted. I supply it as well as I am able.—EDITOR.

† I believe that an article for the *Philological Museum* is alluded to.—EDITOR.

The laborious pursuit of the law proved, however, more than his health would bear; circumstances did not compel him to continue to struggle for it, so, reluctantly, he abandoned it. Literature, more especially classical literature, and subjects connected with politics, continually occupied his mind. His contributions to various periodicals were frequent, especially to the 'Classical Museum,' the 'Museum Criticum,' and 'Black and Young's Foreign Quarterly Review.'

The next letters that we print were written on one of his journeys, taken to the south of France, that he might avoid the inclemency of an English winter.

Paris: Oct. 9, 1832.

My dear Father,—We were not sorry to arrive at the fourth story of the Canterbury Hotel, although we came very well from Calais, the roads being positively good till within a few posts of Paris when the pavement begins, and the horses being passably quick. The journey to Lyons looks very appalling in prospect, I do not know what it will be in reality; sixty-two posts, at the rate of nine or ten posts a day, is something fearful. The Master of the Rolls* called on my mother to-day, who has just come from that part of the world; he gives a good account of the steamboats, so that we shall, if possible, embark at Châlons, which will save eight posts before Lyons. We dined yesterday at Lord Granville's; there were no English people at dinner, except the persons belonging to the embassy and Leach. Several persons came afterwards, among others Lord Rivers, who is just set out on a tour somewhere; and Talleyrand, who was to move towards London to-day.

* Sir John Leach.

I saw Senior to-day, who is come here for about a fortnight partly on a speculation about French charities. He showed me a long and very able letter he has written to Brougham (privately) about the results of their investigations. Brougham, it seems, wishes to bring forward some measure on the subject. Senior's principal suggestion is to take away the controlling power of the magistracy, and to vest it, together with the duty of revising and auditing the accounts, in paid local authorities, who might also be employed for other purposes. Everything, I think, now shows that something is wanted in the rural districts more efficient than the amateur services of the justices. He says that their returns show that over the greater part of England and Wales (particularly North Wales) things are in a much worse state than he imagined; and you know that he did not think very highly of the condition of the labouring poor.

Soult was yesterday declared president of the Council, and overtures have been made to Dupin to join him, who, I hear, will probably refuse. Dupin has a strong party in the Chambers, and will probably hold out in order to force the King to make him prime minister and give him carte blanche as to his cabinet; so that he will come in under nearly the same circumstances as our Ministry. By the way, when you go to London do not omit to read the last article in 'Blackwood's Magazine' for September. It is far the best thing on the present state of parties and the state of the Tories which I have seen. It is almost worth sending for into the country. There is nothing in the appearance of Paris which indicates distress to a wayfarer like myself. Possibly, a person accustomed to walk the streets might recognise more shops or houses to be let than usual; but the number is too small to be discernible by an inexperienced eye. Even in London one might make a sad story about eight or ten houses to be let in a street, and say that it is a proof of distress. I have no doubt that they have suffered severely, particularly by the loss of many English families, who, now that the charm is once broken, will probably never return. The prices of eatables, drinkables, and books (the latter especially) are certainly lower than in England; I cannot understand why. The number and size of looking-glasses and gold clocks, even in bedrooms, is very striking. The weather is getting cold, and I have been perishing by a smouldering wood fire; they were moving the orange trees from the Tuileries gardens, under cover, to-day. * * * You must, I fear, have had a great deal of trouble with my books; I would have made a catalogue myself if I had thought that it was worth while.

My mother is gone to-night to the opera to see the Cenerentola.

Your affectionate son,

G. C. L.

Thursday, Oct. 11.—I had written so far on Tuesday, not knowing that the ambassador's bag did not go till to-morrow. It did not surprise me to hear that there is no intention to appoint a commission to inquire into penal law; for, as I collect from Senior, the Home Office are very sulky at the activity of the Poor Law Commission, and see the subject taken out of their hands, at the same time that they are placed in such a situation that it will be difficult for them not to do something. They have set one stone rolling which they cannot stop, and probably will not commit the same error again. If you will give 5*l*. out of Knight's draft to Gilbert, he will pay with it so much of Britten's bill some time this winter. Dupin has refused to join Soult, and a regular doctrinaire ministry has been formed, which, I fear, cannot stand. The philosophers are more obnoxious in France than in England, if possible. They are very strict about passports now, and it will be necessary for both me and Frigo (his courier) to show ourselves to the police, in order to convince them that we are not Carlists. Frigo has had a tumour on his knee lanced, and I saw yesterday his doctor, who seemed a respectable man, a hospital physician. After speaking to him, it seemed to me that we had only two alternatives, either to get a new courier if we went to-morrow, or if we kept Frigo, to wait till Monday. As the doctor positively assured me that there would be no danger of his falling ill on the road if he went on that day, and as I could not see that he had any interest in deceiving me, we settled to postpone our departure till Monday, particularly as the weather is stormy and changeable, and we are assured it will improve. The swelling was certainly on or close to his knee, and the doctor called it *tumeur blanche*; whether that means what we call white swelling I know not, but conclude that if it was a question of amputation, he would not have talked so confidently of a speedy recovery. The streets and all the public places and barrières absolutely swarm with soldiers: I was told that there are more than 20,000 in Paris, and 60,000 within short notice. If all these warriors are to be depended on, we shall have no more grand weeks in a hurry. They are making some additions to the Tuileries, and workmen are employed in several other buildings; this is on account of the want of employment. Nevertheless, it is very striking to a person just come from a country where the poor laws have had their full swing, how rare an article a beggar is in Paris: now and then a Savoyard boy, and that is all. Even on the road, where the beggars beset the carriage at the post-houses, I have not seen any except cripples blind men, old women, and now and then young children; in short, only persons who are incapable of getting a livelihood by labour. Of such a thing as a sturdy beggar, or a tradesman out of place, asking for alms, I have not seen a trace. This difference *must* be owing to the poor laws, for there is certainly a greater demand for labour in England than in France. I went to-day to the Louvre and spent a couple of hours in the statue gallery. As in all other collections, there is a great deal of trash, and a number of Roman Emperors which have no value except as portraits; but there are many statues of the finest period of Greek art; they have, however, been, for the most part, sadly doctored, patched, and restored, and the partially corroded surface of the face rubbed down to a polish. The collection is well arranged and catalogued and in handsome rooms, which put our Elgin marble shed to the blush.

Your affectionate son,

G. C. L.

I do not write to Gilbert, as I conclude you will act as interpreter.

Cannes: Nov. 7, 1832.

My dear Father,—To-day, I am happy to say, is the last day of our captivity, and to-morrow we shall be released from this execrable fishing village, where meat appears to be almost unknown, and fish, sparrows, and roasted chestnuts are the staff of life. The fine weather has lasted, since we reached Avignon, into November. In the last three days we have strong cold winds, and have considerable difficulty in our frail tenement, where none of the doors and windows have an idea of shutting, and the floors are bare tiles, in contending with the enemy. Nice, I conclude, will furnish more hospitable quarters. There are orange trees here in the open ground, so I suppose it cannot freeze much in the winter. The country in this neighbourhood is by no means fertile; the hills are chiefly covered with low firs (pinasters); the valleys with vineyards mixed with olive trees; there is no grass or grain. Here and there two or three stunted half-starved cows are to be discovered: and, rari nantes in gurgite vasto, some sheep and goats. The sheep in this part of the world are as often, perhaps more often black than white. The chief products of this immediate neighbourhood are oil and dried figs: perfumes are also made at Grasses, a considerable town ten miles in the interior, to which I made an expedition in a cabriolet a couple of days ago; and lest Gilbert should think that the Hereford horses have a monopoly of *the slows*, let him be assured that I was three hours in going, and two and a half hours in returning, after having baited there nearly two hours. With the exception of getting rid of rain, we did not feel the effect of change of climate till we were south of Lyons. The sun indeed shone during most of the day, but there was a piercing cold wind, and after sunset it seemed to me quite as cold as average October weather in England. There is this difference between travelling in England and on the continent. In England the cold is on the road, the warmth in the inn; on the continent the warmth is on the road, the cold in the inn. Lyons is, as you know, the second town in France; it is placed in a striking situation, on a wedge of land that separates the Rhône and Saône just before their junction; both which rivers are crossed by numerous and tolerably handsome bridges on each side of the town. As the site of Lyons is thus limited by nature, the space has been economised, and the streets are for the most part wretchedly narrow. This has been an extraordinarily dry year, and neither the Saône nor the Rhône were navigable except by small barges. At Avignon we heard that the oldest inhabitant did not remember the Rhône so low as it has been this year; there had been no rain in that part of the country for three or four months, nor on the coast of the Mediterranean has there been any for seven or eight months. It has rained here last night and to-day a little, but not enough, as far as I can see, to lay the dust. The springs here are nearly all dry, and the bad water we get is brought from a distance of two miles. Avignon is a well-looking town, preserving some relics of its ancient grandeur which have been spared by the revolution. Like Conway, it is surrounded by its walls, which are in a tolerable state of preservation. The population now consists of 30,000 natives, a garrison of 4,000 soldiers, and 200 Polish emigrants who were sent there by the French Government. Every town and almost every village which we have come through swarms with soldiers. Lyons, of course, has its seven barracks well filled after the revolt of the workmen last winter. Aix likewise has its full share. Marseilles, being a large town, requires to be kept in order, and Toulon is a naval arsenal, and therefore requires a large military garrison. Even in this fishing station there are some soldiers posted; and while I am writing these words, I hear the voice of the drill-sergeant at his daily work ; so that if there is to be a war, France seems to be well provided with troops so far as numbers are concerned. Of the rest I know nothing. The tract of country from Châlons to Marseilles is very important, both on account of its productiveness and its communications by land and water : and the Romans seem to me to have done very wisely in establishing a chain of towns from Autun along the Saône and Rhône to the sea. There is the greatest facility in obtaining good stone, both for building and for road-making, in the whole of this district ; nevertheless the roads in many places are so bad, that even in this dry season they are only just passable. Nothing can more forcibly prove the viciousness of the French system than the state of the road from Lyons to Avignon, from Avignon to Aix, and from Aix to Marseilles, one of the most important lines for the purposes of trade in all France. Marseilles has nothing very remarkable except an oblong, perfectly landlocked port of considerable size. It is the least striking port I ever walked along, which, I suppose, arises from two reasons, one because there is no tide in the Mediterranean, the other because the extreme dryness parches up everything putrid. The weather at Marseilles was as warm as a fine summer day not of the hottest kind in England. Toulon is one of the places where the French convicts are employed in government works. There are now 4,000 of them in the arsenal. From what I could learn, their punishment is almost identical with our confinement in the hulks ; only the duration is longer, the greater part being sentenced for ten years, and many for life. They are not allowed any meat, which is very dear at Toulon, and for the first year they are constantly, day and night, chained two and two. I suspect that on the whole they are rather worse off than the convicts in the hulks. As soon as we are established at Nice we shall get rid of Frigo, who is more helpless and useless every day. My mother received to-day a letter from Aunt Hereford. Pray tell Gilbert I don't write to him as he would have to pay the postage of the letter from London.

Your affectionate son,

G. C. L.

Nice: Nov. 14, 1832.

My dear Head,—I received a few days ago your letter, and was glad to hear that my papers reached you in safety; not indeed that they incurred much risk. As Thirlwall is in distress for matter, I am glad I sent them, though a 'rudis indigestaque moles.' I trust to your fostering hand to warm the dead seeds into life. With respect to *thrall*, I suspect the custom of piercing slaves' ears, although mentioned both in Exodus and in Juvenal, would lead one on a false scent. From *thra* A.S., the same as the English *throe* and the Sc. *thrae*, signifying woe, pain, calamity, &c., thra-el is formed. El is as much the termination as in thyril from thyr. It is difficult to say in what relation thur and thra stand to one another: they *may* be distinct roots; or thra may have originally meant *pain* from *piercing*. This is, however, so uncertain, that it would be safer not to attempt to connect them unless you can get some further link. Query, the English throat and Latin terebro, which cannot come from tero. τόρνος in Greek (whence thro, in Latin turnus, I suppose, torno tourner, tourneur, turner, &c.) probably stands in the same relation to θορ or τορ, as drill to dur. I can make nothing of tur-ren, tur-st (in

Hajen's Glossary to Nib. Lied), thir-st, &c., which must, I suppose, belong to the same family. In Provençal *traou* is a hole, and *traoucar* is to make a hole. This would seem to show that there was a form tralla or trallus, or some such word (or else tral or dralle German), as the Provençal changes the e into ou (the Italian u), thus doutre from alter, aoubo from albus (aube du jour), aoutar, to raise, from altus, &c. Grimm's remarks on composition will make a good article, particularly if you add something of your own. There are not, I think, many English improper compounds; cutthroat, daredevil, makeshift, wagtail, skinflint, cutwater, breakwater, are instances. Also proper names, as Shakespeare, Drinkwater, Thirwall ('Marmion,' Canto i. xiii.) You had better give the whole passage in a note for me. In French they abound; see in the dictionary the various compounds with *garde*. Hôtel-Dieu, Palais Bourbon, Hôtel Meurice, &c., may also be regarded as compounds, and they are improper. As far as I can make out all the Celtic compounds are improper; at least, such seems to me the case when Welsh names of places are translated to me, but it is difficult to judge when one knows nothing of a language. It is important to remark that no modern Latin language has, as far as I am aware, formed a proper compound. If on examination you should find this to be true, it is a remarkable fact. Some morning, when you go to the Bodleian, you will find it worth your while to verify the following references: Archæologia, vol. v. p. 306; vol. ix. p. 332. With respect to French negatives there is a good deal in Raynouard's works, which I can show you when I return to England. It is remarkable that in the Provençal there are no double negatives, but they have dropt the *ne* and preserve only the *pas*. It would be a pity to make a separate paper about yea and yes, if it should spoil your general paper on the subject of affirmatives and negatives. Or in that you might confine yourself to the Latin languages, and bring in anything else by way of illustration. By so doing you would avoid meeting οὐ and μὴ in face. Could you not stir up some Oxford man to write a review, generally the easiest work?

My mother and I, after having passed a deplorable week at a wretched village, where we were forced to do quarantine 'in the worst inn's worst room,' food being scarce, the cold not contemptible, and the rooms so small and the wind so high that we could not always bear a fire, have now established ourselves in lodgings, where we are fixt for a month at least, and probably till the end of December. It is warm enough out of doors, but never warm enough for my satisfaction in the house. I am not surprised to hear of Johnson's blunders; for I strongly suspect he was the author of the translation of Niebuhr, which Talboys sent me, and of the 'ächte Enkelinnen' (the 'Eight Granddaughters').* He seems to have a fatality in the medical line, for I remember one of his translations was 'der Arzt,' the *artist*. It is lucky for Talboys that nobody has taken the trouble of comparing his translations with the original. 'Galignani' gave the other day, from the 'Courier,' a charge of a certain Baron Smith to the Dublin grand jury, in which I find this passage: —'Every legal claim is a right, and every right is a just one; for just is right.' I hope you are convinced by this exemplary argument, as the potato-headed jury doubtless were. I see advertised in the French

* I cannot recollect the title of the translation from the German in which this blunder was made.—EDITOR.

newspapers a pamphlet against the government with this motto, 'Indignatio' (Juvenal). Query, whether a reference to the dictionary would not have been equally effective. My studies for the last few days have been 'Vidocq's Memoirs,' a most entertaining, curious, and instructive book, at least to those interested about police and the ways of thieves. It is a fine commentary on the effect of promiscuous intercourse in prisons. The French system is much the same as ours, minus transportation and the penitentiary.

It surprises me to hear that agitation has made such progress at Oxford. I feel convinced, however, that as the Catholic question made way for reform, so reform will make way for the church. Another thing I am convinced of is, that the church has a thousand times more to fear from the dissenters than the infidels, those who have a *different* faith than those who have *no* faith. An infidel will not avow his disbelief, and the church gets the benefits of all the doubts; a dissenter feels himself a rival, and is proud to own himself as such. A dissenter says that he has got a better faith than yours, whereas an unbeliever looks on all with equal contempt. Consequently I do not expect much zeal on the part of the Radicals, who are chiefly like the French; they have (as a person said to me at Paris) *une irréligion complète.* But from the dissenters a loud, strong, and well-concerted opposition is to be expected. I shall be curious to see if they can bring in Lord Henley for Middlesex. If Villiers* is at Oxford, remember me to him; I will write to him *when* a little news accumulates.

Ever yours,

G. C. L.

* The Honourable Edward Villiers, brother to the Earl of Clarendon, died October, 1843.

Nice: Nov. 20, 1832.

My dear Gilbert,—I have not written to you before chiefly because I thought that you would prefer reading the letters written to my father to paying the value of a tithe pig for a private despatch. Now that your revenues are come in, I shall venture to address you in particular. Not indeed that I have anything particular to say, for it would be difficult to find any place less fertile in subjects than Nice. In comparison with it, Hereford is lively and active. Nice is a small town, containing about 13,000 inhabitants, situated in a sort of oblong basin, surrounded by hills which gradually pass into the Alps and become mountains. The suburb, or faubourg, where most of the best houses are, and where we live, is separated from the town by a wide bed of gravel, in the middle of which trickles a narrow stream of water, but which is subject to sudden and violent floods, when it becomes a large stream and covers the large space of shingle which in common times is bare. The consequence is, that the narrow valley down which this torrent runs, instead of having green meadows or trees at the bottom, is nothing but a bed of gravel. There is nothing remarkable in the town—no fine buildings, no handsome walks, no marks of affluence or attention to ornament. The shops are poor and bad except the confectioners', who shine in their department. There is no English society here now, as there appears to have been in some former years: my mother knows nobody except a sick Lady Elizabeth Lowther, who never goes out, and has lived many years in the south of France on account of her health. All this may give you a bad idea of Nice. On the other hand, the climate deserves all the good that has been said of it. Considering we are, as it were, at the very foot of the Alps, and that for some time several of the mountains in sight have been covered with snow, the perfect mildness and serenity of the weather is extraordinary. For the last ten days we have had the rainy season, and more rain fell during that time than I ever saw fall in an equal time in England; nevertheless the air during the whole time, although the sun never showed itself, was perfectly mild, without the least feeling of cold or dampness in the air. Vegetation appears never to be interrupted. We have peas at dinner almost every day, and fresh flowers and vegetables are now coming up in all the ill-cultivated gardens about the town. The oranges are now hanging on the trees in great abundance, some green, some half yellow. The orange is a small tree, and a very free bearer; in its present state it is the most beautiful fruit tree I ever saw. The fruit is picked in February for exportation. The olive tree, which grows wild in this neighbourhood, and with which all the hills are covered, is so like an evergreen oak that one might easily be mistaken for the other. Its colour, however, is rather darker, and it has no particular beauty, except that, as it does not lose its leaves in winter, it prevents this country, which it covers, from ever looking bare. There are no timber trees in this neighbourhood, no cattle, and no grain. Carts and wagons moreover exist, but by no means abound. The common people all speak a vile patois, neither French nor Italian, perfectly unintelligible to strangers. Nothing but one or two motives could induce any person to establish himself at Nice, viz. health or economy; and for those two purposes, as far as I see, it is admirable. It is now only November 20, but you may judge of the warmth when I tell you that hitherto we have dined with perfect comfort in a room without a fireplace, and that the flies torment a horse so much as to render slow riding disagreeable. In January it is of course colder, but in ordinary years, during the day, the thermometer is seldom under 50, and generally about 60. As to economy, I saw a house in which a mother with two or three daughters took a second floor, besides a kitchen below, the whole sufficient for a family, probably with a maidservant and cook, for 1,000 francs a year, *i.e.* 40*l*. This included furniture, plate, crockery-ware, linen, &c.

* * * *

I cannot say that I look forward with great pleasure to a journey in the dead of winter, as the inns are so fearfully cold; but my mother is anxious to leave this place, which she naturally finds very dull, and to see the lions of Italy. There seems some prospect of my being able to go by sea from Genoa to Civita Vecchia.

* * * *

Your affectionate brother,

G. C. L.

Not long after his return to England, Sir George Lewis was employed for the first time in public business. Questions relating to Poor Laws both in England and Ireland, in consequence of the defective state of the law, occupied general attention; and he was named to act upon a commission to inquire into the condition of the poorer Irish resident in England and Scotland. Thus employed he visited many of the largest English and Scotch towns.

I insert a letter from Sir T. Frankland Lewis, written to his son, Sir George Lewis, in 1834, because the next letter of Sir George Lewis, dated from Manchester, where he was pursuing his inquiry into the condition of the Irish resident there, refers to the principal subject which it contains.

T. Frankland Lewis, Esq. to George Lewis, Esq.

January, 1834.

My dear George,—You have often heard me talk of the Poor Law Committee, of which Sturges Bourne was the chairman, and know how anxious a part I took in all its proceedings. Nothing of importance passed which I was not acquainted with during the sitting of the committee. And when the bills were passing which resulted from our recommendations, though the committee sat no longer, I continued in constant communication with Sturges Bourne on the subject of their provisions, &c. If, therefore, there had been any such understanding as there has been imputed to us, I must have known it. Had there been such an understanding in the House it is absolutely impossible that I could have been ignorant of it. That the laws should only be partially put into operation which were to prevent the Irish from coming over to England, and fastening themselves on the Poor's Rate, was as far as possible from being the wish or understanding of the committee or the Parliament of that day. I may say that it was of all others the evil that they dreaded most, and strove most to contend against. It was particularly Sturges Bourne's object to establish the most effective means of preventing the evil, and I know that he thought the mode resorted to would be effectual though expensive.

* * * * * *

Judge-made law would fill many volumes. Magistrate-made law is generally provided for the occasion; in this instance Manchester will never shake off its effects.

Your affectionate father,

T. Frankland Lewis.

Manchester: Feb. 2, 1834.

My dear Father,—Gilbert left me yesterday for Hawarden, having gone in the morning with me to see the silk mill of a person who had imported raw Irish human beings from Connaught to a considerable extent. I was much obliged to him for his visit, as it was a very agreeable break to me.

What you say about Sturges Bourne's act is quite satisfactory; I had not indeed any notion that such an understanding had prevailed, or that so important a matter could have been left to a vague understanding; nor indeed if it had, do I conceive that any person was bound to acquiesce in it contrary to his judgment. The loss to this town in a *pecuniary* point of view is not very great; whether such an opulent and flourishing community as Manchester pays 10,000*l*. a year more or less in poor rates cannot be a matter of much import; but in a *moral* point of view I conceive that the practice has been most mischievous; in the first place in promoting laziness, fraud, dependence, and improvidence among the Irish labourers who are already here; and, secondly, in attracting from Ireland the most beggarly and worthless part of the population. The public charities, which have been lavished with the most indiscriminate profuseness, have assisted in producing the same effects.

What you say about the views of the Catholic priesthood is no doubt true of the Irish Catholics in Ireland; I question, however, whether it is true of the Irish Catholics in England. In the first place, most of the priests on this side of the water are English. Out of three priests at Birmingham, one was Irish, educated in Portugal. Out of eight (I think) at Liverpool, one only was Irish, educated at Maynooth; and I must say that he is a very respectable man, and gave very fair and candid evidence. Here out of about six priests there are two Irish Maynoothians; and though one whom I have seen is, in my opinion, an insincere man, yet I hear a very high character of him on all sides, and among persons quite above suspicion of interest or caprice. The priests have taken a very decided part against the Trades Unions, and all societies bound by secret oaths; and I believe that their influence has in many instances had great effect. They dissolved the union of the Irish bricklayers' labourers in Manchester this autumn; and it has never been formed again. Altogether, in the contests between the masters and workmen (which are the conservative and destructive parties of these manufacturing districts), they have sided with the former, and that in the most open and uncompromising manner. The Irish occupy so low a place in the scale of society in the large English towns, that it is difficult to imagine that the most enthusiastic or far-sighted among them could ever entertain the project of supplanting the English on their own soil. If they are like the Jews a *separate*, they are also like the Jews a *rejected* caste; they are emphatically in this country what Tacitus says of the Jews among the Romans, 'despectissima pars servientium,' the most degraded of the working population. The Irish do not associate with the English, not because they dislike the English, but because the English dislike them. They are glad enough to perform their drunken orgies with any Englishmen who will descend to their level, and herd with them. All the reluctance is on *our*, not *their* part. The very children in the mills complain of being put to work next to an Irish child; and in the Sunday-schools the English move from them. All this has a tendency to lower the Irish in their own estimation *as Irish*, to make them wish to wear off the marks of distinction, and to adopt the habits of persons by whose opinion they are approved or condemned. I went to-day to several houses and cellars in Little Ireland, which is about the worst sink of Irishism in Manchester, and several persons said that such a boy did not like to go to chapel, and the other child was not sent to the Sunday-school, for want of shoes and stockings. No such motive would occur in Ireland: as no child would have shoes and stockings, the want of them would not be felt a disgrace. I have no doubt that the priests strive, and strive successfully, to keep them within the fold of the true church; but I am inclined to think that the accurate separation between the lower Irish and English in Birmingham, Liverpool, and Manchester is owing rather to an exclusion kept up *against* them than *by* them; and that if they were more frequently to rise in the world, and to become assimilated in habits of order, and cleanliness, and decency to the English, they would not be more distinguishable from them than the English Catholics are now. The Irish keep up all their national, and provincial, and religious feuds; the Ulster men turn out against the Connaught men, as they might in Dublin. There was a great battle here last autumn between County Leitrim and County Roscommon. Not long ago one Irishman, who quarrelled with a countryman of his own, drinking in a pot-house, about the *real presence*, finished the dispute by stabbing him to the heart with a knife which lay on the table. But I do not find that they ever array themselves as a body against the English, unless they consider the English as Orangemen. They do not seem to have any notion of viewing the

English as a common enemy, who is to be extirpated or undermined; on the contrary, I am inclined to think that, on this side of the water, the English are generally the aggressors, and that the Irish, whenever their acts are organised or premeditated, usually act on the defensive. Now and then, it is true, they issue from the drinking houses, mad with gin, and scour the streets; but these are outrages which a good police and a law armed with an effective sanction (now altogether wanting) would suppress; and even if, as at present, not suppressed they could not ultimately lead to very serious consequences. The English labourer, on the contrary, views the Irish with hate and jealousy, as the means of lowering his wages; and though it is my firm belief that such has not been the effect of the Irish immigration (except in some peculiar and narrow departments of industry), yet it is very natural that the natives should think so. A few years ago a battle took place at the entrance of Chester between the natives and a band of Irish reapers, in which the latter were (I understand) fairly beaten and driven back.

I have long been aware that my picture would be very imperfect if not only London but also Bristol is omitted. I thought it, however, prudent not to propose too much at first, lest people should be alarmed; I shall see how things turn up in Ireland, and shall watch my opportunity, and, unless something unforeseen happens, I expect to despatch Bristol on my return. If after that enough time remains, I can complete my inquiry in London. It is possible that I may go to Leeds, which is forty miles from this place; I hear contradictory reports about the number of Irish there. You may direct to Manchester till you hear from me again.

I send you puff the second in the 'Manchester Guardian,' and an admirable letter written by Sedgwick, in order that you may see what is meant by *sledge-hammering* a man. Pray return it to me. The 'Quarterly Review' is abusing the government for its *remissness* in taking up the Poor Law question. Oh the matchless impudence of the sentimental, humanitarian, anti-Malthusian, anti-philosopher, charity-depending organ! There is a long, stupid article in the 'Edinburgh Review' about secondary punishments. It by no means supersedes my pamphlet. There is also a dull attack on Whewell's 'Bridgwater Treatise.' Macaulay writes about Lord Chatham, and McCulloch about the Corn Laws.

Your affectionate son,
G. C. L.

Glasgow: July 23, 1834.

My dear Head,—Villiers sent me a few days ago some Homeric verses on the Duke of Wellington's election. They are rather well done; some of the hits are very good, as, στῆσε δ' ἄγων ὅθι Πηλείδεω τάξαντο φάλαγγες, and φοξὸς ἔην κεφαλήν from the description of Thersites. Gaisford's criticism on them probably was, if I may surmise at this distance, that ἀεὶ in the first page ought to be αἰεί. I bought at Manchester Baden Powell's 'History of Philosophy,' in order to pass my evening hours, and, what is more, I have read it. It was scarcely fair on his unlearned readers for him to quote Diogenes Laërtius in the original *Latin*, with a reference in the note which might even puzzle a learned reader (p. 21). He is not, however, always equally fortunate in his quotations of Latin authors; thus, in p. 58, he cites from Pliny of Hipparchus, 'Ausus rem etiam Deo improbam, annumerare posteris stellas,' which, I suppose, means, 'having attempted a task difficult even for a god to accomplish, viz. to count the stars for posterity.' B. Powell translates it thus, 'who ventured also to do a thing wrong in the sight of the Deity, to enumerate the stars to posterity.' Another equally felicitous translation of Bacon's famous aphorism, 'Antiquitas sæculi juventus mundi,' occurs in p. 91; that is, he says, 'We are more *ancient* than those who went before us,' which is exactly what we are not. Reckoning the life of the world as we should reckon the life of an individual, we are *older* than those who went before us, but we are evidently not more *ancient*. Antiquity is counted backwards, *age* is counted forwards. For example, take any individual, as Socrates; the *older* he becomes, and the greater is his *age*, the less is the *antiquity*. If you wish to have a clear and concise definition of logic, I refer you to p. 86, where, speaking of the Aristotelian philosophy, he mentions 'the systematic forms which it gave to dialectical logic or the theory of conclusiveness.' He does not, however, seem to have an equally clear idea of other parts of Aristotle's writings, even those on physical subjects; for the Meteorologies are transmuted into 'A Book on Meteors' (p. 175).

I see no advertisement of the 'Philological Museum,' and therefore conclude that Thirlwall's attempts to get money from the delegates have failed.

This is now about the tenth day since I came to Glasgow. I may go across to Edinburgh for a few days; I shall then return, and sweep the western coast by Paisley, Greenock, and Ayrshire to Portpatrick, and so to Ireland. Will you send the enclosed paper to Talboys?*

Ever yours truly,

G. C. LEWIS.

* A bookseller at Oxford.

In the summer of 1834 Sir George Lewis received a second appointment. Differences had occurred in the House of Commons and in the Cabinet relative to changes which many members desired to effect in the Established Church in Ireland; and, with a view to get over them, Lord Althorp announced in June that the King had issued a commission to inquire into the state of the Church property and Church affairs generally in Ireland. The names of the persons of whom it consisted were the Chancellor, the Home Secretary, the Secretary for Ireland, Thomas Doyley, T. N. Lister, John Wrottesley, G. B. Lennard, E. C. Tufnell, Daniel Maule, George Cornewall Lewis, W. H. Curran, W. T. Hamilton, Acheson Lyle, and Wm. Newport.

Sir George Lewis next writes from Dublin, where he was engaged with the inquiries which he had undertaken.

He subsequently published an 'Essay on the Irish Church,' which he appended to his account of 'Disturbances in Ireland.'

Dublin: August 6, 1834.

My dear Father,—I received last night an invitation from Sir (Wm.) Gosset to dine with him to-day, which, I suppose, was in consequence of a letter from you; I had intended to call on him to-day at the Castle. My commissioners were very tame when I came to an explanation with them; not one of them hazarded a remark. To-day I intend to read Le Marchant's letter to them, which I have just received, and then I shall leave them to their meditations.

Yesterday I saw Curran, who seems to have been very active, and to have done as much as could have been expected in so short a time and with so laborious a task. All the blank returns have been sent out, and the commissioners will probably begin their work at the end of September *at the earliest.* I have therefore nearly two months clear for the Poor inquiry; and, although it may be troublesome, I am, on the whole, glad that I have not withdrawn my neck from the yoke, which I might easily have done. For, in the first place, these people would have abused me, and have attributed the ill results of their own inefficiency to the desertion of their assistant commissioners; and, secondly, there is such a want of any person who can reckon up twenty without a fault that I hope to be serviceable to them, however thankless the service may be. My present notion is to take the Terry Alt country, and to direct my inquiry particularly to the connection of poverty, vagrancy, and the pressing want of land, with crime and outrage. You are aware that the Terry Alt were the people who dug up meadow land at night, in order to get it for potatoes. From what I can learn of the run [not clearly legible in original] of the evidence as hitherto collected, the evils of the present system of maintaining the destitute poor in Ireland (viz. vagrancy, mendicancy, intimidation, and theft) appear so great, that a well organised workhouse system would be far preferable. The difficulty is, under the circumstances of the country, to *work* any system well, however good the *law* may be. When More O'Ferrall came to Dublin, and saw how things were going on at the Commission, and how utterly worthless were the reports of the assistant commissioners, he moved that they should consider everything hitherto done as nothing, that the whole business should be entrusted to the Secretary, that the Board should adjourn *sine die*, only to be called together by the Secretary if he wished for instructions; that fresh instructions should be prepared, and everything be begun afresh. The paid commissioners in Dublin and the busybodies of course would not agree to this, but I think virtually this is the present state of things. The Board meets *pro formâ*; no business of importance is transacted by it; Whately has long since ceased to attend or to take any cognizance of the business; the Secretary has prepared a long detailed string of queries, which, in fact, are new instructions; and the assistant commissioners are going to start with them on a new plan of inquiry. The reports received are, moreover, as far as I can learn, mere waste paper. Of course you will not mention any of this private history, as it is not fitted for the world at large.

I think that you were right in not giving yourself the trouble of going to London before you knew whether the palpable and prominent objections could be removed. I can form no guess what are the wishes or intentions of the Government, and how far they are prepared to concede.

My present intention is to leave Dublin next Monday.

Your affectionate son,

G. C. LEWIS.

Dublin: October 13, 1834.

My dear Father,—I returned yesterday morning by the mail from Clonmel, having been to Carrick-on-Suir for one night and examined into the poverty of that most miserable and decaying place. To-day I went to the Church Commission, and found the commissioners preparing to start, in general well pleased with their instructions and making no difficulties. One benefice near Dublin was examined on Saturday containing six parishes; there were only fifteen Protestants in it. Hitherto the number of Protestants has turned out to be very small, smaller than was anticipated.

I am glad to hear that you have had some sport in overseers throwing up, &c.; it would have been very dull if everything had gone off smoothly.

* * * *

The district allotted to me to examine is the dioceses of New Ross, Waterford, Lismore, and Cork. I shall not, however, start for three weeks at the earliest, and it is possible by that time that circumstances may have arisen which will make some fresh arrangement necessary. Our great object has been to make the commissioners as much automatons as possible, to leave nothing to discretion, as we have some men who want to show up the Protestants and others who want to show up the Catholics. My notion is that we shall make such a damning case against the Church as must in the end produce an entire remodelling of its ministers and revenues. In this case, as in that of the Poor Law Commission, a measure intended as a temporary stop-gap will produce permanent effects. I do not see how our report can be delayed beyond February at the latest.

* * * *

Your affectionate son,

G. C. LEWIS.

The next letter is written to Mrs. Austin, whose powerful intellect, accurate judgment, and varied knowledge made her society attractive to many of the wisest of her contemporaries. George Lewis enjoyed her friendship, and became her correspondent early in his life. Most of his letters to her have unfortunately been destroyed, but Mrs. Austin has been obliging enough to give me some which she has preserved, and which will, I think, be found interesting.*

No date, but probably written in the autumn of 1834.

Dear Mrs. Austin,—You do me too much honour in supposing that I wrote an article in the 'Quarterly Review' (query, on fox-hunting or horse-racing) in which you are mentioned with praise. I am altogether innocent or guilty, as the case may be, never having written a word in that review. The only praise I have at present to bestow on you is for your translation of Sismondi, the chief part of which I read with great pleasure, as far as the *style* is concerned; I only wish that our original histories were always written in as good English. In proof of my diligence, I send you some errata, which you may burn or use, at your pleasure. Whenever you feel inclined to attack Raumer, I have found you a bookseller, but as you have only just finished Sismondi's *superfétation*, I shall say nothing for the present on the subject. In the summer I made a journey for the Poor Inquiry Commission in Munster through the counties of Tipperary, Limerick, and Kerry. Among other places I went to Kenmare, which I saw under unfavourable circumstances, on account of bad weather; but I think it fortunate that you did not go there, as the climate is moist, and this summer was remarkably cold and cloudy in that part of Ireland. For the last six months I have been in Dublin, demolishing the Church. Our

* A short time after these words were written, Mrs. Austin's death occurred, and an interesting notice of her appeared in the *Times* of Monday, August 12, 1867, in which her warmth of heart, her intellectual power and desire to maintain high principles of action are very justly recorded.

proper style and title is the Public *Instruction* Commission, which the friends of the Church in this country changed into Public *Destruction* Commission. It is a mere statistical inquiry, and proceeds very satisfactorily, but, as you say, proves only what everybody knows. Nevertheless it is something to establish disagreeable truths beyond the power of contradiction. Whately is supposed to have said that the clergy had been long revelling in the Book of *Job*, but that now they were forced to take a spell in the Book of *Numbers*.

I can only return Mr. Austin's and your kind salutations, for I fear that there is no chance of my crossing the Channel in the year 1834. At any time that you have leisure to write, I should be happy to receive even a few lines from you, particularly if anything turns up promising better things in the way of a scheme of codification. A letter would at any time reach me enclosed to the Under Secretary, Castle, Dublin, with 'Public Instruction' on the corner of the outside cover.

Ever yours sincerely,

G. C. Lewis.

Dublin: November 22, 1834.

My dear Father,—It is very likely that the King may have had reasons for ejecting his ministry which are not known to the public, and they may be good and sufficient reasons; but I confess that Lord Althorp's move seems to me to have been laid hold of as a pretext, and could not have been the real motive for the change; and if Lord Melbourne was willing to try whether Lord Althorp could be dispensed with, and the King had no objection to the principles of his ministers. I do not think he acted fairly by them. It seems quite impossible that the Tories can stand if they remain Tories; and if they do not remain Tories, I cannot see why they should wish to come in. Altogether the thing is a mystery to me, which a few weeks will now clear up. Whatever happens, I hope that a provision will be made for the Irish Catholic clergy. Have you seen Croly's pamphlet? If you have not, I will send it to you.

We have made great progress with our business. We have circulated queries in every parish in Ireland, and have got answers in most. We have also employed an enumerator in every parish to amend the census of 1831 by inserting the religious persuasion of each individual; and we have received notifications that about 1,700 (out of 2,600) of these are already completed. The commissioners have been nearly all through Leinster, and have *reported* on about 250 parishes (these reports are ready for the press). If everything goes on as it has gone, our inquiry will be completed, and all the parochial reports will be ready for the printer by the beginning or middle of March. The chief expense (namely, that of employing the enumerators) has been already incurred, as *they* must be paid If the Government were to decide to revoke the commission, they would have to suppress the information already collected, and to pay 4,000*l.* for nothing. Moreover, if it was known that information was in existence which was withheld, it would be said that the Government dared not to produce it, lest it should damn the Irish Church; that it told a story too horrible to be disclosed, which would be a most potent argument, on the principle of *omne ignotum pro magnifico.* It seems to me that the revocation of the Church Commission would (in this country at least) be considered so decided an indication of a reaction, so evidently the first step of a counter-revolution, that in a minor degree it would be like proposing to repeal the Reform Bill. I am not deluded by objects near my eyes into a mistaking their relative importance; but you know that the Irish Church Question was the touchstone of the late Government, and that it will inevitably to a certain extent be the touchstone of the new Government, and that the revocation of the Church Commission would be equivalent to a declaration that nothing was to be done. It is a very different thing *not issuing* a commission and *recalling one already* issued. There must be some strong and cogent necessity to justify the latter step.

I enclose you specimens of the form in which our parochial reports will be set up; each will be divided into three parts, and they will be printed like the queries of the Poor Law Commission, with one set of heads on the margin, which will serve for the whole volume. We are very well pleased with the appearance of the reports which have been set up, and think that they are very clear and usable. We do not profess to show them, so you had better not let them lie about.

I expect to be in Dublin some time longer. Lord Wellesley, the Chancellor, the Attorney and Solicitor-General, and Littleton have resigned. Gosset stays in, or at any rate will wait to be turned out.

There has been no exultation hitherto among the high Protestants; to-day the men who come from court say they are downcast on account of an article in the 'Standard.' O'Connell is in Dublin, and is in a perfectly quiescent state on the subject; his present language is that repeal is not to be mentioned on the hustings: the watchword is to be, 'Opposition to an illiberal ministry;' and that all Liberals, Whigs, and Repealers are to unite till the present crisis is decided in favour of them, and forget all minor points of disagreement. He has been ostentatiously saying this to everybody who would hear him in the hall of the four courts to-day.*

Your affectionate son,

G. C. L.

Dresden: October 1, 1835.

My dear Father,—Since I wrote last we have made a long journey in the diligence from Frankfort through Gotha, Erfurdt, and Weimar to Leipzig, where we staid a day, and thence to Dresden. There was nothing remarkable in this line of country, at least in that part of it which we passed through during the day. The only interesting sight at Leipzig is the field of battle, which is completely seen from the observatory. The celebrated bridge over the Elster is about as large as the bridge over the Somergill at New Radnor. The river itself is scarcely wider than a brook; but it is deep, and the sides are steep, so that a horse cannot leap it. We have passed just a fortnight at Dresden, and go to-morrow to Berlin. A great part of our time

* On July 9, 1834, Earl Grey relinquished the office of Prime Minister, and Lord Althorp likewise resigned the Chancellorship of the Exchequer. In the same month Lord Melbourne was named First Lord of the Treasury, and Lord Althorp rejoined the Cabinet. At the death, however, of Earl Spencer, which took place in the following November, Lord Althorp's removal to the House of Peers broke up this already tottering government. The Duke of Wellington then carried on the business of the country till Sir Robert Peel, who was staying in Rome, was able to return to England. In December Sir Robert Peel formed a Cabinet which was, in turn, but short-lived; it was broken up in April 1835, and Lord Melbourne succeeded him.

has been occupied in seeing the picture gallery, which I suppose is the completest in Europe next to the Pitti. It is peculiarly rich in Venetian pictures, and in Correggio's; it also possesses many paintings of the Bolognese school, but scarcely any of much merit. The chief part of the collection was purchased from the Duke of Mantua by the Elector of Saxony in the first quarter of the last century. There is little colour in the Madonna di San Sisto, and the engraving gives a better idea of it than of any picture I ever saw. It has been recently cleaned, and it is said to have been rubbed down and spoilt; but neither Head nor I could discover any strong trace of damage. A theory has recently been started that it was intended to be used as a flag at processions, which explains why it is painted on silk. It is not a highly finished picture; at least it does not appear that Raphael took any extraordinary pains with it. There is nothing remarkable here in the way of architecture; the situation of the town and its bridge are extremely beautiful. There is a collection of views of Dresden and some other places in the neighbourhood by Canaletti, who, it seems, passed some years of his life here. We made an excursion of two days to a mountainous district called 'the Saxon Switzerland,' within a few hours of Dresden. It is a very beautiful and remarkable tract of country, both in a geological and picturesque point of view, and is not half enough celebrated in England. It has the merit of being accessible at a very small outlay of time, labour, and money.

Saxony has a sort of constitution; there are two chambers, which meet every year and exercise some control over the Government. But a much more powerful control is exercised by Prussia, which overlays all the small states of central Germany, and is perpetually interfering with their internal affairs. For example, at the Saxon revolution of 1830 the censorship of the press was removed, but it has been subsequently re-established in consequence of a requisition from the Prussian Government. The result of this oppressive conduct of Prussia in all its external relations is, that it is intensely hated by the other German states, and that in case of a war with France they would be most unwilling to join with her, however strong their interest might be to keep France on the other side of the Rhine. Prussia has, with great perseverance and adroitness, carried a most important measure, viz. a commercial union, in respect of custom duties, of the German states. Instead of the duties being levied at the boundary of each *state*, as formerly, they are now levied at the boundary of the Confederation. This of course necessitates the adoption by the small states of the Prussian tariff, which is so arranged as to protect the manufactures of Prussia. All the German states will have joined this union next January, except Austria, Hanover, Brunswick, and Hamburg. It will probably give rise to an uniform system of weights and measures and of coinage. However England may suffer by this union, it is of extreme convenience to travellers. I should not be surprised if some arrangement of the same kind was made between Belgium and France. It is said that proposals have been made to Belgium to join the Prussian union. Our present intention is to return by Hamburg, as we shall scarcely have time to make the long journey to the Rhine; it is necessary to go as high as Cassel in order to get to Cologne. We had wished to go direct to Dusseldorf through Elberfeld, the Prussian Manchester, but it seems that there is no post on that road. All travelling in Germany is a Government affair, and is extremely inconvenient, at least everything except posting. In France the diligences are private speculations. We shall probably leave Berlin about the 20th, and hope to be in London on one of the first days of November.

The weather has latterly been fine without interruption.

Your affectionate son,

G. C. LEWIS.

Berlin: October 7, 1835.

My dear Father,—We arrived at Berlin four days ago, and intend to stay till about the 23rd or 24th, when we shall go to Hamburg, and by the steamer from thence to London; the ordinary passage is about sixty hours. I have seen Abercrombie, the Secretary of Legation, and I find that he sent home, during Peel's administration, the answers to some queries on the management of ecclesiastical matters in Prussia which I drew last autumn, and which were forwarded to the Home Office by the Irish Government. They contain a tolerably complete account of the subject, but want further elucidation, which I hope to be able to get by means of the letters given to me by Lord Minto. I have seen Boeckh,* who is a middle-aged man, with nothing remarkable in his appearance.

The King is now at Töplitz, as well as Ancillon, the foreign minister. Berlin is a fine modern town, with long wide streets and large Grecian buildings—what Regent Street would be if the architecture was not barbarous. The neighbouring country is a sandy plain, so barren that it can only just repay its cultivation.

* Augustus Boeckh, whose volumes on the 'Public Economy of Athens' Sir George Lewis translated.

I received your letter at Dresden, at the time when I put my own letter into the post, so that I could not acknowledge it. I was glad to hear that your bow-meeting had gone off well, and that the weather in Radnorshire was better than on the Rhine. It is now beginning to feel cold at night, but the days are clear and sunny. Berlin is intensely cold in winter. I enclose a letter from Head* for his father. If my mother wishes me to bring her any *music*, I can do so without difficulty to any extent; only pray let her write the day this letter arrives. The difference in the price of books between England and Germany is enormous.

Your affectionate son,

G. C. Lewis.

17, Henrietta Street: Feb. 15, 1836.

My dear Head,—Raumer, in his book on England, after some remarks on defects in the English government, proceeds as follows:—

'Ueberhaupt hat meine obige Bemerkung über die Mängel und Gefahren constitutioneller Formen nicht dem Absolutismus der Camarilla Oberwasser geben sollen.'

Now you must know that the *Oberwasser* is the stream of water which passes *over* the wheel in a watermill, as distinguished from those mills in which the water passes *under* the wheel. *Oberwasser geben* is therefore 'to give an impulse to,' or more generally 'to be favourable to.'

Mrs. —— takes a different view of the meaning. In another sheet of her translation, which I received yesterday, the passage stands thus:—'My remarks indeed on the defects and dangers of constitutional

* His friend, Edmund Walker Head, Esq., with whom he was travelling.

forms do not at all tend to the absolutism of Camarilla Oberwasser.' I was thinking of changing Camarilla into Camilla, and adding a note stating that Camilla Oberwasser, though her name was not as well known as it deserved to be, had in fact been Queen of the Bernese Oberland, and had governed her subjects very tyrannically, until she was justly dethroned by the Papal Hohenstaufens.

If anything could compensate to me the loss of a journey with you, it would be the acquisition of this information about Queen Oberwasser, as well as the remark of a friend of yours and mine, who said a short time ago, in a large party, with an authoritative tone, that it was all very well talking, but that there was only one book in Spanish literature worth a farthing, and that was 'Gil Blas.'

The only news I hear is that the Duke of Buckingham is dying, which will produce a contest for Buckinghamshire. The Irish Municipal and Constabulary Bills will be brought forward this week; the Irish Church Bill is not expected till after Easter. Let me hear how you go on.

Ever yours truly,

G. C. LEWIS.

The book alluded to in the following letter, which Sir George Lewis states that he could fill with *more* evidence, but could not make clearer or fuller, contains two essays, the one on 'Irish Disturbances,' the other on the 'Irish Church,' which he published in this year. They contain facts which came to his knowledge, and opinions that he formed, during the time that he served on the two Irish Commissions of Inquiry. It does not appear that in 1836 he would have gone so far as altogether to disendow and disestablish the Irish Church, but in his opinion the changes that were then requisite were very extensive.

London: April 9, 1836.

My dear Head,— I am much obliged to you for your account of the Vulcanian whiteboys of South Wales; like causes produce like effects, and I am thankful for any parallel to so anomalous and singular a state of things. The trade unions, so far as they went in this country, are the best analogy; but they are an associated and definite body, guided by intelligent sharp-witted men, and having large funds at their control. The curious thing in Ireland is that the system should be so extensive, so successful, and yet so devoid of means.

I have just been looking over the evidence of the Irish Poor Law Commission on the subject of disturbances; there is confirmation of what I have written without end, but I do not find anything contradictory or inconsistent with what I have stated, nor indeed anything additional. If I had now to write the book again, I could make a stronger case by giving *more* evidence, but I am not aware that I could make it *clearer* or *fuller*. As yet I have found nothing to make me think that I have not exhausted the subject. You will doubtless have seen, and perhaps have attempted to read, the Irish Poor Report in the newspapers. It sins both in excess and defect; it does NOT contain an account of the state of the people, the causes and extent of their poverty, and the effects which it produces on them; and it *does* contain all kinds of absurd projects which I hope that no sane Government will ever think of introducing. What do you think of the landlords of the commission refusing to sign unless there was a clause recommending that a part of the rate should be paid by the *mortgagees*? One of the most monstrous propositions which ever proceeded even from a landlord, and still more, even from an *Irish* landlord. It is probably too late now for the Government to do anything more than move some resolutions about Irish poor laws; and people say that the Lords will throw out the Irish Church Bill, and that they will put Peel's scheme into the Irish Municipal Bill, which the Commons will reject; so that the Irish measures of this year do not seem to promise much. There is an inimitable dialogue on theory and practice in the new number of the 'London Review' by old Mill in the character of Plato. A keeps up a running fire of truisms, which B answers (being entirely convinced about the second page against all his former opinions). 'How true, how just, how incontrovertible! What magnificent notions you give me of the importance of knowledge; how my mind expands; how I wish that I had known all this before,' &c. &c. *Per contra* there is an article on civilisation by John Mill which is worth reading.

Before I went to Ireland I had very strong opinions as to the influence of *race* on the Irish character. But when I came to look at things more nearly, and to see all the demoralising influences to which they have been and are subjected, I asked myself whether a people of Germanic race would have turned out much better; and I really could not answer in the affirmative. There is a great difference in the physical appearance of the peasantry in different parts; the Celtic blood is purest in the mountains, in Kerry and Galway. On the other hand, in Kilkenny and Tipperary the peasantry have not the Celtic stamp strongly marked; they are large-limbed and fair-haired. The genuine Celts are small, with stiff black hair and dark flashing eyes; Curran is a perfect type of this cast of features. Yet Tipperary is the most disturbed county in Ireland, and Kilkenny one of the worst. Cork, a very Celtic county, is in general pretty quiet. I remember talking to Beaumont about the negroes in the same manner, and he seemed to have undergone a similar change of opinion, and to think that *external* influences had been far too much disregarded in forming an estimate of the negro character. *Cæteris paribus*, I would sooner have a German than a Celt, and a Protestant than a Catholic; but I have no doubt that a peasantry of Catholic Celts may be so governed and placed under such moral influences as to be peaceable, industrious, and contented; and I have no doubt that a peasantry of Protestant Germans might, if properly oppressed and brutalised, be made as bad as the Irish. You remember the German Bauernkrieg.

I have written an article for Hayward on La Roncière;* it is a stupid affair, but having once undertaken it, I was bound to finish. The evidence is nearly balanced, and it is difficult to make out anything with certainty; so that one wants the exact words, and the

* See the *Law Magazine*, vol. xv. p. 241. Monsieur de la Roncière was charged with having annoyed the family of Monsieur de Morell, at Saumur, by writing them anonymous letters; and with afterwards, by means of a ladder, scaling the wall of his house, to the bedroom window of Mademoiselle de Morell, which was on the third story, entering her room, committing a criminal assault upon and wounding Mademoiselle de Morell. Mademoiselle Morell was subject to fits which deprived her during a great part of every day of the full possession of her faculties. The circumstances of the whole case are very extraordinary. The jury found La Roncière guilty, and he was sentenced to twelve years' imprisonment. The evidence, however, does not appear to justify such a conclusion.

report I had was so loose that one could affirm nothing with confidence. The story is in truth a marvellous one; the only result I have arrived at is that both La Roncière and the lady are mad, or as good *as*. It seems to have been much discussed at Paris, and there is now a considerable *minority* who think La Roncière ought to have been acquitted.

* * * *

I heard from Beaumont a short time ago; he is writing a book on Ireland,* and intends to come over to England this season. I wish you could see him again; if he wants to learn about poor laws, I shall send him to you.

* * * *

Georgiana Gordon has got some Scotch songs to send you.

Ever yours truly,

G. C. Lewis.

33, Hertford Street: May 13, 1836.

My dear Head,—

* * * *

Politics seem very quiet, although there have been reports of disagreements in the Cabinet on the Irish Municipal Bill, one party wishing to break with the Lords and the other not. It seems to me most likely that the affair will be compromised by the Commons assenting to the Lords' amendments, but saving five or six large towns, viz. Dublin, Derry, Limerick, Waterford, and Cork. Belfast is not a corporate town. The Government will probably do nothing this session about Irish poor laws; the Irish Liberal members are almost to a man *adverse*, and therefore ministers, being them-

* *L'Irlande sociale, politique et religieuse.* Par Gustave de Beaumont. 2 vols. Paris, 1845.

selves reluctant, can afford not to act. As to the Irish Church Bill, the Lords will certainly throw it out; and it is expected that the English Tithe Bill will founder in the Commons. This, therefore, will not be a very innovating session, according to all appearances.

In the new number of the 'Edinburgh Review' there is an excellent article on 'Irish Tithe,' which I advise you to read. I believe it to be written by one of my colleagues on the Irish Church Commission. There is also a good article on Newman's Arians, against the new sect. Arnold's performance on Hampden and the Oxford malignants seems to me both violent and weak. In the 'Quarterly' there is a very able article against Napier, the author of which is not known; but it is said to be by Sir George Murray, or written under his direction. There is also a strange collection of all the worst parts of the worst French novels, written by Croker; it will save many people a great deal of trouble, and will probably add greatly to the popularity of the said novels. I hear that a novel was put in a shop window with the inscription, 'One of the novels reviewed in the last "Quarterly."' There is a new review, called the 'Dublin,' intended to serve as the organ of the Irish Catholics. The tone of the first number is, on the whole, moderate; there is a complete demolition of the stories about the 'Black Nunnery,' published by a woman named Maria Monk.

I enclose you my article on La Roncière. My father has read it, and he thinks that Mdlle. de Morell wrote the letters, the motive being to force her parents to marry her to La Roncière. I incline very strongly in favour of this explanation; when I wrote the article, I thought the probability was in favour of the girl having written the letters, but I could not find an adequate motive. It was a desperate game, but I think it explains everything. Pray read the trial with this view; the letters are not those of a man, but of a *woman*, and of a woman viewing the facts from the supposed standpunct of Mdlle. de Morell, and guarding the suspicious points with preconcerted excuses. The governess was doubtless in the plot.

I am thinking of beginning Sanscrit, and indeed have done something, but am terrified by the number of letters. Rosen is willing to be my instructor. There is an interesting article by him on Buddhism in the 'Penny Cyclopædia.' I see there are nearly three times as many Buddhists as Christians in the world. I have also some thoughts of writing on 'Transportation,' but I fear it is hopeless to gain attention to the subject. My book on Ireland has not sold much; there is no market for books on Irish subjects unless they are full of religious bigotry. I have not heard my father make any remarks on your mode of doing business,* except expressing satisfaction with it. If anything falls from him, I will not fail to mention it to you.

Johnstone told me he was going to Radnorshire and Brecknockshire, but he did not mention Herefordshire.

* * * *

Ever yours truly,

G. C. LEWIS.

London: July 15, 1836.

My dear Head,—

* * * *

I have been occupied during the last ten days with writing remarks on the report of the Irish Poor Commissioners. They will, I believe, be printed privately,

* His friend, Sir Edmund Head, as this and following letter show, had now been appointed an Assistant Poor-Law Commissioner. Mr. Frankland Lewis was the Chief Poor Law Commissioner.

for the use of the Government; but on this subject you must keep a *βοῦς ἐπὶ γλώσσῃ μέγας*, as the Irish Commissioners would probably send over a detachment of Whiteboys to despatch me if they found out that I criticised their performance in so insidious a manner. I flatter myself that I have made a complete smash of them, but of this you will judge when I show you in the country what I have written. Their utter misconception of the entire subject, both the state of Ireland and the English poor law, is less provoking than the impudent way in which they beg the question while professing to argue it.

Tufnell has got me a very good statement of the causes which induce the sailors to prefer the merchant service to the navy. The writer says that the wages are nearly equal; if anything, the King's wages are rather the lowest. He attributes the preference mainly to the short period of service, and doubts as to the effect of discipline. I suspect, however, that he is wrong. Would you tell me exactly what your Bay of Biscay friend said to you? It appears that the foreign merchant trade is much worse than the coasting trade; the men are worse fed.

I want any facts or arguments to show that it is not safe to give out-door relief to the *impotent* poor, and that the workhouse acts with nearly as much effect upon them as upon the able-bodied. I am afraid that, having no workhouses, you can tell me nothing. My present intention is to leave London with my mother on the 28th, and to be at Harpton on the 29th. I should like very well to go to Cardigan; how, and by what road, will you go? But why during the assizes? We should have to bivouac.

I have been reading Wordsworth's 'Athens and

Attica.' It is a very good book.* He makes an ingenious attempt at a passage in the 'Politics'† at which Niebuhr and many others have tried their hands: Κλεισθένης πολλοὺς ἐφυλέτευσε ξένους καὶ δούλους μετοίκους. Some have inserted καὶ after δούλους; but why should he put the slaves between the two classes of aliens? Niebuhr reads ξένους μετοίκους, καὶ δούλους. The expression ξένος μέτοικος occurs, but ξένος seems scarcely necessary. For ΔΟΥΛΟΥΣ Wordsworth reads ΑΦΥΛΟΥΣ: the letters are very close; but query, were any metœci *in* the tribes? This is hardly a fair question for an assistant commissioner who has to settle about rents of cottages.

Ever yours, G. C. L.

Sir George Lewis to Nassau W. Senior, Esq.

Harpton: August 7, 1836.

My dear Senior,—I should be very sorry that you should think me unreasonable about the Malta Commission, but I am fully resolved to have no share in it, in any shape or manner, unless I am recognised by the Colonial Office. How would it be possible for me, if I were to go merely as Austin's friend, to take a part in the business? My presence would be an impertinent intrusion. What could I say to the authorities of the place? That I had taken upon myself to institute inquiries into the state of the island and its government? It seems to me that I might as well seat myself on the bench in a court of law, and say that I was come to assist the judge in trying causes. It is very true that I should be there with Austin's consent; but what would that matter to the persons whose

* Wordsworth's *Athens and Attica*. Murray, 1836. See page 222.

† See Aristotle's *Politics*, chap. III., ii. 4. Eaton's edit. p. 108.

conduct might be called in question? They would say that I was come into the island as a volunteer spy, as a self-appointed inquisitor; that their cause was tried *coram non judice*. If the Government offered to give me a commission in the middle of the proceedings, I might then consider whether I would join Austin; but after what has happened about the Poor Law assistant commissionerships, should I be justified in thrusting myself into such a position, upon the speculation of having my acts legalised, and rescued from absurdity and ridicule by the arrival of an authority which after all might be withheld? I can conceive no temptation strong enough to induce me to face such risks as these; and in the present case there is so little that is alluring, that if it were not for the circumstance of Austin being the commissioner, I doubt whether I would go as the colleague of any other person if the appointment were offered me on the most unobjectionable terms. The few hundred pounds I could make are no great object to me; the subject is not one of great interest or importance, and Austin is perfectly competent to the task without *any* assistance, to say nothing of *my* assistance. I have neither the prospect of doing myself good, nor of serving the public. The only reason why I feel any regret is that, knowing how liable Austin is to attacks of ill health, I think that the presence of a colleague on whom he could to a certain extent rely would relieve him from a good deal of occasional anxiety, and perhaps shorten the duration of the inquiry. But, although I would never lose an opportunity of serving him in any way in my power, I cannot help feeling that, in going out on the terms suggested, I should be making a sacrifice which no man can be expected to make.

It does not seem to me that the difficulty about the King could amount to much if there was any wish to appoint a second commissioner; but if the Colonial Office have decided to appoint only one, I do not see what should now induce them to alter their decision.

I am fully sensible of the kindness which you have shown me, and the interest you have taken about me on this as on other occasions, and I only regret that I should have been unable to follow your advice.

Ever yours truly,

G. C. Lewis.

I have asked Edward Villiers to send you my paper on the 'Irish Poor Law Question;' when you have read it, pray let Tufnell have it at the Admiralty.

Soon after the foregoing letter to Mr. Senior was written, Lord Glenelg, who was then Colonial Secretary, proposed to Sir George Lewis to be joint commissioner with Mr. Austin to inquire into the affairs of the island of Malta, where confusion existed and discontent prevailed. At first he hesitated whether he would accept the appointment, but chiefly, I think, for the three following reasons, he consented to do so—that he could assist in making great improvements in the government and administration of justice in the island—that he had for a colleague Mr. Austin, of whose talent and knowledge he had the highest opinion, and with whose views he mainly coincided—and that the weakness and disorder of his lungs would be benefited (as indeed proved to be the case) by his passing one or two winters in a warm and dry climate.

In the autumn the commissioners left England, Mrs. Austin accompanied them. Their journey was tedious, and the quarantine at the end of it annoying; but the cordial reception which they met on the island was satisfactory and encouraging. There are at Harpton two lithographs designed and printed at Valetta commemorating the ovations of the inhabitants when the commissioners drove from the landing place to their hotel.

The following letters, some written by Sir George Lewis on his journey, and others after his arrival at Valetta, contain much that is interesting:—

Paris: September 23, 1836.

My dear Father,—We left London on Tuesday as we intended by the steamer for Boulogne, and arrived there duly at the end of twelve hours. On the following day we slept at Abbeville, yesterday we went to Beauvais, and this morning we came on to Paris, and arrived in time for an early dinner. We intend to stay here to-morrow, and the next day to continue our journey towards Marseilles. The weather has been fine till to-day, when it rained a good deal; and Austin has had pretty good health, and there has been no grievance.

* * * * *

Our journey has been so devoid of incidents that I have really nothing to say further, except that I will write from Marseilles and let you know what we do about sailing, and how soon we may expect to be at Malta. At present we do not intend to stay at Lyons even a day, but to go on to Avignon without stopping.

Your affectionate son,

G. C. Lewis.

Avignon: October 4, 1836.

My dear Father,—We left Paris as we intended, and went to Chalons by Dijon, having turned from the

Auxerre road by a newly-made line, which, though longer, saved us both time and *pavé*. From Châlons we descended the Saône in the steamer to Lyons in about eleven hours; stayed a day at Lyons, in consequence of our carriage being delayed, and then went in another steamer down the Rhône to Avignon in about thirteen hours. The country is seen to much greater advantage from the rivers than by the road, whence I had seen it before. In particular the entrance into Lyons by the Saône is extremely striking and beautiful. The Pont St. Esprit which we passed under in going down the Rhône is a long but common-place stone bridge of eighteen arches. The only thing remarkable about it is, that from the width of the piers and the rapidity of the current, it produces a fall like that of old London bridge, which it is dangerous for small boats to pass. We found at Avignon a letter from the English consul at Marseilles (to whom we had written), stating that the ship of war had not arrived, and accordingly we hired a calèche and went to Nismes, a drive of six hours, and have returned to Avignon to-day. The amphitheatre at Nismes is externally almost as perfect as the day when it was built; internally it has suffered considerably. If my memory does not deceive me, it is much larger than the amphitheatre at Verona, and must be one of the largest Roman works in existence. The Maison Carrée is a well-preserved Corinthian temple, of small size, built by Agrippa, the grandson of Augustus. Nismes is a thriving manufacturing town, containing 45,000 inhabitants, and is altogether a different place from what I had expected. It would, on many accounts, be an agreeable residence. On our return we saw the Pont du Gard, which is at a short distance from the road: it is an aqueduct, consisting of three tiers of arches crossing the valley of the river Gard. From its height, and the massiveness of the masonry, its effect is very fine. To-morrow we shall sleep at Aix, and on the following morning go on to Marseilles. Austin has unfortunately had a great deal of bad health, and has, I fear, suffered much from the journey. We have likewise not been lucky in our weather; it has rained, more or less, nearly every day since we left Paris. Nothing can exceed the appearance of prosperity in the parts of France through which we have travelled. A vast number of suspension bridges have been erected over all the streams in this part of France within the last few years: there are now not less than fourteen bridges between Châlons and Lyons. The pillars are made slender, and the chain light; and the expense must be very small. There are steamboats every day up and down the Saône and Rhône; and they appear to load almost to excess. I received my mother's letter at Lyons, which arrived the day that we were there. I will write again from Marseilles before we sail for Malta.

Your affectionate son,

G. C. L.

Marseilles: October 8, 1836.

My dear Mother,—We arrived at Marseilles the day before yesterday, having slept at Aix on the road; and I have received your's and Gilbert's joint composition.

* * * * *

My former visit to Marseilles was made under much more favourable auspices than my present one. During the whole of yesterday there was a hurricane of wind and rain, with lightning, such as I never witnessed before; and the rain, having lasted through the night, continues this morning with almost unabated vigour, though the storm has diminished. Going out was next to impossible; the water in the streets was in some places up to a man's knees. Having seen the town before, I do not so much care; but it is unlucky for Austin and Mrs. Austin, particularly as the former is much exhausted by the journey, and wants some fine weather to set him up. The despatches sent out by the Admiralty to the commander of the Mediterranean squadron were forwarded from Malta to the Levant, and a ship arrived here the day before yesterday from Smyrna, the consequence of which is that it will have to perform quarantine at Malta when we arrive, and we shall be detained eight or ten days in the lazzaretto. It is a frigate, the 'Vernon,' commanded by Captain Mackerbie. It is now lying in quarantine three miles from the harbour. We shall embark to-morrow, and if the wind is fair, shall be at Malta in five days. Our journey has in every respect been prosperous, except the bad weather and Austin's bad health. We have sold our carriage here for 800 francs—two pounds more than we gave for it, and have only lost a few pounds for the repairs. Nanni has turned out very well as a courier.

Mrs. Austin has a brother settled here as an engineer; Austin and she are staying at his house. I dined with him yesterday, and he told me much about the commercial state of the town, with which he is thoroughly acquainted. He describes the mercantile class as extremely narrow-minded, jealous, and timid, utterly unable to act together from distrust and suspicion. The administration of the Custom House laws is vexatious and uncertain in the extreme. The officers themselves are in some cases aware of it, but say they must obey their orders from Paris. There is a sort of trade union of portefaix here, which overawes the Government, and does what it pleases. It has even prevented the erection of a single crane for unlading vessels. Nothing can exceed the weakness of the Government in this respect; the English Government, as compared with it, is Hercules to a pigmy. He thinks that if the French commercial code was improved, and administered in an enlightened spirit, the increase of the trade of this town would be enormous; as it is, the progress is very considerable. The rent of houses at Marseilles is higher than at Paris, and provisions are exceedingly dear. It must be one of the most expensive places in the world to inhabit. The Marseillais call the French 'étrangers;' they call themselves Provençaux. Mr. Taylor has had some English and some Parisian workmen; he says that the natives dislike the latter more than the former. There is a vast deal of superstition among all classes—as much as in Italy; the mass of the people are in a very brutish state. It seems to me that the parts of France that I have seen are in a more thriving state than any part of England, except the manufacturing districts. Nothing can exceed the look of comfort among the peasantry. It is a terrible contrast to Ireland.

Your affectionate son,

G. C. Lewis.

Lazzaretto, Malta: October 25, 1836.

My dear Father,—We arrived in the harbour of Valetta, after a tedious voyage of ten days, on the 20th, and immediately went into the lazzaretto, where we have been imprisoned ever since. We had every variety of weather on our voyage—strong wind, no wind at all, contrary wind, and even a fair wind for a few hours. The 'Vernon,' in which we were, is the largest frigate in the British navy, and is said to be the largest in the world. She is a beautiful ship, and an admirable sailer; had she not been a remarkable sailer we should probably have been driven out of our course towards Gibraltar. She was built by Captain Symonds, who seems to have begun a new era in naval architecture. We saw a good deal of the western coast of Sardinia, and passed close to its southern point, a single rock. The next land we saw was Maritimo, a small island at the north-western extremity of Sicily; and we were afterwards driven to Pantellaria, a little island half-way between Cape Bon and Sicily, from which, after a couple of days' calm, we made Malta. We were towed into the harbour of Valetta by a steamship. The day was beautiful, and there was a general turn out of the inhabitants to see us arrive. The size and extent of the fortifications, the amphitheatrical appearance of the town, and the fleet lying at anchor in the harbour, altogether made nearly the most striking sight which I ever witnessed. Austin, I am sorry to say, has been a good deal shaken by the journey, and the voyage on the top of it. There is something in the perpetual noise and restlessness of a ship, particularly when there is much tacking, which is exceedingly trying to a person in an irritable, nervous state. For this reason I am not sorry that we have had to go into the lazzaretto, as it has enabled him to recruit his strength. We go to-morrow to the hotel, and shall stay there for a few days, till we have arranged about our house and servants. I think that we shall probably have a large house, which will serve both for dwelling and office.

A house with seventy or eighty rooms in Valetta lets for about 60*l*. a year. An ordinary house fetches about 30*l*. I have seen the chief authorities here, viz. Col. Evans, the temporary governor; Sir Frederick Hankey, the secretary and virtual governor; and Sir John Stoddart, the chief justice. The latter is a hot-headed man, who once wrote the new 'Times.' Hankey is a man of ability and of pleasant, frank manners. In person he is something like Lord Harrowby. There seems to be considerable excitement among the people at our arrival. They wish to give us something like a public reception on our release from the lazzaretto, which, I hope, may not take place. Mitrovich, the Maltese O'Connell, seems to me, from his letters, to be a well-meaning, but exceedingly weak man. It is evident that he wishes the Government to buy him. I suspect that he might be had body and soul for 200*l*. a-year. The people, of course, think him a giant. The real grievance of the Maltese, I am sorry to say, lies beyond the reach of commissioners and governments, viz. the excessive population of the island. I fear that in that respect it greatly resembles Ireland, and I hear it said that the priests recommend early marriages on the ground of virtue. There is something melancholy in witnessing an evil of this magnitude, which a Government can do no more to arrest than it can control the winds. The increase is still going on. We shall begin our business in the first days of November; our first step will probably be to hear what the agitators have to say against the Government. This letter will go to Marseilles. I will write by the packet, about the 8th or 10th of next month.

Your affectionate son,

G. C. Lewis.

P.S.—If a parcel should be sent with copies of my article on the Church question in the 'London Review,' will you send some copies to some of the members of the Government?

Malta: November 5, 1836.

My dear Head,—The only novelty which I saw on my road to Marseilles, was the remains at Nismes and the Pont du Gard. The Maison Carrée has been a good deal spoilt by restorations; it is, however, still a pretty copy in miniature of a Greek temple. The amphitheatre is exceedingly fine, and the exterior is still so perfect that the top of the wall is preserved for a large part of the circuit. The interior has been much damaged. It appears to have been used as a fortress or castle in the middle ages; and has, moreover, been damaged in the common way, by being used as a quarry. The Pont du Gard is an aqueduct over the river Gard or Gardon, consisting of three tiers of arches: the lower tier has been disfigured by the application of a modern bridge to it. * * * At Marseilles we embarked on board a frigate which had come from Smyrna, and therefore subjected us to the necessity of performing quarantine on our arrival at Malta. I found it quite a mistake to suppose that there is no motion in large ships; a small vessel has, moreover, this advantage, that it is worked without there being a crew of four hundred and fifty men to walk over one's head during the chief part of the night. We had all kinds of foul winds and calms, and were ten days in reaching Malta. We saw the southern point of Sardinia, the north-west coast of Sicily, and a part of the coast of Africa near Cape Bon. We also remained about two days in sight of a hateful little island called Pantellaria. Valetta is on the whole the most striking and beautiful town I ever saw: the indentations of the harbour, the extent and grandeur of the fortifications and their combination with the rock, and the terrace-like arrangement of the houses, form a collection of objects which no town that I know can equal. It resembles Edinburgh in some points, viz. the mixture of buildings and rock, and the rising of the streets in stages one over another. In other respects it is, of course, very different. The French, of course, did much mischief in Malta, as in all other places which they occupied: among other things they stripped the leaden roofs of the *barraccas*—large porticoes in which the knights used to walk in hot weather. They now serve for the same purpose in cold weather, as their uncovered walls exclude the wind while they admit the sun.

We found ourselves on our arrival, much to our surprise, floating down the full tide of popularity. We made a sort of triumphal entry (of course against our will) into the town; the streets were illuminated at night, and we were annoyed with all kinds of marks of respect. This state of things, however, has not been of long endurance; and we are already beginning to think of rotten eggs and dead cats. The people evidently thought, or were told, that we came out with a Maltese Magna Charta in our pockets; and when we summoned the chief complainants, and began to talk of inquiry, they were manifestly quite surprised, and seemed to think that we had merely to give a grind or two, and out would come a whole code of laws ready made. After three days of inane declamation on the parts of the complainants, and of damnable iteration on our part, they have at last begun to perceive that it will be necessary for us to investigate a subject before we report on it, and that, in order to investigate, we must take evidence. This sequence of propositions, which in England may seem tolerably clear, has only become manifest to our gentlemen by means of a long succession of the severest intellectual throes. It would have edified you to see the gravity which we maintained during the most ludicrous parts of the touching patriotic pathos addressed to us. The two main evils of Malta are, for the upper classes, practical exclusion from office, and brutal treatment by the English in society; and for the lower classes over population. On the latter subject, nearly the same opinions and the same morality seem to prevail as in Ireland; the priests recommend early marriages on the score of what they are pleased to call virtue. The consequence of virtue being to cover this little rock with people so thickly, that already carrubas have become an article of food; and if the increase goes much further, the people must starve if they are not fed by English charity. I have seen Hookham Frere, who found himself in Malta fourteen years ago, at his wife's death, and has forgotten to return to England. He has translated four plays of Aristophanes, and will, I imagine, publish them. The society here appears to consist almost exclusively of persons in government offices, and military and naval officers. Let me know how the unions go on.

Ever yours truly,

G. C. LEWIS.

Valetta: November 8, 1836.

My dear Father,—Since I finished my letter to you, the packet has been respited till to-day; and we have, in the meantime, seen the leaders of the complaining party several times, and have arranged to begin with the question of the liberty of the press. In many respects the people here, I am sorry to say, remind me of the Irish. They have in common mistrust and mendaciousness among the upper classes, and superstition and prolificness among the lower, and its consequence, over population. The jealousy and distrust which the complaining party have shown to us were perfectly ludicrous; the deportment, however, of the deputation which waited on us was quite irreproachable, and far superior to anything to be met with in Ireland. Everybody describes the suffering of the poorer classes as extreme at certain seasons; but it is a subject on which no information has been collected. We shall probably send out some queries in the course of the winter, and for this purpose I should be obliged to you to send me, through the Colonial Office, the thin volume, published by Fellowes, containing Cowell's report, and Arrivabene's account of the poor in Belgium; and Senior's volume on foreign poor laws.

* * * *

Your affectionate son,

G. C. Lewis.

Malta: December 6, 1836.

My dear Father,—I received your letter and my mother's by the last post, and was sorry to hear of the illness of my godchild. In this island it is quite a singularity to have less than ten children; the place is a perfect human warren, and with regard to the numbers of families, the upper classes are just as bad as the lower. Starving nobles with fine sounding titles, and a couple of hundred pounds a year, marry at twenty, and beget twelve or fourteen children. You may judge, with an upper class multiplying in this manner, of the intense hatred with which they regard the English, who fill all the well-paid offices; and of the eagerness with which they look forward to the time when the places will be given to Maltese. The people have contracted such a habit of dependence on the Government, that their only notion of improvement in their condition seems to be the multiplication of moderately paid offices to be given to Maltese. The Government, instead of attempting to give the people feelings of self-reliance, have intentionally kept them in a state of pupilage, have discouraged all movement, have stifled all inquiry, have perpetuated ignorance, and have even discountenanced trade as being troublesome. On the whole, the Government of this island has hitherto strongly resembled the Austrian Government in Lombardy, except that it has done nothing for primary education, and that it has not oppressed the upper classes. The chief secretary, who has virtually governed the island for the last ten or twelve years, was a secretary of Sir Thomas Maitland, who appears to have been an ape of Bonaparte, and to have added to the mistaken principles of his model a brutality and coarseness of deportment which Bonaparte had not. There are a certain number of English here, who admire what they call Maitland's vigour and energy: but the more rational among them are now quite aware that his system of driving and kicking mankind into obedience is, in the long run, mischievous and absurd.

We have been hitherto engaged in inquiring into the liberty of the press; we have completed our oral examinations, and are now drawing the report and the law. The present system is as close as anything can well be. The Government permit no press, except one in their own control, and all political discussion, on all sides of every question, is prohibited. We shall report in favour of the freedom of the press, but shall recommend strict regulations in the way of punishment for libels on private character and on foreign states. The great dangers here are the attacks on private character —which in so small a society, and one with so voracious an appetite for slander, would render the island a perfect hell—and the attacks on foreign Governments by Italian exiles settled here, which might induce the Governments to retaliate, and so to vex the trade of the island. The latter is a serious consideration with an overflowing population already hanging over the verge of subsistence. The leaders of the popular party are for the most part poor creatures, although there is one man, an advocate, of very considerable ability. Among the Government people there is scarcely anything remarkable. There is one Maltese judge of excellent sense, and in other respects a sound and able man. The two greatest demagogues in the island are the chief justice and the attorney-general, who are in a state of perpetual feud with the Government. The former is Dr. Stoddart, once editor of the *Times*, and endued with all the pestilent habits of mind and conduct engendered by newspaper-editing. He is open-mouthed on the subject of a free press, and I have no doubt that he looks forward to a free newspaper as a means of writing against his colleagues, like Brougham. There is a good deal of dinner-giving here, pretty much in the Dublin style. One meets the same people again and again; and it is merely the same pack re-shuffled. The dinners are formed of the English Government employés, of the officers of the garrison and fleet, and Hookham Frere. There is no intercourse whatever in small parties with the Maltese. As to the mass of naval and military officers, it is, of course, unnecessary to say anything; among the employés there is nothing agreeable except Nugent, who is a great circumstance in such a society, and has preserved his mind from the narrowing and corrupting influence of a small town. Hookham Frere has been very civil and good-natured to me, and has lent me his Aristophanes, and so forth; but he has disappointed me exceedingly. I expected a man of humour in conversation, and of terse, pointed expression; instead of which, he is slow, hesitating and long, and without a glimmer of wit. His *opinions* are, of course, puerile, and worthless in the extreme, just what one would expect from a small littérateur shut up for twelve years in a small island. The Maltese are narrow, uninteresting, frivolous, and illiterate for the most part; but their manners and deportment are, almost without exception, unobjectionable, and very superior to those of some of the vulgar English wives of naval men and Government officers, who find themselves in an unwonted position of power and importance, and therefore think it incumbent on them to trample on the Maltese with all the weight of their vulgarity. If an Englishman is to preserve any vestige of sympathetic feelings towards his own countrymen as such, he should certainly never see them out of England.

I enclose some drawings of Malta stone vases for gardens and hot-houses. The prices are very reasonable, and they can be sent to London for a trifling expense. Pray show them to Lushington, who wished me to buy him some, and to Lady Grenville, or any other person who may be likely to wish for any. They are made with great ease and rapidity, and according to any pattern.

* * * *

I shall be curious to know what Mr. Nicholls has reported on an Irish Poor Law. The Government, I fear, will not be disinterested enough to do anything effectual; it is clear that the English landlords would carry whatever they propose.

Your affectionate son,
G. C. Lewis.

Malta: January 10, 1837.

My dear Head,—Many thanks for your long letter. I did not understand you to express yourself as being dissatisfied with your present employment; but, as I thought that you might have some misgiving about the rectitude of your choice, I gave you my reasons, founded on experience, for thinking that to a man who has an English career open to him, Colonial Office is a miserable *pis-aller*. This would not be the case if the colonial appointments were not so scandalously bad as they have been, and as, I fear, they are likely still to be.

Your account of your district is on the whole prosperous, and I am heartily glad to hear that the joint ménage goes on so prosperously.* The Poor Law agitation seems now, in great measure, to have subsided. The landlords probably begin to find that their rents are better paid, and prefer the satisfaction of filling their purses to that of abusing Whig commissioners and Malthusian legislation.

It is so long since I read Pascal's Provinciales that I scarcely remember them. The only distinct recollection I have of them is that the early letters are a masterpiece of clear and almost popular statement and exposure of subtle verbal sophisms. I have lately read Mill's 'History of British India.' A great many of

* Mr. Head was then living in Herefordshire with the Editor.

the details about the squabbles and wars with the petty Indian princes are invincibly dull, but the work is, on the whole, both interesting and instructive. It must be said that the English Government in Hindostan during the last thirty or forty years of the last century was one of the most detestable that ever existed. Omnipotent for the purpose of fleecing the people, it was powerless to protect them. The tax-gatherer extracted the last rupee from the wretched ryot, but there was nobody to save his person and property from the attacks and depredations of armed ruffians. It is curious to observe how invariably the governors fall out among themselves when there is not a strong public opinion to keep them in awe. The history of Indo-English administration is a history of disputes between members of the same governing body. I question whether the Colonial Office are sufficiently aware of this unquestionable truth. If it was merely for their own ease, they ought to seek to raise up a sound and powerful public opinion in the colonies. Pray thank Gilbert for his letter. I expect to leave Malta now in no very long time, certainly before Easter.

Ever yours sincerely,

G. C. Lewis.

Malta: April 3, 1837.

My dear Head,—I sent you by the last packet a specimen of Maltese engraving, which seems to me very respectable. Mrs. Austin found in the ancient cathedral of this island—in the Città Vecchia (the capital in former times)—some designs in inlaid wood which are attributed to the eleventh century. She had a copy made of one, which I saw, and the style seemed to me at least not earlier than the sixteenth century. There is nothing in this island, either ancient or remarkable, in the way of art. The knights appear to have thought of nothing but building new forts, and enlarging the defences of Valetta. They have been so successful in this ambition, that the very extent of the fortifications is a source of weakness, inasmuch as it would take 20,000 men to man the works if the town was regularly invested. This contingency, however, is most improbable, one may say almost impossible, so long as England retains the command of the sea. Nevertheless, the Ordnance are not satisfied unless they keep the place in a perpetual state of siege; and I hear that orders have lately come out from England to cut down some mulberry trees in one of the ditches. A well-fortified town may be an excellent contrivance in time of war, but it is an excessive inconvenience in time of peace. It takes between a quarter and half an hour of walking through narrow gates and across ditches, and up steep steps, and under covered ways, to get clear of the defences, whenever one wishes to breathe some air. You can conceive Ehrenbreitstein on the scale of a town large enough to contain 50,000 people.

The native language of the Maltese is an Arabic dialect, which agrees pretty nearly with the Arabic spoken on the coast of Barbary as far as Egypt. It has never been written, and cannot even be said to have an alphabet. There are not, as far as I am aware, any literary compositions in it preserved by tradition. The people are an Arab race, descended from the Saracens, who obtained possession of the island; their physiognomy bears a striking resemblance to the Jewish. They are a gloomy people; they never seem to laugh, or sing, or dance; their amusements, if such they can be called, are of a religious cast, such as processions on saints'-days, &c. I hear that the country people pass the chief part of their Sundays and giorni di festa in the churches. They are exceedingly ignorant; and not unnaturally, as there has been no education for the poor, very little for the rich, and no free press. They are, however, by no means wanting in acuteness and ability. Their *practical talent* is indeed remarkable; and in this respect they appear to great advantage, even by the side of the English, who (with their descendants) excel all other nations in this quality. There is a pernicious race of nobles who transmit their titles to *all* their sons, together with fortunes varying from 500*l*. to 40*l*. or 50*l*. a year, and a self-imposed inability to follow any money-making occupation. These people are ignorant, narrow-minded, stupid, and rapacious of public money; and it would be well if their titles could be abolished.

As, however, they are now excessively poor, and they have no means of recruiting their fortunes by rich marriages, a few more descents and divisions of property must confound them with the middle and working classes. There is also a numerous body of priests, more than 1,000 (including the regulars) to a population of 120,000. The priests are for the most part bigoted and ignorant; but their influence has considerably declined of late years, and their incomes are most pitiful, varying from 10*l*. to 30*l*. or 40*l*. a year. The merchants, the advocates, the doctors, and the Government employés form the really valuable part of the population. From the narrow policy of the Government in discouraging education and discussion, there is a great want of *knowledge*, both of facts and principles, in these classes; but there is a very fair sprinkling of intelligence, and on the whole I should be very sanguine of the influence which might be produced upon them by a Government which looked to improving the condition of the community, and not merely to raising a revenue in order to divide it among English heads of useless departments.

The misery which prevails among the mass of the people is caused by the excess of their numbers. The great unnatural commerce drawn into Malta by the Berlin and Milan decrees gave a stimulus to population, and also accustomed the working classes to a higher standard of living, from which they have now fallen. But the main cause of the over-population is the ignorant recklessness of the people, and the pernicious morality inculcated by the Catholic clergy as to the necessity of early marriage in order to prevent irregular intercourse. The world, always ready to find bad motives for every action, attributes this doctrine in Ireland and elsewhere to the desire of the clergy to augment their fees. In my opinion, their advice is perfectly disinterested; and is founded on a sincere conviction (however mistaken) that they are discharging an imperative religious duty. I am not at all clear that Protestant clergymen would not give just the same advice, if the practice of confession afforded them the *means* of enforcing it.

I agree with you in what you say about the Irish Poor Law Bill; but it seems to me that the whole will ultimately *shake down* into the English system. The refusal of the *express* right to relief will be quite illusory: practice will establish what the legislature does not grant. Mr. Nicholls's report seemed to me feeble and confused in the expression, but generally right in the opinions and recommendations.

The vulgar adjective from Malta, used by sailors and

others in this island is Maltee. I suppose they argued that as the singular of *bees* is *bee*, so the singular of Mal*tese* is Mal*tee*. Carrying their principle one step further, it seems to me that *cheese* ought to be plural and *chee* singular.

Whenever you are tired of novels, buy 'Colletta Storia di Napoli' (in four duodecimo volumes, price about 15*s*.), and *read it*, particularly the last volume, containing the history of the revolution of 1821. Also observe a passage about kangaroos.

Ever yours truly,
G. C. LEWIS.

I shall be excused for inserting Sir Edmund Head's interesting letter, written after the receipt of that which I have just printed.

Hereford: April 27, 1837.

My dear Lewis,—I answered a letter of Mrs. Austin's a few days ago respecting the works of art in Malta, and therein expressed an intention of waiting to see whether I heard from you by this packet before I wrote. You will see what I have said to her respecting the date of the wood work. I should think that the designs (if the drawings sent by her are faithful), about 1,500, perhaps a little, but certainly a very little earlier.

I fear that I can be of no use to her in what she wanted, viz. searching for a publisher. You know that my acquaintances in that line have not been numerous, and my residence, if residence I have, is not very favourable to any exertions which I would otherwise willingly make.

I will buy Colletta and read it forthwith. I have just read Hallam's new volume of 'Introduction to the Literature of the 14th, 15th, and 16th centuries.' I think the book poor—entertaining it was not perhaps likely to be. There is none of that overflow of the man's own reading, and that internal evidence of his thorough acquaintance with the book he treats of, which alone raise a work of the kind above a mere dry compilation. His digression on the Romance languages is not 'gründlich,' and considering that your book* is the only one in English on the subject, he might have quoted it or referred to it. The Biographie Universelle is his great authority. The history of the Roman law and universities is meagre from Savigny. He is more at home on polemical points at the time of the Reformation; but while he makes justification by faith the test of Protestantism, and the point at issue between Luther and the Romish Church, he either knows not or mentions not that very curious schism in the bosom of the Church which Ranke so well describes. Though he has the names of Contarini and Sadoletus, he says not one word of their holding justification by faith, nor of their attempt to force it on the Pope at the time of the Council of Trent. I suspect Hallam's German is very slight, and though he quotes Meiners and others, I very much doubt his intimate acquaintance with them. If this be so, think of a man writing a history of literature, and virtually leaving out German. Hamlet, with a part of Hamlet omitted, is a joke to it. The omission of Ranke is the more inexcusable, because Milman reviewed it not long since in the 'Quarterly.'

I quite agree in your view of the morality which the Church of England would inculcate, if they could, as to marriage. They act upon it a good deal them-

* An Essay on the Origin and Formation of the Romance Languages, by Sir George Cornewall Lewis. Parker, 1835.

selves, if one is to judge by the number of curates who die and leave large families. Your definition is very good. It is precisely the suppression of the majors which makes the difference between the very high Church and the Romanists.

George Clive ended a letter to me not long ago with the following pious and benevolent ejaculation, writing from the depth of Wales: 'That the devil would fly 'away with this miserable race of Celtic savages, is the 'fervent prayer of yours sincerely, G. C——.' I need not say how heartily I repeat 'Amen' to the above petition—reckoning, of course, that Wales begins just beyond New Radnor.* The gradual action of Boards of Guardians, railroads, and other opportunities of intercourse, may civilize them in about three centuries.

* * * *

Yours very truly,
E. W. Head.

Malta: June 2, 1837.

My dear Head,—I enclose a letter from Mrs. Austin intended, I suppose, to explain about her marqueterie, the history of which she has made out. It seems to be curious in a historical point of view, and some of the figures are by no means wanting in merit. George Clive is, I have no doubt, quite right in his opinion of the intelligence of the Welsh. And how that intelligence is to be raised, while they retain their villainous Celtic language, it is not easy to see. What you said in a former letter about the *cowardice* and timidity of the Welsh is, I suspect, true of all ignorant and *borné* communities. It prevails here to a remarkable degree. There are not half a dozen people in the island who

* Sir George Lewis's family residence is close to New Radnor.

have an idea of speaking out freely, or acting with boldness. Limited and 'routinier' people look only to the particular consequence of the act, instead of trusting to the general effect of their conduct.

* * * *

I have read Hallam's book, which is dry, meagre, and ill written, with a few misplaced patches of laboured rhetoric. So far from understanding any one *subject* well, he does not seem to understand any one book well. His text is a mere digest of compilations and biographical dictionaries. I believe that he knows a little German, for a governess who lived in his family went afterwards to Lady ——, who told me that Hallam had learnt of her. Probably he spells through a book by the help of a dictionary with about the same success that he translates 'das Bücherwesen,' 'the being of books.' It must be confessed that charlatanerie is marvellously successful. I do not think Hallam had seen my essay on the Romance languages till after his lucubrations on the subject had been printed; for he spoke to me about it at the end of last London season, when, I believe, most of his book was through the press.

I have lately read Thirlwall's fourth volume,* which perhaps is the best. He has thrown much new light on the history of Athens at the close of the Peloponnesian war. After all, however, the history is so uncertain that one scarcely knows what to believe. He has succeeded in shaking Xenophon's credit to a greater degree than I should have thought possible. The next volume will, I suppose, complete the work with Alexander's death.

The policy of the Government about their bishops

* Thirlwall's 'History of Greece.'

has been thoroughly absurd. Why not appoint Arnold and Thirlwall at once? However, the House of Lords seem determined to resist to the last; and it is clear that liberal bishops will not convert them. It is, in my opinion, impossible to foresee the issue of the present struggle.* It depends on so many uncertain elements, such as the King's life, the price of corn, &c., that one can only see that, sooner or later, the Lords must go to the wall.

Do not miss the passages about the kangaroos, and about Caraccioli outsailing Nelson, in Colletta. I will write to you soon again.

Ever yours truly,
G. C. Lewis.

Malta: July 15, 1837.

My dear Father,—Your letters of the first of this month arrived to-day, and I have just time to acknowledge them (together with my mother's, which came some time ago by Marseilles) by the French steamer which goes in a few hours. My reason for writing is to relieve you from any apprehensions which you may have conceived from hearing exaggerated reports of the mortality caused by the cholera in this island. The cholera has now been in the island about five weeks, and has, by this time, killed nearly 2,000 people. The alarm has been great; doctors and all persons called on to act have generally neglected their duties: the people have shown the utmost want of prudence, combined with the most stupid and selfish cowardice, and accordingly the disease has made much more havoc than it would otherwise have made. The deaths are

* Chiefly respecting Irish affairs, Irish Municipal Corporations, Irish Tithes and Poor Laws.

now from 100 to 120 a day in a population of 120,000. Several of our servants and messengers have lost relations, and our housemaid has been attacked, but is now nearly out of danger. The disease, however, has chiefly confined itself to the working classes; the few persons of a higher station who have died have owed their death to some known and manifest imprudence or folly, such as over-fatigue, exposure to sun, or refusal to take medicine. The people here very generally refuse to take medicine, from distrust of the doctors and the Government. Reports also have been very industriously circulated, that the bread has been poisoned by the Government. A charitable society has been formed for the distribution of soup, on the committee of which I have acted. The distribution commenced yesterday, and a complaint has been already made that there is reason to fear it was poisoned. The people are in such a brutish state of ignorance, and their moral state is so degraded, that it is perfectly 'désespérant' to have anything to do with them. Such are the effects of a paternal military despotism, which rules people by keeping them in ignorance and dependence. I do not conceive that persons who lead a regular wholesome life are in any greater danger here than they were in London during the prevalence of the cholera, and you remember what that chance amounted to.

I will answer your letters by the next post. The manufacturing distress in England is a terrible evil; I do not see my way out of it; and I trust the Poor Law Act may survive it and the general election. I hope you will stick firmly to the principle, and that you will nail your colours to the mast.

* * * *

Your affectionate son,

G. C. Lewis.

Malta: July 31, 1837.

My dear Head,—Your last letter gave a very gloomy picture of the prospects of the Poor Law Act. From the account of the proceedings of the committee in deciding on the Report, I cannot help suspecting that many people who find it convenient to join in, and make use of, the clamour, would nevertheless flinch from approving out-door relief when it came to a question of aye or no. There is not, I am confident, a maxim which more commonly deceives in practice than the current one, that people are, in the long run, guided by their pecuniary interests. The truth is, that the interest of prejudice is, nine times out of ten, quite as strong as the interest of money, and very often far stronger. Nevertheless, the interest of money is excessively powerful; and when one remembers with what tenacity the landlords cling to the corn laws, and how they mould their opinions in order to support their supposed pecuniary interests on this subject, it is difficult to believe that the landlord majorities of the two Houses of Parliament will ever seriously entertain a project which is likely to make so deep a cut into their incomes.

The difficulty of introducing the measure into the manufacturing districts seems, at present, insuperable; the distress must make the working people ten times more alert than they would otherwise be on the subject. A trade union, supported by a poor-rate, is one of the prettiest pieces of machinery that can be conceived.

I am glad you thought my paper on Irish Poor Laws was worth publishing.* The argument against the com-

* Abstract of Final Report of Commissioners of Irish Poor Inquiry, with Letters to Ministers, by G. C. Lewis and N. Senior. F. C. Wesley, 162, Piccadilly.

missioners' plan (if plan it can be called) seems to me conclusive to any candid reader as it stands. But my own suggestions are very imperfectly developed, and are not fitted to stand hostile and captious criticism, although they seemed to me fitted for their purpose, viz. to assist persons, not sitting down to object, but desirous of information. If I had been in England, I could have made this part much more complete; and I think I could have shown that the objections of Whately and others, if good at all, are good against every kind of poor law, their own included; and that the choice lies between such a measure as I have suggested or none. I am confident that any plan of out-door relief in Ireland would simply amount to a very inconvenient mode of transferring the net revenue of the land from the landowner and tithe-owner to the peasantry. I prefer Raumer's plan of converting the tenants into 'Eigenthümer' directly; and, indeed, I agree with him so far, that if I looked only to particular expediency, and put out of the question the dangerous example of an extensive invasion of the right of property, I should prefer this change to the present state of things. I have no doubt that if the Irish peasantry were a proprietary class, like the French peasantry, habits of frugality would be formed to which they are now strangers. But adopt what plan you will the question always recurs, how are you to strike at the root of the evil—the improvident habits of the people with regard to breeding? Such an insuperable wall of prejudice is opposed to all improvement on this head, that one almost despairs. For this reason it seems to me so important to settle the Church questions in Ireland. It is not so much for the sake of quieting the tithe agitation, as for un sentimentalizing the cause of the Catholic clergy, and for making it possible to gain a hearing for some other than the theologico-ethical opinions with which they poison men's minds. It seems impossible to make the Catholic priests see that early marriages do not, on the whole, prevent the limited evil which they are intended to guard against; that adultery of the husband and of the wife, and prostitution of the children, are the natural consequences of them. The Maltese priests, although these consequences are developed under their eyes in the most lucid manner, are nevertheless utterly blind to them.

* * * *

I have been reading Helvetius' works lately ('De l'esprit de l'homme'). His system of ethics is, as a system, narrow and false, and he was not capable of a close and long-sustained train of reasoning; but his writings contain a vast number of admirable remarks and suggestions, and cannot be read without profit, even if it was merely for the sake of the excellent tone in which they are conceived. The French Revolution and Bonaparte have terribly spoilt the French philosophy, and have filled it full of inane declamation and national prejudice. Latterly, too, they have attempted to borrow some of the maddest speculations of the German mystical philosophers.

We have had occasion lately to look at some French laws, and to look at some reports relating to the concoction of them. It must be confessed that they do their legislative work in a most masterly manner in France as compared with England. There are certainly now men in France who can draw laws in a manner in which laws could not be drawn in England. If the French were guided in practice by rather better *maxims*, they would run us a very hard race in most things, and would excel us in many. It is remarkable enough that in a country which boasts so much of its practical talent as England, everything that comes from the Government and legislature seems to be written between asleep and awake.

We have had cholera lately in Malta, and the disease being clearly non-contagious, we have been put in quarantine by every port in the Mediterranean, Gibraltar and the Ionian Isles included. Sir Howard Douglas, in the latter place, refused even to admit into the lazzaretto the passengers in the Government steamer, and sent them all back to Malta. The cholera has likewise been raging in Sicily, and there have been riots in Messina and Syracuse.

* * * *

Our inquiry is now drawing to a close, and I expect to be in England before the winter. There is, doubtless, a great deal to be said against Brecknockshire[*] and Herefordshire, but I think you have had a great escape in not plunging into a colony. It would be fearful to feel one's self cooped up in the 'kleinstädtischer Geist' for life.

What do you say to the translation of the title of the fairy tale, 'Prince Chéri et la Princesse Belle Étoile,' into 'Prince Cherry and Princess Fair Star?'

Ever yours,

G. C. LEWIS.

Malta: September 2, 1837.

My dear Father,—I wrote you a few lines by one of the French steamers to tell you that the cholera was nearly extinct in Malta. Since I wrote to you it has gone on steadily diminishing, and it can now scarcely be

[*] Sir Edmund Head's district, as Assistant Poor Law Commissioner.

said to exist (five deaths in the last two days), except for the purpose of keeping us in quarantine with all the Mediterranean. The Boards of Health, among whom all exploded errors are carefully preserved, persist in treating cholera as a contagious disease, contrary to the most manifest facts and to the almost unanimous opinion of medical men. After the governor here had been threatening the doctors and scolding the people for treating the cholera as contagious, Sir Howard Douglas, in Corfu, refused to allow the passengers to land from the Government steamer, and sent them back to Malta; and Sir Alexander Woodford, at Gibraltar, subjected ships from Malta to a quarantine of sixteen days. Such is the union between the three military governors of the English colonies in the Mediterranean.

There is a strange rambling book on the Ionian Isles, written by Colonel Charles Napier, the brother of the historian, which I have lately read. Many of his opinions are wrong, but, on the whole, he has a sound judgment, and he seems to have that most rare quality, public spirit. I should judge him to be an abler man than his brother. * * * I fear, however, that it is necessary to have some special interest about Mediterranean colonies to care for the book. A Mr. Slade, a naval man, has lately written two volumes about the Mediterranean. The part relating to Malta is mere gossip, which he must have heard at different dinners and have written down without examination. I have not looked at the rest of the book, but I hear that it is full of nonsense about the power of Russia. I am confident that there never was a more groundless alarm; and I can scarcely think that any ministry would be so absurd as to go to war with Russia upon such grounds as Mr. Urquhart and Mr. Slade and such politicians treat us with. I confess that I have a much greater fear of an American war, if the Government persist in their measures against Canada. Whatever the American *Government* may do, the American *people* are sure to assist the Canadians if we begin coercing them by an armed force, and then we shall have the old follies and abominations over again. What possible advantage England derives from the possession of Canada, I confess I am unable to see. If, however, the ministers irritate the Canadians into expressions and measures insulting to England, they will be able to appeal to the silly national pride of the people, and will probably be supported in a war. Perhaps, too, they may find it convenient to divert people's attention from internal to external politics. The only security against the most pernicious folly, both on the part of the Government and the people, seems to me to be the expense of a war and the disturbance which it would occasion to trade. It is fortunate that the concerns of individuals are managed with a little more prudence than those of nations; otherwise most men would be beggars before they were thirty.

I was much obliged to you for your information about the sentiments of the Government on the question of the liberty of the press for Malta. They accord very closely with what we had anticipated. Profound indifference to everything but the party interest of the moment is the characteristic of the present ministry, and, I fear, of any ministry which is likely to succeed them. We have written to request permission to return to England when we have finished our inquiry, which cannot occupy us much longer. I expect, at any rate, to be in England by the end of the year. It seems absurd to talk of the great difficulty of an inquiry in such a little place as Malta; but the truth is, they have here a set of ancient complicated institutions, founded upon a totally different set of legal and political principles from those of England, and consequently every subject requires a special study before one can feel certain that one is not making mistakes. Having undertaken the inquiry, and having finished a large part of it, I should not like to slur over the remainder for the sake of being in England a few months sooner. Moreover, the inquiry does not simply concern the government of 120,000 people. We hope that if our recommendations are acted on, the moral influence of England in the Mediterranean would be increased, and that her character for good faith would be raised, which must stand very low in the Mediterranean after her conduct about Sicily, Genoa, Parga, and Malta; to say nothing of Nelson and Caraccioli. As to a free press in Malta being an European question, the notion is perfectly absurd, and I am confident that Metternich (if the case has been properly represented to him) cannot consider it so. Probably he objects to everything, on the principle that he may gain and cannot lose; and if the measure was introduced he would doubtless acquiesce in it without remark. The pretension is too monstrous to be maintained, and I am convinced that the House of Commons would not support the Government in deferring so much to the chimerical fears of Austria.

We have had a long continuance of hot weather, and are to have a month of it more. Nobody thinks of going out in the sun. We dine at three o'clock, and I usually ride in the evening about seven o'clock. The heat produces languor and lassitude of body and mind, but I never had better health.

Your affectionate son,

G. C. Lewis.

Malta: October 3, 1837.

My dear Head,—I am glad to hear from Gilbert that you and he have set up a joint-stock ménage; it must be a great advantage to him in every way, only I should fear that you are not often at home. The more I see of colonial life, the more I am satisfied that you did rightly in preferring your present employment, with all its drawbacks, to the colonial service. The scum of England is poured into the colonies: briefless barristers, broken-down merchants, ruined debauchees, the offal of every calling and profession are crammed into colonial places. You probably saw that O'Connell, in his letter about Ruthven, after denouncing him as a swindler and a scoundrel, unfit for the society of gentlemen, went on to say that he had done his best to give him a colonial appointment. This may be taken as evidence of the general opinion as to the qualifications for colonial service; and, although the Government may not have been able to stomach Ruthven, many of the people who have been sent out quite recently are only one degree better.

* * * *

This is the sort of society in which, if I am not much mistaken, you would have found yourself plunged had you accepted a colonial appointment.

* * * *

I confess it seems to me that no man who is not in debt, or has not a large family, is justified in going out to a colony. If I was Gilbert, I would rather be rector of Mornington than bishop of Calcutta.

The Government here have lately been making some changes in their charitable institutions, which we have recommended. The expenditure in charities is now 16,000*l.* a year out of a revenue of less than 100,000*l.*

One of the institutions which we recommended to be gradually abolished was (what in Italy is called) a Conservatorio, that is, a charity boarding-school for girls, who remain in it till they can get places, or are married. On examining the girls in the Conservatorio somewhat more closely than had hitherto been done, it has recently turned out, that although they have been regularly taught to read Italian, they never learnt the meaning of the words; and although there are some who have been undergoing this process for several years who can pronounce Italian to perfection, they cannot understand or speak a word of it. I hope this is not the way in which English is taught in Welsh schools.

The Government press of this place has recently reprinted an account of the blockade of Valetta by a French knight named Ransijat, who had been finance minister under the order; and having sympathized with the French revolution, was placed by Bonaparte at the head of the French commission of government. The man himself is a great curiosity, being a French Jacobin under the mantle of the chivalrous monk of St. John; and his book would, I think, interest those who have no special interest about Malta. I will lend it to you when I return to England, and you can try whether you can read it.

I begin now to doubt whether I shall be in England before the spring: we have still some work to do, and after a hot Malta summer, I am rather afraid of plunging suddenly into an English winter. My hopes of seeing Greece have all vanished; quarantine makes all rapid movement impossible.

Ever yours truly,

G. C. Lewis.

Malta: November 15, 1837.

* * * *

My dear Father,—The change in the commercial policy of this island which we recommended has been recently carried into effect; and I enclose you a copy of our Report which we have printed in Italian, and the law giving effect to our scheme. Now that it is finished, it goes into a nutshell, but I can assure you that the trouble which it cost was not small. In order to fix a system of custom duties, it is necessary to consider all the alternatives; and the combinations are so numerous, and the variety of projects so great, that nothing can be fixed without great consideration.

A Mons. Bailly has lately been in Malta on a mission from the French Government to examine their line of Mediterranean packets. He has given us a copy of a book lately published by him on the finances of England. It contains the first attempt I have seen to give a complete account of the taxation of England; that is, of the taxes levied by subordinate authorities as well as by the supreme Government. He reckons the annual taxation of the United Kingdom at two milliards of francs, or eighty millions sterling, which, he says, is rather under than over the truth. However large the revenue raised in England, I am confident that the evils caused by the abstraction of the money are as nothing when compared with the evils caused by protecting and discriminating duties, and by vexatious regulations for securing the collection of the revenue. I have been lately reading Sir Henry Parnell's book on financial reform; parts of it are rather feeble and confused; but, on the whole, he is successful in making out that an immense improvement may be effected in raising the revenue in England. One of the greatest obstacles to financial reform is the routinier prejudices of official persons. I have observed this in Malta, where all sinister interest was out of the question.

I have read Macaulay's article on Lord Bacon in the 'Edinburgh Review.' It is written in his usual sparkling, lively, and antithetical style, and the historical part of it is interesting and amusing. His remarks on the ancient philosophy are, for the most part, shallow and ignorant in the extreme: his objections to the utility of logic are the stale common-places which all the enemies of accurate knowledge, and the eulogists of common sense, practical men, &c., have been always putting forth. There is generally throughout the article a want of soundness and coherency, and a puerile and almost girlish affectation of tinsel ornament, which, coming from a man of nearly forty, convince me that Macaulay will never be anything more than a rhetorician.

We have had a rainy October, but latterly the weather has been finer. The thermometer, however, gets gradually lower; it now falls to a little below 60°, and a fire at night is not uncomfortable.

* * * *

Ever your affectionate son,

G. C. Lewis.

Malta: December 13, 1837.

My dear Father,—Since last post went out I have received two letters from you and two from my mother.

* * * *

I have been sorry to hear of the death of the ass,[*] a finer one I will undertake to say never ate an English

[*] Sir George Lewis had purchased for one of his father's friends, at the price of 50*l.*, a large Maltese ass, which died on its passage to England.

thistle. I should hope that Mr. Raymond will turn up. I will send you, by next post, an account of what I paid. There is his keep for some time, besides the crib, and the payment for his freight and food when on board.

* * * *

We were much obliged to you for your hints about the spirit duty, and we had actually prepared a statement for the colonial office which was to have gone by this post, requesting them to send out an English exciseman. It is, however, very difficult to do anything satisfactory in the matter, and I fear that the Government must suffer for its past imprudence and neglect, by incurring a present loss.

I read a volume of Pickwick, which, I believe, did not contain above half what has appeared; it is an imitation of Theodore Hook's novels, with descriptive passages imitated, half in jest, half in earnest, from the descriptions in Walter Scott's novels. The wit (if such it is to be called) chiefly arises from caricature, broad farce, and practical jokes, such as a man who never handled a gun going out shooting, &c. Its popularity, though rapid and extensive, will, I think, be short lived. His parodies of speeches are amusing, though too much exaggerated.

Pray tell Miss Ashton I have received all her translation, and have revised a good deal of it.

Your affectionate son,

G. C. Lewis.

Malta: January 9, 1838.

* * * *

My dear Father,—I am sorry that you should have had the trouble of reading our report on the customs in Italian, as I could, without difficulty, have sent you an English copy. The new tariff has now been in force just two months, and experience has hitherto proved that we were right; for there has been an increase of revenue as well as an improvement of trade. I read a long article in 'Galignani' from the *Times*, full of ultra-radical topics, and abusing us for beginning with a tariff taxing the food of the poor. It was written by some person wholly ignorant of the facts of the case, *e.g.* he speaks of the free trade which the island enjoyed under the order, whereas the most important articles of consumption were then monopolized by the Government; there were heavy discriminating duties on articles which could be imported, and there were numerous monopolies granted to individuals as in England in Queen Elizabeth's reign. The principle of our tariff was an unpopular one; but on the whole it has been well received, even by the public at large (if such a term be applicable to Malta); the mercantile classes are almost unanimous in its favour on account of its simplicity, and the small number of articles included in it. I believe it to be the only tariff in the world framed exclusively for the purpose of raising revenue. The duty on grain is certainly liable to the objection which you mention. The quantity of wheat annually imported is about 60,000 quarters, the quantity of wheat annually grown in the island is about 20,000 quarters. It was impossible to raise a revenue in any other way, and we were aware that we were putting a large sum annually into the pockets of the landlords; but the notions about protecting native industry, which prevail in Malta as in other countries, prevented this effect from being considered as an evil, and therefore we said nothing about it in our report. The distinction between superior and inferior wines was preserved from the former tariff, and I have not heard that it has given rise to much difficulty in practice.

* * * *

It is, however, quite a mistake to suppose that the Maltese are disaffected to England, and that there is a Russian party in Malta. If the whole community could vote by ballot to-morrow on the question of England or Russia, I question whether Russia would have six votes, though there is no doubt that she constantly keeps her eye on the island, and sends agents and spies from time to time.

We have now got to finish our laws on the liberty of the press, and have a few points of trifling importance to settle. We shall then begin a report on part of the judicial system, and when that is finished I shall go to England, leaving Austin here to finish the inquiry into the courts and the state of the law. I will not fail to let you know as soon as I am able to fix a time for leaving the island. I shall probably go by a French steamer to Marseilles, and travel across France in malle-postes and diligences. I should like to see Cadiz, and Cosmo Gordon, and Gibraltar, and Lisbon, but I dread the long passage necessary for seeing them. Edward Goulburn has come out as aide-de-camp to Sir Henry Bouverie.

* * * *

I have looked through Mr. Nicholls' Second Report on Irish Poor Laws. It seems to me less twaddling than the first, and to show a better acquaintance with the subject. I cannot, however, agree with him in thinking that there is as much destitution in the north as in the south of Ireland (the difference as to White-boy offences proves the reverse), nor do I see how the law can directly prevent the subdivision of land, as he implies in i. 32. No attempt seems to have been made to rehabilitate the commissioners' report; it appears to be set aside by common consent.

Pray thank my mother for two letters.

* * * *

We have had fine, clear, blue weather lately. The clover is already high, and the almond trees are in blossom.

Your affectionate son,

G. C. Lewis.

Malta: February 8, 1838.

My dear Father,—The English mail is now expected hourly, but has not yet arrived, so that I have not heard from you since I wrote last. The French steamers have, however, brought us 'Galignani' down nearly to the end of January, containing the news of the suppression of the insurrection in Canada and Lord Durham's appointment.

On the whole the country has shown more good sense and more moderation about Canada than I gave them credit for. It remains to be seen whether they will sustain their character, or whether, after a painful period of self-restraint, they will not break out into some violence and folly.

I have been reading lately as much as an ordinary reader can digest of the Duke of Wellington's despatches. The rapidity and justness of his decisions, his unvarying good sense, his profound feeling of public duty and of regard for public interests, are most strikingly displayed in them. If his political views had not been so narrow, and if he had had more knowledge, he would have been the greatest English statesman as well as the greatest English captain.

* * * *

In some of his letters the Duke of Wellington shows a talent for speculating on general questions which, if cultivated, might have borne great fruit. I could point out two or three instances in which this power is displayed; one that will most interest you is in a letter dated Bombay, April 11, 1804, to a Major Graham (vol. ii. p. 202), in which the workhouse principle (*i.e.* of making relief disagreeable by accompanying it with restraint) is very distinctly stated.

The papers bring accounts of intense frost in London and Paris, and I hear that the Rhône, rapid as it is, has been frozen down to Avignon. The month of January in Malta has been remarkably fine; blue sky nearly the whole day, and little wind, which is the bane of this island. The thermometer has been rarely under 50°. Since the beginning of this month there has been a change for the worse, the temperature has been lower, and there has been a good deal of wind and rain. But it is perfectly ludicrous to talk of severe cold in Malta at any time of the year. A small fire is always sufficient in the house, and a great coat is never required out of the house, even for riding.

Everything here is as still as death. We were at one time a little afraid that the Italian exiles would make use of the liberty of the press to attack their own Governments, but there are only one or two in the island, and it has been intimated to them that if they attempt anything of the sort, they must be off, and I have no idea that they can venture to run this risk. The Italian Liberals are for the most part a most imbecile and odious race; nothing, indeed, would induce people to tolerate them except the sanguinary ferocity of their stupid Governments.

I cannot yet fix any time for leaving the island. I do not now expect to move before the beginning of April. Your affectionate son,

G. C. LEWIS.

Malta: February 22, 1838.

* * * *

My dear Father,—This is the carnival week, and there is a great deal of amusement going on in the shape of balls, regattas, and what not. The officers of the army divert themselves in various ways. A few days ago they were all in motion to see a wager between two midshipmen, who undertook to race one another, each floating in a half barrel, the one drawn by six geese and the other by eighteen ducks. But the ducks and geese spoiled the sport, for (as a person present described it to us) 'non volevano camminare.'

The Canada business has, on the whole, ended well. It remains to be seen what Lord Durham will do in the way of a new constitution. The radicals have certainly acted very ill. However bad the conduct of the Government might have been, it afforded no reason for inciting to rebellion, or for approving it when it had taken place.

Everything is going on well here. I enclose a pamphlet relating to our new tariff which has been just published. As yet, I cannot say when I shall return. I hope by next post to be able to foresee more nearly. Pray remember me to Head if he is still in London. Has he had the misfortune of becoming a baronet?

Your affectionate son,

G. C. LEWIS.

Malta: March 23, 1838.

* * * *

My dear Father,—We have received a letter from the Colonial Office, desiring us to wind up our commission as soon as we can; and we have now reported or finished our reports upon everything except two subjects, viz. the question of a *consiglio popolare*, or representative assembly, and law reform. On the former of these we have collected our materials, though the report is not written. The latter will take time, as it will involve the formation of codes which Austin is ready to undertake if the Government wish it. I intend to leave the island shortly, so that you need not write to me in Malta after the receipt of this letter.

* * * *

On the whole the English Government have behaved very well with respect to Malta. There were two great obstacles to overcome, viz. indifference about so small an object, and interest in maintaining numerous jobs, and abuses, and blunders.

I send some acorns from a famous oak at Belgrade; pray sow them.

Your affectionate son,
G. C. Lewis.

Paris: May 9, 1838.

My dear Mother,—I left Malta on the 27th of April by the French steamer, and arrived at Marseilles on the 3rd of May. On the following day I left Marseilles by the diligence, and arrived at two o'clock this morning at Paris, being a slice out of the fifth night that I passed in the diligence.

* * * *

I intend to leave Paris not earlier than the 12th,

and not later than the 14th. You can judge from this when I am likely to be in London.

*　　*　　*　　*

Your affectionate son,
G. C. Lewis.

The changes effected by this Commission in the government and laws of the island of Malta were, as had been anticipated, very extensive. In the administration of justice, in the method of taxation, in the regulations relating to education, to the press, the police, as well as in other important matters, many alterations were made by which discontent was removed, and satisfaction given to the inhabitants.

The dry genial climate in which George Lewis had spent a year and a half had been beneficial to his health; the languor produced by excessive heat during a summer had been more than compensated for by the freedom from cold which he had enjoyed during two winters.

On his return he writes to his friend Sir Edmund Head, who was still acting as an Assistant Poor Law Commissioner in Herefordshire.

London: June 2, 1838.

My dear Head,—I am glad to hear from Gilbert that you are likely to be in London in about a fortnight from the present time; but I fear that you will not stay more than a few days. You are, of course, aware that the 18th is just a week before the coronation.

The principal change which I observe in London since I went to Malta is the increased number of omnibuses, hack cabs, &c. They are now so numerous as almost to make it disagreeable to walk in the streets. By-the-by I heard that somebody moved the Court of Queen's Bench the other day to grant two mandami.

I have heard two lectures of Carlyle's on the literature of England and France in the eighteenth century. He is interesting and even instructive to hear; though he belongs to a class whose business it is to deny all accurate knowledge, and all processes for arriving at accurate knowledge, and to induce mankind to accept blindly certain mysterious dicta of their own. It is clear that so long as this set of opinions prevails the great mass of every community, even those calling themselves the educated classes, must be, for most practical purposes, in the same state of enlightenment as Sir William Courtenay's late followers in Kent. The decryers of reason, logic, science, theory, speculation, pride of human intellect, &c.; and the eulogists of common sense, moral sense, intellectual humility, &c., form two great classes, whose respective opinions assume very various forms, but amount in the end to the same thing.

Arnold has published the first volume of his 'History of Rome,' and Thirlwall the fifth of his 'History of Greece.' Both of these are decidedly democratic works, and will, no doubt, have their influence. Thirlwall's fifth volume does not finish the reign of Philip; I suppose his sixth will end with the death of Alexander. I will talk to you about Arnold's book when I see you.

What a picture of Walter Scott's character is exhibited in Lockhart's life of him. How low and vulgar his objects and how sordid his view of literature. He contracted to deliver novels as a Manchester manufacturer might contract to deliver bales of calico; and he received the money in advance in order to buy farms or pay for gilt furniture.

Ever yours,
G. C. Lewis.

In January, 1839, George Lewis succeeded his father

as one of the three principal Poor-Law Commissioners; thus we find the next letter to Mr. Austin alluding to a conversation which he had held in the Poor-Law Office.

29, Hertford Street: December 2, 1839.

My dear Austin,—You are aware that it has been the practice in our colonial system to consider the governor as the mere representative of the Crown, as a mere viceroy; and, consequently, that when a House of Assembly has been established in a colony, the colony has ceased to be a Crown colony—in other words, the Crown has lost its power of legislating in the colony by Orders in Council. Nevertheless, it is quite clear that it might be expedient to impose upon the legislative power of a colonial governor the check of a popularly elected body, though it might not be expedient to abandon the power of legislating in the colony by Orders in Council. The notion that the two powers must be simultaneously abandoned seems to have arisen from a clumsy application of Whig doctrines about 'taxation and representation,' and 'the influence of the Crown.'

The only exception to this rule in our colonies is furnished by British Guiana, which is a Crown colony, but the governor's legislative power is checked by two councils—one a *general* council, composed half of elected and half of official members; the other a *financial* council, composed exclusively of elected members styled *financial representatives*. The chief secretary of Guiana, a Mr. Young, is now in England. He is a friend of Lefevre's, and I had a long conversation with him a few days ago at the Poor-Law Office. He gave a favourable account of the working of these bodies, and said that the governor had never found any difficulty with them. They had passed every financial measure which the Government had proposed. He said that it had never been, *in fact*, necessary to resort to an Order in Council in order to pass a measure rejected by the councils; but he added, that the councils were well aware that the Colonial Office would interfere by an Order in Council if they resisted the reasonable demands of the Government. He stated that the Crown had sometimes legislated in the colony, but not in contested points.

I have doubt that if a similar power had been reserved to the Crown in Canada, Jamaica, and the other colonies, we should have avoided the difficulties into which they have fallen. If a House of Assembly is factious, the governor and Colonial office are powerless; but, unwilling to apply to Parliament, they struggle on and allow matters to proceed from bad to worse, until an Act of Parliament becomes absolutely necessary. Little as the Colonial Office may know of the state of our colonies, it is the only part of our government which *does* know anything about them. Parliament is as ignorant as it is indifferent. Consequently, if the Colonial Office is unable to legislate when it will, the time for legislation is lost, the colony falls into confusion, till at length the fear of downright anarchy compels the unwilling Ministry to bring a bill into Parliament. The result is that the only direct interference which the mother country exercises on a chartered colony is by occasional and capricious acts of the supreme legislature.

There is nothing in our recommendations which ought to suggest the idea that Malta would, in case of their adoption, cease to be a Crown colony. You will be able to judge whether it will be advisable to make an express remark to that effect. If they were to get an elective council, and if the Government were to acquire the habit of deferring habitually to its opinion, a question *might* possibly arise as to the power of the Crown to legislate alone. Provided this power was distinctly reserved, and there was a good governor, I should have little fear of giving them their 'consiglio popolare.'

Ever yours truly,
G. C. Lewis.

Poor-Law Office: December 18, 1839.

My dear Head,—

* * * *

Your account of Hampden's book* makes me curious to read it. I always suspected that it was more heterodox than Senior and others were willing to admit; for the Oxford people do not in general make a great stir about nothing. It is very probable that Hampden did not himself see the consequences of his own arguments.

I passed an evening a few days ago with Austin and John Mill. We had a long conversation on the effects of the Reformation, Austin (who was in good health) arguing strenuously that the Reformation has, on the whole, been an evil to mankind. His chief arguments were: First, that it has produced sectarianism, with all its concomitant evils of hatreds, divisions, persecutions, &c. He thinks that the bitterness between parties in the Catholic church (as Jansenists and Molinists) has been mainly owing to the Reformation. Secondly, that it has rendered theological questions popular. He says that, before the Reformation, theology was confined to the schools, and that if it had not been for

* Hampden's Bampton Lectures.

the Reformation, people would not dispute about free will and grace more than they dispute about nominalism and realism, or syllogism and induction. He says that the Catholic church is entitled to the gratitude of the world for having handed down the torch of knowledge and resisted barbarism during the middle ages; but that no person actuated by the spirit of Protestantism has ever rendered any service to mankind. He says that reason was advancing before the Reformation, and that it would have made more steady advances if the Reformation had not taken place. He doubts whether new opinions would have been proscribed and condemned by the Church; but he thinks that free speculation would have been permitted as under Leo the Tenth.

What he now wishes to see is a truly Catholic and comprehensive church—a church which does not act on the maxim 'compelle entrare,' but which treats every person as a member, unless he refuses to be so treated; which views every man as a Christian, as the State views every man a subject. For this purpose he would not change the articles and symbols of any church, but would get rid of all tests, subscriptions, &c., and carefully exclude all condemning and anathematising priests, all men such as Philpotts, from the endowments of the clergy.

This outline will give you an idea of his opinions on the subject. I fully assent to the conclusions, but I feel great difficulty in forming any confident opinion respecting the effects of the Reformation. It is a great thing that the Church has no official organ for condemning opinions.

Ever yours truly,
G. C. Lewis.

London: January 4, 1840.

My dear Head,—I agree with you in dissenting from Austin's views concerning the effects of the Reformation; at least, to the extent to which he carries them. I think it true that a great deal of the mischief done by the Church of Rome since the Reformation is imputable to the provocation which this great schism gave to the Catholic party. I also think that the reaction against Protestantism which took place at the end of the sixteenth century was in some degree owing to a disappointment as to the effects of the change. But I cannot bring myself to believe that the persecuting and obscurantist spirit of the Church of Rome would have been ever got the better of by any other means than open resistance. I do not believe that the rulers of the Church would ever have seen that it was their interest to tolerate freedom of thought and discussion. If so, open resistance, with all its attendant evils of sectarianism, mutual persecution, and so forth, was inevitable. I am every day more and more inclined to attach weight to the destruction of the executive portion of the Church, and to the silencing its speaking organs of doctrine. I see constantly abortive attempts to procure authoritative declarations and condemnations by the Church, without people being aware precisely what they are aiming at. They feel the want, but they do not quite see how to satisfy it.

There is another most important consequence of the Reformation as to the diminution of the hold of the clergy on men's minds, viz. the secularization of the Church property.

Milman was saying the other day that before the Reformation nearly the whole of Westminster belonged to the Abbot of Westminster. Macaulay, who was present, added that the revenues of the Abbot of Glastonbury would be now equal to at least 500,000*l.* a year. Conceive what power over opinions would be exercised by a spiritual aristocracy with such mighty possessions as these. We see what power of this sort is exercised in this country by a comparatively torpid and uneducated aristocracy solely by the means of rents and money; how much greater power would be exercised by an aristocracy equally rich, containing many active and educated men, and having spiritual associations and sanctions to back it.

I confess that I have great doubts whether the *popularization* of theological controversies has been exclusively owing to the Reformation. The Reformation and the *general diffusion* of printing are nearly contemporaneous; and I attribute to the latter, and to the spirit of discussion which it created, much of the polemical spirit which arose at this time. The disputes of the Jansenists and the Molinists show that polemics may become popular in an age of general reading in the bosom of a Catholic country.

Austin argues in nearly the same tone against the French revolution, and doubts whether the world would not have advanced more quickly without it. I have also heard him question the good effects of the American War of Independence.

With regard to the French Revolution his case is stronger than with regard to the Reformation. There is no doubt that the terror excited by the atrocities of the democratic and infidel party in the French Revolution has given great strength to the anti-popular and clerical party. Still it is difficult to be too grateful for the utter annihilation of the old aristocratic institutions and opinions in France, and a large part of Germany;

and a peaceable reform would not have effected this. A peaceable reform in 1789 would probably have produced in France the same ultimate effect as the Revolution in 1688 in England. It would have curtailed the power of the king and the privileges of the nobles; and it would ultimately have transferred the governing power from the court to the territorial aristocracy.

I bought the other day a 'Dictionnaire du bas langage.' It contains the following article—Mèche, *découvrir la mèche*, éventer un complot, un dessein, une entreprise, que l'on tenait secrète. The same word is in Roquefort, but is not so clearly explained. It is clearly connected with to *mich*, and is perhaps the origin of it. Skinner derives a *micher*, a covetous man (I suppose because he conceals, hides, hoards money) from *mica*, in French *miche*, *because he counts all the crumbs that fall from his table.* This etymology, Mr. Richardson says, is undoubtedly the true one. There is a slight objection to it to which Mr. Richardson does not advert, viz. that the French form of *mica* is not *miche* but *mie*, like *pie* from *pica*.

It occurred to me the other day that the Roman maxim respecting slave-children, 'partus sequitur ventrem,' is *partly* founded on the ground that 'hors le mariage il n'y a de certain que la maternité.' Slave women, of course, were not married; and even where a free man had intercourse with a slave, it was uncertain who might be the father of her children. The maxim was doubtless in part founded on the interest of the masters.

* * * *

I am glad to hear that Tremenhere is likely to make an interesting report.

Ever yours truly,

G. C. LEWIS.

The glossary referred to in the two next letters is a glossary of provincial words used in Herefordshire and some of the adjoining counties which Sir George Lewis had himself compiled and published in the preceding year.*

Wilton Place: January 25, (probably) 1840.

My dear Head,—I have sent the Herefordshire glossary to Day,† and have received from him, in return, a list of Shropshire and also of Sussex provincialisms.

Among the former is *songowing* for gleaning, which he spells *song-going*, and derives it from the practice of singing the harvest home.

You will see that in page 122 of the glossary, *songal* or *songle* is noticed as having been formerly used in Herefordshire in the sense of a handful of gleaned corn. *Songow* is doubtless formed from *songal*, according to the Cheshire practice of changing *l* into *w*.

Is it possible that songle can be derived from the French *sangle* (lit de sangle), which means a girth, and is probably the same as the Latin *cingulum*?

The resemblance of the sound is close, and the meaning is tolerably near.

Query, is the expression *songle* now known in any part of Herefordshire?

Ever yours truly,
G. C. Lewis.

'In many of the Dutch towns, *cingel* or *singel* is the name of a street in the suburbs without the walls, situate at a certain distance and concentrical with them or a part of them, thus surrounding them like a *cingulum*. This is the true etymology of the singel at Meldorf, which was doubtless outside the old city wall.'—*Niebuhr*, 'Nachgelassene Schriften nicht philologischen Inhalts,' p. 43.

* Murray, 1839.
† Mr. Day was an Assistant Poor Law Commissioner.

June 10, 1840.

Dear Mrs. Austin,—There is an article in the *Times* to-day on your translation of Ranke.* I think that you will be pleased to see the high terms in which the writer speaks of Ranke's work; the spirit or nature of which he appears to understand and appreciate justly. I should certainly say that the reception which this important work has hitherto met with is an encouragement to undertake something more by the same author. There is more probability of sweetening the bitter theological and sectarian spirit of this country by indirect than by direct means.

Murray, however (with whom I dined yesterday), is very desirous that you should undertake some *original* work. Do you feel a *Beruf* of this sort?

Ever yours truly,
G. C. Lewis.

Harpton: September 28, 1839 (probably) or 1840.

My dear Head,— I find in your copy of the Herefordshire glossary the following addition under *scallage*, '*skilling*, a lean-to or shed built against a building (E. Field).' There is a Scotch word *shiel* or *shieling* for a shed which may be connected with *shelter*; as *shade* and *shed* are the same word. Possibly *skilling* or *shieling* may be connected; and *scallage* is perhaps a corruption of *skilling*. There is no Scotch dictionary here, and therefore I can find nothing about *shieling*.

In a list of words which appear to be in Mr. Dyke's writing, there is the following remark under 'lich-yat,' which is the common name for churchyard gate in his part of the country: 'I am told that *collims* is another term for the same gateway, but I never heard it used.'

* Ranke's 'History of the Popes,' translated by Sarah Austin. Murray, 1840.

The word *collions* is written in pencil, and Mr. Dyke seems to be doubtful whether he has got the right form. I suspect that he means *scallenge*, or some similar sound. Would you or Lady Head have the kindness to write to Mr. Dyke, and direct his attention to the article *scallage* in the glossary, and ask him whether that is the word to which he alludes?

Perhaps this question may bring out some other form of the word which may throw light on its etymology. I suspect that the etymology given in the glossary is wrong.

When you go to London, pray do not forget to call on Grote, at 4, Eccleston Street, Belgrave Square.

* * * *

Ever yours truly,
G. C. Lewis.

Similarity of literary taste, study, and knowledge gained for Sir George Lewis the intimate friendship of George Grote. He valued Mr. Grote's opinion and judgment so highly, that few, if any, of his pleasures exceeded that which he took in discussing with the learned historian of Greece, not only subjects connected with early history and philosophy, but likewise topics connected with politics and passing events. He had also great enjoyment in the society of Mrs. Grote, with whose varied and brilliant conversation he was always entertained. A visit from them at Harpton was a welcome event, so likewise was the receipt of their letters.

The next letter that we print was written to Mr. Grote; and in the further correspondence others will be found, some of which are addressed to him, and some to Mrs. Grote.

January 23, 1841.

My dear Grote,—I am sorry that you took the trouble of sending to inquire after me. I have this evening reached the *crapula* of a headache; which, though more or less unpleasant, is a far better thing than the headache itself.

I hope that Mrs. Grote is recovered, and that she has escaped the transition state.

I return two out of the several books of yours in my possession. If you are by chance sitting in your own room, pray send me the volume of Seneca the philosopher, which contains a treatise styled *Apocolocyntosis*. If you are sitting upstairs, pray put it out for me to-morrow and I will send again.

When you are next within reach of the Odyssey, pray see if you can satisfy yourself as to the connection of the two verses xvii. 322–3, *ἥμισυ γάρ τ' ἀρετῆς* &c., with what precedes. The use of *πότνια* in Od. i. 14 disproves Hawtrey's theory about the word viz., that it means *wife*. Query, why is it never used in the masculine gender?

How inartificial and forced the beginning of the Odyssey is, as compared with the beginning of the Iliad! Ægisthus, in v. 29, is lugged in by the head and shoulders without there being any apparent reason why Jupiter should be thinking of him and Orestes, rather than of any other conceivable thing. The speech of Minerva, beginning at verse 45, is, however, quite worthy of the author of the Iliad. The verses 55–62 are, in particular, most beautiful.

Ever yours truly,

G. C. LEWIS.

The following letter from Sir George Lewis to his

cousin, Miss Duff Gordon, illustrates the readiness to explain and give information which I mentioned in the preface. He had always great pleasure in the society of his present correspondent.

London: September 3, 1841.

My dear Georgiana,—By the science of æsthetics, the Germans (who introduced the word from the Greek) mean that science which deals with beauty considered as the subject of the fine arts. Hence comes the adjective æsthetical, which has a corresponding sense. Thus it might be said that a picture which showed great knowledge of colouring, drawing, anatomical details and so forth, but was composed without taste or a sense of beauty, had *technical* but not æsthetical merit. Mr. Price's essay on the Picturesque, Mr. Knight's essay on Taste, Burke's essay on the Sublime and Beautiful, are æsthetical treatises. Æsthetics may be shortly defined as the *science of taste*.

You will find a full explanation of the meaning of the word in the article *æsthetics* in the first volume of the 'Penny Cyclopædia.'

The Greek word from which æsthetics is borrowed means, 'that which concerns sensations,' and therefore does not describe very correctly the subject of the science of taste and the fine arts. But the word is convenient, and seems now pretty generally adopted both in France and England. It has, however, the disadvantage of not being as yet generally understood; a fact which is proved by your question.

The weather is very fine, and will, I hope, enable the harvest to be got in fairly. London filled a good deal for the meeting of Parliament; but the battle is now over, and people are going away. They are to meet on Monday to adjourn to the 24th, when Peel will probably continue the Poor Law Commission for a year, and ask for a loan of four millions. It is expected that there will be no opposition to either of these proposals, and that after a very short time Parliament will adjourn, or be prorogued, till February.

I am told that Fielden has received the sobriquet of the 'Self-acting mule.' I hope that you will be able to see the wit and appropriateness of this name.

Your affectionate cousin,

G. C. Lewis.

I cannot resist inserting the following characteristic letter from the Rev. Sydney Smith to Sir George Lewis which I found among his papers.

Combe Florey: September 11, 1841.

Dear Lewis,—You appear to be awkwardly situated, both as respects your future colleague, and the duration of your office. I shall not leave this place for London till about the 22nd of October. We are popular, and have a run upon the road to the *Rector's Head*, which, in our case, is often more full than you philosophers suppose rectors' heads ever to be; but if you can come, write and name your day, and I will tell you whether we can receive you or not. I shall be sincerely glad to see you if we are free.

What shall we do when our friend Mrs. Grote returns from Italy? We must get models of the Antinous and Apollo. Common gestures and human postures will not do. You must look like a dying gladiator, and I must set up in my old age for a Sacerdos Belvidere. I am very sorry she is going; there will be no philosophy, but in Pantaloons, till her return.

Yours, my dear Lewis, very sincerely,

Sydney Smith.

London: December 3, 1841.

My dear Father,—

*　　*　　*　　*

No material change has taken place in Mrs. Hare's state. . . . . It is certainly not at all desirable that you should think of returning [from Rome] at present, and in this opinion Guthrie* concurs, who is now attending me for a slight cough, which I made worse by my journey to Cheltenham. I shall stay in the house for a day or two, and leave the office to Head, by which means I shall avoid all risk.

There are indications that Peel intends to make some concession to the manufacturing interest. Whatever he proposes this session (if it be tolerably fair) *must* be carried; for there is no other party now strong enough to form a Government. But if he cannot suggest a reasonable compromise between the agricultural and manufacturing interests, his Government will become involved in difficulties, which will undermine it before many years are over. It is impossible to foresee what new combination may be formed; but I am satisfied no Government can stand against the restless desire of the large towns to obtain a relaxation of the present restrictions on the import trade. I am afraid that Peel will allow himself to be influenced by taunts about changing his opinions on the Catholic question.

*　　*　　*　　*

Guthrie says that the disease of the girl at Venice is ichthyosis, or fish-skin, a very rare disease, of which, however, he saw an example no long time ago. He says that it is so rare as to be a curiosity. Its

* The eminent surgeon, G. J. Guthrie, Esq.

cause is unknown, and it does not appear to affect the general health.

* * * *

Your affectionate son,
G. C. Lewis.

Note.—Mrs. Hare, the mother of Sir T. Frankland Lewis, died early in 1842. Sir T. Frankland Lewis received his son's letter in Rome.

Chester Street: March 13, 1842.

My dear Grote,—I was greatly interested by your last letter, written from Rome, and delight to find that you have set to work so methodically and made yourself master of the ground-plan of Rome. I suppose that Bunsen's and Gerhard's works give everything that is known, together with much that is not known. Never having been at Rome, I have seen none of Raphael's *profane* works; but I can easily believe that your judgment of them is correct. Nothing can be more exquisite than the beauty, and grace, and sweetness of his Madonnas; but the subject is a limited one, and scarcely bears such frequent repetition. However, I suppose that the Dresden Madonna is his finest picture. If you can contrive it, you should see the Nismes amphitheatre and the Pont du Gard on your way home. These provincial buildings give one a lofty idea of the solid, commanding character of Roman architecture. What grand railways the Romans would have made if they had been invented in old times!

I knew that some attention was paid to modern history and physical science in Italy; but I am surprised to hear that there is any speculative philosophy. Such pursuits are not much encouraged in countries where the 'Times,' and 'Morning Herald,' and 'Bell's Life in

London' reign supreme; but even the indifference and ridicule of an ignorant mob are heavenly, as compared with the iron hand of a jealous, priest-ridden, people-fearing Italian Government. Bentham has an Italian admirer and imitator, named Gioja. I have lately bought one of his works, a treatise on the compensation of wrongs. There is, I believe, very little knowledge of Greek in Italy. Micali, who wrote a history of the 'Antichi popoli d' Italia,' is ignorant of Greek. I doubt whether there are half-a-dozen Italians who could read a page of Xenophon's 'Anabasis.' Probably, most Italians who have any pretensions to education can read Latin. It is remarkable that the knowledge of Greek is now nearly confined to the *Protestant* countries. This was not so formerly. However, Greek never made its way into Spain. I do not remember having seen or heard of a Greek book printed in Spain, or edited by a Spaniard.

Peel's corn-law measure is a slight improvement on the present scale, but it retains a prohibitory duty, and makes no *essential* change in the existing system. The agriculturalists, however, were at first a good deal alarmed by it, and many of the more unreasonable among the country gentlemen have been inclined to kick against it. The friends of the Government say that it will raise much more revenue than the present scale, inasmuch as wheat will be imported without waiting for the low duty. The harvest this year will probably not be an abundant one. The budget is, I think, on the whole a good one. I like the income-tax and the amendment of the tariff. The timber-duties part seems to me ill-managed. Peel's speech on the budget is considered very able; all important discussion on the corn laws is at an end for this session.

The case was, in my judgment, ill-argued by the Opposition, and Peel is certainly stronger now than he was on the first day of the session. I see nothing which is likely to shake his Government for many years to come.

There is something perpetually stirring in Parliament about Poor Laws—a question, or a return, or some small matter, but sufficient (with the current business) to occupy my time so completely that I have hardly been able to read or do anything for myself, except correct the proofs of the reprint of my translation of Boeckh.* There has not, however, been any debate in either house, except in the House of Lords, in a case brought forward by Philpotts. Duncombe has a motion for a committee on Local Acts, and Gilbert Unions, next week, which the Government will resist. I do not expect that the Government will make any essential concession, but that there will be a good many modifications of the law. We have been revising all our legislation lately, and re-issuing our orders, which has cost us much labour. We have just made a new order, to quiet the doctors, who are very clamorous. On the whole, I consider the prospects of the Poor Law Commission much brighter now than they were this time last year. Graham has been very kind to me, and I like him much as a man of business. I need not say anything of Head as a colleague; I only wish I could feel easy about his health. He has lately been, by Graham's desire, to Paisley, to ascertain the amount of distress there, and he has discovered that the relief fund has been grievously mismanaged. Chadwick has been

* Boeckh's 'Public Economy of Athens,' translated by Sir George Lewis, and first published by Mr. Murray in 1828.

writing a long report on the means of preventing disease by drainage, cleansing, &c. It contains a great deal of good matter, and, on the whole, I prefer it to anything else he has written. We shall present it shortly as *his* report, without making ourselves responsible for it. Lister has had a severe pulmonary attack, from which he is slowly recovering. Senior has written an article for the 'Edinburgh Review,' on the national character of France, England, and the United States—I should rather say their *international* character, as shown in their conduct to other countries. John Mill is about to print his work on Logic, which is completed. I have been reading a controversial work on Ancient Christianity, written against the Puseyites. It is an exhibition of the *bad* doctrines and spirit of the primitive Church, written by a person who seems deeply read in the Greek and Latin Fathers, but to have no acquaintance with classical literature. It is a curious work, and I shall like to talk to you about it when I return. The writer is a strenuous *Low* Churchman. Eastlake has published a useful translation of the first part of Kugler; and Mrs. Jameson an account of the picture-galleries in or near London, which is said to be very good.

I fear that I have deferred writing until it is doubtful whether this letter will reach you before you leave Rome. Pray remember me to Mrs. Grote. I am glad to hear so good an account of her health.

Ever yours sincerely,

G. C. LEWIS.

Wildbad: August 17, 1842.

My dear Head,—By a singular accident, I have been prevented from answering your letter of the 7th until to-day. A travelling servant whom I took with me, fell sick at Heidelberg. A medical man saw him there, who pronounced that he had a little fever, and gave him some calomel. I waited a day at Heidelberg, and the next I started with the Austins, in a Lohnkutsch, for Stuttgart, whence they were to go to Carlsbad, and I to Wildbad. However, he continued ill upon the road, and I left him at Heilbronn, with instructions to follow me to Wildbad. I stayed a day at Stuttgart, and when I arrived at Wildbad, I found that the man had come the day before, and that the small-pox had made its appearance on him. The consequence of this discovery ought, strictly, to have been that the hotel and all its inmates should be put in strict quarantine until the man was convalescent, viz. about four weeks. The king's commissioner at Wildbad had, however, taken upon himself to dispense with the law so far as to send the man, in the custody of a surgeon, to the hospital at Stuttgart, and to seal up the room in which he had slept. Your letter for me had been given to him before my arrival, and was lying upon the table in his room; but, although I used all my eloquence to obtain it, I was unable to get the seals removed until to-day. Small-pox is treated in this country like the plague in the Mediterranean, which, considering that vaccination is compulsory as well as gratuitous, seems to me to be carrying the paternal principle of government rather too far.

* * * *

The national hatred of England seems to be almost at its height in Germany. The newspapers (particularly the 'Allgemeine Zeitung') abound with articles advising the establishment of a separate manufacturing system and the exclusion of English manufactures.

The party who would naturally resist the demands of the German manufacturers (viz. the landowners) are reduced to silence and despair by the exclusion of their corn from England. The cry for protection in Germany is unquestionably the consequence of the corn laws, and a retaliation against them. A body of delegates from the Zollverein is now sitting at Stuttgart, and one of the subjects for their consideration is the exclusion of foreign cotton twist. They will probably resist this cry for the present, as Prussia, with a strong body of weavers, is against it; but if our corn laws are persisted in, the blow will infallibly come. We seem to be on the eve of a *war of tariffs*—a war by which Germany, France, and America will more certainly damage England, with less suffering and loss to themselves, than by a war of fleets and armies. Minute accounts of the distress in England, from the speeches of Cobden, &c., in Parliament, and from the extreme newspapers, are given in the German papers, with an intimation that they come far short of the truth. These accounts are dwelt upon with the most evident satisfaction; the distress is attributed to the diminution of our foreign trade, and it is argued that foreign nations have only to persist in their protective policy (imitated from England herself) in order to lower the proud superiority of England, and bring her to the verge of a revolution.

In the case of a French war, we may rely on the *interests* of the Germans, but certainly not on their *affections*. Their hatred of England is only second to their hatred of France. I am sorry to say that there is no doubt about the correctness of the above view.

I saw Zachariä,* in passing through Heidelberg.

* Karl Salamo Zacharia, the learned author of 'Vierzig Bücher von Staate,' &c.

He has married a pretty, simple-mannered German woman, and has one child. He has published an account of his travels in the Levant, and particularly of his stay at Salonichi and Athos. There is a new law-lecturer at Heidelberg, named Vangerow, a man of much eminence. He has at present engrossed nearly all the law students. Strauss is living at Stuttgart; he is about to marry a Dresden singer.

We intend to move to Kissingen, in Bavaria, in a few days. Pray direct there until you hear from me. But as it is possible that we might be detained here, if the subject should be of importance, pray write me a few lines to both places. Mr. and Mrs. Villiers desire to be remembered to you. I am glad to hear that you are well. The weather is excessively hot.

Ever yours,

G. C. Lewis.

Wildbad: August 22, 1842.

My dear Head,—

* * * *

I hope that you will appreciate the following story. When Voltaire was in Germany, he was one day talking against the Jews of the Old Testament, and was particularly severe in his condemnation of Habakkuk, against whom he brought various specific charges. On a subsequent day, a person who had been present at the former conversation returned to the subject of Habakkuk, and offered to prove, by reference to passages in Scripture, that Voltaire had wholly mistaken his history and character. Voltaire listened to this proposal with considerable impatience; at last, he cut it short, by saying, 'C'est égal, Habakkuk était capable de tout.'

The news of the disturbances in the manufacturing districts of England will be received with exultation from one end of Europe to the other, and the appointment of the Duke of Wellington to the Horse Guards will probably be taken to mean that the country is placed under military government. All this will encourage the manufacturing party to press for further protection. There is scarcely anything too extravagant for the German public to believe about England, provided it be to our discredit. The English news in their newspapers is almost exclusively confined to detailed accounts from the 'Sun,' and such like authorities, of the distress and riots in the manufacturing districts. This is not confined to the papers which incline to liberal politics, if, indeed, such can be said to exist in Germany, It is equally true of the absolutist organs. The censorship permits this, in order to create a horror of a free government. Not a word against Russia would be allowed to appear, although the Germans hate the Russians, if it be possible, even more than they hate the English.

I took a letter for Malta, the other day, to the Wildbad postmaster, and gave it into his hands, saying that it probably ought to go by Baden and Strasburg to Marseilles, as I had written *viâ Marseilles* on the letter. He looked at it for some time, and then said to me, with a sort of inquiring air, 'Malta ist in England, wahrscheinlich, oder in Irland.' Since Lord W—— ——'s remark, that he had been too sick in crossing from Dover to Calais to allow him to think of crossing the Simplon, I have not heard of so choice a bit of geography.

* * * *

Ever yours truly,

G. C. Lewis.

Kissingen: September 6, 1842.

My dear Grote,—My principal reason for not having before written to you is that I had very little to say; and I fear that my stock of memorabilia has not been much increased by delay. I travelled with Villiers* and his wife, by the ordinary railway and steamer line, as far as Bonn, where I landed, and left them to go on to Wildbad. At Bonn I found the Austins, and, after staying a couple of days at Bonn, travelled with them up the Rhine, as far as Heidelberg, and thence to Stuttgart, where I parted from them, they going to Carlsbad, and I to Wildbad. Austin had quite made up his mind as to the Malta project; his principal reason seemed to be that the salary was not sufficient to enable him to save anything, and he had enough to live upon in Germany. Moreover, he seemed quite uncertain about his health. He talked a great deal about all he had seen and heard in Germany, particularly the latter. He thinks that the mischief done by our corn-laws, in encouraging the Germans to set up a manufacturing system of their own, and to exclude foreign manufactures (chiefly English), cannot now be undone, although the progress of their prohibitory policy would probably be arrested by judicious legislation on our part. Even the Austrians are now beginning to manufacture for themselves, and to think of encouraging native industry by duties. The Austins intend to pass the present month at Carlsbad, and after going to Dresden for a short time, to pass the winter at Berlin. He meditates an article for the 'Edinburgh Review,' on Prussia. I found Wildbad a quiet, secluded watering-place in the Black Forest, where there are natural baths, which people take upon the sand,

* Hon. Edward Villiers, brother to the Earl of Clarendon.

through which the water rises. Villiers derived no benefit from the baths, and, after I had stayed there about a week, we came through Würtzburg to Kissengen, where we have been a few days, and which I shall leave this week. Kissingen has some mild chalybeate saline waters, which attract a large number of Badgäste during the season, but the number is now much diminished, as the season ends in the middle of this month. The king of Bavaria has built a fine kursaal, decorated internally in the Munich style, and also a handsome colonnade for peripatetics. The neighbouring country has little beauty or interest. Much distress has been created in Germany by the hot summer; the hay harvest has failed, so that there is not sufficient food for cattle in the winter. A large number of cattle have, in consequence, been brought into the market, and the price of meat is now extraordinarily low, as it will be extraordinarily high in the winter. I saw a statement in a newspaper, that sheep are selling, in some part of Prussia, at eight gröschen a-piece (less than a shilling), and oxen at three to four dollars. If cattle are not imported into England from Germany at these prices, when will they be imported?

Dr. Strauss is now living at Stuttgart, and he is about to be married to a Dresden Sängerin (older than himself), whose name I forget. It is said that he received 30,000 florins (= 60,000 francs) for his 'Christliche Glaubenslehre,' and that the booksellers will give him five Friedrichs d'or a sheet for all that he writes. He is still a young man—not much above thirty, I was informed. I understood that he had nothing like a party or sect in Wirtemburg; his writings had created some 'Verwirrung' among the younger Theologen, but had made no converts. His last work, in which he openly repudiates, not only Christianity, but also all that is considered essential to natural religion, appears to have alienated even moderate sceptics from him. He has no professor's office, and is not likely to obtain any; but he appears to enjoy the most entire toleration, both political and social. His writings have certainly been read over all Germany. I have met with a very interesting book, which I will show you when I return to England, viz. 'A History of English Deism in the last Century,' by a Dr. Lechler, published last year at Stuttgart. It has, doubtless, been called forth by Strauss's writings. The book throws much light upon the progress of philosophical speculation in England during the last century, and is important with reference to the influence of Locke's Essay. It is not very creditable to us that the book should have been hitherto unnoticed in England. It is written in a perfectly candid and impartial tone, which will account for its neglect. I intend to stop at Dusseldorf in my way down the Rhine, and to see Elberfeld; also to visit Utrecht, Amsterdam and the Hague, and to embark at Rotterdam, so as to be in London on the 19th or 20th.

Pray remember me to Mrs. Grote, and believe me

Ever yours truly,

G. C. Lewis.

After Christmas, 1842, difficulties connected with the administration of the Poor Law in Ireland required Sir George Lewis to go to Dublin for a short time. Thence he writes thus to Mr. Grote:—

Bilton Hotel, Dublin: January 11, 1843.

My dear Grote,—Since I have been in Dublin the weather has been wet and windy, and I have scarcely done more than walk from the hotel to the office and back again. I have, however, dined out two or three times, seen a certain number of people, and read the newspapers, and I have now obtained a pretty good idea of our position in this country. Everything in Ireland is carried on with such a hubbub and noise, and there is so much insincerity in a vast deal that is said, that there is no finding out the truth except by coming to the place and selecting one's informants.

The principal and most formidable opposition to the Poor Law in this country proceeds from the *landlords*; it is, in fact, an anti-democratic movement. The boards of guardians are extremely popular in their constitution, and, I need not add, are quite new. The ex-officio guardians are limited in number; they must not exceed one-third of the board. The elected guardians are chosen annually by a suffrage nearly universal, inasmuch as every occupier of land or houses is rated, and every ratepayer has a vote. Moreover, the ratepayers can, if they wish it, vote secretly by returning the voting paper in a sealed cover—a practice which, I understand, is often followed. The consequence of this state of things is, that the elected guardians are virtually returned by the priests, and the landlords have no control over their election. The boards of guardians, consisting thus of a majority of tenants appointed by the priests, decide upon all matters within the scope of the Irish Poor Law. Although these matters are not so extensive as those that are managed by an English board, they are nevertheless important. The guardians prepare a valuation, make a rate, give relief (which, though it is confined to a workhouse, amounts to something), and appoint a clerk, collectors, and workhouse officers. What, however, is, perhaps, most important, they establish the principle that certain municipal powers relating to the affairs of the poor are to be administered, not by the landlords exclusively (as hitherto), but by a board consisting partly of landlords and partly of tenants; and in which, at present, the tenants always have a majority. The Irish landlords (as is natural considering what has hitherto been the rural *régime* in Ireland) cannot stomach this; moreover, they dislike excessively paying a tax for the poor *at all*. They would hate a poor law, even if it were administered by a grand jury. The consequence of all this is, that the gentlemen have done and are doing their best to defeat and obstruct the law, and to persuade the Government to relieve them, if not of the whole law, at least of its most distasteful provisions. In this attempt they are assisted by the resistance made to the payment of rates. Every person is here rated, and the number of ratepayers under five pounds often exceeds half the entire number of ratepayers. These cottiers are wretchedly poor, and they derive no consolation from the doctrine of the political economists, that the rate ultimately falls on the rent. Primarily it is paid by *them*; *their* goods are distrained if it is not forthcoming; and such is the competition for land, that somehow or other the landlord can contrive to throw additional charges on the tenants, although any but an Irish landlord would suppose it impossible to shave them closer than they are already shorn. Hence has arisen the resistance to the poor rate and the necessity of collecting it at the point of the bayonet; a necessity which throws great doubts upon the expediency of rating the small occupiers. The danger of an exemption is, that it may offer a premium to the sub-division of holdings.

So far as there is any middle class in the country, these persons (viz. the *strong* farmers, as the Irish call them) are generally favourable to the poor law. Its chief supporters are the priests, who are extremely favourable to it, on account of the decisive influence which they possess over the election of guardians.

From this account you may judge of the sincerity and patriotism of O'Connell's proceeding in taking the field against this measure, and using it as an argument for *repeal*—in other words, for *rent*.* As a measure tending to strengthen and consolidate the power of the Catholic or popular party in Ireland, it certainly ranks next after Catholic emancipation, the Reform Bill, and the Municipal Bill, to say the least of it. Upon the management of rural affairs it has a more direct and searching influence than any of these measures, and if the Board of Guardians could be firmly established, and take their rank among the settled institutions of the country, a way would be opened for modifying the power of the grand juries. Already a Commission has proposed the transfer of some of the functions of grand juries to the Boards of Guardians.

* * * *

I have taken your advice and returned to the 'Athenæum,' but I wish that you would use your influence with the editor to induce him to give an abstract of the contents of each number on the first page, as is done in the 'Spectator:' perhaps Mrs. Grote will take this matter in hand.

* * * *

Ever yours sincerely,
G. C. Lewis.

* So the fund was called raised by O'Connell for the promotion of repeal.

Dublin: January 29, 1843.

My dear Grote,—I agree with you in thinking that we shall probably weather the anti-poor-law storm in Ireland; but I can assure you that the wind is blowing very hard, and we are close upon a lee shore. It is true, as you say, that no substitute is likely to be *ultimately* more popular than the present law; but that does not diminish our difficulty, which arises from the general resistance to the execution of the law as it stands.

Your description of Feuerbach's book has interested me much: I will certainly read it. I see that the 'Deutsche Jahrbücher' have been suppressed by the Saxon Government in consequence of the interference of Prussia and Bavaria.

I send you by to-day's post a copy of an Irish newspaper, in order that you may read a report of a speech by a Mr. Conner on fixity of tenure. This is another instance of the practice of discussing the causes of the poverty of the working people, the part of Hamlet being omitted. It is strange this man does not see that if the present precarious occupiers are converted into owners, a new set of precarious occupiers will grow up under them, unless all tenancy at will is prohibited. Pray keep this paper, as I wish to show it to my father.

I leave Dublin to-morrow, and hope to be in Chester Street on Tuesday night.

Ever yours truly,
G. C. Lewis.

From the next letter, written to Mr. Austin, it appears that Sir George Lewis found it necessary to pay special attention to his health. Had he taken more exercise he might have been stronger—but he was very sensitive to cold, and had consequently an aversion to going out much in winter; and what with the requisite attendance at the Poor Law Office, and his usual literary occupations, his constitution suffered from his too sedentary habits. He was recommended to consult Dr. Jephson at Leamington, from whence he now writes; he found benefit from the strict diet which the doctor enjoined, coupled with injunctions to ride daily.

Dale Street, Leamington: October 23, 1843.

My dear Austin,—A letter which I received lately from Mrs. Austin contained an expression which leads me to hope that you are meditating the publication of something more upon jurisprudential subjects. I cannot forbear from writing to you to express my great satisfaction at your having formed this intention. I do not know whether you intend to continue your general course of lectures, or to finish your papers on codification. Brougham's pamphlet has had the effect of calling attention to the latter subject; and I think that the prejudices against a digestion of the law, as well common as statute, have been softened of late years. But whatever you may decide to publish, I shall be equally thankful for the additional instruction. I have long thought that no living person is so competent as yourself to instruct the world upon ethical and legal subjects; and I am satisfied that if you would unlock your stores, you would find that your teaching would gradually make its due impression.

It has been a great vexation and disappointment to me to be absent from London at the time when you are there. I wish that you could be induced to remain a few weeks longer; if you could, my house, if it should be any convenience to you, is entirely at your disposal. I retain it till the end of the year, but I shall go to my father's house in Grafton Street when I return to London. I shall probably come to London in about a fortnight. My health has got so much out of order, that I found it necessary to do something for it, and I have derived very decided benefit from the strict regimen upon which Dr. Jephson has put me, and which I have now pursued nearly three weeks.

I should not be surprised if he could do good in your case; his chief skill lies in chronic disorders of the digestive organs. People come to him from far and wide; he makes at least 16,000*l.* a year, which is an extraordinary *provincial* income.

Ever yours truly,
G. C. Lewis.

Grafton Street: August 14, 1844.

My dear Head,—Last night I was reading Sprengel's 'Geschichte der Medicin,' and I found in it two singular facts. One is that a certain Dr. Veit was publicly burnt at Hamburg, in 1522, for having attended women in childbirth disguised as a midwife.

The other is, that according to Cardan's statement, necromancy was up to his time taught as a science in the University of Salamanca, and that the lectures upon it had only been then lately prohibited. Cardan died in 1576.

I imagine that the belief in necromancy in Western Europe was a tradition from Greece and Rome, confirmed by the story of the Witch of Endor.

It seems as if Salamanca always kept a little behind Oxford.

Lyell, in his work on Geology, mentions that lectures founded on the Ptolemaic system of the world had been delivered at Salamanca in this century.

Ever yours truly,

G. C. Lewis.

Harpton: Saturday, September 14, 1844.

My dear Head,—

* * * *

* * * *

I quite agree with you about O'Connell's speech. It was a masterpiece of demagogical oratory, but showed manifest signs of fear, and an absence of all fixed views as to future policy. He now sees that the Government are not afraid of indicting him, and that if they get a verdict they *can* shut him up. It looks to me as if his *present* intention (for he varies from day to day) is to give up striving for a completely separate Irish party, and to attempt some sort of co-operation with the Whigs and Liberals in England. This is the best thing that can happen. Perhaps he may think that he may be strong enough to turn out the Tories, and bring back a Government which he can control. After all, it is a sorry triumph for a great demagogue, the would-be leader of a nation, to celebrate his liberation from gaol by a decision on a technical point of law, due to the legislature whose oppression he is always denouncing. He cannot pretend to say that it is due to his own party and followers, and therefore being unwilling to ascribe it to an English party, he gives it to *Providence*. I hope you observed an inimitable passage about Providence acting by secondary causes, and that one of the chief of these was—'The Morning Chronicle.'

It is very difficult to arrive at any confident conclusion after reading a French trial. The witnesses are never pressed home, and there is so much hearsay evidence, that almost any rumour might seem to be proved. But certainly the impression left on my mind by the rambling investigation at the two trials of Fualdès'* murderers, was, that the conviction was right.

* This singular murder, which made a sensation throughout France, took place on the night of the 20th of March, 1817. A woman dressed in man's clothes entered a house of the lowest reputation, inhabited by one Bancal and his wife and Colard and Anne Benoit, in the town of Rodez, in the south of France. As she reached the top of the stairs, a noise was heard at the bottom, and she, anxious to be concealed, and Madame Bancal wishing to conceal her, placed her in a small bedroom adjoining the kitchen. The noise proved to be that of five or six men forcing up Monsieur Fualdès, a magistrate of the town, into the kitchen, where, after having compelled him to sign some papers, they laid him on the kitchen-table and murdered him. The principal assassins were Bastide Gramont, Fualdès' godson, and Jausion, a banker and agent, at Rodez; the others were hired for the purpose. When the murder was ended, Bastide, a man remarkable for his height and strength, heard a noise in the small bedroom, out of which he drew the woman in disguise. He would have killed her on the spot, as a dangerous witness of what had taken place, but Jausion interfered in her favour, and they were at length content with her swearing a solemn oath by the side of the corpse, that she would reveal nothing that she had seen or heard. She was then permitted to depart. The murderers proceeded to carry the body of Fualdès to the outskirts of the town and throw it into the river Aveyron; where, however, it was found on the next morning.

Suspicion fell upon Jausion, Bastide, the Bancals, Colard, and others, and they were arrested and examined. The man Bancal afterwards fell ill, made a statement which compromised his fellow-prisoners, and died.

About the same time, a certain Madame Manson, the wife of a French officer, whom, according to her own words, she had taken for a husband 'comme on prend une pilule,' and from whom she was separated, a lady of very doubtful character, admitted to a young aide-de-camp, that she was the woman who was concealed in the small bedroom at Bancal's. She was arrested as a possible accomplice in the murder, or as, at all events, a probably important witness in the case. During her many examinations, her assertions were continually withdrawn or modified. She prevaricated and contradicted herself, partly, it is supposed, from shame; partly from fear of revenge on the part of the prisoners; at length, however, it appeared pretty clear that she was the woman who was concealed,

Madame Manson's story comes out at last pretty clearly, partly from herself, and partly from her confidantes; and it is so little creditable to her, and there is so much reluctance to tell it, that I can hardly doubt its truth. I do not see what plausible theory can be invented for explaining it on the supposition of its falsehood. You ought to read the trial in the French collection.

We went yesterday to see Sir Harford Brydges. What a pretty place Boultibrooke is!

* * * *

Ever yours truly,
G. C. Lewis.

In the autumn of 1844 Sir George Lewis married Lady Maria Theresa Lister, the widow of Thomas Henry Lister, Esq., a sister of the present Earl of Clarendon; an union which contributed largely to his subsequent happiness. Many of his letters are now dated from Kent House, in Knightsbridge, the lease of which belonged to Lady Theresa, and which they now jointly occupied.

The next letter is written to the Hon. Mrs. Edward

that she had seen the murder through cracks in the door, had sworn the oath, and had been allowed to leave the house as I have described.

After a trial at Rodez, some of the prisoners were found guilty, but the trial was proved to be informal, and a fresh trial ordered to be held at the neighbouring town of Alby. The result of this second trial was, that Bancal's wife, Bastide, Jausion, Colard, and Bach were condemned to death, but Bach recommended to mercy. Other prisoners had lighter punishments; Madame Manson was acquitted. Bastide, Jausion, and Colard were executed.

The vehement interest which was felt in these trials, arose partly from a belief that the murder of Fualdès was a political murder; this clearly was not the case, as the motive was robbery, which Bastide and Jausion in fact committed. The position and evidence of Madame Manson likewise tended in a great degree to increase it.—See 'Causes Célèbres,' published by Lebrun, rue des Saints Pères, Paris.

Villiers, who, by his marriage, had become his sister-in-law.

Kent House: February 3, 1845.

My dear Elizabeth,—I return the letter on mesmerism and Miss Martineau which you have had the kindness to send me. The writer of it wisely abstains from confident and sweeping conclusions on the subject. I cannot say that it has at all altered such opinions as I have been able to form on what is called mesmerism and its influences. There is much in the view of the writer which appears to me very reasonable; but there is one expression in his letter which I must quarrel with. He calls *mesmerism* 'a new science.' I cannot admit it to be new or a science. It is not *new* in the ordinary acceptation of the word, for it was introduced by Mesmer before the year 1780, more than sixty years ago. Nobody would now think of calling vaccination a new discovery, and yet it is posterior to mesmerism. Moreover, at the time when mesmerism was introduced, its claims to be considered as a valuable scientific discovery underwent a most careful and conscientious investigation by a Commission of competent persons appointed by the French Government, and their report, drawn by the celebrated Bailly, denounced it as a delusion either useless or mischievous. Instead of a new science, therefore, I should be inclined to call it an old imposture, long since exploded by the decision of competent and disinterested judges.

Nothing can be a greater mistake than to suppose that the subject of mesmerism requires investigation, or that it has not attracted the attention of the medical profession. I believe that a respectable library might be made of books on the subject; and that almost as much has been written upon it as upon judicial astrology, witchcraft, the art of interpreting dreams, phrenology, or homœopathy. Miss Martineau's complaints of want of investigation and of indifference to truth, and her tacit assumption throughout her letters that the year 1844 is the year one of mesmerism, only prove her utter ignorance of what had been written or done, long before she was born, with regard to the mock science upon which she has undertaken to instruct the world.

But those who have seen or read of the effects of mesmerism, or animal magnetism, say that these effects are something real and unquestionable, and that it cannot be set aside as a mere imposture and imagination, like astrology or palmistry. That certain effects are produced on certain persons by what is called mesmerism is undeniable; but it does not thence follow that mesmerism is a *science*, new or old.

The original theory of Mesmer with regard to his pretended discovery is fully stated in Bailly's report. Great changes in that theory, and in its practical application, have been made since his time, and the language of the mesmeric writers is so mystical and unprecise (not excepting Miss Martineau's), that it is very difficult to make out what they intend to teach, or whether they agree in any common doctrine. It seems, however, that they all conceive the essence of mesmerism to consist in this: that when two persons are brought into relation with one another (generally by means of contact, or close approach), some physical influence is exercised by one body upon the other. This physical influence was compared by the early mesmerists to magnetism, and metallic rods and conductors were used in order to convey it. Of late years all agents, except the hands and looks of the mesmerizer, have been generally abandoned.

Now, it appears to me that there is no evidence of the existence of a specific influence, or fluid, or occult agency such as the mesmerists assert. If it was a physical agency communicated from one body to another, it ought to act according to natural and invariable laws, like a contagious disease. Yet we know that this is not the case. We know that women, and young women, are much more susceptible of mesmeric influences than any other class of persons. This is not the case with those influences which we know to be purely physical. If a philosopher, or a weather-beaten soldier, and a hysterical girl were vaccinated, the former would be as likely to take the cowpox as the latter.

The claim of mesmerism to be considered a science, and a useful or important discovery, rests entirely upon the assumption that it works by a specific physical influence. But as soon as the imposture and the exaggeration are cleared away, it appears to resolve itself into one out of the many well-authenticated examples of strange nervous affections produced by the imagination.

It is a matter of certainty that various circumstances, having apparently nothing in common, can, through the imagination, give such an impulse to the nervous system as to produce various phenomena, some of a hysterical or convulsive character, and some connected with somnambulism, or sleep accompanied with imperfect consciousness. Instances of these strange and eccentric affections are afforded by the dancing madness of the middle ages, the Tarantism which prevailed in Southern Italy in the sixteenth and seventeenth centuries, the paroxysms of the French convulsionnaires in the beginning of the eighteenth century, and the convulsive seizures of the English Methodists and other religious fanatics. In all these cases women are said to have been more easily affected than men; and the propagation of the nervous hysterical convulsions was wonderfully assisted by sympathy and the presence of many persons. It is to be observed that Mesmer's original experiments were made upon assemblages of persons, and not upon single patients.

It is possible that the power of producing hysterical symptoms, or of bringing on a state of semi-conscious sleep, may, if employed by skilful and scientific physicians, be turned to some good account. I cannot say that I have any expectation that such will prove to be the case; my belief is, that if any good could have been elicited from it, some progress towards the discovery of that good would have been made in the sixty or seventy years which have elapsed since the quack Mesmer tried to make money by his pretended discovery. Nevertheless, I can conceive that some means may be found of guiding and restraining a power which seems now so liable to abuse, that no one thinks of applying it except in cases where all other means have failed.

I am, however, utterly incredulous as to the pretensions of mesmerism with respect to mental phenomena. I do not believe that we shall ever learn any new truth, either as to matter of fact or matter of opinion, from any mesmeric patient in a state of somnambulism. I have no faith either in mesmeric clairvoyance or mesmeric intuitions; and I fear that, notwithstanding Mesmer and Miss Martineau, we shall never be able to acquire knowledge by any other than the tedious and painful means of observation and reasoning.

As to Miss Martineau's own case, nothing in my opinion can be safely inferred from it in respect to the virtues of mesmerism. In the first place, even if there had been a perfect cure, no safe conclusion could be built upon a single case. Our knowledge of the animal economy is too limited to enable a person (and that person unskilled in medicine) to pronounce with confidence upon the effects of a process of treatment tried in one instance. But, in the next place, it appears clearly from Mr. Greenhow's pamphlet, that Miss Martineau had begun to improve before she was mesmerised; that she was then taking a medicine (iodine), from which she was likely to derive benefit; and, what is most important, that after all she was not cured of her malady. The nervous symptoms of pain were mitigated; but the displacement of the organ still continues, and may, for aught that we know, reproduce the same symptoms on some slight provocation.

With regard to Jane and her somnambulistic revelations, I must be allowed to suspend my belief until I know a little more about Mrs. Montagu Wynyard. Miss Martineau, already a believer in mesmerism, of an enthusiastic and credulous temperament, and nearly stone deaf, is formed by nature for a dupe. Mrs. M. W. may, perhaps, be desirous of notoriety, or she may be amused by deceiving the world, or she may be practising a pious fraud on Miss M., thinking to do her good. Half-witted girls, such as Jane is described to be, have sometimes a large dose of cunning; and it is not unlikely that Jane may be something between a dupe and an accomplice.

Such is my confession of faith with regard to mesmerism. I believe that the mesmerists have discovered that there is a power of producing, principally in young women and boys, certain hysterical and nervous affections, which had previously been supposed only to arise spontaneously. There appears to be nothing novel or unexampled in the phenomena of mesmerism, as regards either the convulsions or the somnambulism, except that they are produced by an external agency. It is possible that by a vigilant observation of these phenomena, some means of controlling them and rendering them useful may be discovered. A strong presumption against the probability of success is, however, created by the fact that since 1780 no person of a truly scientific spirit has felt inclined to pursue this line of enquiry.

Believe me, ever yours affectionately,

G. C. Lewis.

London: July 25, 1845.

My dear Head,—Sir Robert Inglis made an exceedingly confused, dull and unimpressive speech yesterday to about sixty members, on the grievances of the tithe-owner in respect to rating.* He evidently did not understand the question, and certainly nobody could understand his speech. He was answered by Sir James Graham, who stated the opposite views with remarkable clearness and in a small compass. The House seemed to understand him—indeed, they could not well avoid it; and he evidently satisfied his audience. Lord John Manners said a few words about bringing forward the Stock-in-Trade Bill earlier next session, and nobody else spoke. The Bill was then read a second time without a division.

Inglis has not advanced the case of the tithe-owner by this move. The probability is, that unless some

* For Sir Robert Inglis's speech, see 'Hansard,' 3rd series, vol. lxxxii. p. 1042.

more vigorous hand takes up the subject, it will never be revived. Sir James Graham seemed quite satisfied with the result. The Scotch and Irish Bill went through committee last night with little opposition, and no division. I was not in the House. There are one or two verbal amendments to be made, and the report is to be brought up to-night. I expect it will be read a third time on Monday. The Valuation Bill is not to be proceeded with to-night. The report is still to be brought up. Probably it will be taken on Monday. Power is still in attendance.

You have heard of poor Mr. Clive's death.* I understand that he had had some warning previously, and that he had even been advised not to go to George Clive's house by the railway.

* * * *

The Commons Enclosure Bill will certainly pass this Session. It ought to have a great effect in Wales.

Thank you for Horner's letter. I will show it to Clarendon.

There is a curious pamphlet by Baptist Noel, recommending the Voluntary system for the Irish Protestant Church. It is addressed to the Bishop of Cashel, who must be highly pleased with it.

Ever yours sincerely,

G. C. Lewis.

Ems: September 15, 1845.

My dear Head,—

* * * *

Ems is now beginning to thin, but it does not expire till the end of the month. We intend to leave it this week, and to go through Schwalbach and Schlangenbad

* Edward Bolton Clive, of Whitfield, Herefordshire, member for the city of Hereford.

to Biberich,—down the Rhine to Coblentz, stay a day there, in order to see some of the Moselle, and afterwards give a day to Andernach in order to see Laach.

* * * *

The German papers are full of information relative to the schism in the Catholic Church; the Deutsche Catholiken, or the Christkatholische Gemeinde, as they call themselves. It took its rise in a letter written by a Silesian priest, named Ronge, remonstrating against the exhibition of the sacred tunic at Trèves. The Bishop of Trèves and his clergy worked this imposture beyond all reasonable limits of prudence, and a serious reaction amongst all the more honest and rational Catholics has been the consequence. I have seen some of Ronge's pamphlets; he is said to be a perfectly sincere, honest and determined man, a sort of little Luther; he writes in a homely popular style, with every appearance of strong feeling. His principal point is *separation from Rome*; and this topic coincides with the national patriotic movement now alive in Germany, which, moreover, all the Governments encourage. Hence they call themselves *German* Catholics. They permit marriage of the clergy, communion in both kinds, celebration of mass in German, and they reject confession. They call themselves Catholics, but are substantially Protestants. They have formed a sort of free Church, with funds of its own, to which Protestants and even Jews have contributed; and which Prussia, Baden, and Wirtemberg have recognised as a legal Church. Their numbers are said to exceed 30,000, and I hear that sixty priests have joined them. Many of these have given up livings of considerable value. They are favoured by some of the higher Catholic clergy, particularly by the Archbishop of Freiburg.

They are just the reverse of our Puseyites, who are Catholics calling themselves members of a Protestant Church; these people are Protestants, calling themselves members of a Catholic Church. They differ moreover from the Puseyites in two other respects; one, that many of their priests have sacrificed their emoluments when they changed their opinion—the other, that the converts are chiefly among the middle class, merchants, tradesmen, &c. My belief is that the movement is of genuine importance, and that the Catholic Church of Germany is in a critical position as respects its connection with Rome, and the maintenance of some of its characteristic doctrines. Much will depend on the conduct of the leading men: the Catholic Governments are doing all they can to stifle the movement. I have read a historical investigation into the sacred tunic of Trèves, by two professors of Bonn. It seems that there are about twenty other sacred tunics, particularly one at Argenteuil, in France, which has been recognised by the Pope, and on which Lord Clifford has written a book. Moreover, they profess to have seen at the late exposure of the tunic, that the vesture without a seam has seams in it. The whole affair is far too ludicrous to endure solemn criticism; the Church of Trèves forgot that while they were hoodwinking the multitude, they were committing the capital error of outraging the reason of the upper and middle classes. They have already smarted pretty severely for this piece of dishonest folly; and I feel convinced that they have not yet seen the last or the worst.

The Germans seem fonder of the Zollverein and the exclusion of foreign manufactures than ever. We may expect to see the prohibition stricter every year.

*　　*　　*　　*

Have you heard the anecdote of some person calling on Guizot, and asking him if he was recovered from his attack of illness? 'Je me porte beaucoup mieux' (was his answer). 'Regardez, je lis des romans,' showing Thiers' history of Napoleon.

* * * *

Ever yours truly,
G. C. Lewis.

Downing Street: March 11, 1846.

My dear Grote,—I tried to find you on Sunday, but unluckily failed, my object being, among other things, to thank you for the copy of your twelfth and last volume, which has safely reached me. You have, I think, every reason to look back with satisfaction upon the time and labour which you have devoted to this great enterprise.

You have effectually accomplished the object which you set before you, and your success has been generally recognised by competent and impartial judges, and indeed by the general voice of the public.

All other histories of Greece are superseded by your work; and those who treat the subject hereafter must take your treatment of it as their starting point.

The established character of your history at our universities, where its political principles would not make it acceptable, is a remarkable fact, and is creditable both to you and to them.

Ever yours sincerely,
G. C. Lewis.

Kent House: March 16, 1846.

My dear Grote,—The parcel containing the copy of your history, with the volume of the Seneca and my article, arrived safely; and I am much obliged to you for the present of your book. I have looked through the whole of it so as to see its general plan and structure, and I have also read consecutively a portion of the first volume. Your mode of treating the mythological part is, I think, quite successful. You have contrived to give a correct view of the character and contents of the religious and heroic legends of the Greeks without losing yourself in endless detail.

I feel satisfied that your work will occupy a very high place in the historical literature of the country, and that it will influence the opinions of all studious persons upon the nature of what is called early history.

Thirlwall's first volume is based upon sound principles of criticism; but, in the first place, his citations of authorities are insufficient; and in the next place, his views are scarcely expressed with distinctness. He always seems, like Lord Eldon, to exercise his ingenuity in evading a decision of the question. You have fairly stated the case, and argued and illustrated it so as to meet every objection and remove every obscurity.

I do not know whether you are acquainted with Otfried Müller's articles—*Attika*, *Eleusinia* and *Pallas*, in Ersch and Gruber's Encyclopädie. They are well worth reading, particularly that on the Eleusinia. There is likewise in the same Encyclopaedia (which is in the London Library) an article on the Odyssey, by Nitzsch. I would also recommend to you the articles *Inspiration* and *Orakeln*.

There is a new work on Greek mythology and religion by *Heffter*.

Ever yours sincerely,

G. C. Lewis.

Kent House: April 5, 1846.

My dear Grote,—I cannot resist writing to express to you the satisfaction, as well as instruction, which I have derived from reading the two last published volumes of your history. You have, in my opinion, accomplished the task which you have undertaken, and although particular parts might be developed, you have succeeded completely in placing the whole question of the mythology and legendary narrations of the Greeks upon what I believe to be their true footing, without the omission of any material part of the subject, and without leaving any possibility of mistake as to your conclusions and the grounds of them. The subject of the Greek mythology, and the mode of its treatment, is, as you know, of great attraction for me; and I offered Macvey Napier to review your book, intending to be full on this part of it, but he wrote me word that John Mill had already undertaken the article. Your chapter on the state of society described in the Homeric poems is very successful; perhaps you might have said a little more on the state of the mechanical arts, and the ideas about external nature, than you have given. Everything on the latter head is collected in Voelcker's Homerische Geographie. The chapter on the Homeric poems is most interesting, and in the chief part of it I concur. But I cannot agree with your view of the early books of the Iliad, and I doubt the possibility of distinguishing between an Achilleid and an Iliad. In particular, the ninth book, which you consider of inferior execution, seems to me one of the finest parts of the poem, and at all events it relates mainly to Achilles. Inconsistencies do not convince me that the poem was not the work of one poet. They merely prove to me that his plan was not perfect. There is an article by Colonel Mure in the 'Foreign Quarterly Review,' showing that the Æneid is full of inconsistencies. There are gross inconsistencies and incoherencies in the plot of several of Walter Scott's poems and novels. The examination of the plan of the Iliad seems to me too detailed, and too full of very doubtful matter, to have a place in a *general* history of Greece. It somewhat breaks the course of the preliminary part, and it would be better suited to a history of Greek *Literature*. The first glimmerings of history, where almost every fact is insulated or disputed, form the least interesting portion of your subject. Your chapter on the Spartan constitution, however, quite satisfies all I could have wished, and your theory about the lots, as to which I never could make out anything, seems to me both novel and sound. I enclose on a separate paper a few remarks on individual passages, which have occurred to me.

Ever yours sincerely,

G. C. Lewis.

In consequence of dissensions in the Poor-Law office, and of difficulties attending the administration of the law, the Government found it desirable to re-model the commission in the early part of 1847. In the month of July in that year, Sir George Lewis resigned the office of commissioner. Allusions to these changes will be found in the following letter to Mr. Grote :—

Kent House: Jan. 26, 1847.

My dear Grote,—I am sincerely obliged to you for your very kind and warm letter. You will, I am sure, not suspect me of making empty professions when I say that I value your good opinion and your esteem infinitely more than I care for the abuse of ten thousand brawlers or writers in newspapers. There is, however, nothing in the change announced by the Government of which I disapprove. On the contrary, they appear to me to have taken the best step both for the public and the commissioners which the circumstances of the case admitted. Lord John completely threw over the report of the Andover Committee, and said that the Government intended to found no measure upon it. But he added that there was a state of feeling in Parliament, and a relation between the Home office and the commissioners, which rendered a change in the constitution of the department expedient, when the question of the renewal of the commission came before the House. He proposes to retain the present central control unimpaired, transferring the issue of general orders to the Queen in Council; constituting the department differently, and enabling it to be represented directly in the House of Commons. At the same time, I believe, the department will be made perpetual, instead of being, as at present, only temporary. It has been my great object to prevent the attacks of the last session from being used as a means of destroying the central office, and subverting the existing administration of the law. Although —— and his friends had *personal objects*, the aim of Wakley and the *Times* and their adherents was more extensive. If the Government make a good arrangement of the *personnel* of the new department, the amount of *public* injury done will not be great. For my own part, nothing but a consciousness of the impossibility of resigning would have induced me to hold my office even up to the present time. To be exposed to the insults of all the refuse of the House of Commons without the power of defending oneself, and to have one's chief opponent as the secretary of the board of which one is a member, without the power of dismissing him, is a position which nothing but necessity can render tolerable, and which I only submit to for the present because I have no alternative.

If it should be found on experience that the direct representation of the Poor-Law commission in Parliament leads to the abandonment of some wholesome regulations which are now in force, and renders the administration less impartial, this change for the worse must be imputed to our parliamentary constitution, and not to the Poor-Law department or the existing administration. Parliament is supreme, and we cannot be better governed than Parliament is willing to govern us. It is vain for a body of subordinate functionaries to attempt to enforce, on such a subject as Poor Laws, opinions which are repudiated by the majority of the sovereign legislature.

Pray remember me kindly to Mrs. Grote, and thank her for her good wishes.

What progress are you making with your two new volumes?

I presume that you have not yet begun to reprint your two first volumes; I have a few notes on Vol. II. to send you, but they are not written out.

Ever yours sincerely,

G. C. Lewis.

There is an article of mine on Local Taxation in the last number of the 'Edinburgh Review.' There is also an excellent article by J. Austin on Centralization.

We have taken Villiers Lister from Mr. Youldon's

and sent him to Harrow this school time. He seems very happy at the change.

In the next letter, written to the daughter of Mr. Austin, Lady Duff Gordon,* who by marriage was the first cousin of George Lewis, he bears testimony to the great merits of the article on Centralization,† mentioned in the last letter, which Mr. Austin had contributed to the last number of the 'Edinburgh Review;' and, at the request of my much lamented friend, Mrs. Austin, I append another letter on the same subject, which, by doing honour to her husband, had given her great pleasure; it is written by Mr. J. S. Mill to Sir Alexander Duff Gordon.

Kent House: Jan. 24, 1847.

My dear Lucie,—I have read with great pleasure and profit your father's article on Centralization. It says all that can be said on the subject within the limits of a review; indeed, I wonder that he was able to pack so much matter into so small a compass. It will assist materially in clarifying people's ideas on this much misunderstood subject, and will serve to diminish the unreasoning antipathy with which centralization, as distinguished from excessive or injudicious interference of the central government, is regarded in this country. I seriously hope that he may fulfil a sort of half-promise which he makes, of writing a second article on 'The legitimate province of the governing power.' Local authorities are in general less skilful and more weak

* Lady Duff Gordon is well known for her contributions to literature, especially by her lately published letters from Egypt, which have been read with so much entertainment. Lady Duff Gordon's lamented death took place at Cairo in July, 1869.

† *Edinburgh Review*, Jan. 1847, vol. lxxxv. p. 221.

than central authorities; and, therefore, if the interference is *wrong*, local authorities are likely to do less mischief. This seems to me the substance of the popular objection to centralization.

*   *   *   *

Ever yours affectionately,
G. C. LEWIS.

From Mr. John Stuart Mill.

India House: Jan. 27, 1847.

My dear Sir Alexander,—I regret to hear that Mr. Austin is again suffering from illness, which has, perhaps, been brought on by the application required in writing his admirable article in the 'Edinburgh,' and by the very natural and intelligible reaction after it was finished. In his bad health he must at least have the consolation of feeling himself useful, for the article is exactly one of those things which he can do so well, and which so few are capable of doing at all—a *thorough* discussion of the subject it treats of, going down to the roots and fundamentals of a matter never treated in that way before—eminently calculated not only to give clear ideas and to correct vague feelings and confused notions on that particular subject, but also to educate the minds of those who wish to *study* such subjects—a class that would probably be much more numerous if there were not so lamentable a paucity of such helps to them. One of the persons of greatest intellect that I have known said, after reading the article, 'What a pity the same man does not, in the same manner, *precisionize* other and even more important questions of political morals;' and I do hope that he will now be encouraged to do so. There is really some hope of this now that he has actually *finished* something; for his inability to satisfy *himself* is the only thing except ill health which has ever seemed to me to stand in the way.

Very truly yours,

J. S. MILL.

Desirous to remove a slur which he thought had been unjustly cast upon his administrative ability during the later part of the time in which he had acted as Poor-Law commissioner—released from an office the tenure of which was incompatible with his sitting in Parliament, Sir George Lewis now sought a seat in the House of Commons. A vacancy was about to occur in the county of Hereford; his mother's family resided in that county; his father's residence was close upon the borders of it; he was well known there by many friends; and when it was understood that he was willing to come forward, a requisition was sent to him, which he accepted. In the following letters he speaks of his canvass; he was elected on August 4, without opposition.

Hereford: July 2, 1847.

My dear Head,—

* * * *

To-day I canvassed the outskirts of Hereford, and I do not go to Ross till next week. Hereford alone will occupy about five days. I propose now to be absent all next week, if you have nothing to say to the contrary.

The number of voters for the county exceeds 7,000, and it is difficult to make much impression on so large a body without giving some time to the work. I have no reason to fear a contest, but the mere act of canvassing suggests the idea of starting fresh candidates;

and if the dissolution should be deferred much longer, I should not be surprised if somebody started on a sort of forlorn hope. The yeomanry of the county are numerous and independent, and are a good deal under the influence of the small proprietors. Fortunately, however, there is no subject on which they feel strongly. I have scarcely heard anything about Poor Laws in Hereford. Both the Low Church and Dissenters have, however, taken up the *Protestant* cry; and I have been asked several questions about Maynooth, Endowment of the Catholic clergy, Education Grant, &c. One of the relieving officers of the Hereford Union refused his vote to-day because I would not promise to be against all endowment of Popery.

* * * *

Ever yours truly,

G. C. Lewis.

Mornington: July 6, 1847.

My dear Head,—

* * * *

I have had to-day some reminiscences of my ancient pulmonary enemy. I think it was owing to the great heat of the last few days, and to standing in the sun to canvass. The consequence probably will be that I shall be able to do less this week, and that I may not be able to return till the week beginning on Monday, the 19th. Pray let me know if this will be at all inconvenient. If you should see Brand, pray let him know that my return will not be so soon as I expected.

Ever yours truly,

G. C. Lewis.

P.S. The debate* in the Lords on Friday night was worth reading. The arguments *pro* and *con* were well stated. I was much struck with Lord Stanley's speech, who appeared to me thoroughly to understand the question. It was curious to see in what a summary manner they did execution upon Borthwick's and Etwall's clauses.

Hereford: Aug. 5, 1847.

My dear Head,—My election passed off quietly yesterday, notwithstanding the alarms of Feargus O'Connor and Oastler.† * * * Nothing could go off better or more peaceably than the whole affair. * * * I hope you will write the Settlement ‡ article in the 'Edinburgh Review.' I see no necessity for making it very long. You might begin with a reference to my article on Local Taxation, at the end of which the subject is adverted to, and the intention to appoint a committee is mentioned.

Ever yours sincerely,

G. C. Lewis.

Harpton: Aug. 16, 1847.

My dear Head,—I have received a letter from Lord John Russell announcing his intention to offer me a parliamentary office before the beginning of the session. I shall not mention this to anybody but my own immediate relations, as circumstances may arise to prevent the intention from being fulfilled (although Lord John

* Debate of Friday, July 2, on the Poor-Law Administration Bill. See *Hansard*, 3rd Series, vol. xciii. p. 1130.

† Reports had been circulated that Feargus O'Connor or Oastler would oppose him.

‡ The article may be seen in the *Edinburgh Review* of April, 1848, vol. lxxxvii. p. 451. It was reprinted and circulated by the Government when the law of assessment was altered in 1865.

himself expresses no doubt), but I lose no time in communicating it to you, as showing what his intentions are to the commissioners. It seems to me that the great difficulty in your case is to find an office that will suit you.

* * * *

Have you come to any understanding with Empson about the Law of Settlement?

Ever yours truly,

G. C. LEWIS.

Sir George Lewis was appointed Secretary to the Board of Control in the following month of November.

Grove Mill House: Sept. 28, 1847.

My dear Head,—I cannot tell you how glad I was to receive the account of Lord Grey's offer, for, although, after Lord John's letter, I felt convinced that the Government seriously intended to provide for you, I did not feel sure how soon a fitting opportunity would arise amidst the pressure which is kept up from all quarters upon the Government.

Lord Grey's letter is quite satisfactory, and I collect that you have made inquiries which satisfied you as to the eligibility of the appointment. I know very little about the place; I fear it is terribly cold, but I suppose pine-wood is cheap, and stoves are capacious. It is odd it should be in North America. You must take some lessons about *hoisting the British colours, &c.*

I cannot make out why they keep the Poor-Law appointments so long open. Are they waiting for Hawes to find a seat?

Ever yours sincerely,

G. C LEWIS.

Lord Grey, then Colonial Secretary, had offered to Sir Edmund Head the Governorship of New Brunswick. His offer was accepted.

Grove Mill House, Watford: Oct. 31, 1847.

My dear Grote,—I was very glad to receive your letter, and to find that you were so well and so agreeably employed. I shall read your pamphlet on Switzerland with much interest.* My mind is not in the blank paper state, but in a state much worse, that is, a number of confused blots and scratches have been made upon it by various contradictory articles which I have read in newspapers, out of which I can decipher nothing clear.

A short time ago I made an excursion into Herefordshire to attend some agricultural societies, and to deliver my sentiments on subjects of which I was considerably ignorant; with that interruption I have been here since the end of September, and have not lost sight of my intended review of your third and fourth volumes. I found, however, that I could do nothing without books of reference, and therefore I postponed my article till the April number. This abominable meeting of Parliament,† however, deranges me in every way, and will, I fear, render much of what I have written useless. I have, however, carefully read a second time your last two volumes, and am ready to write the article as soon as I am within reach of my books. The task is not a light one, for the quantity of material in your two last volumes is immense. At present I am writing on a subject on which I had previously collected some notes, a subject not strictly of logical science but connected with it, viz. *the legitimate province of au-*

* 'Seven Letters on the recent Politics of Switzerland.' Newby, 1847.

† Parliament in November, the Session began on the 18th.

*thority in matters of opinion and practice.** The problem is to determine the cases in which we can properly believe anything, not on appropriate evidence, understood by us, but merely because another person thinks so and so. It opens a great variety of questions connected with ethics and politics, which have never been looked at from this point of view, and it interests me to pursue the various threads of speculation. I have, however, very much lost my faith in the advantage of *abstract* speculation on morals and politics in the present state of knowledge and opinion, and I write it rather for my own sake than from any idea of being useful. It seems to me that there is too little consensus about elementary facts in the moral sciences for any abstract treatment to be of much avail; and I have come to the conclusion (particularly after reading your four volumes) that an enlightened commentary upon historical data, well ascertained, is the best form in which instruction on such subjects can be presented to the public. A series of good histories would be the best foundation and preparation for a really scientific treatment of politics and morals. My best regards to Mrs. Grote.

Ever yours sincerely,

G. C. LEWIS.

Grove Mill House: Nov. 3, 1847.

My dear Gilbert,—I have written again to Empson about your article,† and will let you know his answer. I quite agree with what you say about gardening, as to the distinction between flower-gardens and wild thickets—such as a *jardin anglais* was supposed to be.

* His essay on the 'Influence of Authority on Opinion,' was published by Parker in 1849.

† *Edinburgh Review*, vol. lxxxviii. p. 403.

Would it not be well to look into Mr. Price's book on 'The Picturesque'? He was a great *enemy* of formal, regular gardens.

I have an idea that there is an epigram of Martial which speaks of hothouses—of plants kept in an artificial state under glass. If I am not mistaken, it is quoted in 'Beckman,' but under what head I do not remember; I think I could find the passage if I was in London. The gardens of the ancients were for the most part mere shrubberies, with statues, like their idea of the Elysian fields, as described in the sixth Æneid. Horti, in the plural, in Latin, meant a villa. Horti Cæsaris is Cæsar's villa—*i.e.* a large palace, with grounds laid out, close to Rome. They had, however, flower-gardens to a certain extent. The ancients had some exotic fruits, '*Persica* mala,' &c.; but few, if any, exotic flowers.

Whately, the author of the book on gardening, was either the father or the uncle of the Archbishop of Dublin.

I am afraid that this detestable meeting of Parliament will accelerate my start at the Board of Control, and that I shall have to leave this place and go up to London very soon. My only consolation for this anti-Christmas session is, that I hope there will be six weeks interval afterwards.

Yours affectionately,

G. C. L.

Grove Mill House, Watford: Nov. 5, 1847.

My dear Grote,—I received yesterday the volume on 'Swiss Politics,' which you were so good as to send me. I have since read it with great interest, and feel much indebted to you, both for having written the book, and having sent me a copy of it. The narrative is lucid and flowing, and the view taken of the whole series of events appears to me perfectly just and discriminating. It carries one back to the seventeenth century, and seems to place one in the midst of the Thirty Years' War. Open lawlessness, free bands, religious zeal producing political revolutions and wars, priests leading the people in council and in the field—all this is very unlike the present century. The anticipations to which your narrative leads are very gloomy, and I see by yesterday's paper that the seven cantons have formally seceded from the Diet, and that civil war is declared. The cause of the mischief is religious bigotry working upon an imperfect federal constitution. Probably neither would have led to open war without the other. Unless one party can defeat the other in the field, and a settlement can be effected by force, I see no escape from the present complication but a division of the present confederacy into two leagues. In this case the larger and more Protestant section might make a *better* federal constitution than they now possess. I subjoin one or two remarks which occurred to me in reading your work.

In p. 22, line 12, there is a misprint, which obscures the sense—some such word as *defend* or *justify* is apparently omitted.—Page 121. It might have been desirable to explain why the Legislative Council of the Canton de Vaud was so obstinate in rejecting the reasonable prayer of the petition. The constitution was then popular, and the canton is, I believe, chiefly Protestant. There is an apparent absence of motive for making so decided a resistance to the strongly-expressed opinion of the great body of their constituents. —Page 128. It seems clear from the narrative that the principle of *arms*, imported into the Sonderbund, and distinguishing it from the previous league of Sarnen, was a retaliation against the Corps francs, and partly in self-defence. The Protestant party had previously shown a disposition to resort to arms. If this be so, it is a point in the case of the pro-Jesuit cantons to the statement of which they are entitled.

I forgot when I last wrote to you to answer what you had said about the Poor Law Commission. The truth is, that I have been so glad to emancipate myself from the subject lately that I overlooked it in writing to you. Lord John Russell decided to retain Nicholls as Permanent Secretary in the Poor Law Office, on the ground of his being the Senior Commissioner, and of his having given up a lucrative office under the Bank of England upon his first appointment. I hope that he may prove an efficient Secretary. They offered Head the Governorship of New Brunswick, which is 3,000*l.* a year for six years. It is complete banishment into the backwoods, but the climate is better than Canada; and, after all that had passed, Head accepted it without hesitation. The employment is honourable and sufficiently lucrative. For my own part, I regret very much that he could not be appointed to some office in this country. The Government have offered me one of the Secretaryships of the Board of Control, and I have virtually accepted it, but I have not yet been up to London to see Hobhouse. I do not apprehend that the office is a very laborious one. I hear that Jones Loyd was favourable to the Government interference with the Bank, but I have still to learn how bankrupt merchants are to be made richer by more bits of paper.

Ever yours sincerely,

G. C. Lewis.

Kent House: Dec. 21, 1847.

My dear Gilbert,—I hope that you have arrived safely after your several journeys, and that your household derangements have been set to rights. The Dean * has been publishing in the 'Times' his memorial to the Queen, and is doing his best to prolong the agitation. I suppose that it will end in Hampden being installed, and in the Government offending a large part of the Church for no conceivable object.

I send you a copy of the 'Epigram' of Martial, and also a passage from the postscript to Mason's 'English Garden,' which contains an abstract of the poem. You should by all means procure Mason's 'Poems,' which I believe is not an uncommon book, and read this poem, as it sets forth his principles very distinctly. He is an *anti-formalist*, or *naturalist*, but pins his faith to the doctrine of sweeping curves; and is opposed to the Dutch or French garden, formed on the pattern plan, on the one hand, and to the modern school of *unimproved* nature, founded by Knight and Price, on the other. You will also be amused by Mason's 'Heroic Epistle to Sir William Chambers,' which very successfully ridicules his work on 'Oriental Gardening.' Chambers, I believe, built Somerset House, and therefore must have been an architect of no common powers; but I suspect his book on 'Oriental Gardening' was a piece of charlatanism.

* * * *

Your affectionate brother,

G. C. Lewis.

* Dr. Merewether, Dean of Hereford.

Grove Mill: Dec. 28, 1847.

My dear Gilbert,—

* * * *

I am glad that you have made so much progress with your article. The subject is an interesting and agreeable one. Sir William Temple's 'Essay,' at which I looked the other day, contains a good deal of matter. I see that the remark about the climate of England enabling one to go out more days in the year than any other is given there to Charles the Second. Sir William Chambers's work may safely be set down as a piece of charlatanism.

With respect to Oriental gardening, I enclose you some notes from a book of authority which I have borrowed from the India Board, and am now reading. Duhalde's book was in the London Library after all. It is in the catalogue as large as life.

The Dean of Hereford has suddenly become a hero, a capacity in which I did not expect to meet him. The 'Times' of to-day, by the pen of Mr. Mozley, nearly deifies him. I cannot understand what should have driven him to such extremities. We shall all be anxious to hear what were the proceedings of to-day. Julius Hare has written a pro-Hampden pamphlet, which the 'Chronicle' praises.

Pray thank my father for his letter received to-day. I will write to him to-morrow.

Your affectionate brother,

G. C. L.

Grove Mill: Jan. 14, 1848.

My dear Gilbert,—The passages from the 'Jesuits' Letters' are curious, and I do not see how it can be doubted that the Chinese had at that time attained to considerable skill in laying out gardens on a large scale. They had no theory to support (like Chambers), and the utmost that can be suspected is, that there is exaggeration. It does not, however, follow that the English style of landscape gardening (of which Stowe * may serve as the model) had anything to do with China, or was in the remotest manner borrowed from it. The description of the *canals* in the Chinese gardens resembles that of the Indian gardens in one of the extracts I sent you. In the note at the end of Mason's 'Garden' is a reference to the article, *Architecture du Jardinage*, in the French 'Encyclopédie.' This work is at Moccas,† and it might be worth your while to look at the article.

* * * *

I suppose that something will be done about the Militia, and that there will be a small increase of the army in consequence of the Duke of Wellington's letter.‡

Ever yours,

G. C. L.

Grove Mill: Jan. 5, 1848.

My dear Head,—I have been so often assisted by you on points about pictures, that I am tempted to trouble you again about a picture at the Grove which puzzles me. Theresa is collecting materials for a catalogue of the pictures, and we have been examining them closely for purposes of description. You may perhaps remember a fine half-length portrait something in the style of Bronzino, which hangs over a door in the inner

* In Buckinghamshire: the residence of the Duke of Buckingham.

† In Herefordshire: the residence of Sir George Cornewall.

‡ 'The Duke of Wellington's letter to Sir John Burgoyne, on the defences of the country.' See *Annual Register* vol. xc., for 1848.

library. It represents, apparently, a young Italian or Spanish cavalier or gentleman, in the dress corresponding to that of Queen Elizabeth's time—but *black*. He wears a sword, and a dagger on the loins, with chased gold and steel hilts. The face is remarkably handsome. It is painted on panel. On the back, on the rough wooden surface, is an old inscription, the letters of which seem to have been branded in with hot iron, and afterwards traced with some plaster or white substance. The upper part of it can now be read with difficulty, and a portion of it may have been planed off. As far as I can make out, it is as follows:—

PERARI DE REVONA
KEYE PINXIT
A° 1556

The letters under which I have put a dot, in the first line, are indistinct. Something also *may* have been lost at the end of the line. The second and third lines are quite distinct, and every letter certain. The first line seems to contain the name of the person represented; in which case the mysterious word in the second line is the painter's name. Or the whole may be the name of the painter. But as the word before 'pinxit' is quite unintelligible to me, I can make out nothing. The date, which is certain, ought to give the clue. I have no books of reference here, and therefore have nothing to assist me.

The 'Times' failed altogether in making a hero out of Merewether. I do not know whether you saw the articles in the 'Chronicle' against him. They were remarkably pungent, and there was no answering them; so the 'Times' let their man drop. The affair, I hear, is not yet over; but it is clear that bishops and deans in these degenerate days have no taste for martyrdom, and dislike flying in the face of power. The Government will prevail; but the victory will be dearly bought, and will cost much too high a price. I have sent for Hampden's 'Lectures,' and am going to follow Wilberforce's example, and read them.

I cannot believe that steam-navigation has made so great a difference in our coast defences as the Duke of Wellington's letter throughout assumes. His whole argument is based on the assumption that the defences which were sufficient from 1815 to 1845 are sufficient no longer. He does not enter into this question upon which everything seems to me to turn. I should like to see it discussed by *gens du métier*. At all events, the advantage cannot be *all* on one side. Our steam navy is in proportion as much stronger than theirs as our previous sailing navy; perhaps, counting private steamers, even stronger. No doubt, if the French could land a large army with artillery, matériel, &c., we are in a scrape. But this is the question and always has been.

I recommend to you Ricardo's book on the Navigation Laws:* it is essential as to colonial trade. The case against them is stronger than I supposed.

I hope that Lady Head and your children have escaped without influenza. I direct this to Chester Place, hoping it will find you.

Ever yours,

G. C. L.

* Important discussions on the Navigation Laws took place in Parliament in 1848 and 1849, the result of which was an Act effecting great changes, which passed in May 1849. The book alluded to is the 'Anatomy of the Navigation Laws,' by John Lewis Ricardo, M.P. London, Gilpin, 1847.

Kent House: Feb. 8, 1848.

My dear Gilbert,—The passage in Pliny, about which you wrote to me at Grove Mill, is in his 'Natural History' (book xix. ch. 23). Translated, it as follows:—'The cucumber is of a pulpy nature, and its fruit is out of the ground. The Emperor Tiberius was extremely fond of it, and it was served every day at his table. For in fine weather his gardeners wheeled the plants out into the sun on moveable frames; and in winter placed them under the protection of *glass*.' Specularia may mean any transparent substance, as talc or glass: specularis lapis is used by Pliny for talc. Juvenal applies the word specularia to the glazing of a lectria or sedan-chair. The passage is quite unambiguous as to forcing cucumbers in winter under some vitreous substance.

Martial has also an epigram (viii. 14) in which *specularia* is applied to a hot-house for forcing fruit. The Romans must certainly have been familiar with the practice of forcing fruits and vegetables, and even flowers, but the dearness and scarcity of glass and talc must have confined the use of hot-houses within narrow limits.

* * * *

Yours affectionately,

G. C. L.

The following letter was addressed by Sir George Lewis to Mrs. Austin in Paris, where she and Mr. Austin were residing when the disturbances broke out in February 1848.

Kent House: March 4, 1848.

My dear Mrs. Austin,—I have heard intelligence of yourself and Austin several times during the last few days, but I cannot refrain from writing to enquire after you in the present state of things, and to express my hope that you have not been subjected to any serious inconvenience by the late alarms. All accounts, both public and private, represent the town as perfectly quiet; and I suppose to those who staid at home while the disturbances lasted, there was only that annoyance which arises from a feeling of uncertainty. Even in quiet times, and with a settled Government, it is not easy to see very far into the future, and he must be a bold prophet who will undertake now to predict the course of events on the Continent. Of one thing, however, we may be pretty sure, that the future will not be a copy of the past, and that things will not follow the same course now as either in 1789 or 1830. There appears to be no tendency to propagandism at present. All the movement is Ashleyite or Walterite. It appears to be not merely a *social* but a *socialist* revolution. Somebody has said that a *provisional* government is a government which supplies the people with *provisions.* We shall now see the system of out-door relief, limitation of hours of work, interference between employer and workman, tried on a large scale. This seems destined to be the modern *protectionism*, now that corn laws and protective custom duties are giving way. There is a strong party ready to try the experiment in this country, but no principle of that sort is ever carried to its full extent at one blow in England. Both in our wise and foolish acts we generally do things by halves; and considering the large alloy of folly in public opinion, perhaps the existence of this perpetual drag-chain which we put on in going *up*, as well as going *down* hill, is not to be lamented.

During the last few months I have much changed my mode of life, having commuted a very laborious office into one with little labour, and having besides had to attend in Parliament. India is a very interesting subject from its magnitude, but the government is mainly in the local authorities and the Court of Directors, and the Board of Control is, as its name imports, merely a controlling body. It originates very little, and all the preliminary work is done at the India House. However, it is the link with Parliament, upon which everything ultimately depends; and since the abolition of the trading functions of the Company, the Court of Directors is assuming more and more the character of a sub-department of the Government. There is a growing feeling, I think, against the retention of our American colonies, the West Indies and Canada; and more disposition to look to the East, where all our recent acquisitions have occurred. The overland journey contributes to this.

Louis Philippe will be treated here with respect, but there is no real sympathy with him. It has been said that, although he would not allow the people to have their *dinner*, he has had his dessert.

I read with great admiration and assent Austin's letter, which Lucie * mentioned to me. Pray give him my best regards, and believe me,

Ever yours sincerely,

G. C. L

Kent House: April 16, 1848.

My dear Head,—I was extremely glad to receive your letter written in Halifax harbour, describing your safe arrival, and, on the whole, favourable passage. The time of year was not propitious, and you had a narrow escape of a terrible storm on leaving the port of Liverpool. You were lucky in not having many fellow-passengers.

* Lady Duff Gordon, Mrs. Austin's daughter.

By the time you receive this letter, you will have reached your destination and have assumed the government of the colony. Judging from the weather in England, the winter cannot have yet relaxed its grasp, and you will have a cold journey from St. John's.

I shall be very anxious to know your first impressions, and how you and Lady Head like your new life and habitation. I always regret that I have not seen America, which I am never likely to see now.

Since you left England, the consequences of the French revolution have been working themselves out rapidly, but nothing has yet assumed a definitive shape, either in France or elsewhere. The French Provisional Government has continued its communist course, acting under the dictation of the working classes in Paris. The financial and commercial crisis has in consequence been immediate—production is diminished, trade and credit are almost paralysed. An extreme system of out-door relief, at the cost of the general Government, is established in Paris. The town has, however, been kept quiet, and the Government appear to wish to consolidate their own power as far as they can. They are very despotic, but not yet warlike. They have thrown cold water on the Irish mission to Paris, and have not yet interfered in any foreign quarrel. Milan, however, has successfully rebelled, and has expelled the Austrian army, which now occupies Verona and Mantua in strength, and will not abandon Lombardy without a struggle. The King of Sardinia has marched to the assistance of the Lombards, but no engagement with the Austrians has yet taken place. Vienna has expelled Metternich, and concessions have been extorted from the Government; but the quarrel with the people is now settled, or at least suspended, and Hungary has obtained terms with which it is satisfied. The power of Austria is still great; and if she resolves to fight for Lombardy, the French will probably march an army over the Alps, to assist the insurgents in Sardinia. The Prussian revolution has gone further than the Austrian —there is to be a free constitution, with a parliament and liberty of the press. A Liberal Ministry has also been called to power. There is a strong movement towards the *unity of Germany*—an attempt to strengthen the Diet, and change the Staatenbund into a Bundestaat. Whether this will be effected is still doubtful. At home, the chief feature in politics has been the more decided split between the Government and the Radicals, and the attempt of the latter to form a separate party, and to gain possession of power by the extension of the suffrage. Much opposition has been offered by them to a bill lately brought in for altering the law of Treason and Sedition.

A threatened movement of the Chartists, which was to take place on Monday last, and to bring about an English revolution, was completely frustrated by the preparations of the Government and the voluntary organisation of the upper and middle classes. There was more genuine alarm in London on that day than I ever remember to have existed. People hardly doubted of the event, but they feared a bloody conflict in the streets.

My Sattara debate came on a short time ago, and is adjourned. It is too unimportant, luckily, to excite attention in these stirring times. Your article appears in the new number of the 'Edinburgh Review,' and reads very well; but people are thinking of nothing now but extension of suffrage, the five points of the Charter, repeal of the Union, risings of the people, and such like pressing questions. John Lefevre has been appointed Clerk of the House of Lords; he succeeded Le Marchant, according to the intention announced to you by Lord John Russell. The Under Secretary's office, held by Le Marchant, is political; I have not heard who is to have it. My best regards to Lady Head.

Ever yours truly,

G. C. LEWIS.

Sir George Lewis having been for rather more than six months Secretary to the Board of Control, was now requested to change his office and to become Under Secretary to the Home Office. The second post was considered of somewhat greater importance than the first, and he was more familiar with the subjects with which its business required him to deal, but the necessary attendance at the office was more close, and he much regretted the inroad thus made upon the leisure which he had been in the habit of devoting to literary work.

Kent House: May 14, 1848.

My dear Head,—Since I wrote to you I have received your second letter from Halifax, and also have heard of your safe arrival at Fredericton, and your installation as Governor, together with sundry compliments from your new subjects. By this time I suppose that even the winter of New Brunswick has relaxed its grasp, and that you are able to go about and see the new country. You have the 'regni novitas,' without the 'res dura' which is its usual accompaniment; for the causes which shake European society do not reach across the Atlantic.

* * * *

There has been lately a shifting of offices, which has reached me in its effects, and has transferred me from the Board of Control to the Home Office. John Lefevre having become Clerk of the House of Lords, Le Marchant has succeeded to his place. I have succeeded to Le Marchant's; and Wilson, the editor of the 'Economist,' is my successor. Stanley, who is Foreign Under Secretary, is called up to the House of Lords,* so that Hawes and I are the two Under Secretaries in the House of Commons. The change is not one which I particularly desired, as the Board of Control was a quiet nook, which left me a good deal of liberty during the recess, and there is more to be done and more attendance at the Home Office. The subjects at the Home Office are, however, more familiar to me, and they are better suited to a county seat.

* * * *

Our Chartist commotions are gradually subsiding; but there is a strong tendency in the direction of an extension of the suffrage, in consequence of the progress of events on the Continent. Hume is to bring forward a motion on the subject at the end of this month. I do not think that anything will be done this session, but I have great doubts whether public opinion will be satisfied without *some* advance in the popular direction. The small boroughs, which are chiefly under the influence of large landowners, form the main ground of objection.

Since the ridiculous scene† at Limerick the ultra-Repeal party in Ireland has become contemptible, and the State trials now about to commence have lost half their interest. But the repeal feeling through the country is strong, and is rather increased by the Poor

* Created Baron Eddisbury.

† See the account of the attack made in Limerick on Messrs. Smith O'Brien, Meagher, and Mitchell: *Annual Register* for 1848; *Chronicle*, p. 59.

Law, which alienates the affections of the smaller Protestant gentry. Twisleton has been in town this week, and I have seen him; but he has nothing new to say. I also met Whately at Senior's at breakfast, but he talked of nothing but craniology, mesmerism, and bad etymologies.

The Danish question will probably be settled, but the Italian mess is thicker than ever. The Austrians occupy Verona, and Mantua, and the north-east angle of Lombardy; and if Charles Albert cannot dislodge them with the help of the Pope, the French will probably march over the Alps. The Italians do not wish to invite them, but they will perhaps appear some day soon as unbidden guests. Macaulay has resigned his seat in the Cabinet. I hope his 'History' may flourish the more in consequence. My best regards to Lady Head.

Ever yours sincerely,

G. C. L.

Kent House: June 20, 1848.

My dear Head,—I had the pleasure of receiving your letter from Fredericton, dated April 21; and I have delayed answering it for some time in consequence of the incessant occupation of my day as well as night, which my present office combined with Parliament produces. The business is not of any great importance. The Home Office is a sort of central point for an immense number of offices and officers, commissions, lord-lieutenants, magistrates, &c.; all their correspondence with the Treasury and other departments, and all their applications for instructions or money, pass through or are made to the Home Office. It is also a house of call for numbers of people who wish to receive information, or to communicate it. Then there is a great deal of routine parliamentary business, arrangements about returns, and the like. The time of the Secretary of State is very much occupied with Cabinets and interviews; and it is only by constant attention on the part of the Under Secretaries that at a moment of pressure, such as has been lately caused by the Chartists, the routine minor business of the office is kept going. The Home Office is likewise a Colonial Office for the Channel Islands and the Isle of Man; and although these are not large communities, each of them has a governor and a little government complete in itself, which gives rise to the various questions which a separate government invariably creates. On the whole, although the Home Office subjects are more familiar to me, and I feel that I am more in my proper place, I regret on many accounts the easy life which I had at the Board of Control.

The state of the Continent has not altered very materially since I wrote to you last. The Danish question will be settled without a general war; but the German States are in confusion. There have been fresh disturbances at Berlin; the Prussian Government is without strength. The Court of Austria is still in a fugitive state, and has virtually emigrated from Vienna. Belgium and Holland keep their heads above water, and have suffered less than any of the continental countries. France is still only one degree removed from anarchy.

The charlatans who got to the head of affairs are utterly discredited, but there is nobody to take their place. John Austin, who is just come over, describes the state of mind of the French as one of perfect political scepticism and indifference. They have no rallying point. They have no confidence in any public man, and no attachment to any political institution. They care no more for a republic than a monarchy. He says that if they were really in earnest about republican institutions, there would be much more chance of their re-establishing order and stability. He thinks that there is no active vindictive revolutionary spirit among them. The Revolution consists in a vast commercial crisis. Everybody is poorer than he was. The landowner does not get his rents. The manufacturer dismisses his workmen. The skilled artificer receives twelve instead of forty francs a week. If he will not work for this sum he must go to the ateliers nationaux: i.e. receive out-door relief, with an illusory labour. But my expectation is that we shall see a succession of weak Governments in France, and a succession of men at the head of affairs for some time to come with no fixed policy or system, but living by shifts and expedients, sometimes putting down anarchy by force, sometimes appeasing the popular anger by bribes and dishonest concessions. In short, I look forward to a state of things similar to that in Spain, varied by the difference of national character. The Italians have shown more good sense and self-command than the French. The King of Naples has quarrelled with his subjects, and Sicily has declared itself independent. But the Pope is still on his throne, and the Roman State holds together. Charles Albert has made himself virtually king of northern Italy; and his recent defeat of the Austrians will probably lead to their expulsion from Italy without French interference. The Italian patriots dread the French, and will not call them in until an absolute necessity arises. I had a short conversation with Lord Palmerston about Italy a week or two ago, and he then was very confident that the

Austrians would be driven out of Italy without a general war. It is curious how entirely the continental revolutions have turned upon secular interests: for the most part they have resolved themselves into *economical* questions. Indeed the question of *out-door relief* seems likely to be worked out over the Continent on a large scale. The Pope has only maintained himself by placing himself at the head of a *political* party: his government has lost its ecclesiastical character. The Church everywhere now plays second fiddle to the State. The quarrel between Palmerston and the Spanish Government has been a nine days' wonder; and although it is not yet settled, and indeed in appearance the breach is now wider than ever, yet I do not anticipate anything serious from it at present.

* * * *

At home, public business is neither in a very satisfactory nor a very unsatisfactory state. The great difficulty of the finances remains where it was—certainly not diminished, perhaps rather increased. The country will not bear an additional income-tax, and no more money is to be got out of the indirect taxes. The West India proposition of the Government is acceptable to no one. It affords no substantial relief to the colonists, but it sacrifices revenue, and it is doubtful whether it will be carried. The repeal of the navigation laws has been upon the whole well received. It will not pass this session, but I look upon its success next session as nearly certain; at least, if there is not a change of Administration.

* * * *

The Repeal party in Ireland is full of internal dissension and distrust. The priests do not like the Jacobin section, who are the most forward and enterprising. On the other hand, this portion contains all the real energy and talent of the party. There is a vast deal of genuine suffering and a general disaffection to the English connection among the Catholics—and this it is which constitutes the real danger. If the provinces were sound, the brawlers in the large towns would be contemptible.

In England the slackness of trade has produced much distress in the towns and manufacturing districts; and this, combined with the events on the continent, has given a real importance to the question of parliamentary reform. Nothing will be done now; but I fully expect that four or five years will not pass over us without sweeping away some twenty of the small boroughs, and transferring their members to more populous places.* The great weakness of the present system is, that the minority of the *property* as well as of the *population* of the country has the preponderance in the representation.

Your account of your colony and its government is very interesting, and implies, I fear, that your first year will bring you a good deal of delicate arrangement. American society is now a very interesting study, for it is clear that its democratic institutions are becoming more and more a model to Europe.

My best regards to Lady Head.

Ever yours sincerely,

G. C. Lewis.

London: August 6, 1848.

My dear Head,—I have to acknowledge two letters from you, dated June 14 and July 9, which I have received with much pleasure, as I think that your new life proves both interesting and agreeable, and you

* This expectation, long foreseen, has since been fully verified.

have every reason to be satisfied with your decision as to going out. I had intended to write to you sooner, but you will, I am sure, forgive me when you recall the delights of the last six weeks of the session, with which we used to be familiar, though not from personal experience. There has been a more than usual allowance of tedious talk this session; and what with late nights and morning sittings, and the necessity of attendance of the subordinate members of the Government, I really had hardly a spare quarter of an hour for some weeks. The Government is not very strong, and does not exercise much personal ascendency in the House. The schism in the Conservative party has likewise led to a practical secession of the natural leaders of that party from the debates, and has thrown the Opposition into the hands of a set of men who, being destitute of real talent, can only succeed by occupying time and multiplying cavils and objections.

Our old friend * * *, the village lawyer, has been very prominent and busy in this vexatious petty warfare. The only man of genuine talent among the Protectionists is * * *, and his talent consists mainly in good comedy. He is a sort of Brummagem Sheridan.

Owing to these two causes, the waste of time and protraction of debates this session has been fearful. The Government made a fatal mistake in meddling with the sugar duties—this has been the great blunder of the session. They ought to have stuck to the settlement of 1846, which the House never would have disturbed if they had stood by it. Having committed this leading error, they proceeded to follow it up by a profusion of technical errors in the arrangement of the details of a most complicated set of scales of duties, the discussion and correction of which has occupied many a weary hour, and brought much discredit on the Government. In the course of these debates, they started an attack upon Hawes for suppressing a despatch, and upon Lord Grey for misquoting a memorial. These attacks were pursued with the usual zeal which belongs to personal questions, and created a great deal of interest for some time, quite disproportionate to the importance of the subjects. The result of the whole series of attacks and debates has been that the Colonial Office is in bad odour, and that some other arrangement of the office is a probable event.

It is certainly a defect that the Colonial Secretary should not be in the House of Commons. The Under Secretary does not speak with sufficient authority. This, however, cannot be avoided, so long as the rule remains about two Secretaries of State only being in the House of Commons. Sir George Grey and Lord Palmerston must both be in the Commons. Molesworth has been making a speech on colonial policy, which you will read with interest. It is an elaborate attack on our entire colonial system, and he has taken advantage of the present unpopularity of the Colonial Office to attribute to its influence what are in fact the evils inherent in dependance. When he talks of abolishing the interference of the Colonial Office, and giving self-government to the colonies, he means in fact the abolition of the influence of *England*, and the grant of *independence* to the colonies. This is not quite fair—but he has shown very clearly the cost of the colonies, and has drawn up a better debtor and creditor account than has ever been exhibited before. The repeal of the navigation laws would have passed the House of Commons this session, but it was sacrificed to the sugar duties—a measure which pleased nobody, did no good, and gave up revenue. I expect that it will be carried next session unless the House of Lords pluck up courage to throw it out. It is a subject, however, in which their *prejudices* rather than their *interests* are concerned, which makes some difference.

The French Revolution has now passed into the stage of military despotism—at which it was pretty sure to arrive; but it will not long remain there, as Cavaignac is not a man of much capacity, and he has no military reputation independently of the late conflict in Paris. Bonaparte had both these qualifications after the 18th Brumaire. I expect that there will be a succession of weak Administrations, despotic in their measures, but guided mainly by civilians. Hitherto the Chamber has not been sufficiently tranquil and orderly for debates of any magnitude. Everything seems to be decided by ejaculations and conversational remarks. The bourgeoisie seems thoroughly sick of the Republic, and of its fraternity and equality; but they have cracked the china jar of royalty, and cannot, I suspect, mend or replace it. People still talk of the Comte de Paris; and Louis Philippe, I am told, expects to be sent for every day; but I have no faith in a restoration. In the first place, I doubt whether it would have any practical effect; in the next place, the French are too deeply imbued with the phraseology and cant of republicanism to wish for a restoration of royalty even for a practical benefit. The Austrians are driving back the Italian army, and the French have been asked to interfere. This struggle is still uncertain as to its event. The probability is that Austria will retain the north-east angle of Italy for a time, but will be driven across the Alps in the end. The Holstein affair hangs fire, but

Palmerston is still very confident that it will be settled The Queen of Spain has miscarried; the King wishes that she should have a child, but they are quite estranged from one another.

At home, Chartism has for the present been extinguished by the convictions of Ernest Jones and his colleagues; the main subject of interest lately has been the (so-called) Irish rebellion. The leaders of the confederates utterly miscalculated their strength, but they defied the Government, and it was necessary to give them the honours of rebels. The Habeas Corpus Act was suspended in a day, and the Irish Government was armed with all powers necessary for suppressing an insurrection; but, unluckily for the rebels, it turned out that the priests were against a rising, and the rebellion has, as it appears, been suppressed by forty-five policemen firing one volley at a few hundreds of a ragged regiment, and without calling in the aid of the military. Smith O'Brien has not been taken; he is, or was, hiding himself in the north of Tipperary, and there is an idea that he has succeeded in getting on board a ship in Galway Bay, which will take him to America. Ireland is in a more distracted state than ever, but I hope that the events of this year will do for Repeal what 1745 did for Jacobitism in Scotland. The extended Poor Law is eating deep into the margin of the incumbered properties in many parts of the country, and extensive changes of ownership of land are, I think, impending. The Poor Law of Ireland is exercising a most powerful influence on the social state of the country. In England the Poor Law is no longer heard of. The experiment of direct responsibility to Parliament has been decidedly successful. This is Graham's opinion as well as mine. Charles Buller has carried a

Bill making vagrants and irremovables a union charge. He was forced to give up the proposition of altering the principle of calculating the common fund.

* * * *

I will send you the book you wish. Have you got Campbell's two last volumes? A good discussion of American democratic institutions, with reference to their fitness to European society, would be of great value and interest now. Pray keep your eye on this subject. It has never yet been well treated. I hope that Lady Head is better; my kind regards to her.

Ever yours,

G. C. L.

Grove Mill House: Sept. 28, 1848.

My dear Head,—I sent you a short time ago a copy of Brougham's Bill containing a digest of Criminal Law, which you wished to have. Hawes promised to forward it in your bag, and I hope it has reached you safely. I dare say the Criminal Law of New Brunswick is in a most incondite state; probably nobody knows what is law and what is not.

The last part of the session was tedious, and prolonged beyond the usual time, but uneventful. The Peelites nearly all went away, and there remained some Protectionists, some Radicals, and the members of the Government, with a few supporters. This made the attendance more strict. A long time was occupied with the estimates, and economy is now the order of the day, as Charles Wood was at last compelled to propose a loan of two millions. All establishments are now to be reduced to the lowest footing compatible with efficiency. The best part of the session was muddled away by the discussions on the sugar duties, a change which satisfied nobody, and solved no problem. The real difficulties of the case remain untouched, and the question about the maintenance of the African squadron will come on for decision next session. A committee has investigated the case, and has reported *against* the efficiency of the squadron for its purpose; still, there is a reluctance to withdraw it altogether and leave the slave trade to its natural action. The unwillingness to continue the large expense necessary for maintaining the squadron is at the same time very great.

Gladstone made a very able speech against the Colonial Office arrangement relative to Vancouver's Island. The feeling of the House, so far as there was one on the subject, went, I think, with him. For my own part, I cannot see what advantage we could gain from a new settlement in this remote region—six months' sail from England, and far distant from any of our foreign possessions; for practically it is in a different world from our provinces on the *western* coast of North America. If any people can colonise it with advantage, it must be the Americans. I should be glad to know your opinion on this subject. There has not been any really important legislation this session affecting England, unless the Act enabling the Queen to send a Minister to Rome deserves that name. The Scotch Entails Act is an important measure for that country. The Health of Towns Act passed after a multitude of changes, and Chadwick has at length been installed as the paid Commissioner, where I hope he may remain quiet. The Act does not apply to the metropolis or the large towns, and will, I presume, have no important operation. It was so emasculated by Henley in Committee that its powers will not amount to much in practice. Some cases of cholera have occurred at Hull, so that they will start at a lucky moment. The change in the Poor Law has, so far, been decidedly successful. Buller carried some short Bills, making a few changes in details, but everything of importance remains as it was. He is trying to deal with the subject of vagrancy. The horrors of workhouses, and the blessings of out-door relief, are now as much forgotten in the House of Commons as if they had never been mentioned. Since the French Revolution of this spring and Louis Blanc's doctrines, even the 'Times' is very shy upon the subject of the right to relief and employment by the State. The Irish rebellion, wherever it ventured to show itself, has been crushed by a few policemen. The military have never been called on to act. What the event of the trials at Clonmel * will be, remains to be proved. No jury trial in political cases can be satisfactory in Ireland. The jurors are either political friends or political enemies, and an acquittal does not seem to prove innocence, or a conviction guilt. It is just such a tribunal as an Election Committee, when every member voted according to his party, and not according to the evidence. For the present the Repeal party is on the ground, and the problem is, how to prevent a new organisation of the same sort being formed on an anti-English basis?

The continent is in confusion, but not yet at war. The Holstein question is settled, but there has been a bloody *émeute* at Frankfort. Northern Italy is on the brink of war, and the French Government is said to be

* For an account of the trials at Clonmel before the Special Mission which had been issued, see *Annual Register* for 1848, p. 389. Smith O'Brien, McManus, Meagher, and O'Donoghue were found guilty of high treason.

living only from day to day. England now is the only fixed point in Europe; for, although Holland and Belgium are sound, they are too weak to form a *point d'appui.*

I have been living at Grove Mill since the end of the session, going up occasionally to the Office, and writing some of an 'Essay on Authority in Matters of Opinion,' which I hope to print this winter. I regret very much that I am not able to show it to you, and profit by your advice and knowledge.

Sir George Grey has been with the Queen in Scotland. My father and Lady Lewis have been making a Scotch tour, and have seen the *other* half of the Chancellor Clarendon's pictures at Bothwell Castle. Theresa is working hard at her catalogue. Graham is at Netherby. Lord George Bentinck's death was awfully sudden, and without apparent cause. I do not think that it will unite the Peelites and Protectionists, who are essentially dissimilar. My best regards to Lady Head. I hope you are well, and not frightened at the approach of the enemy, winter.

Ever yours sincerely,

G. C. L.

Grove Mill: Nov. 24, 1848.

My dear Head,—I am really quite ashamed of having allowed so long a time to elapse without writing to you. I have three letters of yours to acknowledge, two containing a most interesting account of your peregrinations, and all showing that your new life is anything but unpleasant. My only excuse for this long interruption is, that for some time past I have been going daily to London in order to attend the Office, and returning by the evening train, so that I have been oscillating like a pendulum, and my whole time has been thus filled up. Early in October I went for about ten days into Herefordshire, where I had the satisfaction of acting as Steward at Bromyard Races, and attending at two public dinners. I then returned to Grove Mill. Waddington, my colleague, went to Brighton, and did not return to the Office till yesterday. During that interval I was forced to be present every day, in order to sign letters and keep things in motion. Everything is quite quiet now in England. The Chartists, both in London and the provinces, are reduced to silence; all the prosecutions against them prospered, and they had no support from the middle classes. Manufactures and trade are somewhat reviving, and the revenue is said to be improving. The circulation is in a sound state; there is no rash speculation, but good bills are discounted on easy terms. The railway companies have been pulling in; their shares have undergone a great depreciation, and they are taking steps for limiting their expenditure and placing their management on a sounder basis. We have, I think, passed the worst; but with the present state of the continent, and the great destruction of potatoes which has again taken place this year, also a harvest under the average, the demand for our manufactures must be curtailed. Everybody is retrenching his expenditure, and the Government among the rest. Economy is the order of the day in all the public departments. The Treasury thinks a grant of 100*l.* is now a great concession to anybody. All estimates are undergoing a severe revision. The Admiralty have been reducing establishments, and stopping works at the dockyards, and all the offices are preparing for an *economical* session. The demand for retrenchment is the popular cry: people feel themselves pinched by the pressure of the times, and, as usual, attribute it to a wrong cause, viz. the weight of taxation. They therefore think that, if taxation were diminished, they would be relieved. It is as if anybody thought that the cold of a Canadian winter would be diminished if the days were lengthened without the sun's power being increased. Finance, however, both as to estimates and as to ways and means, will be the great question of next session. Ireland, of course, will occupy a large space. Rebellion is crushed, certainly for the present, and, I hope, permanently. This year *ought* to be the 1745 of Ireland. The writ of error* is now under argument before the Irish Queen's Bench. I hardly expect that so important a conviction will be set aside on technical grounds. There are, however, grave doubts whether the refusal to give the panel and list of witnesses was right. The great practical subject in Ireland now is the Poor Law. This is the third (or rather fourth) year of scarcity; the potato began to fail in 1845; and I suspect that this winter will, for the landlords, be the true Irish crisis. Renewed demands come upon exhausted means; the patience and finances of England are dried up, and its assistance will be furnished with reluctance and parsimony. The Poor Law is now better organised than ever; the collection proceeds regularly; and it is finding out all the weak places. Connaught is fairly insolvent, but in Munster many of the unions are in a struggling state; and it is clear that an entire change, partly in the *personnel* and partly in the habits of the proprietors, is

* The writ of error respecting the Irish trials for high treason was disallowed by the Irish Court of Queen's Bench. The case was afterwards carried into the House of Lords, by whom the judgment of the Court below was confirmed. See *Annual Register* for 1849, p. 351.

impending. All the social elements of Ireland are now in an unsettled state; they are all moving about as in a great seething caldron of impurities. The conviction that Ireland never can be settled until the priests receive an endowment is gaining ground, and, strange to say, notwithstanding Exeter Hall and the Dissenters, I am inclined to think that, as far as *England* is concerned, the question might be pushed through. The great difficulty is the hostility of the Irish priesthood themselves. No doubt their opposition would, in the great majority, be insincere; but they are so committed, so wrong-headed, and *so afraid of offending their flocks without making sure of their endowment*, that they will declare against it as a body, and thus put an almost irresistible argument in the mouths of the English Anti-Catholics. The Irish Protestants are beginning to look upon Catholic endowment in the light of an insurance for their estates, and many people see that we should soon save the amount in the army and police, to say nothing of prestige abroad. It is curious to observe what a Nemesis oppressed nations have it in their power to inflict. The Irish not only torment us at home, but carry a hatred of England wherever they settle, and thus fill America with enemies of our Government. So the Poles are scattered over Europe, and furnish revolutionists to every continental State. I understand that they have been most active both at Vienna and Berlin; and they are in league with the Rouges in every metropolis in Europe. If the Government had seen any reasonable prospect of carrying the question of Catholic endowment this session, they were, I believe, quite prepared to make any sacrifice of power or party connection for the purpose. But to propose it without a fair chance of success, would be to gain no present advantage, and to increase the difficulties of a settlement hereafter. The English Poor Law has ceased to occupy attention as a national question. The management of workhouses now takes its place with the management of prisons, &c., as a question of local interest and detail. A good deal is said about vagrancy, and the number of Irish vagrants is much increased. They are beginning to refuse relief at the workhouses; but the trade of vagrancy is really kept up by the *public*, not by the *vagrant wards*. There is to be a general measure on turnpike trusts and highways introduced by the Home Office next session; and I am preparing with Coulson a Bill on the subject of valuations for local taxes. There is to be a committee on the Irish Poor Law, and about thirty or forty new unions are to be formed in Ireland. Large alterations are likewise to be made in the electoral districts. By the way, Lord Courtenay has accepted the Chiltern Hundreds, and has been appointed a Poor Law Inspector. * * * The new Board of Health have been issuing very voluminous decrees and instructions about cholera. Hitherto, however, the cholera has made but little progress. only a few cases on the banks of the Thames, and those have now nearly ceased. Some of the doctors, I hear, doubt whether it has been the Asiatic cholera; but I suspect that it has been the real disease, though to a very limited extent, and not in a very severe form. There has been a great deal of discussion in the newspapers of the Conservative side as to the possibility of re-union since George Bentinck's death. The discussion, however, has only served to widen the breach. There is a genuine repugnance and difference of *Grund-ansichten* between the Peelites and Protectionists. If they shook hands over the corn-law quarrel, they would part company upon some new question within a month. A junction between the Peelites (or some of them) and the Whigs is possible: a junction between the Peelites and Protectionists, I look upon as impossible. Lord John Russell has not shaken off the weakness of his trachea which he had during last session; this is a dangerous defect for a person who has to make so much use of his voice.

* * * *

Windischgrätz is a man of decision, and he has settled the Vienna democrats for the present. But great concessions to the popular party will, I suppose, be inevitable, and how anything like a popular form of government is to be reconciled with the disjointed state of the Austrian Empire is more than I am able to comprehend The Slavonic race hang upon its rear, as you say, in great force; and there is no making Lombardy and Venice bind up with the Tedeschi. The Frankfort Parliament still go on with their debates, and call themselves the central *power*. What their power may be, I have never discovered. If they were the only popular Assembly in Germany it would be different. At Berlin the King has at last plucked up a little courage; he has allowed the army to disarm the burgher guard, and silence the Assembly. The Democratic party have had the sense to understand that for the present they are beaten, and have not attempted to fight. But Prussia must end in having a very popular form of government. In France, Louis Napoleon is considered nearly certain of his election as President. Thiers supports him—and I am told that the *paysans* will vote for him to a man. Many of them believe that he is the Emperor himself, so vague are their notions of historical events. I hear that the army is the only real *puissance* in France, the only organisation and compact body; and that they are not impatient, but quite resolved to get the supreme power into their hands. Bugeaud is their man. They wish for fighting, but would prefer a *civil* to a *foreign* war. Manet altâ mente repostum, I suppose, the affront they received in February, when Louis-Philippe was bowled over so unceremoniously.

There has been a check to our arms in Moultan, on the north-west frontier. Hardinge's settlement with the Sikhs appears to be unsound, and I suppose it will end in the old story of annexation. Those half-occupations of a country never answer. The more I observe of Indian affairs, the more I am convinced that there is no real resting-place between entire government and perfect non-interference, as far as we are concerned. We are so powerful, and stand on a level so much higher than the natives, that remonstrances, representations, advice from our agents, though intended bonâ fide, have to the public opinion the effect of commands. Cum rex implorat, precibus præcepta colorat. That monkish verse ought to be written at the top of all instructions to our Residents at the semi-dependent courts.

I have read lately Hampden's 'Bampton Lectures,' which, in point of ability and knowledge of the subject, seems to me the first theological work which has been produced for a long time in this country. Parts of it are obscure in point of conception. His metaphysics and logic are not in fact very profound; but his accounts of the origin of some of the doctrines—particularly the Trinitarian and Eucharistic—are admirable. It is a book quite worth reading. But as to the question of orthodoxy, I confess I cannot defend him. He has been unskilfully and dishonestly attacked, and has been charged with opinions which are not in his book. He cannot be convicted of heresy on any one doctrine —it cannot be proved, for example, that he is a Socinian. But his argument goes distinctly and fully to the rejection of every system of dogmatic theology—above all, to the rejection of every creed involving the use of scholastic phraseology, such as the Nicene and Athanasian creeds. As these creeds are recognised in our articles as well as liturgy, I do not see how his orthodoxy can be maintained unless he abandons a part of his book.

Macaulay's 'History' is announced; two volumes are ready, which bring the history down to the arrival of William. He reckons on thirteen volumes. Grote also announces two more volumes, which are to go as far as the Athenian siege of Syracuse. I hear that literature is suspended for the present in Germany. They were thinking of breaking up the University of Bonn. Colonel Mure (who wrote some travels in Greece) is about to publish a history of Greek literature. The early part is a very full discussion of the Homeric question.

I wrote to Beaumont about a copy of the French report on the fight of June; but got no answer from him. I will send you a box of books at the end of the year. When you write next, pray tell me how far I am to go as to price. Would 10*l*. be too much? I propose to send you Lord Hervey's 'Memoirs' as one book. Lord Talbot, I am sorry to say, is at the point of death, and Lord Melbourne is also dying. Gilbert and Jane are gone to Cheam. The Clarendons have been over in England for about a month. Both are looking very well. He is to have the Garter, vacant by Lord

Carlisle's death. The approbation of his administration in Ireland is universal.

Theresa and I desire our best remembrances to Lady Head.

Ever yours sincerely,

G. C. Lewis.

Grove Mill: Jan. 8, 1849.

My dear Head,—It is a long way to wish you and Lady Head a happy New Year across the Atlantic; but letters now travel so fast, that to correspond with Fredericton is like writing to Rome or Vienna a few years ago. I have received your last letter, for which I am much obliged, and will soon make up your parcel of books and attend to your other commissions. I hope that you will not find the severity of the winter a serious inconvenience. Probably furs, stoves, and thick walls keep out the enemy cold effectually. I am, however, anxious to know how you find it on experience. I should think that after a time the snow must grow very *tiresome*, and you must long to get rid of that incessant white covering to all outward objects.

The newspapers will have told you much better than I can all the public events which have occurred in the last two months. The machine has been working very fast for some time, but at last the engineers seem to have succeeded in stopping its pace, and most of the wheels are now either at rest or turning slowly.

The French, not caring for the Republic represented by Cavaignac, and dazzled by the prestige of the name Napoleon, elected Louis Napoleon as their President.

* * * *

The decisiveness of his majority has had a tranquillising effect, and for the present France is quiet.

They are tired of disturbances, and wish for rest and peace. In Austria, Windischgrätz holds the sword with a strong hand, and everything is just now in a state of compression; but I cannot think that things will relapse quietly into the old despotic régime. Prussia has obtained a democratic constitution, retaining the forms of royalty. This, with some modifications, will probably stick; but I doubt whether she will be able to lay hold of Saxony, Wirtemberg, and Bavaria. Italy is still at sea, but the Democratic party have made fools of themselves, and the Pope will, no doubt, return to Rome. He is too great a card for a small Italian State to throw away. With its historical recollections, it would be madness for Rome to lose its preeminence as head of the Catholic world.

In England there have been two more deaths in public life—poor Charles Buller and Lord Auckland. Charles Buller died of the consequences of an operation, which brought on erysipelas, and the erysipelas was followed by typhus. He will be a great loss in his office. Baines, his successor, is at present only a lawyer. We shall see how he deals with the economical parts of the subject. He is, however, a shrewd, able man. Lord Auckland was very popular in the Navy, and his loss will be felt in his office. His successor is not yet appointed. Lord Normanby, Lord Minto, Francis Baring, Lord Hatherton, and even Graham or Sidney Herbert are talked of for it. I have no idea who is likely to be appointed. The session begins on February 1. Finance will be the main subject; but the revenue has begun to improve and trade is mending. We have, I think, past the worst. It is a remarkable fact that after all the political convulsions of last year, the English Funds were four per cent. higher in January 1849 than in January 1848. The Irish Poor Law will also give rise to much discussion; but as there is to be a Committee, I trust it will be taken out of the House, or at least a good deal of it. The English Poor Law expenditure for the year ending Lady Day 1848 shows an increase of nearly 900,000*l.* over the preceding year.

Everybody is in raptures with Macaulay's 'History.' He gets 500*l.* for six years for his two volumes, and divides the profits after 6,000 copies. This number is *already* sold. It has had more success than any book since Lord Byron's poems and Walter Scott's novels.

Theresa desires her best remembrance to you and Lady Head.

Ever yours sincerely,

G. C. LEWIS.

Knightsbridge: Jan. 23, 1849.

My dear Grote,—It never occurred to me as a possibility that you would re-write your two first volumes—a völlig umgearbeitete Ausgabe seems to me quite out of the question. I never thought that you would do more than modify certain parts and passages which might appear to you susceptible of improvement, when you have the advantage of reading the work in the compact form of print and referring backwards and forwards. I believe that I wrote out everything which appeared to me of any use or importance in the notes which I gave you; but when you come to town, I will send you my two first volumes, which contain whatever notes I have made. When you come, I hope that we may not fail of meeting, as I should be very glad to have a good conversation with you. I have gone once through your fifth and sixth volumes, the first more attentively than the second, as I read it when I was in the country and had more time. On the whole, I am glad that I have reserved my review, as the battle of Marathon made an inconvenient period to stop at, and I can now carry on the history to the consequences of the Persian war, viz. the origin and growth of the Athenian ἀρχή. The Peloponnesian war begins a new phase of history. Your new volumes quite come up to the expectations raised by the preceding ones, which is, I think, as high praise as need be given. Your account of the position of Athens at the end of the Persian war, of her voluntary leadership passing into a compulsory empire, and of the difference between the democratic government at home and the imperial government abroad, is far clearer, fuller, and more instructive than anything to be found in any previous historian of the same epoch, Boeckh and Thirlwall not excepted. As for Mitford and writers of that stamp, it is perfectly inconceivable how they have confounded the national and imperial government of Athens. It is as if anybody were to argue that because the English government in Canada or Jamaica or the Mauritius was bad, therefore it is bad in England. How any tolerably attentive reader of Thucydides—who read him in the original, which I presume Mitford did—could fail to perceive this strongly marked difference, I confess I am unable to comprehend. If I am not mistaken, Mitford quotes the words of Thucydides—τυραννίδα ἔχετε τὴν ἀρχήν; i.e. your relation to your subject allies is that of a τύραννος, or despot to *his* subjects—as a proof that, according to the avowal of the Athenians themselves, democracy is a tyrannical government. Is it possible for the force of blunder to go further? There is a note in p. 480 of your fifth volume, in which you appear to me to have overlooked the fact that the article is wanting, and have construed the sentence as if it were present. Τὰ δὲ δικαστήρια μισθοφόρα κατέστησε Περικλῆς necessarily means, 'Pericles gave pay to the courts.' If the meaning were, 'He established the paid courts,' it would be τὰ μισθοφόρα. I do not, however, think that the sentence implies either that Pericles established the courts, or found them existing. 'As to the courts, κατέστησε μισθοφόρα, he gave the members a daily pay for attendance.' Whether he established them or not, non constat. I need scarcely remind you of the importance which Aristotle attaches to the payment of public officers, and how often he insists upon it as a characteristic of democracy.

It is always pleasant to find ideas shared by one's friends and those whose opinions one respects. I read Lord Hervey's* most admirable work some months ago; and if I had written to you about it, I should have used almost the same words as you have employed. The extreme unfairness of Pope's character, and its universal reception, both struck me forcibly, as well as the parallel with Aristophanes. There is, I think, a distinction to be made between the exaggerations of party writers and the pictures of professed satirists. The latter are so distorted and caricatured, and are painted with so deliberate an intention of rendering the object hideous, that they often give an impression utterly false. Witness, for example, what you refer to—the portrait of

* *Memoirs of the Reign of George II.*, by John Lord Hervey. 2 vols. Murray, 1848. Mr. Grote had written to Sir George Lewis, 'I have recently read Lord Hervey's *Memoirs*, on the recommendation of a friend. If you have not read them, I recommend them to your notice; for they really afford the best *exposé* of the real interior of a court which I have ever happened to light upon—resting too upon evidence which seems above all suspicion.'

Socrates in 'The Clouds.' Many of Juvenal's and Swift's descriptions fall under the same category. In fact, for purposes of *truth*, I distrust the representation of every satirist by profession. Party writers sometimes are, indeed, as bad as satirists (e.g. Junius); but in general they do not write with a deliberate and formed intention of perverting fact. They are under the influence of strong prejudice; they see facts through a coloured medium; but in general their writings, with due allowances and deductions, afford materials on which true history may be founded. E.g. Xenophon was a strong partisan—but nobody can deny that he has left us much valuable history; and so with most modern contemporary historians and writers of memoirs. To return to Lord Hervey. His work has not, I think, been sufficiently appreciated; it contains passages worthy of Tacitus, and altogether exhibits the workings of a masculine understanding. His picture of the English Court in the time of George II. is a curious pendant to the picture of the Prussian Court about the same time in the 'Memoirs of Madame de Bareith.'* There are also some curious memoirs of the Princess of Zell,† the wife of George I.; but whether they are genuine or not, I have never been able to ascertain. I have been told that the Duke of Cambridge (who ought to know something on the subject) treated them as genuine.

The Tooting cholera would, as you say, have been glorious game for the 'Times.' The fact is, that the Commissioners did all they could to get rid of these contractors' establishments, but were thwarted by the

* *Mémoires de Frédérique-Sophie-Wilhelmine de Prusse, Margrave de Bareith, Sœur de Frédéric le Grand.* 2 vols. Colburn, 1812.

† *Memoirs of Sophia Dorothea.* 2 vols. Colburn, 1845.

large London parishes. This, however, would have availed little against the rhetoric of the 'Times.'

Ever yours sincerely,

G. C. Lewis.

Kent House: April 5, 1849.

My dear Head,—It is, I am sorry to say, a long time since I wrote to you, and I have received two letters, which I have not acknowledged, but which I read with much interest, especially as I was very glad to hear of the arrival of your young American and of Lady Head's recovery. If she is not already christened, I propose the name of *Columbine*, as suited to the land of her birth.

Since the beginning of the session, what with Office, and attendance at the House, and the Irish Committee, and correcting the proofs of my book, as well as finishing the manuscript, I have really had no time for writing you a proper letter, such a one as was fit to make a long voyage. I made, however, the selection of books which you desired and despatched them, and will add at the end of this letter the amount of their cost, which I paid. Gilbert was unable to arrange about the apple grafts, and therefore I sent the box without them.

My book is now about to be published, and whenever there is another opportunity of sending to you, I will not fail to forward a copy. Your speech to the Legislature was well suited to its purpose, and your government seems quite successful. I heard Hawes cite you one night as a specimen of one of Lord Grey's appointments: and the relations of New Brunswick with the mother country are now quite satisfactory. I agree with you that the responsible government, though it may be defective in theory, may nevertheless be worked in practice, if the parties concerned are reasonable. But it cannot be worked, unless people in this country see that, pro tanto, it is a concession of virtual independence to the colony. If cases like those under discussion now in Nova Scotia and Canada are not to be tolerated by the Colonial Office, responsible government is impossible; and yet there is an indisposition in many people here to acquiesce in the proceedings to which I allude. Altogether, our colonial relations are in a very unsatisfactory state just at present. There is a constant series of attacks on the Colonial Office, which can end in no good result, inasmuch as they are founded on no intelligible or consistent view, and, in fact, imply that there is to be no interference from this country. Wakefield has recently published a book on 'Colonisation.' It is merely a re-hash of his old opinions, seasoned with some new abuse of the Colonial Office and Lord Grey.

The navigation laws repeal will pass the House of Commons, but whether the Lords will agree to it is uncertain. There is an idea that, if they throw it out, Lord John will resign and the Protectionists come in. The chief subject, however, since the opening of the session has been the eternal Ireland. In one form or another, Ireland has occupied about three out of every four nights. The English has now become practically an Irish House of Commons—Græcia capta ferum victorem cepit; but instead of outshining us with her arts and sciences, Ireland overlays us with her barbarism. The main question has been, how to relieve the distressed unions in the west. The Government began by proposing a small grant. This was reluctantly given, much opposed by the Protectionists and many Radicals, and Graham declared that he would not consent to another vote. It then became necessary to find some exclusively Irish fund, and the Government accordingly proposed a rate in aid of sixpence in the pound from all the unions in Ireland. This proposal has created violent complaints in Ireland. Ulster, in particular, objects to being taxed for Connaught, and nearly all the Irish members speak and vote against this new tax.

* * * *

I have been attending the Irish Poor Law Committee three days in the week. There are twenty-six members, chiefly Irish, and Somerville and I represent the Government. Graham has attended a good deal and has been friendly, but very rambling in his examinations. The evidence has been very incoherent and diffuse. Power and Twisleton have each had four entire days. The subject most interesting to the Irish members is the *area of taxation*, which the large landowners wish to diminish and to make conterminous with estates as far as possible. Every man wishes to have a *close parish*. The evidence is favourable to the workhouse in its strictest form; and the evils of a tax system of out-door relief have been so fully developed in Ireland that the outcry against the English Poor Law has died away. The subject is now nearly forgotten, and its ordinary administration jogs on like that of any other part of the public affairs.

* * * *

Affairs in Italy seem to have settled themselves for the present. Austria retains Lombardy, but grants a paper constitution to her entire empire. How this can work, I confess I am unable to understand. Carlo Alberto has saved his dynasty by abdicating. The Pope is still in exile, and there is no immediate question of his return. The Archduke John renounced his absurd office of the Head of the Empire; and it has been offered to the King of Prussia, who declines it. The Frankfort Parliament must surely dissolve before long. Russia is walking into Transylvania, but in other respects is quiet. In France, things are shaking down. Louis Napoleon appears to have acted with tolerable prudence, and there is no disposition to risk a war, with the certainty of expense and the uncertainty of success.

I have introduced as a Home Office measure a bill altering the entire management of the roads, abolishing turnpike trusts, and placing all roads under the control of a county board of magistrates and the Board of Guardians. It is opposed by the Tory country gentlemen, because they are sulky about the price of corn, and by the clerks of 1100 trusts, so that I am not very sanguine of its success, but it has a good deal of support. Your consolidation of the Criminal Law is very useful, and ought to pass. Do you assume the power of repeating English statutes in force *before* the foundation of the colony?

* * * *

Everybody in this house is well. My best regards to Lady Head.

Ever yours sincerely,

G. C. Lewis.

Kent House: June 10, 1849.

My dear Head,—I have received with much pleasure two letters from you, which I had intended to acknowledge earlier, but you doubtless remember that as the session advances the work by no means diminishes; and I have been so busy and so tired, that I have not had time and courage sufficient to write you a *justum volumen*, as the commentators say. I have had to attend the Irish Poor Law Committee—a committee on the removal of Smithfield Market; and, latterly, a committee on Local Turnpike Bills. These have for some time taken up every day from twelve to four, so that you may conceive my spare time has not been abundant. The General Roads Bill was defeated by the opposition of the clerks to trusts, who are nearly all attorneys, and their influence with members, particularly as there was at Easter some expectation of a Protectionist dissolution, was irresistible. We were forced to withdraw it, and the question must now be settled in some other way. I have therefore been attending a committee on the Renewal of certain Local Acts, in order to make a beginning of reform, and to find out exactly how the present system works. I must say that a more splendid exhibition of the advantages of uncontrolled local discretion can scarcely be conceived. It has convinced me still more strongly of the policy of the Poor Law Amendment, and has made me feel practically what the management of the Boards of Guardians would have been if they had been left to their own devices. I am meditating some plan of overhauling the turnpike trusts, and of establishing some control over them by a standing committee of quarter sessions, without altering the system entirely, or incorporating them with the highways.

The Government has now weathered the danger of the navigation laws, and will reach the end of the session. It is expected that the prorogation will be before the end of July this year, for a wonder. The prudence of the Lords got the better of their desire to restore the corn laws, and they abstained from turning out the Government, which they could easily have done if they had wished it, for Ministers would certainly have resigned if the Navigation Bill had not been carried. There was a great reluctance to place the government of the country in the hands of Stanley and Disraeli. Nevertheless, the opportunity was a tempting one, for the farmers in a mass believe that the present depression of agriculture is produced by free trade, and they would turn out every member who was opposed to a fixed duty on corn. The most acceptable candidate now to many agricultural constituencies, e.g. to the city of Hereford and in some degree to the county, would be a Protectionist Radical—a friend of economy, enlargement of the suffrage, and protection to native industry. This, I take it, would also make a good candidate for the United States. There is no doubt that a dissolution at the present time would give a great gain to the Protectionists, though perhaps not a majority. The triumph of the Protection party would, however, be short-lived: the convulsion would be terrible. There would be a great struggle between the town and country populations, and the former would attempt to gain the superiority by altering the balance of the representation — by diminishing the number of members for counties and small boroughs and increasing the number for large towns. In this they would ultimately succeed, and when the change was once made, good-bye for ever to the power of the agricultural party. From this extremity we have been saved for the present by the prudence of the Lords. If the harvest should prove abundant, prices will, it is true, be low; but the farmers will have a good deal to sell, and if the consumption is brisk, I do not think they will be so ill off as at present. There will probably be in some cases a re-adjustment of rents, and in others a change of tenants; and in this manner the country will gradually adapt itself to the altered law.

Ireland is in a terrible state. The suffering and misery are perfectly awful; but there has been so much lying and so much exaggeration, that people in England do not know what to believe, and the distress passes now comparatively unheeded, though as great, if not greater, than at any previous time. The Encumbered Estates Bill of this session is a really drastic measure, and must, when rents begin again to be paid, cause many of the deeply mortgaged properties in the west to change hands. Creditors, however, have no interest in forcing a sale at a season of depression: they are a sort of partners in the concern, who do not wish the property to be forced into the market at a moment of depreciation. Therefore, unless the potato returns this year in full vigour, I do not expect many sales to be made for some time to come. By the bye, when you write next, would you have the kindness to let me know how far the potato disease has ceased in your province and in North America generally, so far as your information extends. I cannot believe that the disease is likely to be a permanent one, which has now become a favourite theory with many people.

I thought I had mentioned to you some time ago that I was writing on the subject of 'Authority.'* I feel certain that I alluded to it in a letter written about September or October last, which I fear you may not have received. My book has been favourably reviewed in the 'Examiner,' the 'Athenaeum,' and some other newspapers, and nearly 200 copies have been sold,

* *Essay on the Influence of Authority in Matters of Opinion.* Published by Parker, 1849.

which, as the subject is not a very attractive one, and the mode of treatment is not intended to be popular, is quite as much as I could hope for. I had considerable difficulty in dealing with the question of Church authority; and I am glad to find that Milman approves of my chapter, who is an excellent judge in the matter.

I am meditating now a work on the 'Methods of Political Reasoning.' It will take me several years, if I am ever able to complete it. The work which I have in my mind, if I could execute it properly, is an organon for the use of the political enquirer—a manual of rules for the guidance of the historian or politician in the method of conducting his investigations. A work of this kind would dispose of nearly the whole body of political speculators, from Plato downwards, without refuting their conclusions separately, by showing that their *methods* were unsound, and could lead to nothing but error, except, indeed, by accident.*

I have had so little time to read that volume of modern history which the 'Times' puts forth daily, that I dare say you are now more *au fait* of what is going on upon the continent than I am. The French expedition to Rome was an unprincipled blunder. It was intended to be an electioneering move, but it failed of its purpose, and has increased the confusion of Europe. Louis Napoleon's address is an imitation of the American President's Message. It is somewhat feeble and puerile in its style, but is more veracious and honest than such documents usually are in France. It is curious that they talk of extending their Poor Law.

* Sir George Lewis's *Treatise on the Methods of Reasoning in Politics* was published by Parker in 1852.

Germany is all in pieces. There has been a revolution and fighting in Baden, and movements along the Rhine, and the Frankfort Assembly is at last disbanded. Prussia is now attempting again to take the lead, but all is uncertain and fluctuating. The intervention of Russia in Hungary is the great event in central Europe, but hitherto it has led to little result. Italy is awaiting the event of the French interference at Rome. I confess that I have great doubts whether the Pope will ever recover his temporal power. This seems to me one of the changes which is likely to be permanent. The Pope cannot become a constitutional sovereign, negotiating with a parliament, and he can hardly hope to recover his despotic powers, together with an ecclesiastical set of Ministers. The interests now are exclusively political and socialist: the Church, as such, goes for nothing in the revolutionary movements of the continent. There is nothing original or native in any of the continental reforms. Everything is a mere copy of American institutions, as formerly everything used to be a copy of English institutions. In politics they seem to be nothing but a set of grown-up children. I have in vain endeavoured to extract your drawings from Murray. I have kept no copy of what I paid for your books. My best regards to Lady Head.

Ever yours sincerely,

G. C. L.

Garnstone, Herefordshire: Sept. 4, 1849.

My dear Head,—I had intended writing to you and thanking you for your last letter as soon as the session was over, but I have put it off from day to day until now, partly in consequence of a series of duty *gaieties* which I have been going through for my constituents.

I have already attended Leominster and Hereford races, two days of each, and have been to a bow meeting, and have a music meeting in prospect. I have likewise been at Whitfield and Eywood,* as well as at Harpton, and am just returned from Perrystone, where I have greatly enjoyed the society of William Clifford, who a little reminds me of Montaigne transferred to the nineteenth century. Yorke and Mrs. Yorke and Mrs. Hall were there. I never was at Perrystone before, and found it a more beautiful place than I expected. Nothing in its way can be finer than the wooded bank down to the river.

The farmers are in better humour, on account of the abundant produce of the soil and the prospect of a good harvest; all sorts of crops are prosperous, except hops; and the potato blight, though it has shown itself in a very decided form, is not extensive in this part of the country. There is, however, still a great hankering after a revival of the Corn Law, in some shape or other, among the farmers. All classes have felt the uneasiness arising from straitened means. The agriculturists find a remedy in a protection duty on corn; the town populations look to retrenchment and consequent reduction of taxation. Both are equally mistaken in the cause of their distress, and consequently in their remedy. Just now, however, the manufacturers are fully employed, and I heard only to-day that the demand from Leeds and Bradford is now clearing this county of its wool at high and increasing prices. The excitement of the railway speculations has done much harm; and having been driven up by unsound competition far above their proper height, they have now been

* Respectively the residences of the Rev. Archer Clive and Lady Langdale.

as unfairly depressed by the exposure of Hudson's proceedings, which has made people think that *no* railway management is to be trusted. It was very unlucky for Herefordshire that it did not get a railway before the tide turned. It will be several years before railway speculation will revive, and then it will assume a much more sober form.

The Government was, I think, on the whole, stronger at the end than at the beginning of the session. They did tolerably well what was required of them, and the other parties rather lost than gained ground. The Protectionists were unable to show that they had any definite policy, or any confidence in their leaders. Disraeli, though a hard hitter in attack, failed as an exponent of a measure or a system of policy. The Peelites were not only small in numbers, but disunited among themselves. Peel and Graham stood on several occasions nearly alone—Gladstone, Lincoln, and the minor Peelites going off in other directions. Peel appears to me clearly to have abandoned definitively all idea of being a party leader or holding office. He is anxious, however, to maintain his position in the House of Commons, and to be considered as the chief speaker in it when he thinks fit to exert himself. Hume is still very stout, but he had a bad illness this year, and is beginning to show symptoms of failure. Cobden is trying to find some popular cry to take the place of free trade, and has made the most of retrenchment and peace. But he has lost credit for good sense: his notions about arbitration are so erroneous and superficial that many persons see through them; and although the Radical party has a good *avenir*, still it is not making much way in opinion at the present moment. The 'Chronicle' has been for some time a

Peelite paper, and is very ably written. Smyth and Hayward are two of the writers. I do not know whether any copy of it reaches Fredericton, but its articles are well worth reading, and its foreign correspondence is remarkably good, particularly that from Germany.

The Queen's visit to Ireland is a political event of some importance.

Lord John and the Cabinet were afraid, but Clarendon urged it strongly, and they gave way.

Everything turned out better than the most sanguine expectation could have anticipated. The people were enthusiastic, there was no dissentient minority, and the Queen and Prince were most gracious in manner and expression, and were really pleased. There had been a small number of persons who wished to mark their sympathy with Smith O'Brien and the rebels of 1848; but they were overborne by the general feeling, and moreover there was an unwillingness in the citizens of Dublin to permit anything which might have the effect of preventing future visits so advantageous to trade. * * * I am rather sanguine as to this visit giving an impulse to the Irish mind in the right direction, and in assisting the disposition which now exists towards an acquiescence in the union with England, and to a final abandonment of the Repeal movement. The first number of the new 'Nation,' which has just appeared, confirms the idea that the Irish agitators will now apply their exertions to more practical objects, and that they will cease to pursue the phantom which impoverished the whole nation for the sake of filling the purse of one man. The Encumbered Estates Commission of last session is an important measure, but it will not operate suddenly. Some years must elapse before its working can be felt. In a few words, it seems to me to be this: a contrivance for enabling tenants for life to sell a portion of the settled property for the payment of debts, without the intervention of the Court of Chancery.* The land question has now been pretty well exhausted in Ireland, both by enquiries and legislation. A great deal about the management of estates by the courts which was not known before came out during the last two sessions; but it was very technical, and was understood and attended to only by a few. The measures of last session will require patching, and assisting where they are deficient, but the neck of the question has been broken. The Irish Poor Law cannot be much mended; the amending bill of last session contained nothing very material. The chief alteration going on is administrative, viz. a reduction in the size of the large unions and electoral divisions, but this is still in fieri. The only great Irish question now remaining unsettled is the Church question. You know my opinions on this subject, and I believe we are quite agreed about it; and what I thought I still think, but what the practical solution may be I am quite unable to predict. There seems now a greater disposition among the Catholics to say nothing on the subject; but if ever any large portion of the land of Ireland gets into the hands of Catholics, good-bye to the Established Church.

The continental wars are now appeased, and nothing remains to be settled but the results of the French intervention in Rome. The Pope will probably be restored, but his tenure will be a frail one; and, if he

* It is obvious from this statement that Sir George Lewis would not have entertained favourably any approach to fixity of tenure in Ireland, or the weakening the power of the landlord over his tenants.

does not give satisfaction, the next shake in Italy will be sure to see him again in exile. A good many travellers have gone abroad this summer, but nothing like the former number. Twisleton sailed on August 25 for New York, and intends to see the United States; but I suppose he will hardly visit our provinces. I hope your expedition into the woods will have been as interesting as that of last year. My best regards to Lady Head.

Ever yours sincerely,
G. C. LEWIS.

Grove Mill, Watford: Sept. 20, 1849.

My dear Mrs. Grote,—Your letter has followed me from Herefordshire, where I have been lately going through a long course of gaieties, to Grove Mill, to which we returned at the end of last week. I kiss your rod in the most submissive manner, and plead guilty to considerable delay about Grote's 'History'—though I cannot admit that it is *two* years. I do not remember undertaking to review the third and fourth volumes till last year, that is, 1848. I intended to write the review during the session, and made some progress after Easter, but the pressure of business at the end of the session (which, as Grote knows, is very heavy upon official members) prevented me from finishing it. I have brought the six volumes with me to this place, and I have them now all before me. I shall lose no time in finishing my article, and I have every reason to believe that it will be ready before the end of October. I shall send it immediately to Empson, and hope that he will insert it in the next number; but that, of course, will depend on him.

We were much disappointed at losing your visit, but

I hope that we shall contrive to meet before long. I am due in London on October 1, take my turn of attendance at the Office, and expect to remain there during that and the following month. Is there no chance of your leaving the Beeches,* and coming to that unromantic street, Savile Row, where there are no twisted roots, during that time? I have a great deal of frozen-up conversation to inflict on you and Grote.

Believe me ever yours sincerely,

G. C. LEWIS.

Home Office: Nov. 27, 1849.

My dear Head,—I think I wrote you word that I had been in Herefordshire in September, and had made a circuit of divers visits. Since October 1, I have been in London and in constant attendance at the Office; therefore, as you may conceive, I have no adventures to relate which can compare with your excursion up the country, into the woods, and across lakes. During the chief part of the time Sir George Grey and Waddington have been absent; but the country was as quiet as a duck-pond, and the business was quite of a routine nature.

There is now an assembling of official persons; the first winter Cabinet was held to-day. As to internal affairs, the chief subject is the low prices of corn and cattle, and the despondency of the agriculturists, who derive no comfort from anybody who does not tell them that they are finally and irredeemably ruined. Rents are ill paid in some places, and there is great consternation among landlords. The feeling in favour of protection is strong and nearly universal in all the agricultural parts of the community. On the other hand, they are

* Mrs. Grote's residence, near Burnham.

united in nothing except a wish to have their protection restored. They do not like Disraeli, who is their best man, or at least their best speaker in the House of Commons. They do not believe him to be sincere, nor do they confide in his judgment. There is also great difficulty in an Opposition imposing a *new tax* while the revenue exceeds the expenditure. For this is what protection means, when it comes to be translated into an actual motion.

The colonial questions are in a ticklish state. There is much dissatisfaction with the recent management of the Colonial Office, and the state of the Cape at this moment is highly unsatisfactory. Nothing is more likely than a junction of Protectionists and Radicals upon some colonial question; and the Government can at any moment be put in a minority, if two or three parties combine against it. But as no one party is strong enough to form a government, they are not likely to take a step which would put them in the position of having the offer and declining. On the whole, I see no great change in the position of the Government. Though weak in itself, it is relatively strong, and though there is a prevailing feeling in favour of protection throughout the agricultural constituencies, the Protectionists are not in a position to take advantage of it.

The Chancellor* is better, and it is expected that he will go on, for the present at least. Denman has had a second paralytic stroke; he has not sat this term, and it is not expected that he will ever sit again. Lord Campbell is talked of as his successor.

Everything foreign is in a fluctuating, unsettled state, but things are shaking down by degrees. The French

* Lord Cottenham.

are becoming more absurd every day, and are decidedly drifting to leeward in the esteem of Europe. The Germans would be the first continental power, if they could but unite. This, however, is hopeless. Prussia and Austria must remain separate, even if the minor States are swallowed up.

I have written lately an article* on Grote's 'History,' which will, I hope, appear in the next number of the 'Edinburgh Review.' I have also gone on with my political 'Arbeit,' and have been writing on the 'Nature and Treatment of History.' This has caused me to read several interesting discussions—among others, some essays on the speeches in the ancient histories, and in some modern ones, particularly the Italian. I have found a calculation that the speeches in Thucydides are more in bulk than a *fourth* of the work. Does this appear to you possible? If I am not mistaken, one of the speeches in Thucydides answers a speech, argument by argument, delivered elsewhere—that is, for instance, a speech in the Assembly at Athens answers a speech at some Peloponnesian meeting of delegates of allies. Do you remember which speech it is? I have a distinct recollection of observing at Oxford that such was the case in one instance.

My father is, I think, in excellent health; he has lately had his picture painted by Watts. Grant has lately finished my picture, and has greatly improved it, both as a portrait and a painting.

* * * *

Mrs. Edward Villiers is in town with her children. Earnest is at school. The twins are prodigiously fine children—much taller separately than any single contemporary, which seems unfair. I do not believe that

* *Edinburgh Review*, vol. xci. p. 118.

the question of personal identity has ever clearly been made out between them.

Best regards to Lady Head.

Ever yours,

G. C. L.

Home Office: Nov. 29, 1849.

My dear Head,—I have just received your letter of the 13th instant; and as I wrote to you a few days ago, I will only answer your question about Milman. He has been gazetted Dean of St. Paul's, and seems pleased at his appointment. The drawback is the distance of his house from the society of which he is fond, and on which the state of his eyesight makes him quite dependent in the evening.

The Welshmen clamoured for a Welsh bishop, and Lord John satisfied them very dexterously by giving them an Englishman, formerly head of Lampeter, who understands Welsh.

Empson has had a paralytic stroke and renewed bleedings from the nose; he is, however, better at present. Lord Jeffrey assists him with the 'Edinburgh Review.'

Fox Maule has just been added to the Cabinet, an event of no great importance to the public. He has, however, a good deal of weight in the House of Commons, and he is a great man in Scotland. Dalhousie's health is said to be failing, and there is even an idea that he will not remain much longer in India. The great weakness of the Government now is its colonial policy, or rather the state of several of the colonies. The adjustment of the agricultural interest is also an operation which will not be made silently. Even sober-minded persons think that many landlords and a majority of the farmers will be ruined in the process. I am not so desponding myself; but I confess that I look forward to a serious struggle between the agricultural and the other interests before an equilibrium is established.

I have just been included in a commission issued to try to devise some means of changing the site of Smithfield Market. The subject is not an easy one, and I expect that it will give a good deal of trouble before it is over. There has been an immense deal of exaggerated declamation on the subject.

We have just had a thanksgiving as well as your province; but for a different cause—namely, the cessation of cholera. In Hereford diocese they had two thanksgivings—one from the bishop, and a second from the Queen; but they never had the cholera, so their thanks were quite disinterested.

Ever yours,
G. C. L.

Knightsbridge: Jan. 25, 1850.

My dear Head,—I have had the pleasure of receiving your letter of December 20, and as you do not mention the cold, I suppose that your winter had not then promised to be more severe than usual. Here, however, the frost has been longer and sharper than in any winter since 1838. It began a little before Christmas, and has only just now broken up—I hope not to return. The Thames began to be so much impeded with ice, that for a few days the steamers did not ply, which is unusual.

We have stayed till within the last few days at Grove Mill, leading a very quiet life. I have been writing my 'Political Logic,' which, if it is ever finished, few people will read. I shall nevertheless do my best to complete what I fear may prove a somewhat thankless labour.

My article on Grote's 'History' has appeared in the last number of the 'Edinburgh Review;' there is a good review of Lamartine's 'History,' by Senior; and a long dissertation on 'Colonisation,' by Monteagle. Grote is hard at work at his 'History,' and has nearly completed two more volumes. Macaulay's continuation is not promised till two or three years hence.

The session is just about to begin, and there will be a violent explosion of anger from the Protectionists. I have no doubt that the agricultural interest is much depressed. The farmers are suffering universally, and in many places rents are ill paid. This is particularly the case in Herefordshire. The agriculturists are not, however, agreed as to their remedy. They wish, of course, for a restoration of protection, but they are afraid to ask for a duty sufficient to raise prices materially. They talk about the special burdens upon land, but they fail in showing any practicable means by which their pressure can be mitigated. They are not united as to their remedy, and still less as to their leader. They dislike the idea of Disraeli leading the House of Commons, and yet they have nobody superior to him. The session will be an angry one, and the event is uncertain; but although I think it likely that the present Government may be turned out, I do not see what *other* Government can come in.

I shall try to do something about the roads this session, after last year's failure. The turnpikes present the chief difficulty; the highways are more easily managed. A parochial assessment bill, amending the law as to valuations, is also proposed.

I have been working lately at a commission on the

subject of Smithfield and Newgate Markets; the latter being the market for the sale of *dead* meat. The magnitude of the business transacted at these two markets is enormous. The value of the stock sold at Smithfield is estimated at seven millions a year. Both of them are too confined, and ought to be removed. I expect that our report will be ready about Easter.

Chadwick has been preparing a wonderful plan for abolishing intramural interment (as it is called), and making the Government the universal undertaker. This plan has, I believe, been subsequently modified, and it is not likely to be agreed to in its first state; but I have not seen the amended version. Whatever is done, I fear that the subject will give an immensity of trouble before it is settled.

You will be sorry to hear that poor Buckland is in a state of entire mental alienation, so as to be incapable of acting as Dean. This malady is not yet known publicly, but will not, I suppose, remain a secret. His manner was always hurried and a little excited; but I never suspected him of a tendency to insanity. Your story about 'baptismal pants' is excellent.*

The Gorham case is to go against the Bishop; and Campbell is at last to be Chief Justice. Best regards to Lady Head. Ever yours,

G. C. L.

Kent House: April 24, 1850.

My dear Head,—I ought long ago to have thanked you for two interesting letters, and have continued my

* Baptism by immersion is frequently administered in the rivers of the United States; and I believe that the allusion here is to the advertisement of the proprietors of a shop who, anxious to supply garments for the use of persons taking a part in this rite, advertised 'Baptismal Pants.'—EDITOR.

chronicle of events. I quite agree with you in thinking that a federation of the North American provinces is not a likely event, nor is the way to annexation straight or short. I had a conversation lately with Mr. Lawrence, the new American Minister, on the subject, and I saw plainly that the annexation of Canada was a balanced question for the States, and that it could not be carried without a division of opinion, even if the Canadians desired to be annexed. I have lately received a letter from Twisleton, dated at New Orleans, on the subject chiefly of Cuba, and the desire of the Americans to obtain it, as well as on their chance of success. He mentions that he had heard from you and intended to pay you a visit, which intention I hope he will be able to fulfil.

You will have seen from the newspapers the course of the parliamentary debates. The relative positions of parties remain pretty much as they were. No two of them show any disposition to combine, and the Government is stronger than any one other party. The Protectionists have shown that they are afraid to put forward the question of protection and to propose a restoration of the corn duties.

This session has likewise exhibited Disraeli's unfitness for the part of a leader more clearly than before. He was called on to do something *positive*, and has utterly failed. The Peelites hang off and remain isolated. Peel and Graham give a steady support to the Government; Gladstone, Thesiger, and Sydney Herbert are hostile to it, but do not approximate to the Protectionists. Lincoln is in the Mediterranean.

Colonial affairs are quieter. The Ceylon case has passed off for the present. The Cape disturbances are at an end; and the Australian Bill is nearly through

Committee. Lord John has announced the abolition of the Lord Lieutenancy, which had been determined on some time ago. The plan is to have a fourth Secretary of State, and to allow the present state of things to go on till the end of the year. Clarendon is favourable to the change, and it will not be much opposed, so that it will probably pass this session.

My Highways Bill is still in suspense. It is generally approved of: but the difficulty of carrying anything which *appears* to impose any additional burdens on farmers is at its maximum just now, and I do not feel sure what the result will be. I have also introduced a Parochial Assessments Bill, which would make a great improvement in the law.

There is a plan now on foot for making a railway from Gloucester to Ross, which is likely to be executed. The Great Western give considerable assistance; but in these days of railway insolvency, it is no easy matter to carry such a scheme into effect.

My father is in very good health now, but he was a good deal annoyed by a burglary which took place in the house at Harpton while he was there at Easter. The thieves broke in on the ground floor, and carried away a silver inkstand and plate to the value of about eighty pounds. They were probably Birmingham thieves and had no connection with the neighbourhood.* The Dean of Hereford, much to the relief of New Radnor,† has lately died. Many people wish Gilbert to become a candidate, but he prefers remaining as he is, and has no wish to be a Church dignitary. The Deanery

* The burglars proved to be Birmingham men, assisted by a person in the neighbourhood; they came in the hope of finding money collected at a rent-day: but the rent-day had fortunately been postponed.

† Dr. Merewether was also Rector of New Radnor.

of Hereford is not very tempting: 1,000*l.* a year with a house in ruins, and the Cathedral to subscribe to.

Last night Lord John announced the intention of the Government to issue a commission for enquiry into the two Universities; the announcement has created a strong sensation, and the Church will resent it. I have heard nothing of the persons of whom it is likely to consist.

I am sorry to say that Mrs. Villiers has had some severe attacks of pain lately, which have affected her sleep and altogether lowered her health. Ferguson has been very attentive to her.

The article in the last 'Edinburgh Review' on my book* is by Senior. My best regards to Lady Head.

Ever yours sincerely,

G. C. LEWIS.

Sir George Lewis was now (1850) removed, at the wish of his colleagues, from the Under Secretaryship of the Home Office to the more important office of Financial Secretary to the Treasury. He makes remarks upon this change of work and of position in the following letter to Sir Edmund Head:—

London: July 11, 1850.

My dear Head,—Since I had the pleasure of receiving your last letter I have seen Twisleton, fresh from Fredericton, from whom I was extremely glad to have an account of you and Lady Head, as an eye-witness of your colonial greatness. It was an odd accident that you should have met in that distant quarter of the world. Twisleton seems to have enjoyed

* 'Influence of Authority in Matters of Opinion,' *Edinburgh Review*, vol. xci. p. 508.

his journey much, and to have made a careful observation of the state of things and men in America.

I have lately made a change of office, which is a promotion in point of salary, and also as to the importance of the duties. On these accounts I am bound to be pleased with the change. At the same time, I regret the Home Office, the duties of which suited me very well, and I do not feel that I have any particular aptitude for being the *économe* of the Government, and revising the items of treasury expenditure, which is the business of the Secretary of the Treasury. Tufnell * was tired of being the Parliamentary Secretary, and his health has not been good lately. His retirement made a vacancy in that office, which there was a difficulty in filling, until Hayter was induced to take it. I was placed in Hayter's office, and Edward Bouverie has succeeded me. One of the first fruits of this transfer is, that I have to serve on a commission for reporting on closing the country post-offices on Sunday, a subject which has stirred up the Sabbatarian mind of England, and has produced a wonderful quantity of petitioning and agitating. It is a question on which there are two irreconcilable parties, and whatever is done is sure to give mortal offence to one—possibly to both.

Peel's death has been a very sad event. He leaves a great blank in public life; his great experience, his extensive knowledge, his long official career, and his practised habits of debate and power of speech gave him a position in the House of Commons which nobody else filled. He had, it is true, lost his party, and he told for little in a division, but his voice had great

* Right Hon. Henry Tufnell, M.P. for Devonport.

weight in the country, and no speech of his was a matter of indifference even in the House. I cannot say that I prized his judgment very highly, nor do I think that as a *guide* in public affairs, when he had ceased to be an *administrator*, he was of great value. He did not see far before him; he was not ready in applying theory to practice; he did not foresee the coming storm. But, when it had come, there was no man who dealt with it so well as he did. For concocting, producing, explaining, and defending measures he had no equal, or anything like an equal. There was nothing *simile aut secundum*. When a thing was to be done, he did it better than anybody. The misfortune was, that he saw the right thing too late; and went on opposing it when men of less powerful minds saw clearly what was the proper course. Latterly, when he became more of a reformer, he was sometimes too bold, as in his scheme for planting Connaught, which really was very wild and fanciful.

Peel's death will exercise a great influence upon the Peelite party, but I do not expect either that the Peelites will become Protectionists, or that the Protectionists will give up protection and adopt Peelite leaders. Graham is a great sufferer by the change, as he had constantly stood by Peel, when his other friends went different ways.

Upon Gladstone it will have the effect of removing a weight from a spring—he will come forward more and take more part in discussion. The general opinion is, that Gladstone will renounce his free-trade opinions, and become leader of the Protectionists. I expect neither the one event nor the other. I do not believe that Gladstone will give up free-trade, nor do I think that Disraeli will submit to be displaced from the lead.

Even his followers could hardly make such a proposition to him.

Palmerston achieved a great triumph over his enemies. His speech was an extraordinary effort. He defeated the whole Conservative party, Protectionists and Peelites, supported by the extreme Radicals, and backed by the 'Times,' and all the organized forces of foreign diplomacy.

After all has been said and done, the Greek affair was very undignified and unjustifiable; and the principle involved in Pacifico's case is a dangerous one. Unless it is carefully limited, it would lead to the most monstrous consequences.

*   *   *   *

Ireland is beginning to mend, and a good potato crop will set it on its legs again. * * * Colonial affairs are quieter. Less is heard about the Colonial Office, but there have been awkward disclosures of private letters before the Ceylon Committee. * * * I expect that the session will last till about August 20. We shall then, I suppose, go for a short time to Herefordshire, and return to town for the autumn, or, rather, winter.

Villiers * goes to Cambridge next October term.

My father has quite recovered his health; he goes to Harpton in a few days. I have made considerable progress with my book,† at which I employ all my odd hours. I wish I could have the benefit of your revision. My best regards to Lady Head.

Ever yours truly,

G. C. Lewis.

* T. Villiers Lister, Esq., Lady Theresa Lewis's son of her first marriage.

† His treatise on politics, published by Parker in 1852.

Grove Mill: Sept. 15, 1850.

My dear Head,—The latter part of the session was uneventful, though very fatiguing, from the number of hours which the House sat. Since the prorogation, we have been staying at Grove Mill, with the exception of a day's excursion which we made to Combe, Lord Craven's place, near Coventry. It contains a very interesting collection of pictures, chiefly portraits which Theresa wished to see on account of her book.* There are fine full-length portraits of Prince Rupert and Prince Maurice, and also of the Princess of Orange when a child, by Vandyke. There is a good full-length portrait of Charles I., by Mytens, and numerous portraits of the Queen of Bohemia, and all her family, by Honthorst, who seems to have been a sort of court painter to the Palatinate. The collection was made by her and left to her favourite Lord Craven, and it has remained undisturbed since his time. There are several portraits of Sophia, the daughter of the King of Bohemia, and Electress of Hanover—who forms the link between the Stuarts and Georges. I never saw a likeness of her before.

I am supposed to be in attendance on the Treasury during the month of September, and I go up as often as I am wanted, which is about twice a week. There is one junior lord in London: Charles Wood is in Scotland, Hayter is in Ireland, and Trevelyan on the continent. I never knew so profound a stagnation in public affairs both at home and abroad, as far as this country is concerned. The Editor of the 'Observer,' whom I saw yesterday, told me that he had great difficulty in finding topics for his leading articles. Wad-

* 'Lives of the Friends and Contemporaries of Lord-Chancellor Clarendon, illustrative of portraits in his Gallery.' 3 vols. Murray, 1852.

dington told me he had had nothing to do at the Home Office but to protect General Haynau from the brewers.

At the Treasury there has been a good deal of routine business, because people cannot live without money even in the month of September; but it is all of a quiet nature.

The Queen was very well received in her progress to Balmoral; I saw Prescott, the American, who had met her at Castle Howard; like other people he was struck with the intelligence and information of the Prince. The Scotch have been much pleased by her residing for a few days at Holyrood; the Prince made a peculiarly good speech on laying the stone of the National Gallery at Edinburgh. I do not know whether you happened to read it. Clarendon has likewise been acting king in Ireland, and has been making a most successful progress in Ulster. He has had an excellent reception; which, considering what took place about Dolly's brae, proves that the Orange party are down in the world. I look upon it that repeal is now virtually extinct, and Orangeism in a moribund state. The only active and really living movement in Ireland now is that which is represented by the Tenant-Right League. The question between landlord and tenant is a real one, but it is an internal domestic question, and does not concern imperial relations. The religious questions still continue, and the bigoted party has prevailed in the synod of Thurles by a majority of two.

The French President has been emulating our Queen and making visits to the provinces, according to the newspapers, which, I presume, may be relied on; his reception on the whole has been highly favourable. I find myself becoming, what I never expected to be, a strong Bonapartist. It is clear that the French look back with no satisfaction on any part of their history except the Empire. They dislike the *ancien régime*, and its inequalities, besides which it may be admitted that the Government of France, during the last century, was too bad for a civilized nation to endure very long. They are not proud of the Restoration—a Government imposed on them by foreigners. Louis Philippe's was a sordid, self-seeking system, and hence they have nothing to look back on with pleasure but the wars and glory of the Consulate and Empire. A nation must have some recollections, and the Bonapartist recollections alone offer any chance of stability to a new Government. It does not follow that the feeling which grows out of military glory, and creates a prestige for the name of Napoleon, necessarily requires to be fed with fresh military glory. Louis Napoleon seems to be pacific—he is no captain—nor a man capable of leading armies, and he will probably limit his ambition to being Prince President for life. It is clear that he intends to break through the restriction as to his re-election, and to become a candidate at the end of his four years; and as he will no doubt use all the influence of Government, as well as the prestige of his name, to secure his return, I do not see how any one can have a chance against him. It is clearly the best thing for the country that he should be re-elected quietly.

Louis Philippe's death was no political event; it does Palmerston some good by removing the centre of a constant set of cabals and intrigues against him; but otherwise it has little importance.

I have felt very sincere regret, as I have no doubt you will feel, for poor William Clifford's * death. He is quite

* William Clifford, Esq., who resided at Perrystone, near Ross, in Herefordshire.

irreplaceable: he has left nobody behind him like himself; the mixture of benignity, humour, simplicity, knowledge, modesty, and boldness of thought was quite peculiar. His death was sudden, and I have not heard what it was caused by.

Bailey, my colleague, has also died after a long-suffering illness; he was a strong Protectionist, but a perfectly honourable and straightforward colleague. He is to be succeeded by a Mr. Booker, a flaming Protectionist from Glamorganshire, who will, I fear, give some trouble.

Twisleton is gone for a short time to Germany * * * I hope you are quite well.

Ever yours sincerely,

G. C. Lewis.

P. S. Whenever you have another parcel of books, there are two which I should wish to add to your list. One is a little volume lately published by Francis Newman, entitled 'Phases of Faith;' giving an account of his successive changes of religious opinion, and containing a good deal about Oxford and Oxford men which will, I think, interest you. The other is a work in four octavo volumes, by a Monsieur Charles Comte, entitled 'Traités de Législation,' published about fifteen years ago. It contains the best and truest account of the savage state of society and mode of life which I am acquainted with, and I should be glad to know what you think of it with reference to the Red man. I recommended it to Twisleton, who promised me to read it.

Grove Mill: Dec. 28, 1850.

My dear Head,—I have not yet thanked you for the interesting journal of your travels, which you must have had much pleasure in making, and of which I was very glad to have so full an account. You certainly made a terrible stumble* at the threshold; it was very lucky that Lady Head was able to recover so soon, and she certainly showed a most Amazonian boldness in following you so soon. I received the letter to Wortley, and forwarded it to him. I have also given your commission to Cochrane, who undertakes to execute it. It must be confessed that books are very cheap if one watches one's opportunity. The difference between buying a book when it is in the market and ordering a book simply is immense. Foreign books in England are the cheapest of all, when they are not new.

I passed the month of November and nearly all December in London with no incidents in my own life. I went down to Hereford to attend a county meeting for promoting a railway from Gloucester to Hereford. A large sum in shares has been subscribed, and it is *nearly* enough, but I have not yet heard whether it is quite enough. The meeting was well attended, and Brunel came down. It will be a great convenience to all the dwellers in that part of the country if it can be executed. There has since been a county meeting on the Papal aggression, which I did *not* attend. The amount of nonsense which has been talked on this subject has been very large. The creation of dioceses in the ambitious manner in which it was done, was, however, a very wanton attack on the Protestant feeling of the country, which was quite contented to slumber if it had not been roused by the Pope. No

* The sudden illness of Lady Head, as they were about to start from New Brunswick on an expedition to Canada and the United States Lady Head recovered in the course of a few days.

doubt the Pope and his advisers had been misled, by the Puseyite conversions, into supposing that all England was ready to go to Rome. By this time they have probably discovered their error. I do not expect that this row will alter the relation between Catholics and Protestants in this country; the storm will blow over, and both parties will be as they were. But it will bring the Puseyites to their bearings; it will be an instantia crucis to them which will compel them to choose one road or the other. The extreme left will become Roman, the middle and the extreme right will gradually drop the 'ritualism' and the other distinctive attributes of Puseyism, and relapse into old-fashioned High Church opinions, such as used to be held at Oxford thirty years ago. It is expected that the Government will bring in a Bill prohibiting the Roman Catholic bishops from assuming territorial names of sees. If this is done, it will be a very innocent piece of legislation, but it will probably produce an infinite quantity of *déraisonnement*, and bad theological politics. Lord John's letter took advantage of the opportunity against the Puseyites, but there were some unfortunate expressions in it, not necessary for his purpose, which offended the Catholics.

Disraeli's letter was a failure. The Protectionists, as a party, have taken no line in the matter. They would, however, have put themselves at the head of the national feeling if Lord John had not: the Peelites are inclined to inaction. There was an excellent letter in the 'Times,' on the side of indifferences, signed '*Carolus*.' It was written by Charles Greville.

Protection is considered even by its friends as a hopeless cause. Calvert has been returned for Aylesbury, quite an agricultural borough, in the county of the Duke of Buckingham and Disraeli, without difficulty; his Protectionist opponent withdrew. The farmers are, however, really in a depressed and suffering state. The price of wheat has continued for a year at about forty shillings, and it is not likely to advance. Rents must be lowered, but re-adjustment is a slow and painful process, and landlords put off the evil day as long as they can. The agricultural cry now is for relief in the way of taxation, but taxation is not the cause of their difficulties, and a change of taxation will afford them no real relief. The pressure for a transfer of local burdens is stronger than ever. I should not be surprised if some more expenses of criminal justice were transferred. Lunatic asylums are also talked of. My belief, however, is that all these transfers will turn out to be mere moonshine. If prices continue on their present range, the arrangements between landlord and tenant must undergo a general revision. In the meantime the country thrives; the revenue keeps up, trade increases, crime and pauperism diminish.

There is a great interest and expectation about the effects of the Crystal Palace. It is not a popular subject at Knightsbridge, particularly at this moment, when we are overrun with the workmen who stream along the road at meal-times as if a manufactory was breaking up. I have never been able to make out precisely what good it is to do; but it is a 'grand idea,' it 'embodies the spirit of the age,' &c. &c., and so I suppose it will have some effect. It will certainly bring a great many people to London, and increase the profits of hotel and lodging keepers.

I have nearly finished the first draft of my book.* It will make two octavo volumes, and it will take a

* 'Treatise on Politics.' Parker, 1852.

year, or perhaps more, to complete and revise. My wife has begun printing a life of Lord Falkland.* She has also written lives of Lord Capel and Lord Hertford, and will publish them with an account of the collection of pictures at the Grove. Murray publishes.

I wish you and Lady Head a happy New Year. Our winter promises now to be a mild one.

Ever yours sincerely,
G. C. LEWIS.

Brougham says that the *second* epistle of John is likely to cause as much controversy as the *first*. You know that the first epistle of St. John contains the text about the three witnesses.

G. C. L.

Kent House: March 6, 1851.

My dear Head,—I have been putting off a letter to you for some time from week to week, because I had nothing but *little* events to tell you. Now I have got a great event, and I accordingly sit down to give you an account of it. The session opened quietly enough. Everything except agriculture was prosperous, trade was increasing, the manufacturing districts in better work than ever, retail trade thriving, the funds high, credit sound, plenty of gold in the bank, our foreign relations pacific, the colonies without an insurrection, and not even a border war in India. As to agriculture, there was no *statistical* case of depression to be made out. Land maintains its value; farms are re-let, though often at a reduced rent; pauperism is diminishing; and the agricultural labourers, though their money-

* 'Lives of the Friends and Contemporaries of Lord-Chancellor Clarendon, illustrative of portraits in his Gallery,' by Lady Theresa Lewis. Murray, 1852.

wages are in many counties as low as 7s., are admitted to have never been in a more comfortable state. The notice of the Papal measure in the Queen's Speech was likewise brief, and the debate on the Address passed off without any strong feeling. The motion to bring in the Anti-Papal Bill, however, roused the Irish Catholic members, and they combined for the purpose of turning out the Government on the first question which should present itself. This question was Disraeli's motion on agricultural distress, on which the Government had a majority of only fourteen. The next step was the proposal of the Budget, which was coldly received—no great interest was satisfied; and the scheme for the commutation of the window tax into a house tax was received with a violent outcry in the large towns. It now became manifest that the Budget would not be carried without considerable alterations, to the necessity of which the Chancellor of the Exchequer* doubtless looked forward with great uneasiness. A vote of censure for the proceedings with respect to Ceylon was likewise impending over the Colonial Office, and was likely to be carried. At this moment a division took place on a Bill for enlarging the franchise, in which the Government were beat by their own friends by a majority of two to one. This latter event, added to what had already occurred, furnished a ground for resignation. The decision was come to quite suddenly, and was just in time to avert the first debate on the Income Tax. What has passed since, as to resignations and negotiations to form a new ministry, has been all fully explained in the most authentic manner in the debates of the two Houses. Stanley, when first applied

* Right Hon. Sir Charles Wood, now Viscount Halifax.

to, was reluctant to undertake the formation of a Government. He was averse to a dissolution, and without a dissolution he had a minority in the House of Commons: moreover, the question of Protection as well as the Anti-Papal Bill were great puzzles. He advised the Queen to try a union between the Whigs and the Peelites. The Queen then sent for Lord Aberdeen and Graham, but they had committed themselves privately to a strong opinion against any legislation on the anti-papal question; and Lord John could not, after what he had done, withdraw his Bill altogether. The negotiation therefore failed, and Stanley was again applied to. He first tried the Peelites, and offered the Foreign Office to Lord Canning. He afterwards tried to prevail on Gladstone to join him; this latter offer must, I presume, have been made with the intention that he should lead in the Commons. Both refused, and he then tried purely Protectionist materials. Lord Ellenborough was to have the Foreign Office, Disraeli the Colonies, the Duke of Northumberland the Admiralty, Sugden to be Chancellor, Thesiger and Walpole Attorney and Solicitor; Herries, and afterwards Tom Baring, were said to have refused the office of Chancellor of the Exchequer, and Henley of Home Secretary. These two refusals brought matters to a crisis; and upon finding that his own friends would not take office, he gave up the attempt. My belief is that if he had himself been in the House of Commons, he would have formed his Government. * * * When this attempt was abandoned, there was nothing for it but to bring back the former ministers, which was accomplished by throwing over the transition the decent veil of a consultation with the Duke of Wellington. The second reading of the Anti-

Papal Bill is fixed for Friday night, and the war will begin again. The resignation of ministers was, in fact, produced by the defection of the Irish members; and the difficulty of the crisis is to satisfy the Protestant feeling of England without offending the Catholic feeling of Ireland. Graham's course fulfils the latter condition, Lord John's the former. The question is, to devise some course which will fulfil *both* conditions. I believe it might have been done originally, by confining the Bill to England; and as the aggression, as it is called, was limited to England, the defensive measure might fairly have been kept within the same limits. The Bill, however, has been made general, and it is no easy matter *now* to cut it down. Something of the kind, however, must be done, if the Bill is not to be debated continuously till next Christmas.

As to the Budget, there must be some modification, and that is now an easier undertaking. The chief effect of the late move has been to give a deadly stab to the cause of Protection. Among public men Lord Stanley has gained the most, and Disraeli lost the most. The Government is still in an insecure position, but just at present nobody will try to turn it out. Such is our present situation; and I fear that Lord John's solution of difficulties will not be so successful as your move with respect to the Chief Justice.

* * * *

If any copy of Lord Holland's 'Reminiscences' reaches your province, you will find it worth reading; but it is a gossiping book, and his idolatry of Napoleon is positively puerile, and appears in its true light when the grounds of it come to be stated. I suspect, however, that his account of Marie Antoinette, for which he has been so much abused, is true.

Senior is passing the winter at Palermo on account of his bronchitis.

*   *   *   *

Ever yours sincerely,
G. C. Lewis.

Grove Mill: Sept. 1, 1851.

My dear Head,—Since I wrote to you last the session has been brought to an end, and the question about which there was so much speculation, as to whether the ministry would survive the session, has been brought to a practical solution. The last five or six weeks of the session were at least as fatiguing to the official members as usual. I do not think that anybody can know what *bore* is, in its intensest form, who has not been compelled to sit through all the debates, morning and evening, to the last moment, during the last month of the session. Of course it is not so bad as the lot of a Neapolitan State prisoner, or a galley-slave chained to his oar. It is not physical suffering, nor is it even mental pain; but it is *bore*, in the proper sense of the word, and in its highest degree. Of the three parties the Government was, on the whole, *least* damaged by the session. The Peelites made themselves unpopular by their line on the Anti-Papal Bill. As they had not, as a party, distinguished themselves by any peculiar love of religious equality, their conduct was referred partly to love of Catholicism and partly to faction. The Protectionists were weakened by various blunders of Disraeli, also by their ambiguous language on the subject of Protection, and their reluctance to commit themselves to any definite policy on the subject. My belief is, that if they came in they would only temporize; they would not propose to restore any duty on corn, but they would try some relief in the way of changes of taxation, and attempt to quiet their supporters by assuring them that they had their good at heart. If they could once come in (which would not be very difficult), and if, when once in, they could trust their leaders, and agree among one another (which would be far more difficult), I am disposed to think that they might go on for a time upon the plan of doing nothing. However, that is not the general opinion among our people. Hayter, whose business it is to count votes, and to find out parliamentary feeling, thinks that, even in a new Parliament, they could not last through a session. It was certain that when the agriculturalists found that no immediate attempt to recover Protection was to be made, they would cool amazingly.

The Anti-Papal Bill consumed the chief part of the session; as a measure of legislation, it is wholly unimportant. The whole dispute seems to me de nugâ caprinâ. Neither the assumption of the territorial title, nor the prohibition to assume it, is of the slightest practical moment. The English bishops, for the present, submit to the law. The Irish bishops, against whom it was *not* directed, are beginning to make a bluster; but I expect that it will be a fuoco di paglia. Paul Cullen's acceptance of the chair at the Dublin meeting, when he was moved into it as Archbishop of Armagh, was very close to a public assumption of the title. The signatures in the newspapers prove nothing. The titles may have been added by a printer's devil. The real cause of the Catholic revival in this country is not political; it is due exclusively to the Oxford School. They, and their adherents, have made converts among the clergy and upper classes in *England*, upon theological grounds. In Ireland, where the political influences are more felt, there have been no conversions to Catholicism.

* * * *

Gladstone's pamphlet* about Naples has had a prodigious run; it has been universally read, and has made a most powerful impression. For the future, it will do good; but, for the present, it will probably increase the sufferings of these wretched men. The reaction in all the continental Governments is most decisive. The Government is everywhere more coercive and jealous than before the last revolutions. Vienna is still *en état de siége*; so is Lyons, with the guns *braqués* upon the town. Sardinia may, for the present, have gained a little. All people, however, describe Paris as having recovered its former cheerful appearance.

The Exhibition has been wonderfully successful. The foreigners have admired and been pleased. Numbers of French and a good many Germans came over. They stayed only a few days—and spent but little money—and saw as many sights as they could. All the authorities—the Commissioners, the Woods, the Government, and the Court—are in favour of removing the Crystal Palace when its work has been done. There was a sort of popular feeling in favour of keeping it, which found an expression in the House of Commons, but nobody has a purpose to suggest, and the money for purchasing and maintaining it is not forthcoming; so I expect to see it disappear at the fated time. There is really not an intelligible reason to be assigned in favour of its permanence. * * * Coode has lately

* 'Two Letters to the Earl of Aberdeen, on the subject of State Prisoners at Naples.' See *Annual Register* for 1851, p. 138.

written a report on the Law of Settlement, in which he argues the question on general grounds; and strongly urges the abolition of removals. The more I examine the subject the more I am satisfied that this is the right thing to do. I will send you a copy, as you will be interested by reading it. The language is unnecessarily strong, and the tone is exaggerated; but I think that he proves his case, and demolishes the arguments in favour of the law.

The potato disease shows itself again this year, if not in a very destructive, yet in an unmistakable form. Where it is slight, it is confined to the leaves, or to the leaves and stalk. In some parts of Ireland it will, I fear, make a considerable deduction from the crop.

My father and Lady Lewis made an excursion this summer as far as Milan, and were back by the beginning of August. The weather beyond the Alps was not very hot. There is a new essay by Manzoni, on the 'Historical Romance,' which they procured, and I have read. It is written with elegance and good taste, but there is little force or novelty in it. It reminds me of some of Dugald Stewart's essays.

Senior is much the better for his winter in Italy. Macaulay is continuing his 'History' in a leisurely way; there is to be nothing more this year. Grote, on the other hand, works on like a German professor. He has two more volumes, the ninth and tenth, nearly ready. * * * My wife has nearly finished printing her three lives, 'Lord Falkland, Lord Capel, and the Marquis of Hertford.' There is to be a long introduction, containing an account of the pictures, which is nearly ready for the press; and I expect that the work will be out before Christmas.

We went down to Whitfield,* for a bow-meeting, at which all the county attended. The day was beautiful. I have since been staying at Grove Mill, but in attendance at the Treasury, Trevelyan being absent. * * * My best regards to Lady Head. I hope your children are thriving.

Ever yours sincerely,

G. C. Lewis.

Kent House: May 19, 1851.

My dear Head,—I despatched some time ago your box of books, which contained the set of Memoirs, and a few other books, for which I enclose the bill. It is, as you see, paid. I will also pay Cochrane's account, and you can pay me for both. I sent you the second volume of a new periodical, called 'Notes and Queries,' thinking it might interest you. Both Bathurst and I have written some articles in it. His are signed by his initials, mine are signed 'L.' Since that time I have received your letter of March 31, for which many thanks. I will tell my father to write to you. He is very well, and is meditating a summer tour on the continent.

The Government have had sundry reverses and misadventures since the crisis, but their position remains substantially unchanged. Graham's speech on the Anti-Papal Bill gave great offence; it was thought mischievous and dangerous, and produced a general feeling against him, except among the Irish Catholics. It has entirely destroyed the prestige connected with him, and I look upon a coalition between him and the Government at present as impossible. The conduct of the Peelites generally on this question has been equivocal

* The residence in Herefordshire of his friend and political supporter, the Rev. Archer Clive.

and unintelligible, and has done them no good. It has been a damaging question for all parties; and if the Pope wished to produce confusion and do mischief, he could not have taken a more effectual step. The Protectionists are now certainly desirous of coming in; a dissolution would increase their numbers; but if they seriously set about trying to re-impose a Corn Law, they would infallibly fail. My belief is, that they would *not* make the attempt, but would try other measures of (real or supposed) agricultural relief. The country is averse to frequent changes of Government: and it is not unlikely that they might go on for some time if they abstained from any reactionary measures. Their position, however, would be very different from Peel's in 1841. When Peel came in the Corn Laws were still in force, and he began by mitigating them. Moreover, his Cabinet contained three of the strongest men in the House of Commons, which would not be the case with a Protectionist Government at present. My seat in Herefordshire is in a very tottering state; two new Protectionist candidates are announced, viz. Charles Hanbury, a brother of Bateman; and Mr. King King, of Staunton. Wegg Prosser has announced his intention of retiring at the next election. It is possible that the Protectionist feeling may be less strong at the dissolution than it is now; but a good deal will depend on this harvest. Hitherto the great supplies have come from *France*, which nobody anticipated. The life of the Government is precarious, but I think it more likely than not that it will last to the end of the session. The Irish are making the same use of the Anti-Papal Bill which O'Connell made of repeal. They use it as a means of disturbance, and of gaining popularity, but do not wish actually to force the Government out.

The country is remarkably prosperous, with the single exception of the agriculturists. Even in agriculture there is no case for legislative interference. The labourers are well off, and the land is tilled. Landlords and tenants must re-adjust their contracts, and rents must fall. The limitation of the Income Tax to one year will put our whole financial system in the kettle at the beginning of next session. I * * *. The Poor Law Board has now become purely administrative, and has no character or policy of its own. Baines, however, has managed the business very well in the House of Commons, and has disarmed all opposition and hostility. A great change has, however, taken place since our day. This has been partly owing to old ——'s death, and partly to the experience obtained under the Irish Poor Law. Twisleton has now established himself and his excellent library in chambers in the Albany. I do not make out that he is doing anything.

I have myself sometimes formed a project of translating Aristotle's 'Politics.' I wish you would undertake it; but I doubt whether it would be expedient to add notes illustrative of *modern* institutions. There is a good German translation by Stahr, and a new edition of Barthélemi St.-Hilaire's translation is coming out. For the present, whatever spare time I have is occupied with my political treatise, which I expect to finish by the end of the year, so as to print it in the course of the spring and summer of 1852. It will consist of two volumes, and therefore will occupy some time in printing. It will go over the same ground as that treated in Mill's 'Logic,' but will not agree in all his views, and will be fuller and more detailed. Mill's 'Logic' is, as you say, an admirable book. It has not, I think, been sufficiently praised or estimated at its worth. It is a superior book to his 'Political Economy.' In consequence of Mill's recommendation, I have read Comte's 'Cours de Philosophie' twice over. My estimate of the moral and political part of this treatise differs altogether from Mill's, but I think you would find it worth reading.

Grote's 'History of Greece' has quite established itself in public esteem. It is regularly read at Universities by candidates for honours. The two first volumes have reached a third edition, and have been translated into German. The remaining volumes have reached a second edition. He has two more volumes, the ninth and tenth, ready, which bring down the history to the battle of Mantinea. Boeckh has published a new edition of his 'Staats-haushaltung.' It contains many corrections and additions, but is substantially the same work as the first edition. I have heard with great pleasure of Lord Grey's approbation of your conduct, and do not doubt that it is well deserved. As your province seems now quiet, could you not come over this summer and see the Great Exhibition? It is a wonderful sight, quite unlike anything which ever before existed; from its gigantic dimensions, the multitude, variety, the completeness, and the individual excellence of the articles exhibited. It is a complete repertory of the useful arts for the whole world, exhibiting the best works of each country. Its success has been beyond all expectation, the opinion in its favour is unanimous, the *frondeurs* are silenced, and the receipts are immense. Our best regards to Lady Head.

Ever yours sincerely,

G. C. Lewis.

P.S. Did you ever read Volney's account of the Indians in his work on America?

Grove Mill: Dec. 21, 1851.

My dear Head,—I received your letter some time ago, and I have been terribly remiss about writing to you. The truth is, that I have been very much occupied of late with completing my treatise on 'Politics,' which, I am happy to say, is now as good as finished, and the first part is gone to the press. It will make two volumes, each containing 500 closely-printed pages; so you see that I had enough to fill up all my *horæ subsecivæ.* Theresa likewise has been carrying her book through the press, and the correction of proof-sheets, &c., has taken up a good deal of my time. The whole of it is now in the printer's hands, and nothing remains to be printed but the catalogue of the pictures at the Grove, on which she has bestowed much trouble, and which, I fear, will be too long for the non-artistical reader.

The great event of late is the new French revolution. I agree very much with the articles in the 'Times,' which you have doubtless read. Louis Napoleon is a man with a great deal of selfish ambition, and with considerable daring and firmness. The Assembly would not allow him to be re-elected for another term of four years; and being able to reckon on the support of the army, he determined to put them down by force, and establish a mock constitution, but in reality a military Government. The cry about Socialism is mere hypocrisy; the leaders of the Assembly whom he sent to Ham are not Socialists; nor is it true that there was any intention of arresting him. It is clear that the whole affair is a *singerie* of the Consulate and Empire, but the use of force has been more direct than under the Convention or at the 18th Brumaire. The proceedings of the Comité de Salut Public were regular and constitutional as compared with his performance. If the press and the tribune are fairly silenced, and the army has no internal enemies to contend against, they will cry out for their reward, and ask for plunder. This can only be given them by engaging in a foreign war, and such would be the infallible result of a real restoration of the Imperial régime in France. I do not, however, believe in the possibility of restoring the Empire without the Emperor. After all, Napoleon himself was the soul of his own system.

Our domestic affairs are thriving. The revenue keeps up, but there is a falling off in the assessed taxes, on account of the interval between the going out of the Window Tax and the coming in of the House Tax. Interest is low, the funds are high, and speculation in Gold Companies is commencing. The Protection cry has very much lost its *national* importance. If the Protectionists were to come in, they would not venture to propose a restoration of the Corn Law, but would merely dabble a little with shiftings of taxation. As respects *particular seats*, however, the cry is still alive. It can be used with effect for local purposes, as in Herefordshire. The gentlemen for the most part see the inutility of attempting a reaction against the large towns and all the intelligence of the country; but the farmers are more hot-headed and short-sighted, and more easily duped by interested leaders.

I have not yet seen Disraeli's book about George Bentinck, and only know what has been said of it in the newspapers. It seems for the most part to be heavy, as abstracts of debates and speeches always are. It is impossible to make a hero out of Bentinck. He was not really an able man; but he was proud, bold, determined, and honest, and thoroughly wrong-headed on all economical questions, which gave him an influence during the free-trade struggle. He had likewise great arithmetical skill, and great power of cramming statistical details. He was a *painfully* bad speaker, and his speeches were the result of mere cram. He had no resources of his own. The great question for next session will be the Reform Bill, as to which there are great expectations. There will, I suppose, be enlargements of the suffrage, and something will probably be done with the smallest and most corrupt boroughs. The St. Albans enquiry has produced a great impression. The French coup d'état will have anti-democratic effect here, as showing the practical fruits of universal suffrage, in that country at least.

I hardly think that there will be an opportunity of legislating on the Law of Settlement next session; but if any measure is brought in, it will, I believe, be total abolition and not union settlement. I have got a Highway Bill which I want to bring in, but I fear there will be no opportunity. The Customs Board have got into bad odour, in consequence of some rash prosecutions of the great Dock Companies. I had to attend a most tiresome committee all last session, and I am afraid that it will be renewed when Parliament meets.

* * * *

The Kossuth business was somewhat absurd, but his speaking is said to have been extraordinary. I do not suppose that any foreigner ever spoke with so much success to large crowds of people. He had never been in England before.

* * * *

I have not seen Bunsen's work on Hippolytus, but I believe that the object of it is to show that the treatise attributed to Origen, lately published by the Oxford University Press, is not by Origen. Grote told me that he had read the volume, and that it is worth reading. It contains a good deal on the opinions of the Greek philosophers. Shall I send you a copy with your next parcel of books—it only costs a few shillings—or will you wait to your summer visit? I shall be happy of course to back your application, but I should think that it would be granted without hesitation.

My father is remarkably well—very little changed, I think, since you saw him, either in his mind or habits. Gilbert and Jane and their children have likewise been well. Mrs. Villiers* is entirely confined to the house, except for an occasional drive, but she has been better for the last three months than she has been for some time. We had January weather at the end of November, but latterly mild spring weather with southerly winds. Henry Bulwer is going to Florence; I have not heard who succeeds him in the United States.

My best regards to Lady Head.

Ever yours sincerely,

G. C. LEWIS.

In February 1852, Lord Russell's Government resigned, and before the end of the month Lord Derby accepted office; and, in consequence of the prospect of an early dissolution of the Parliament which had been elected in 1847, many members, and among them Sir George Lewis, began a canvass. It had been for some time made known in Herefordshire that three candi-

* The Hon. Mrs. George Villiers, the mother of Lady Theresa Lewis.

dates* of Protectionist principles would be brought forward.

Kent House: April 14, 1852.

My dear Head,—I have postponed writing to you so long, since I received your letter with the intelligence that you would come over this spring, that I fear it is almost too late for me to begin. I intended some weeks ago to write you a long account of the change of Government, but at the time I was much occupied with clearing out and making the final arrangements before the change of office; and since that time I have been so much occupied with my canvass that I have delayed my letter.

The change of Government was not unexpected, but it might, I believe, have been prevented. The division on Lord Palmerston's motion was a surprise, and he himself did not wish to turn out the Government.

* * * *

However, the cup was full, and a little movement was sufficient to make it run over.

* * * *

The chief effect of the change has been that Graham and Cardwell have come to sit among the Whigs—while Gladstone and Sidney Herbert sit below the gangway.

* * * *

The dissolution is likely to take place at the end of May or beginning of June, and I hear that the result will be, that the numbers will stand nearly as at present, though many seats will be changed. My canvass was very good in the towns—the shopkeepers are, for the most part, free traders. The same is also the case with the small freeholders throughout the country; but they

* They were the Hon. Charles Hanbury, Mr. Booker, and Mr. King King.

are generally dependent, and cannot always be relied on for voting.

* * * *

Altogether, I consider my chance a good one; but until the canvassing lists are received from all parts of the county, I cannot feel sure.

I am very glad to think that I shall see you again so soon.

Ever yours sincerely,
G. C. Lewis.

Kent House: July 29, 1852.

My dear Grote,—I send you the the first part of the evidence relating to the Income Tax, which is all that I have received. It is disappointing, as throwing any light on the really difficult parts of the question, but it proves that the principal evasions are in Schedule A—not, as was alleged and believed, in Schedule D—and that they are principally owing to the exemptions.

The American evidence shows that the State of New York is taxed on the same principle on which the County rate is imposed in this country—with this difference, that 'means and substance' is assessed as in Scotland.

I have been thinking again of the plan of a history of Greece and Rome combined, for the post-Alexandrine period, about which we had a conversation; and I feel satisfied that it is the best mode of treating *both* the histories of that period.

There are two main points of union before the wars which ended in the complete subjugation of Greece. One is the expedition of Pyrrhus, the other is the wars with Carthage for the possession of Sicily. These two events bring Greece and Rome into contact.

Alexander the Great died in 323 B.C., and Pyrrhus was born in 318, only five years afterwards. The events immediately following the death of Alexander might therefore form an introductory narrative—the *combined* history being the main theme.

Pyrrhus invaded Italy in 280; and the first Punic war began in 264—sixteen years afterwards. If the Punic wars of Rome are taken in connection with the Punic wars against the Greek cities of Sicily since the Peloponnesian war, they are likely to be regarded with a different feeling. The devastation of the flourishing and civilized island of Sicily and its Hellenic cities, by the cruel and faithless Carthaginian Βάρβαροι, must move the sympathies of every modern reader.

But as the Romans succeeded in defeating the Carthaginians, and treated them with great kindness, we are apt to sympathize with the beaten party. The history of the Punic war is taken as an isolated fact, and not, as it ought to be, in connection with the prior history of the Carthaginians in Sicily.

The wars of Rome against Philip, Perseus, and the Achæans belong equally to Greek and to Roman history; and by a singular accident the two streams of Grecian and Punic warfare are lost in the sea at the same point, for Carthage and Corinth are both taken in the year 146 B.C.

I would therefore take for my subject, the history of Greece and Rome, from the birth of Pyrrhus to the capture of Corinth, a period of 172 years—318–146 B.C.

The proper subject of the history of Polybius is the period of 74 years from 220 to 146 B.C. In his two introductory books, however, he gives a portion of the history of the preceding century. The terminus a quo chosen by Polybius would not suit your purpose—the terminus ad quem might be imitated.

I enclose a note of the two books which I am desirous of procuring. I also add the title of a book which you might find interesting, as throwing light on the conduct of the Athenians in the affair of the Mercuries.

Ever yours sincerely,

G. C. Lewis.

Had the representation of minorities passed by Lord Derby's Government in 1867 formed a portion of our law in 1852, Sir George Lewis would for a second time have represented Herefordshire; but the united strength of three adversaries, combined with the Protectionist feeling which still existed among the farmers, was too powerful for him. His canvassing books showed a large majority, but the smaller voters were so dependent on the farmers, that they could not be polled in his favour, and he was defeated. He was also unsuccessful at Peterborough, which city he contested later in the year.

Grove Mill: Sept. 29, 1852.

My dear Head,—It was very unlucky that my electioneering troubles lasted all the time when you were in England; and now that I have settled down into a peaceable life, and could have enjoyed more of your society, it is unfortunately too late.

* * * *

The feeling of regret at the Duke of Wellington's death has been strong and universal. There have been some good articles on him in the newspapers. There is an excellent characteristic (*sic*) of him in to-day's 'Examiner;' and the life in the 'Times' (written by a Mr. Dod) contained a good *précis* of his history. I see that it is to be published separately in a shilling volume. It is expected that he will have a public funeral, and will be buried in St. Paul's.

There has been a report in the 'Chronicle' of an intended Commercial Treaty between France and England; but I have not heard it confirmed from any authentic source, and it is denied in the 'Moniteur.' I fear it is too good to be true. Louis Napoleon is quietly preparing the way for the Empire; and it is expected that before next spring he will have procured a vote from the electors declaring him Emperor.

Nearly 250 copies of my book have been disposed of; which, considering the time of its publication and its subject, is, I think, a great success.

* * * *

Ever yours sincerely,
G. C. Lewis.

Grove Mill House: Nov. 13, 1852.

My dear Head,—Our two first letters crossed on the way, and I have since had the pleasure of receiving your letter of October 18. I have deferred writing to you until the meeting of Parliament, thinking that there would be something important to write about; but the passage in the Queen's Speech about free-trade is oracular and evasive; and the debate showed nothing except that the Free-Trade party were united and determined. Lord Derby's declaration as to the abandonment of Protection was complete and conclusive; all that now remains is, to see how they will deal with Charles Villiers's motion, and what Disraeli's Budget will be. I own that I am exceedingly curious to see what they will propose, for their surplus is not likely to exceed a million, if it amounts to so much; and I am quite at a loss to know what they can propose which will give any relief or satisfaction to the agriculturists. They *must* try to do something for their clients; and if there is not the reality, there must be the appearance.

There is among well-informed persons now a great alarm and mistrust as to the designs of the President and the probable deficiency of our defences. My own belief is, that he is at this moment sincere in his professions of a pacific disposition.

* * * *

There is also a very bad feeling towards us in the Austrian Government, partly on account of Palmerston's policy and partly on account of the Haynau affair. It is said that the Rhine province is disaffected to the Prussian Government, and that the population would receive a French army with open arms. All these are ugly symptoms, and my belief is that our relations with the continent have never been so bad or so insecure since 1815. All the great Powers are now despotic; and as England is the only exception, its position is the more invidious. It is now the *only* place where truth can be heard and where political refugees can obtain an asylum. When France was an accomplice with us in this offence against the other Powers, the guilt was less.

I have heard nothing new from Peterborough since I wrote to you. Whalley is still a candidate; no Tory has come forward. The writ cannot be moved before the 26th, and the election will take place on one of the early days of December. I do not feel sure of the result, though it would be very bad luck if I were the first to be beat. I believe that the Herefordshire petition is to be prosecuted, but I have heard nothing final.

* * * *

Ever yours sincerely,
G. C. LEWIS.

Kent House: Dec. 12, 1852.

My dear Head,—I have lately returned from a most disappointing journey to Peterborough, having been beat by a majority of fifteen. * * * The debate which took place on Charles Villiers' motion* is quite intelligible from the newspaper report. The passage in the Queen's Speech on free-trade was studiously ambiguous, and rendered a parliamentary declaration on the subject necessary. A moderate resolution had been prepared by Graham, and assented to by Lord John and Gladstone. Charles Villiers was willing to move it, but Cobden insisted on something stronger, in the secret hope that the House would reject it, and thus damage itself in public opinion, thereby promoting the cause of parliamentary reform. Palmerston got possession of the resolution prepared by Graham, and moved it as an intermediate proposition. The House, not wishing to turn out the Government before they proposed their Budget, agreed to this course. It was fortunate that the decision went this way, for it would have been most unwise to prevent the appearance of the Budget, which has since seen the light. The complete and definitive throw over both of Protection and

* In February 1852, Lord John Russell resigned, and was succeeded as Prime Minister by the Earl of Derby. In August the Parliament was dissolved, and a new Parliament assembled on November 4. The reference in the Queen's Speech to free-trade being considered ambiguous, Mr. Charles Villiers subsequently moved resolutions pledging Parliament to a free-trade policy. *Annual Register* for 1852, p. 120.

local burdens must loosen the hold of the Government upon the agricultural body, and upon this their chief strength depends. The farmers do not care much about the repeal of half the Malt Tax, but the extension of the Income Tax and the doubling and extension of the House Tax are unpopular all over the country, and particularly in the towns. It is by no means improbable that the Government may fail in carrying their Budget,* and, considering the flourish of trumpets with which it was ushered in, they can hardly in that case avoid going out.

* * * *

The floods have been dreadful; half the country has been under water.

Ever yours sincerely,

G. C. Lewis.

Sir George Lewis, no longer in Parliament, now occupied himself with literary business, and consented to become Editor of the 'Edinburgh Review.'

Lord Derby's brief Government terminated in December 1852. He was succeeded by Lord Aberdeen; but though Sir George Lewis would willingly have been re-elected to Parliament, had any opportunity favoured his obtaining a seat, he had no disposition for another public office. He expresses himself to that effect in the following letter:—

Kent House: Jan. 2, 1853.

My dear Head,—Since I wrote to you last, two events have happened, of which one is important to me individually, the other is important to the public at large. One is, that I have accepted the Editorship of the 'Edinburgh Review;' the other is, that there has been a change of Government.

* Right Hon. B. Disraeli was Chancellor of the Exchequer.

About three weeks ago poor Empson died, and Longman asked me to be his successor. There is a good deal of work to be done, but it is unaccompanied with the drawback of attendance at an office; and, situated as I was, I thought it wisest to accept. I shall try, if I can, to get a seat in Parliament; but if I was in Parliament, and had an offer of office, I should refuse it, as the work of an office is incompatible with my present employment. Empson left the January number in an incomplete state, and I have been working very hard for the last fortnight in completing the arrangements for bringing it out. I am in hopes that you will be inclined to give me some help—any article on an American subject would be acceptable. There are some new American novels on 'Life in the West,' which are said to be interesting. No review of such a book is worth anything unless it is written by a person who knows something about the life which is described. There was to have been an article on 'Uncle Tom's Cabin' in the January number, but the writer was unable to finish it in time.

With respect to the change of Government, you will have seen in the newspapers all that is material. There was no real anxiety on the part of the Opposition to turn out the Government; the sections of it were divided, and there was none of that 'coalition' which Lord Derby spoke of. The Budget, however, was more than human flesh and blood could bear. The promises of a substitute for Protection which Disraeli had made at the elections, rendered it necessary that the Government should propose something which appeared for the benefit of the agriculturists. They sounded some of their supporters among the county members as to a transfer from the local rates to the

Consolidated Fund; but I believe the answer they got was, that a measure which destroyed the power of the magistrates and the local authorities would not be acceptable to their party. They had nothing, then, to propose but a reduction of the Malt Tax, which created a large deficit, and rendered an increase of taxation necessary. This latter object was effected by doubling and enlarging the House Tax. Disraeli was evidently very confident of the success of his Budget, and impatient to produce it. But when it had been out a week, it was clear that the country would not agree to it. The farmers did not care about the reduction of the Malt Tax: but the towns did care very decidedly for the increase of the House Tax, and showed a strong objection to it. The Government made an energetic whip, and pressed every vote that could be obtained. The proposition was, however, unpopular, and they were beat by nineteen in a very full House. Having made their Budget a means of redeeming their promise to give their party an equivalent for Protection, they could not modify it, and therefore defeat upon it was vital. Lord Derby immediately resigned, and the Queen sent for Lord Lansdowne and Lord Aberdeen. Lord Lansdowne had the gout, and could not go to Osborne. Lord Aberdeen was then sent for alone, and he undertook the formation of a ministry composed of Peelites and Whigs. Nothing can be better than the list of names. All that is doubtful is the number of *votes*.

* * * *

My wife has had a bilious fever, which has kept her in bed a long time, but she is now, I am happy to say, beginning to recover.

Ever yours sincerely,

G. C. L.

Kent House: March 26, 1853.

My dear Head,—I am quite ashamed to think how long it is since I have written to you. I have three letters of yours to acknowledge, which I had much pleasure in receiving. There has been nothing, however, very interesting to write to you about, and I find that my Review work compels me to write so many letters of a quasi-official sort, that I have been remiss about all others. I have to keep a sort of office, without any clerks. There will be some good articles in the next number of the Review; but it will be chiefly political, not literary. There is great difficulty in finding persons who can write well on literary and general subjects. Besides, my acquaintance lies chiefly among politicians. There is to be a good review of Alison's recent trashy 'History,' and also an estimate of Disraeli's political career; an amusing article moreover on the 'Welsh Clergy,' by Conybeare, a son of the Dean of Llandaff, now vicar of Axminster. There will also be articles on 'Education' and the 'Income-Tax.' I shall be glad to know what you think of the number, as it is the first number really edited by me. If you wish, I can send you a copy. The only interruption to the monotony of my life has been a visit to Oxford, where I went in order to examine for the Ireland University Scholarship. I was asked to accept, and thought it right to go, although it cost me a good deal of trouble, and came at an inconvenient moment. I was disappointed, on the whole, by the exhibition made; some of the mistakes made even by the best men were amazing, and there was no great talent displayed by any one. Butler, a scholar of University, son of the Dean of Peterborough, a Rugby man, was the successful candidate. All the best men belonged to Balliol or University, and their eminence proves the success of the system of open scholarships, which must gradually spread to all the Colleges. Christ Church and Brasenose have lost all their distinction as places of learning, and Oriel is not very eminent.

Gladstone's connection with Oxford is now exercising a singular influence upon the politics of the University. Most of his High Church supporters stick to him; and (insomuch as it is difficult to struggle against the current) he is Liberalizing them, instead of their Torifying him. He is giving them a push forwards, instead of their giving him a pull backwards. As he has just joined a Whig ministry (for such it is, in fact), this is the critical moment. If he does not move, his Oxford friends must either follow him or separate from him. *In general*, they have chosen the former alternative.

* * * *

The chief point which the most ultratractarians now contend for is *confession*, but the bulk of the party are merely very high-churchmen. They are against Rome and its distinctive tenets, but wish to have a powerful hierarchy, with extensive powers and exalted position of bishop and priest, great funds at their disposal, mute acquiescence on the part of the laity, and so forth; but no union with Rome. There is a Tutors' Association at Oxford, where speeches (and very good ones, too) are made. The Commission has stirred up the University, and I see that the University has new life in it. Among the junior tutors there is a well-marked Liberal party; small in numbers, but strong in talent, and evidently not timid. I expect to see great changes in Oxford before ten years are over. I have begun to read Lord

Grey's book,* which has been favourably reviewed by the newspapers, and is well spoken of. It is written in a conciliatory tone, and all controversy is, as much as possible, avoided.

Ever yours sincerely,

G. C. Lewis.

P.S.—What do you think of writing an article for the 'Edinburgh' upon the following work: 'Histoire du Canada depuis sa découverte jusqu'à nos jours'? par Garneau; three vols. 8vo: Quebec, 1852. It would be in time if ready for next summer. G. C. L.

Kent House: April 26, 1853.

My dear Head,—I have just received your letter of the 4th, and I had previously received your letters containing the information about the Spirit Law, for which I was much obliged. I sent the account of the Spirit Law to Conybeare, who has used it for an article on 'Teetotalism.'†

There is no occasion for you to be in any hurry about the Canada article. You can defer it till you return to England, and we can get over the book from Quebec. Nobody thinks of anything now but war, and all eyes are turned Eastward. The colonies are so well governed and behave so well that nobody thinks about them.

I shall be very happy to see you again in June. I do not understand that there is any intention of recalling you, and I presume that you may prolong your stay as long as you wish it. Do you intend to bring away your things in June, and to break up your establishment, so as to leave yourself no option of return-

* 'The Colonial Policy of Lord John Russell's Administration,' by Earl Grey. 2 vols. Bentley, 1853.

† *Edinburgh Review*, vol. c. p. 44.

ing? The Duke of Newcastle seems to take a long time about filling up vacant Governments. With respect to the stability of the present Government, which must be an element in all your calculations, I should say that, now that the Reform Bill is given up, the chances are that it will last till the beginning of another session. There is no strong party at present ready to take the Government, and therefore the object will rather be to discredit, to damage and to undermine, than to turn out.

* * * *

You doubtless saw the fate of the Poor Settlement Bill. Palmerston made an indiscreet promise about Irish removals, which alarmed the English members, and the Bill was virtually thrown out for this session. The plan of a Union rate (which is very much borrowed from your article) has also offended many of the country gentlemen. The abolition of removal simply is (as is natural) chiefly opposed by the members for large towns. I see that there will be great difficulty in carrying the measure, but I am told that the House would agree to reduce the term of irremovability from five to two years. This would make a great practical difference.

We have just completed our report on the City of London, and are to sign it this week. We recommend a plan for dividing the entire metropolis into municipalities, which will be attended with important results, if it is ever carried into effect.

I suppose that the weather in America and that in England have little to do with each other. We had severe cold with much snow in December and the first part of January, but since that time the season has been unusually fine, particularly March and the first half of April. I have little domestic news to tell you. There has been the usual allowance of influenzas, coughs, etc. Mrs. Villiers has been confined several weeks to her bed, but is now recovered. Addington has lately retired from the Under Secretaryship of the Foreign Office, and has been made a Privy-Councillor. His successor is Hammond, a senior clerk in the Office. Milman has just published a 'History of Latin Christianity,' i.e. a history of the Western Church, in three vols. It comes down to about 1300. My best regards to Lady Head. Your reign seems a very peaceable one.

Ever yours sincerely,

G. C. LEWIS.

Sir George Lewis's next letter is to his friend Mr. Greg, whose frequent contributions to literature he continually read with satisfaction and interest.

Sir George Lewis to W. R. Greg, Esq.

Kent House: June 10, (probably) 1853.

Dear Greg,—

* * * *

C. Wood's* Indian speech reads well as a history of internal administration of India. The subject of the Government does not seem to me to have been well discussed hitherto. Every Government of a dependency is of a necessity a double Government. There is a local element and an imperial element to be reconciled. Where there is a white population in the colony we give them a local legislature, as in Canada. The local element is then provided for by the local body in the colony. The imperial element is provided for by the Governor plus the Colonial Office, together with occasional legislature in Parliament. This is, to all intents and purposes, a double Government, in which

* Now Viscount Halifax.

the constituent elements are constantly coming into collision, unless care and forbearance is exercised.

In India the people are not sufficiently civilized and intelligent to admit of this solution of the problem. They belong to the coloured races, and when they were independent they were always governed despotically. There cannot be a Hindû House of Assembly. Nevertheless, there is a local element in Indian Government which must be provided for. According to the present system, the Directors,—who are chosen by the proprietors of Indian Stock, and are supposed to be acquainted with the circumstances of India, to have been servants of the Company, or to have dwelt there—represent the local element. How far they may do this effectually or satisfactorily, is a question open to debate; but it seems to me that the present form of *double* Government for India is an attempt to solve a problem which *must* be solved in one way or another for *every* dependency. The interference of Parliament is no solution at all; for Parliament has no local knowledge or interest, and it represents the imperial element as much as the President of the Board of Control.

I am afraid that the prospects of the *wheat* harvest are very bad.

Ever yours truly,

G. C. Lewis.

Kent House: July 31, 1853.

My dear Head,—

* * * *

The Government has gone on successfully on the whole; the Budget and the India Bill have been the two questions of the session. Gladstone has managed the former admirably; but his measure for altering the interest of the debt has failed, in consequence of the recent fall in the funds. The tax on the succession of real property was generally popular; and the Lords, though Lord Derby did his best to whip up his party, were afraid to throw out the Bill. The India Bill is, I believe, the best measure which could have been proposed. It prepares the way for a gradual extinction of the Company, which will come at last, and when it comes will be no great improvement.

The Russian question is still unsettled. My belief is, that the Emperor will not this time attempt to march against Constantinople, and that, after keeping his troops in Moldavia and Wallachia for a time, he will make some agreement and evacuate them. What has taken place will give a shake to the Turkish Empire, will have loosened its cohesion, will have displayed its weakness, will have unsettled men's minds and have prepared them for a more decisive catastrophe hereafter. All this is a decided gain to Russia, without going farther. At the same time, the language of the Emperor is still unfriendly and was recently threatening, and it is dangerous to predict what his course may be if anything should occur to irritate or offend him. Russia is, after all, a semi-Oriental country, and we must not expect it to act in perfect accordance with European maxims of policy.

* * * *

The camp at Chobham has been a subject of great interest this year, and numbers of people have been to see it. There has been a good deal of grumbling among both the officers and the soldiers about the wet and hardships, merely in order to play at soldiers. The season—an unusually wet one—has been unlucky, but I believe the game has been worth the candle. During the last few days the principal topic has been the secession of the cabmen to the Mons Sacer. The Government measure was, in my opinion, hasty and ill-considered, and I believe that the cab proprietors had a real grievance, which might by proper precautions have been prevented.

I shall be anxious to hear an account of your life in the woods; the effects of your accident* will, I hope, gradually wear off. Our best regards to Lady Head.

Ever yours sincerely,
G. C. L.

Sir George Lewis to W. R. Greg, Esq.

Kent House: Aug. 1, 1853.

My dear Mr. Greg,—My views as to the Voting Paper question agree very much with the letter of Mr. Enfield. I fear, too, that the letter from Leeds correctly describes the working of the system under the operation of strong party spirit. If properly-paid collectors were employed by the returning officer, opportunities for fraud would be less; but I fear that with ignorant and illiterate voters all sorts of tricks would be played. Friends and agents of the candidate would get access to the voting paper before it was returned to the collector, and would write upon it, and so render it unfit for use. It would be necessary to enable the voter to obtain a *second* paper; and this permission would create all sorts of questions. Great difficulty would likewise be experienced in construing Clauses 8 and 12 of the Bill. It is not stated that the collector must receive the paper from the voter, or from his servant or agent, or even at his house. How,

* A fall from his horse, by which he was much bruised and had a rib broken.

therefore, would the 'default' mentioned in Section 12 be determined before four o'clock? Anybody, so far as I see, might deliver it to the collector, wherever he might be, before the clock struck *four*. It is scarcely possible to exaggerate the ignorance and helplessness of some of the poorer class of voters in the backward part of the country. My belief is, that the system is impracticable where there is strong party feeling and large funds for the purposes of corruption and intimidation. This conclusion has, however, been forced upon me by facts, contrary to my wishes; for I should gladly see the mode of voting in question extended to parliamentary elections. It solves the problem of treating, which cannot, as far as I see, be solved in any other way, and it is an effectual solution.

* * * *

Ever yours truly,

G. C. Lewis.

Worcester: Sept. 14, 1853.

My dear Head,—

* * * *

I have had lately the offer of the Government of Bombay, which was made me in a flattering manner by Charles Wood. It was, however, impossible for my wife to leave Mrs. Villiers, and there was a difficulty about taking Alice;* so that I decided at once, on domestic grounds, to refuse. I was not personally much tempted by the offer, notwithstanding the large amount of the salary. India is an interesting field, especially at the present moment; but it would have cut short a great many threads which I have begun to spin. I therefore remain constant to the 'Edinburgh Review,' and am just about bringing

* Miss Alice Lister, Lady Theresa Lewis's second daughter.

out another number. We passed nearly the whole of the month of August at Harpton, and are now staying a few days with the Cradocks* at Worcester, after having made some Herefordshire visits. We intend to be at Kent House in about a week, which will enable me to perform the obstetrical services for the October number of the Review. The article on the 'Income Tax' in the April number, to which you refer, was written by no other person than ——. I had a great deal of bother with his illegible scraps of MSS., but it contained much solid thought and analysis, and the actuaries who were so roughly handled, and who more or less humbugged the Committee, never ventured to reply to it. The tone of the article was suggested by me, but all the detail was worked out by —— himself. * * * Everything is in a perplexed state at Constantinople. Russia is ashamed to recede, but afraid to strike. The Turks have collected a large army, and have blown up their fanaticism, and, reckoning on the support of France and England, are half inclined to try the chances of war. France and England are desirous of peace. I think that both parties are in the wrong—Russia in making unjust demands; Turkey in resisting a reasonable settlement.

War is quite on the cards, but I still persist in thinking that it will be averted, unless some accidental spark fires the train.

The harvest will be pretty well got in, but will be *under* an average.

Ever yours sincerely,

G. C. Lewis.

* Dr. Cradock, now the Head of Brasenose College, Oxford, and Mrs. Cradock, Lady Theresa Lewis's sister-in-law. Dr. Cradock was at that time a Canon of Worcester.

Kent House: Oct. 7, 1853.

My dear Head,—Since I wrote to you I have been staying a few days at Birmingham, and also made one or two visits in that neighbourhood; and we returned to town towards the end of September, in order that I might bring out my October number, which is now, I am happy to say, accomplished. There are some good articles in it, but too long.

Prolixity is the *bête noire* of an editor. Every separate contributor has some special reason for wishing to write at length on his own subject.

* * * *

The Turkish question is now approaching a crisis, and the Derbyites are sanguine that it may break up the Government and let them in again. The position in which we are placed is a very complicated one. Russia has acceded to the terms which we proposed, and Turkey has put herself in the wrong, so far as we are concerned, in this particular quarrel. Yet we are called upon to assist Turkey in a war against Russia, in order to prevent Constantinople from becoming Russian. France has behaved very well throughout the whole dispute, and has shown no disposition to make terms for herself by playing a separate game. The Danube is now the only security for peace; neither army dares to cross it, and while this broad river rolls between them, there can only be a *constructive* war, and negotiation may still be effectual. Even now I do not despair of peace, though the chances are greatly diminished. I think it possible that I may attend the annual dinner at the Hereford fair on the 19th, which will give me an opportunity of sounding the Protectionist feelings of the farmers. I hear that they have finally abandoned all idea of recovering a Corn Law, but some of the ex-Protectionists have, I fear, cast only the protection slough, and remained Derbyites, having previously been Liberals.

On the 21st, the first meeting of my City Commission is to be held. Labouchere and Sir John Patterson are my colleagues. The principal object seems to be to throw the municipal franchise open to a larger number of persons. My father and Lady Lewis are at Harpton; Gilbert is at Monnington; his little girl has lately been unwell, and it will be necessary to take her to the sea-side. We have had one of the wettest and darkest, though not one of the coldest, summers I remember; at the same time the amount of heat has been small. The harvest will, in many parts of the country, be deficient by a third or a fourth. With my best regards to Lady Head.

Ever yours sincerely,
G. C. Lewis.

Kent House: Oct. 14, 1853.

Dear Mrs. Grote,—I agree with all you say about John Mill's article, and I hope that Grote will think as you do; at the same time, I could have wished that he had said a little more about the volumes which he was reviewing. I rejoice to hear of the steady sale of the work, but I would not print more than will supply the market until an edition in eight volumes can be brought out. I am in favour of stopping at the death of Alexander, and of making the continuation a separate work. I have often talked to Grote about this continuation, which ought, in my opinion, to include all the civilized world of that time—Italy, Spain, Carthage, Greece, Asia, Egypt. This would be really interesting; but what is called the history of Greece—from Alexander to the taking of Corinth—cannot be made interesting or instructive if treated by itself. Witness Thirlwall's volumes for this period.

I think that you ought to notice volumes five and six of Moore. They will be sent to you as soon as published. The article* ought to appear in January; if it is postponed longer, Croker will be as much forgotten as the Talmud. I do not think that a regular biography is needed, but, above all, pray study brevity, for people will not read long articles, however good. I am writing on 'Fox.'

Ever yours sincerely,
G. C. LEWIS.

Kent House: Dec. 1, 1853.

My dear Head,—

* * * *

The article on 'Church Parties' is by Mr. Conybeare, the son of Conybeare, Dean of Llandaff, who wrote a volume on 'Geology.' He is a very clever writer, and his article has made a great sensation in the ecclesiastical world. The extremes of all parties dislike it. The 'Reform' article has also been much read. The review of Grote is by John Mill.

My time during the last month has been principally occupied with an enquiry into the affairs of the City of London, of which there have been long reports in the 'Times' and other papers. The subject has excited more interest than I expected; we found ourselves compelled to admit the reporters, and as the newspapers have plenty of space during the recess, they have been

* 'On Moore's Life,' by Lord John Russell. *Edinburgh Review*, vol. xcix. p. 494.

glad to fill it up with evidence on a subject which concerns so many persons. It is evident to me that the City have continued their old system just a little too long, that public opinion among the great body of the community has got ahead of them, and that when the exposure has arrived they find themselves with scarcely a friend out of their own ranks. They are like Louis Philippe when the day of adversity and trial is come: they have nothing to look back upon but a long course of selfish and sordid conduct, and there are no acts which enlist any public sympathy in their favour.

The Eastern question still drags its slow length along. No subject ever produced so much writing; so many despatches, projects, proposals, mediations, suggestions, couriers, and telegraphic despatches. The electric telegraph is a most fertile mother of lies. It has added to the number and currency of false reports immensely. The principal feature of the present phase of the question is, that Turkey desires war. Her Government is in almost a desperate state. Her finances and internal affairs are in hopeless confusion; and the Divan wish for a war, in order that they may involve France and England in it, and that, when the kettle has been stirred, something may come out of it for the benefit of Turkey. A desperate policy is always a bad policy, and such is now the policy of Turkey. My own belief is, that England has little or nothing to fear from a Russian occupation of Constantinople, but this is a heresy which it is scarcely safe to utter.

A Reform Bill is on the anvil, and will, I suppose, be announced in the Queen's Speech, and introduced early in the session; whether it is lost or carried, it will probably produce a dissolution next summer.

* * * *

I have been writing a review on the 'Memoirs of Fox.' I shall have much pleasure in reading your *Abhandlung* on 'Shall and Will.'* You should dedicate it to the Scotch and Irish nations.

Ever yours sincerely,

G. C. LEWIS.

Kent House: Jan. 4, 1854.

My dear Head,—I wish you and Lady Head a happy New Year. All Januarys are, I suppose, equally cold at Fredericton; but we have already had an extra allowance of winter, and every prospect of its continuance. Since I last wrote to you there has been the strange escapade of Palmerston. He disliked the Reform Bill, partly as being too extensive to suit his taste. He therefore resigned, solely upon this measure; but he probably expected that a threat of resignation would bring his colleagues to terms, and was surprised at being taken at his word. When he was out, he found that the country took his resignation very coolly, and that he was so much courted by the Derbyites that he could not avoid becoming their leader in the House of Commons in the next session. He could not hope to occupy a neutral place; and so, finding that his position was a bad one, that it was too late in life for him to set about forming a new party, he changed his mind, and intimated to the Government that he wished to return. His colleagues were glad to take him back, and so the affair was patched up.

Everything in the East looks warlike; and if our fleet

* 'An Essay on *Shall and Will,*' by the Right Hon. Sir Edmund W. Head. First edition published by Murray in 1856; second edition published by Murray in 1858.

does not come into conflict with the Russian fleet, it will be next to a miracle. My expectation is, that before long England and France will be at war with Russia; and as long as war lasts all measures of internal improvement must slumber. The Reform Bill must remain on the shelf, if there is war; for a Government about to ask for large supplies and to impose war taxes cannot propose a measure which is sure to create dispersion and to divide parties at home.

I have just finished my January number, in which there are some good articles, including that on the 'Ottoman Empire;' the review of 'Fox's Memoirs' is by me. In the next number but one there is to be an article on '*Teetotalism*;' and I have promised the author of it to ask you for information respecting the New Brunswick Liquor Law, as well as the similar law in Maine. Are these measures effectual? and do they really prevent spirit drinking? If there is anything in print on the subject which you could recommend, perhaps you might be able to send it to me.

I expect before long to hear of your being able to fix some time for coming to England. Political prospects are uncertain in the extreme, on account of the imminence of war. If war is averted, there will be a Reform Bill, which is likely to lead to an early dissolution. If war arrives, the Reform Bill and all other similar measures likely to produce party struggles and divisions must be postponed. This is all I can tell you by way of guiding your conduct: I am sorry that it is not more definite.

Ever yours sincerely,

G. C. Lewis.

Kent House: March 4, 1854.

My dear Head,—I have had the pleasure of receiving your two letters, and am much obliged to you for the documents relating to Temperance, which I will use as you desire. They give exactly the information which I wanted. The result is just what might have been anticipated, but it is extraordinary that such a prohibition should ever have been enacted. I shall be much obliged to you if you will write such an article on Canada as you describe; a view of its present state and prospects, with only slight references to its early history, would suit the 'Edinburgh Review' best. Both the last numbers were out of print almost immediately. The next number will be ponderous, unless it is redeemed by an excellent article on 'Mormonism,' by Conybeare.

The war still hangs fire in an extraordinary manner; but as a messenger was sent to St. Petersburg last week with an ultimatum, the uncertainty must soon be dissipated. Our Government have no hope of peace; but the Emperor will fight with tremendous odds against him, and one does not see where his hope of success lies. What is singular in this matter is, that the French Government are not eager for war and the French people do not take it up warmly. They like fighting for plunder or territory, not for the balance of power, however much they may talk of glory. The Turkish question occupies the attention of the public almost exclusively; even the new Reform Bill, which disfranchises 70 seats and almost doubles the existing constituency, has been received with comparative indifference. It was put off last night till after Easter, in consequence of the unwillingness of many supporters of the Government to vote against a dilatory motion in the present state of our foreign relations. The Government, however, intend, if they are able, to bring it on after Easter. The great difficulty about it is, that as it affects so many seats, the House will get rid of it, if it can; and the country are so well satisfied with the existing state of things, that they will not put a sufficient pressure on their members to compel them to support it. There has been much stir at Oxford in consequence of the adoption by the Hebdomadal Board of a plan of Pusey's for their own reform. It was a complicated contrivance for a combined court in certain cases. It was carried in Convocation; but the Government have announced that they will not accept it. An excellent pamphlet has been published by Vaughan, Professor of Modern History, in answer to Pusey's evidence attacking the professional system of teaching.

The remarks on 'Shall and Will' to which you allude are in an article in 'Jamieson's Scotch Dictionary,' in vol. xlvii., or No. xciv. of the 'Edinburgh Review.' I dare say I can get you a copy of it without difficulty; but when I have got it, how shall I send it to you? Will the Colonial Office forward it? or shall I cut out the article?

Baines * has proposed the abolition of the Law of Settlement in a good speech. The Bill consists of a clause abolishing removals, and half-a-dozen clauses embodying a plan similiar to that proposed in your article. The abolition of settlement can be carried, but there will be great resistance to union chargeability.

I am writing regularly on the Roman history,†

* Right Hon. Matthew Baines, Chief Poor Law Commissioner.

† 'Credibility of the Early Roman History,' published by Parker, 1855.

and have just finished Coriolanus. It is slow, tiresome work, and I shall not complete it till the end of the year. I have no domestic news. My best remembrances to Lady Head. I gave your message to Graham. When shall we hear of your intentions of returning?

Ever yours sincerely,

G. C. Lewis.

Kent House: June 6, 1854.

My dear Head,—I have received the letters about the Liquor Law you were so good as to write me, and have given all the information to my contributor. His article will probably appear in the next number. I likewise sent the extract from the old number of the 'Edinburgh Review' which you wished to have. The bookseller whom I employed took some time in finding the number, which caused a delay.

My own life has been lately of the most jog-trot order. I have been working steadily at my Roman history, and been following Niebuhr through all his wonderful perversions and distortions of the ancient writers. I have finished as much as occupies the first seven books of Livy, and have only to go through the three remaining ones. I have never moved from town.

The war continues to be almost the only subject of public interest. The papers are full of nothing else; and I hear that no subject excites any real interest in Parliament. The Oxford Bill has been much debated in the House of Commons, and the Government expect to carry it. I received only yesterday a note from Lord John Russell, saying that two members are to be added to the five Commissioners already named in the Bill, and asking me to be one of them. I have consented, although the office is unpaid, and will probably be troublesome, difficult and unpopular. The duties do not appear to begin until Michaelmas 1855. It is understood that a fourth Secretary of State is to be appointed, and that the War and Colonial departments are to be separated. I hear that the Duke of Newcastle is to retain the War Department and to give up the Colonies. It seems most likely that Lord John Russell will take the Colonies, but the question is supposed to be still unsettled. If he does not take them, Molesworth is talked of, but Sir George Grey seems to me more likely. There is a wish in a large part of the public that Lord Palmerston should be the War Secretary, but the Duke of Newcastle does not wish to give up this subject; indeed, I hear that he would prefer to retain *both* departments. The Russians are making slow progress on the Danube, and the Turks have hitherto defended Silistria with success. It is expected that some French and English troops will be moved to the relief of the place, if they can reach it in time, but the public, of course, know nothing of the future movements of the army nor of either fleet. France is quite quiet. The good society of Paris growls at the Emperor, and bears with great impatience the suppression of all discussion, both in the Assembly and in the press; but the paysans are satisfied, and there is no Pretender who is a real rival to Louis Napoleon. Austria—that is, the Court and ministry—is anti-Russian at heart, but it is restrained by prudential considerations from taking a decided part against Nicholas. In Prussia, on the other hand, both Court and ministry are Russian, as Bunsen has found to his cost. His recall has been regretted by a large number of people here, as he had become half-Anglicized.

The new Crystal Palace at Sydenham is to be opened this week with a great ceremony. I went to see it a short time ago, and it is an extraordinary erection for a private company. It will contain the largest and completest collection of casts in the world. My best regards to Lady Head. I hope that we shall soon hear something certain about your arrival.

Yours very sincerely,
G. C. LEWIS.

Knightsbridge: July 6, 1854.

My dear Head,—I had heard the welcome news of the offer of Governor-Generalship of Canada having been made to you, but I abstained from writing to congratulate you until I knew from you that you had accepted it. The office is the highest in the Colonial service, and the appointment is in every way honourable to you. It was, I have no doubt, made entirely on public grounds, from the experience of the manner in which you had administered the Government of New Brunswick and from a knowledge of your abilities and character. The duties are no doubt difficult, and the post is conspicuous; but your previous experience in New Brunswick will be of essential use to you, and you will enter upon the undertaking with every prospect of success. It is certainly a very singular accident, that a small society such as that of Merton should have sent out two successive Governors-General of Canada.* It shows the importance of the Commission to which I have recently been added; namely, that for carrying the Oxford Act of this session (for I suppose it will become an Act) into execution. I am not very sanguine

* The Earl of Elgin and Sir Edmund Head

as to the working of the Commission, and do not much like the job; but when the Bill has passed and the Commissioners have met, I will let you know more about the prospects.

It will be impossible for you to write the meditated article. When you have moved to Canada, pray send for the book of which I sent you the title (published at Quebec); and when you have had time to look at it, pray let me know if anything can be made of it for my purpose.

The Government has not prospered lately. The fate of the motion for admitting Dissenters to Oxford * was singular; I have no doubt that the division was influenced by the knowledge of the fact disclosed by the religious census published in the winter, that the Dissenters are about half the population.

The changes of office connected with the War Department had likewise a damaging effect. I believe that the Duke of Newcastle wished to retain both departments; but when his colleagues decided that the two should be separated, he made his election in favour of War. In my opinion, he chose the wrong one. Sir George Grey,† I suspect, was by no means desirous of office. He is, however, now your chief, and your correspondence will be with him. Your appointment was decided on before the change of departments; it was made by the Duke of Newcastle. I wrote him a few lines expressive of my gratification at his decision.

If the 'Edinburgh Review' travels to Canada, pray read the first article in the July number, just about to

* The division was in favour of the Dissenters. See *Annual Register* for 1854, p. 204.

† Right Hon. Sir George Grey succeeded the Duke of Newcastle at the Colonial Office.

appear. It contains a very clear and very authentic account of the negotiations in the Eastern question. You may rely on it as giving the true version of the business. The war might have been prevented if Lord Stratford had advised the Turks to *accept* the Vienna note. The article on 'Minorities' * is mine.

Pray give my best regards and congratulations to Lady Head.

Ever yours sincerely,

G. C. LEWIS.

Kent House: Sept. 21, 1854.

My dear Head,—I am lately returned from an expedition up the Rhine, and have received the two letters which you have had the kindness to write. We took Thérèse and Alice,† and, as bad luck would have it, both of them had feverish attacks, which compelled us to stop a week at Coblentz, and afterwards four or five days at that most uninteresting place Namur. We went as far as Bingen, and then turned; we passed about ten days at Bonn, and there saw much of Tocqueville, who was fortunately staying there. The alienation of the entire upper classes of Paris from the Emperor and his Court, as he describes it, is most extraordinary. They have seceded in a body, and at present there are no defections. Since our return to London, poor little Alice has had an attack of pleurisy (owing to a cold which she caught on the road), and she has been very seriously ill, and we are not able to move far from this house at present.

I am occupied in bringing out the October number of the 'Edinburgh Review.' It will contain some good

* *Edinburgh Review*, vol. c. p. 226.

† Lady Theresa Lewis's two daughters.

political articles. The paper on 'Locke,'* about which you enquire, was by Rogers, of Birmingham.

* * * *

I see that you have just been gazetted Governor-General. It was very unlucky that you did not contrive to pay us a visit, for when once you are installed in Canada you may find it difficult to get away. * * * Everybody is now waiting for the news of the landing of the Sebastopol expedition (a word, you must know, which, according to the Russian pronunciation, has the accent on the penult, like homœopathy, the unmeaning letter being accented). I hear that the strength of the defending forces is imperfectly known; but if France and England make the attempt, they must go on fighting until it is successful. Austria has played a timorous and feeble part; still she must not be confounded with Prussia, for she has committed acts of hostility against Russia, and under ordinary circumstances Russia must have declared war against her. Moreover, her occupation of the Principalities sets the English and French armies free, and enables them with safety to attack Sebastepol.

The cholera has been bad in London and created a good deal of alarm, but is now abating. It has done much harm to our troops on the Black Sea, and still more to the French.

I have just sent to the press the first part of my work on Roman history. There is a great deal of it, but it is now, I rejoice to say, nearly finished.

Our best regards to Lady Head. I hope she likes the idea of being Queen of Canada.

Ever yours sincerely,

G. C. LEWIS.

* *Edinburgh Review*, vol. xcix. p. 383.

Kent House: Nov. 18, 1854.

My dear Head,—I would have written to you earlier, if I had been sure that I should be safe in directing to you at New York. I congratulate you now on taking possession of your new government. The post is important and interesting, and I have no doubt that you will feel at your ease in it after the experience you have had. It is, I think, well that Lord Elgin * has cleared away his own remanets before he resigned.

The atmosphere seems pretty clear in America; I wish I could make you a similar report of things in Europe. It is now unfortunately too clear that, notwithstanding the delusive success of the battle of the Alma, the expedition to Sebastopol has been rash and ill-calculated. The position of the Allies is a most precarious one. Their numbers, never large, have been reduced by disease and the enemy, and they are now the besieged rather than the besieging party. Reinforcements will be sent out, but the Russian army will probably receive equal, if not greater, additions. I do not see how the place is to be taken, or how, if it is not taken, our army can be extricated and our guns brought away. It was said at the beginning that the Russians, though not formidable for aggression, were powerful for defence. In consequence of the momentary success at Silistria, we chose to disregard this truth, and to invade the Russian territory. I hope with all my heart that we may not pay dearly for our imprudence; but I cannot help thinking that the present prospect of affairs is most unfavourable. If you have got a Thucydides, or Grote's 'History of Greece,' you will find in Nicias's despatch from Syracuse a curious parallel to the pre-

* The retiring Governor.

sent state of things at Sebastopol, where he says that the Athenians, who came as besiegers, have become the besieged. It is to be hoped that the parallel will end here. At all events, Lord Raglan will not sacrifice his army to an eclipse of the moon.

What you say of the feelings of the American Government towards England is, I fear, common to most other Governments. They would all rejoice if any great calamity were to befall us. I saw Mr. Ogden Hammond; but he called upon me in September, only a few days before he was to return to America, and therefore I was unable to do anything for him. He seemed a shrewd, sensible man; he spoke very highly of your government in New Brunswick.

* * * *

I have been engaged in Review work, and in revising my book on Roman history, and getting it through the press, which is very tedious work, on account of the number and length of the notes. I expect to complete the printing of the first volume (500 pages) by the beginning of next month. My criticism is purely negative. I set up nothing of my own. One of my objects is, to show that Niebuhr's reconstructive theories are untenable, as well as the accounts which he sets aside.

Macaulay's two volumes are supposed to be completed, and are expected by Easter. Ford has lately sent me an interesting article on the 'Pilgrim Fathers, and the Early History of the United States Settlements,' written by a Mr. Lucas, a friend of his. It is very unlucky that you did not come over to England in your interregnum; but I hope that your new reign will be so peaceable that you will be able to come next summer. The Oxford Commissioners have had a meeting, but nothing has been done. I have omitted to ascertain the facts about the book you mention, but I will send you them in my next letter. Ticknor's 'Spanish Stories' are very curious.

Ever yours sincerely,
G. C. LEWIS.

Kent House: Dec. 29, 1854.

My dear Head,—

* * * *

I am much obliged to you for your suggestion, but I doubt whether there is any use now in printing an article on Canada, for the public attention is so completely occupied with the war in the Crimea and the affairs of the East, that scarcely anybody will turn his eyes to the West.

The little ante-Christmas session has been chiefly important as showing the determination of the country and of Parliament to carry on the war; but what is to be the result of this ill-advised expedition to Sebastopol, it is difficult to conjecture. Our army is in a position at present in which it can neither advance nor recede. It can neither take the town nor re-embark. The belligerents of this country rely upon the effect of fresh reinforcements. But the Russians have greater facilities for sending reinforcements than the Allies; and it by no means follows that the sending reinforcements will alter the *relative* strength of the armies. The battle of Inkerman saved the Allies from a desperate danger. If it had not been for the extraordinary bravery of the Guards, the Russians would have succeeded in occupying the heights, and in that case our whole army might have been destroyed. Even if we take Sebastopol, our object is not much advanced in effecting a settlement, for the Emperor would not negotiate. A permanent occupation of the Crimea is impossible; and if we simply dismantle the fortress and depart, it will speedily be rebuilt. It seems to me that the entire expedition is a mistake, and that, whatever the event may be, it must cost us infinitely greater sacrifices than the utmost success can compensate. I fear that we are still at a long distance from the termination of our war to promote civilization by supporting the Turks.

The clamour about the Foreign Enlistment Bill* was quite unexpected and most unreasonable. The Government only carried it by a small majority, and they would have gone out if they had been beaten.

There is a strong feeling against the Duke of Newcastle as War Minister, founded on the idea that the war has not been carried on with sufficient energy. The fact is, that the Government were urged into the Sebastopol adventure by popular clamour; that they undertook it with an imperfect knowledge of the difficulties of the enterprise; and that the military men anticipated that, if the army could once be landed, the place would speedily fall. This delusion was shared by all the world in September, and even October last; but now that events have dispelled the illusion, the people forget their own mistake, and visit its consequences on the head of the War Minister.

I am just bringing out the January number of the 'Edinburgh Review.' It contains some articles which would, I think, interest you. That on 'Parliamentary Opposition' is mine. I wrote it at Bonn, in the summer. I have likewise completed the M.S. of my

* This Bill was brought in by the Government during the short winter session; it was strongly opposed in the House of Lords. See *Annual Register*, 1854, p. 231.

work on Roman history, and have printed the first, and about a hundred pages of the second volume. It will be finished in about two months. It will, I think, place the question on an intelligible issue, whereas Niebuhr is so capricious and inconsistent as to make everything unintelligible. I had a great hunt at the London Library for the 'Grands Jours d'Auvergne,' in which the Librarian assisted, but we were unable to discover the book to which you referred. Are you sure that it was anonymous? There is no trace of it in the catalogue under this title.

I do not know whether you saw a life of Lockhart in the 'Times.' It was written by Mr. Elwyn (the present editor of the 'Quarterly'), Lady Eastlake, and Milman. It was an *éloge* rather than a biography or an impartial character.

The Oxford Colleges are giving great signs of life. Several revised statutes—or, what is the same, plans of revised statutes—have been sent in to the Commissioners, but no meeting has hitherto been held upon any of them. You probably saw that old Routh has lately died. He wanted only a month or two of a hundred years.

I am thinking of writing an article on the treaty of Tilsit and the intended partition of Turkey between Alexander and Napoleon. There is a good deal about it in Thiers' recent 'History.' I shall be very anxious to hear how you find your new proconsulate, and whether you are satisfied with the state of affairs.

Ever yours sincerely,

G. C. Lewis.

The lamented death of Sir Thomas Frankland Lewis, the father of Sir George Lewis and of the

Editor, occurred at Harpton Court, in January 1855. A short illness of two days terminated unexpectedly a life valuable to his family, his friends, and his constituents. This event caused a vacancy in the representation of the Radnorshire Boroughs, and it became necessary for Sir George Lewis to decide without delay whether he would become a candidate. It was the belief of his friends that he desired again to sit in Parliament; but during the years that had passed since his defeat in Herefordshire he had become more and more indisposed to return to active political life. His preference for literary rather than parliamentary and official occupation had increased. He disliked electioneering in every form, and the having to listen so frequently to long, late, tedious debates; and it was with difficulty that he could be persuaded to re-enter the House of Commons. Indeed, had it not been that Lady Theresa Lewis, myself, and other relatives, urged him, for a variety of reasons, not to abandon a career for which he was so eminently fitted, the probability is that he would not now have stood for the vacant seat or have entered the House of Commons at any future period. His unwillingness was, however, fortunately overcome, and, after a short canvass, he was elected unopposed.

He writes of these events in the next letter to Sir Edmund Head.

Harpton: Feb. 10, 1855.

My dear Head,—Before this letter reaches you, you will have received from Gilbert an account of my poor father's death, which took place so suddenly that I only received the telegraphic message informing me of it a couple of hours after the letter which brought the news of his being ill.

*   *   *   *

The attendance at the funeral was large—although the snow fell all the morning, with a piercing east wind—and the demonstration of respect and regard very general and sincere.

* * * *

After the day on which this mournful ceremony took place I was called upon to take steps for securing the seat in the Radnor Boroughs. I issued an address, and afterwards canvassed Presteign, Knighton, and Rhayader, where I met with a very favourable reception. The election has since taken place without opposition.

* * * *

Ever yours sincerely,
G. C. LEWIS.

Sir George Lewis to W. R. Greg, Esq.

Kent House: Feb. 14, 1855.

My dear Greg,—Many thanks for your congratulations on my return to Parliament, which was accomplished without difficulty, as no candidate appeared against me in the field, and I had not even to make preparations for a contest. My desire for office at present is scarcely above freezing point.

I wish that I could agree with you as well about foreign as I do about domestic politics; but this war has been distasteful to me from the beginning, and especially so from the time when it ceased to be defensive and the Russian territory was invaded. My dislike of it, and my conviction of its repugnance to the interests of England and Europe was only increased with its progress. I shall rejoice greatly if its future course should convince me of error. The ideas put forward in some of the articles of the 'Times' about our possible military power seem to me extravagant. I am glad that you think so too.

Ever yours truly,
G. C. Lewis.

Harpton: Feb. 16, 1855.

My dear Head,—

* * * *

The recent political changes* have produced a prodigious quantity of negotiation and parleying, but have ended in wonderfully small result, for the substitution of Lord Panmure for the Duke of Newcastle is not likely to change the course of the campaign, or to convert failure into success. I have been for a long time very desponding about the siege of Sebastopol, and I have still but faint hopes of the town being taken. The winter, however, cannot last much longer, and fighting must recommence when the spring weather begins. The numbers of the Russian army are immense, and it seems impossible that we should be able to increase our numbers sufficiently to be able to invest the town.

* * * *

Ever yours sincerely,
G. C. Lewis.

The result of Sir George Lewis's return to Parliament was, that Lord Palmerston in the course of a few weeks offered him the office of Chancellor of the Exchequer, which Mr. Gladstone had just vacated. There are many persons who will perhaps discredit the assertion made in the following letter, that he 'most reluctantly made

* In February Viscount Palmerston succeeded the Earl of Aberdeen as Prime Minister, and various changes took place in the Cabinet. *Annual Register* for 1855, pp. 207–208.

up his mind to accept' it; but that such was the fact is well known to myself and all those among his friends who were intimately acquainted with his wishes.

Kent House: March 18, 1855.

My dear Head,—Events have succeeded one another so closely with me of late, that I really have had no time to write to you. Soon after my return to London after my election, I received quite unexpectedly the offer of the office of Chancellor of the Exchequer in Lord Palmerston's Government. I had just returned from the country. I had had no time to look into my private affairs since my father's death—I had not even proved his will. I had the 'Edinburgh Review' for April on my hands; and the last part of my volumes on Roman history. I had been out of Parliament for two years, and I did not know the present House of Commons. I was to follow Gladstone, whose ability had dazzled the world; and to produce a War Budget, with large additional taxation, in a few weeks. All these circumstances put together inspired me with the strongest disinclination to accept the offer. I felt, however, that in the peculiar position of the Government, the office having been already refused by Cardwell and F. Baring, refusal was scarcely honourable, and would be attributed to cowardice; and I therefore most reluctantly made up my mind to accept. I remembered the Pope, put in hell by Dante, 'Che fece per viltade il gran rifiuto.' My re-election passed off without difficulty. I went down to Harpton for two nights, and made a speech in the Town Hall at Radnor. Since my return to London I have been engrossed with the

* A portion of this letter is printed in the preface to Sir George Lewis's historical articles from the *Edinburgh Review*, collected into a volume; published by Messrs. Longmans in 1864.

business of my office, and have hardly had a moment to spare. There is an awkward question about the newspaper stamp, which I have had to plunge into. There are also all the preparations to be made for the impending Budget, and measures to be taken for providing sufficient sums to meet the enormous extraordinary expenditure which the war in the Crimea is causing. Gladstone has been very friendly to me, and has given me all the assistance in his power.

* * * *

The prospects both of the war and of the negotiations at Vienna are in the highest degree uncertain. I can add but little to what the newspapers tell you. The Russian Envoy agrees to accept the four bases, and expresses a wish for peace. The capture of Sebastopol seems as distant as ever, unless we can gain some advantage over the covering army, which renders all close investment of the place impossible. The Emperor Louis Napoleon has been burning to go to the Crimea; and he is said to be still resolved on this move, notwithstanding the dissuasion of all his advisers. It seems, however, that his project is at least adjourned for the present. I had intended to go down to Harpton at Easter, but this will now be impossible.

Ever yours sincerely,

G. C. Lewis.

Kent House: June 10, 1855.

My dear Head,—I am quite ashamed to think how long it is since I wrote to you. The fact is, that events pass too rapidly to allow of my sending you a regular account of them as they occur; and it is difficult to know where to begin making a selection. My Budget was an alarming task, on account of the magnitude of the sum to be raised. The additional taxes were, however, assented to without resistance by the House, who feared a larger addition to the Income Tax, and thought that if they objected to my proposition taxes which they disliked still more would be substituted. I had great anxiety and difficulty about the loan, for (luckily) it had been so long since the system of war loans had ceased that the official traditions were lost, and I could scarcely find anybody to give me any information on the subject who had himself had any personal knowledge or experience. There are few persons now in office who were public servants in prominent positions during the late war. However, I contrived to avoid all pitfalls, and the loan was negotiated upon terms favourable to the public and sufficiently advantageous to the contractors. The money market was in a state favourable to such an operation; for at present there is an abundance of money, but a want of profitable investment for the purposes of trade. No wild speculations are in fashion, so that there is a run upon Government securities. The funds are high and Exchequer bills at a good premium, although the rate of interest upon them has been lately reduced a little.

I have succeeded in carrying the Newspaper Bill, which I received as an inheritance from Gladstone. The effect of it will be, that the 'Times' and other daily papers will be in the same position as the 'Athenaeum.' They will have an unstamped and a stamped edition, the latter of which will be fitted for going by the post. The newspaper press, both in town and the country, has been violently opposed to this remission of duty, which narrows the market and keeps out competitors. My belief is, that their fears will prove groundless, and that the existing newspapers will have an advantage in the new race of competition. I expect that whatever increase there may be in the newspaper circulation will be produced rather by adding to the sale of the old newspapers than by calling new newspapers into being.

You will have seen from the papers the course of the long debate on the war in the Commons. The only real part of the conflict was decided by the division before Whitsuntide, which showed that the House did not wish to bring in Lord Derby. Since Whitsuntide the debate has been resumed for the sake of enabling members to deliver their opinion on the war, but it has had no practical importance; and it ended on Friday night without a division.

* * * *

The general feeling of the country is decidedly warlike. They are not deterred by the pecuniary sacrifices which the war requires, by the burdens which it imposes, or by the small amount of national interest which it involves. They consider the campaign in the Crimea as a duel with Russia, and they will not recede until we have made our utmost exertions to take the place. The last news is favourable. The successes in the Sea of Azof must cut off a portion of the supplies of the Russian army, and the substitution of Pélissier for Canrobert is likely to have almost as important effect. Canrobert was a man unequal to supreme command, and therefore influenced by advisers who gave different counsels, and the result was inaction. Public opinion in France is generally hostile to the war, but the Emperor, who values the opinion of the army, remains firm, and the campaign will now proceed until something decisive occurs.

My book on Roman history has been reviewed in some of the newspapers, but it has not hitherto been reviewed by any competent judge. About three hundred copies of it have been sold, which, for such a book, I consider very satisfactory. I will try to send you a copy through the Colonial Office.

* * * *

The appointment of Liddell in Gaisford's place* gives satisfaction to all the reforming party at Oxford. * * * The Oxford Commission proceeds on its labours. It will throw open the Colleges, so far as restrictions of founders, kin, diocese, country, school, &c., are concerned; but it will leave the exclusively Church character of the University untouched, except so far as new Halls may be created for Dissenters. I have had lately several conversations with Lord Elgin about Canada and other matters. He seems to me a very shrewd and sagacious man.

Ever yours sincerely,

G. C. Lewis.

Downing Street: August 17, 1855.

My dear Head,—The session is at last over, and all the parliamentary difficulties of the Government have been overcome. The great difficulty of Sebastopol, however, still remains, and does not seem to approach nearer to a solution, although the news which has just arrived of the Russians having made what seems a rash attack upon the position of the French and Sardinians looks as if they found themselves in a bad state. As long as our army remains in the trenches before Sebastopol, no Government can have any stability.

* As Dean of Christ Church.

Our domestic politics are entirely dependent on the events of the siege, as they occur from day to day.

* * * *

The resources of the country with respect to taxation and borrowing are immense; the revenue keeps up well to the estimate, notwithstanding the increased rates of duties and the influence of the war upon trade. There is, however, a great difference between the present and the late war, in an economical point of view, which people in general seem to me to overlook. In the last war the funds were low, interest was high, and prices were enormously raised. Now, the Three per Cents. are above ninety, and prices are not materially affected, with the exception of the prices of grain, which have been raised by deficient harvests. The reason of this difference seems to me to be twofold. First, in the late war the continent was ravaged, and the means of exchange destroyed. The continental system of Napoleon likewise shut the ports of Europe against us. Secondly, our own Order in Council produced quarrels with neutral powers, and impeded our trade with countries which the power of Napoleon did not reach. *Now* the continent of Europe is practically at peace. Production goes on as usual. The war is a duel fought between the armies of Russia and the Allies upon a remote and barren shore. We have, moreover, had the good sense to concede the principles of maritime warfare which were asserted in the last war, and have thus remained on good terms with the United States and other neutral powers. Our present war abstracts forty millions a year from the national income, and burns it in gunpowder at the Crimea. But the sources of wealth flow as before. The production of income is unimpeded. Trade and manufactures are not obstructed. If I hold the office of Chancellor of the Exchequer in the next session, it will be probably necessary for me to produce another War Budget, and therefore to lay on new taxes. Among the custom duties it was proposed this year to modify the timber duty. I communicated with Lord Elgin on the subject, but his opinion was against any alteration. Next year it may be more difficult to resist an increase, and I should be very thankful if you would consider the question with reference to the North American provinces. The present discrimination is too large; but an addition might be made both to the foreign and colonial duties, which would preserve a certain interval.

The Queen is to pass a week at Paris, in an uninterrupted succession of festivities. The dislike of the educated classes for Louis Napoleon will probably tell upon her reception. We intend to start for Harpton next week, and to stay there a couple of months. There are, however, to be Cabinets all the summer, at which somebody must attend.

I hope that a copy of my book on Roman history will reach you.

Ever yours sincerely,

G. C. LEWIS.

Sir George Lewis to W. R. Greg, Esq.

Downing Street: Sept. 25, 1855.

My dear Greg,—Neither the Allies nor the Russians are at present moving, and it is quite uncertain what the relative position of the armies will be at the end of the fighting season; assuming, however, that by November next the whole of the Crimea up to Perekop is in the hands of the Allies, what is your plan for the future government of the Crimea? The main objection to the system of counterpoise, as opposed to limitation, was, that it was an armed truce—that it was a chronic state of war in the Black Sea—and necessitated the maintenance of fleets and armies in those regions. Would not the same objection apply to an occupation of the Crimea by the Allies? Is the occupation to be joint, by France and England? If so, on what terms is such a joint government to be conducted? Are there to be two consuls, one named by France and one by England? Or is the government to be named alternately by the two powers? Could the Crimea be handed over to Turkey? Would this be a measure in the interests of civilization, or would Turkey be able to hold it if France and England were otherwise occupied? The main object of the expedition may now be said to have been accomplished; but now that it is accomplished, the promoters of the expedition do not seem to be agreed as to the use to be made of the success.

* * * *

Ever yours truly,
G. C. Lewis.

The following letter is written to Henry Reeve, Esq., Clerk of Appeals in the Privy Council Office, who had long been a valued friend of Sir George Lewis, and who had succeeded him as Editor of the 'Edinburgh Review.'

Downing Street: Oct. 17, 1855.

My dear Reeve,—I acted on your friendly hint, and accelerated my journey to London by a week. I had previously intended to come up on Saturday next. As it was, however, it turned out luckily, for —— is come over on a sort of mission from the Bank of France; and I had an opportunity of conferring with him while he is in London. The drain of bullion upon the Bank of England has been greater and more rapid than I anticipated. It has been caused mainly by the remittances for the war, and the action of the Bank of France, to which some other accessory causes have been added. The Bank has not behaved imprudently, nor has the Government done anything which can be complained of. The balances in the Exchequer are large, and the payments have been made without pressing on the resources of the Bank. There has not been over-trading, and stocks are low. In order to act upon the exchanges, the Bank must resort to measures of a stringent kind for contracting a trade which is not otherwise than wholesome. This will produce distress, but the policy is inevitable. The high price of corn will also affect the revenue by diminishing the consumption of tea, sugar, spirits, beer, and other similar articles. I fear, therefore, that if the war is to be prolonged for any considerable time, we must look to carrying it on under less favourable financial conditions than those which have hitherto existed. The revenue and trade of the country are in a sound state. The difficulty arises solely from the drain of bullion, and from the measures to which the Bank is driven in order to counteract it.

The news from Kars * is important. It is another blow to the Russians, but it is evident that they do not intend to evacuate the Crimea without a struggle. All the recent information tends to this conclusion, and it remains to be seen whether the allied generals will be

* The Russians had attacked Kars, but were repulsed by our troops, leaving 4,000 men killed, 100 prisoners, and one gun.—*Annual Register*, 1855, p. 157.

able to expel the Russians from the Crimea before the winter.

I have not yet had time to read your new number, which seems to contain interesting articles.

Ever yours truly,

G. C. LEWIS.

Sir George Lewis to W. R. Greg, Esq.

Kent House: Nov. 27, 1855.

My dear Greg,—The number of the 'North British Review' only reached me yesterday, and I have not been able to answer your letter till to-day.

I have read your article,* but I do not feel sure that I thoroughly understand your meaning, or that I see how you would make your system march. You appear to assume that the Government is to be a Government of departments—that each man is to do what seems best to himself in his own department, provided he can carry it in Parliament, even against the opposition of his colleagues. You put the case of a Foreign Minister, now, in favour of continuing the war, and a Chancellor of the Exchequer in favour of making peace. See p. 190. Now, in the first place, it seems to me that your system would render meetings of the Cabinet useless or mischievous. Ministers would meet to dispute, and part to differ. Besides, how would it be safe to read confidential despatches before persons who were in communication with men of an opposite party, and would immediately go and disclose the information? However, I will suppose that no Cabinets were held and that each minister acted for himself, according to the best of his judgment. What I do not understand is,

* *North British Review* for 1855, article 'Cabinets and Statesmen.'

how a war could be conducted by a warlike Foreign Minister if the Chancellor of the Exchequer was peaceful. He would say, I am against war; I think it impolitic and mischievous, and I shall prepare a peace Budget. When the estimates came in from the War Departments to the Treasury for approbation, he would withhold it, unless they were reduced to a peace scale. The same argument might be extended to every other department in succession. Nearly all new measures involve some question of expenditure—new salaries, new pecuniary arrangements of some kind. Suppose that the Colonial Secretary wished to give 20 millions for emancipating the negroes, but the Chancellor of the Exchequer opposed him; he could not stir. It is this power of the purse which has made the First Lord of the Treasury the Prime Minister and head of the Administration.

In the manner in which Cabinets are now formed, he and the Chancellor of the Exchequer act together, and no difficulty arises. But if the Foreign Secretary was in favour of war, and the Chancellor of the Exchequer opposed it, and the Prime Minister supported either one against the other, the one whom he did not support must go out.

It seems to me that your plan would virtually abolish the office of Prime Minister. I do not see what power he would have with a set of colleagues who, on all the great subjects of the day, differed from him and from one another.

There is much more which I could say to you on the subject, if we were to meet. Moreover, I do not agree in your estimate of individuals. I believe the Duke of Newcastle to be a laborious and public-spirited man, and to have been most unjustly run down last winter. * * * You must remember that one of the first qualifications of a minister is to obtain public confidence; and no amount of brilliancy in speaking will supply this capital defect. Fox, and Burke, and Sheridan are remarkable proofs of this truth. It is not necessary to have a great orator at the head of each department, as you may see by looking at the list of the Cabinet in Pitt's long administration, which lasted seventeen years, against an amount of talent which, as it was at its commencement, has never since been equalled.

The French are becoming very pacific in their language, and are beginning to take a new view of the progress of the war. There is no truth in the statement that Russia has offered us terms of peace.

Ever yours truly,

G. C. Lewis.

Sir George Lewis to Henry Reeve, Esq.

Kent House: Dec. 2, 1855.

My dear Reeve,—Bright's speech, in which he proposes a heavy Income Tax upon all realized property, has revived in me the idea of reviewing a similar plan published in a work called 'The People's Blue Book,' which abounds with fallacies, and which may be taken as a sample of this system of finance. I think I could expose the whole scheme (Bright's included) in about a dozen pages. If I have time to write it,* should you be disposed to insert such an article? and if so, how soon must it be ready? I have no wish to say anything against the Income Tax. On the contrary, to the extent of seven-pence in the pound, I think it as little

* I believe that he had not time to write it. I do not find that it was published. [Editor.]

objectionable a tax as can be levied when so large a revenue is required as our present armaments demand.

Ever yours sincerely,

G. C. LEWIS.

Kent House: Dec. 13, 1855.

My dear Head,—I must begin by thanking you for your interesting letters written during your progress, and giving a very satisfactory account of your dominions.

* * * *

I have been a good deal annoyed lately by a dark spot which came suddenly in one of my eyes, and which Guthrie has treated by making me go through a course of mercury for several weeks. He has done me no good, but he has prevented the mischief from increasing or taking place in the other eye, which at first he apprehended. He attributes it to over work of eyes and brain; as to which I have considerable doubt, as I had not been working much this autumn. At first he interdicted me from reading and writing, but I have been unable to obey this injunction long. The object of mercury is to promote vascular action, and thus to produce absorption. He thinks that the spot is owing to the rupture of a small vessel in the retina, or in the brain near the optic nerve.

Poor Molesworth's end was very sudden.* His death was, I believe, caused by peritonitis, which required stronger remedies than his constitution would bear. I doubt whether he would have produced that golden age in the colonies which the newspapers anticipated from his advent; but he was a courageous man, with independent opinions, and, though not a man of business,

* Right Hon. Sir William Molesworth, Bart., Secretary of State for the Colonies; born 1810, died October 22, 1855.

might have settled important colonial questions on right principles.

There has been a good deal of uneasiness in the money market lately, on account of the large shipments of gold to the East, but at present things are quieter. Parliament will not meet before the usual time, and there will be no dissolution until the Government is brought to a stand-still. The country is still very warlike, and desirous, as it seems to me, of continuing the war, rather for glory and prestige than for any solid object. Louis Napoleon, however, and the French generally are pacific, and terms of peace have been arranged between France and Austria, to which England has acceded and which Austria will offer to Russia. I do not expect that they will be accepted; but if they are peremptorily rejected, the refusal can scarcely fail to draw the bonds closer between Austria and the Western Powers. The reluctance of France to continue the war on the present scale of expense is great and must influence our farther joint proceedings, whatsoever may be the issue of the proposal about to be made.

I found it necessary to resign my seat at the Oxford Commission, and Twisleton* has been appointed my successor—a very good choice. The recent changes in the Cabinet—Stanley and Baines—are not of great importance.

Ever yours sincerely,

G. C. L.

Kent House: Dec. 14, 1855.

My dear Reeve,—I have devoted a considerable portion of the day to the examination of Bright's scheme.

* The Hon. Edward Twisleton

The subject is essentially dry; but I think I have made my argument intelligible to anybody who cares about such matters; and it is important that a plan proposed by him, and supported by such a paper as the 'Daily News,' should be understood.

You can judge whether you think it worth adding. I am totally at a loss even to conjecture how the large sum which he states was calculated.

* * * *

Ever yours sincerely,
G. C. LEWIS.

Kent House: Dec. 15, 1855.

My dear Reeve,—Many thanks for your remarks, which are just. I have gone too far in saying that a high Income Tax would put a stop to investment, though such is its *tendency*. I will modify the passage in the proof.

In the 'Almanac de Gotha,' the 'contributions directes' for the French Budget of next year are taken at 469 millions, equal to about 18 millions sterling. This, compared with our Income Tax, Land Tax, Assessed Taxes, and other direct taxes, is not a very large sum.

I am inclined to think that an Income Tax of 15 or 20 per cent. upon Schedules A and C exclusively would operate in some such way as this. It would be a deduction from the income of all *existing* owners and holders of stock.

But with respect to *purchasers* it would operate by depreciating the value of the property. People would not invest without getting something like 3 per cent. on their money. The consequence would be, that land would sell at 20 (perhaps), instead of 30 years' purchase, and that the Three per Cents., instead of being at 96, would be at 76. As to land, it would approximate to the system of the Indian Land Revenue. As to the funds, it would be in effect a fraud upon the existing creditors. It would be a forcible withholding of the part of the annuity which had been sold. With respect to the future, the Government would neither gain nor lose—as, in case of a new loan, they would borrow on so much worse terms: the increased Income Tax would be allowed for in the terms offered.

It would have a curious effect upon the Indian debt. For the past, it would be a fraud on the lender; for the future, it would be a virtual diminution of the credit of the Indian Government, and a forced contribution of the Indian to the English Exchequer.

* * * *

Ever yours sincerely,

G. C. Lewis.

Downing Street: Jan. 28, 1856.

My dear Head,—Since I last wrote to you the death of poor Mrs. Villiers has taken place. * * * It has been a great blow to Theresa, who has lived with her from childhood in the closest intimacy.

The meeting of Parliament is now impending, and I am about to attend a Cabinet at which the Queen's Speech will be settled. The peace negotiations* have made steady progress from the beginning, and I do not see any rock ahead on which they are likely to founder. The draft of terms was prepared by France and Austria in concert, and proposed to England. It underwent some slight modifications, and was proposed, as you have seen, to Russia. When the terms were

* Sebastopol had fallen on Sept. 9, 1855.

prepared, and indeed when the proposition was made, scarcely any hope was entertained that they would be accepted. The chief advantage of the arrangement was thought to consist in involving Austria, and causing her to break off friendly relations with Russia. The Russian Government, however, wisely preferred not to take another ticket in the lottery of war. They probably thought that, after a year or two more fighting, they might have to submit to terms as much worse than the present terms as the present terms are worse than the Vienna terms. Nesselrode is believed to have been the main promoter of pacific counsels. The only point of importance which remains unsettled is the non-fortification of the Aland Islands, which we insist upon. Paris is to be the place of meeting, and England is to be represented by Clarendon and Cowley, Russia by Brunow, and France, I believe, by Walewski. When the preliminaries have been signed, the first point will be the settlement of an armistice; and when this has been agreed upon, they will proceed to negotiate the treaty. My belief is, that this will not occupy a very long time, as the subject has been thoroughly threshed out during the last year. All peaces are unpopular, and all peaces, it seems to me, are beneficial, even to the country which is supposed to be the loser. How greatly England prospered after the peace of 1782, and France after the peace of 1815! I suppose that this peace, if it takes place, will be no exception to the rule. On the whole, it will be unpopular in England, for all the nonsense of the country, which is well represented in the Press, wishes to continue the war for the sake of military prestige. In France, indeed, the peace will be popular; nor has the war ever been popular there, as it has been in England.

* * * *

As to the timber duties, all financial arrangements must remain suspended until we know what the result of the negotiations is to be. There is a deficit upon the present year which must be provided for; but the provision for the coming year, from April 1, cannot be made until we know whether we are to have peace or war.

Macaulay's book has had a prodigious success. It is exceedingly interesting, and throws a flood of light upon the period; but it is too long, and it is overdone with details. All the part about Ireland is excellent. He is peculiarly strong upon ecclesiastical and controversial questions of all sorts.

I am about to take steps for enclosing* Radnor Forest; its present state is an evil both economically and morally.

My best regards to Lady Head.

Ever yours sincerely,

G. C. LEWIS.

Kent House: April 13, 1856.

My dear Head,—

* * * *

The signature of peace was accomplished with less difficulty than might reasonably have been anticipated. Russia had suffered more than we were aware of, and was sincerely desirous of bringing the war to an end. She made concessions which, when they were first promulgated, all the agents of Russia on the continent and all the friends of Russia in England treated as out of the question. France wished for peace, in order to prevent additional expense, and to close the drama

* This important local improvement was completed in 1866.

with a triumph for their arms. Austria wished for peace, in order to put an end to her costly armed neutrality. England was content to make peace upon fair terms; but the public opinion of this country was not averse to the continuance of the war, if satisfactory terms were not procured. Clarendon has conducted the negotiations with great ability, and with acknowledged success, on the part of England: he has been both firm and conciliatory.

There is some discussion now going on upon miscellaneous topics, of which Italy is the principal. I do not know that anything of much consequence will emerge from these subsidiary conferences. The House of Commons is tolerably quiet. The Opposition are looking for an opportunity of putting the Government in a minority. Their notion is, that this can be done by finding some question on which the Peelites and Cobdenites will vote with them. A division of this sort would, however, probably lead in the first instance to a dissolution. The question which stands in the worst position at present is that of the American recruitment. We hear that the publication of Marcy's despatch* has produced a great effect in the States, and that the whole mass of public opinion is now with him. I do not believe that Pierce ever wished to provoke war, or that he wishes it now; but in picking a quarrel for political objects, and in deliberately pursuing an offensive course when all grounds of complaint have been removed, he is playing with edge-

* For an account of the dismissal of Mr. Crampton, the British Minister at Washington, and of Mr. Marcy, the American Secretary of State's letter to Mr. Dallas, the American Minister in England, on the subject of enlisting American citizens in the service of England during the war with Russia, see *Annual Register* for 1856, p. 277.

tools. People in this country are grown familiar with war; they would enter upon it more lightly than they would have done a few years ago.

* * * *

There is to be an article on my book on Rome, by Bunbury, in the new number of the 'Quarterly.' I am told that it is a qualified defence of Niebuhr. It is remarkable that Niebuhr has not yet found a champion, although more than a year has elapsed since my work was published, nor has anybody taken up the cudgels in defence of Macaulay and the ballad theory.

Ever yours sincerely,
G. C. Lewis.

The next letter is from Sir George Lewis to the Honourable Edward Twisleton, for whom he entertained both a high opinion and a sincere friendship. Other letters to the same correspondent follow.

Sir G. C. Lewis to Hon. E. Twisleton.

Kent House: June 2, 1856.

My dear Twisleton,—Many thanks for your note. The instance which you mention of Niebuhr's exaggeration respecting a book which he did not know to be a spurious* production is very characteristic of his mind. His 'Roman History' teems with cases where he has built a vast imaginative super-structure upon a foundation of error. If you would have the kindness to draw up such a note as you propose, I should be

* Niebuhr believed the Abbé Soulavie's spurious *Memoirs of the Minority of Louis XV.* to be Massillon's, and called it 'the best historical work in French literature.' See *Notes and Queries*, vol. iii. p. 401.

very glad to insert it on any future occasion when I may be able to resume the subject.

Yours very sincerely,
G. C. LEWIS.

A German professor at a College at Liége has undertaken to translate my work into German, and I shall send him some corrections and additions.

Sir G. C. Lewis to Hon. E. Twisleton.

Kent House: June 9, 1856.

My dear Twisleton,—I am greatly obliged to you for the note on Niebuhr,* and will certainly avail myself of it whenever I have an opportunity. An example of this sort, taken from modern history, will enable people to form some idea of the license of his imagination in ancient history, where the quantity of certain information is comparatively so scanty.

Yours sincerely,
G. C. LEWIS.

Kent House: July 6, 1856.

My dear Head,—I am much obliged to you for your two letters. I have likewise received your note about Ticknor,† who is arrived, and whom Lady Theresa has seen; but we have not yet met. He is to breakfast with us this week, and I shall have much pleasure in making his acquaintance. I was much interested by reading your official and private letters about your ministerial crisis, which were sent round to the Cabinet. You were doubtless right in remaining passive, and

* See note on previous page.

† Ed. Ticknor, of Boston, U. S. A., a gentleman of learning and leading position in his own country, author of an excellent account of Spanish literature, &c.

throwing the responsibility upon the ministers and the Assembly. It seems to me that half the mistakes which people make in politics arise from doing too much. 'Ne quid nimis' is an invaluable maxim for a person who is constantly called upon to act under the influence of excitement, both in himself and others. The imperfect fusion of the provinces and the necessity of a double majority is an evil which is sure to make itself felt from time to time. To a certain extent we have it at home. We are often told that an Irish measure was carried against a majority of the Irish members; a Scotch measure against a majority of the Scotch members; a measure affecting the manufacturers against a majority of the manufacturing members, and so on. It is, I think, clear that Canada is in a sound state, and that the difficulties in the way of its Government are such as admit of being overcome. It was very fortunate that your prudence and foresight kept you out of the recruiting business. If your Secretary had done as much as Mr. Howe, we might really have had a war with the United States.

I see from the Blue Book that you had an interview with Crampton and Ströbel. I should like much to know your view of the conduct of our agents in the United States—how far they gave any just cause of offence to the United States Government. You have, doubtless, read Hertz's trial. The disclosures made at that trial have been partly met by general denials, and partly by counter-evidence which discredits the character of the principal witnesses, but we have never heard precisely what Crampton and Howe did. Marcy's object evidently was not to stop the recruiting, but to get Crampton into a trap and to use the case against him as political capital. Dana's lecture on

'Sumner,' which you were good enough to send me, is very interesting. It illustrates the relations of the South and North, and their feelings to one another. People here speak of the outrage on Sumner as a proof of the brutal manners of the Americans and their low morality. To me it seems the first blow in a civil war. It betokens the advent of a state of things in which political differences cannot be settled by argument, and can only be settled by force. If half England was in favour of a measure which involved the confiscation of the property of the other half, my belief is that an English Brooks would be equally applauded.* If Peel had proposed a law which, instead of reducing rents, had annihilated them; instead of being attacked with invective by a man of words, such as Disraeli, he would probably be attacked with physical arguments by some man of blows. I see no solution for the political differences of the United States, but the separation of the Slave and Free States into distinct political communities. If I was a citizen of a Northern State, I should wish it. I should equally wish it if I was a citizen of a Southern State. In the Northern States the English race would remain unimpaired. But I cannot help suspecting that it degenerates under a warmer sun, and that a community formed of Anglo-Saxon masters within the tropics and negro slaves would degenerate. I see no reason why the pure English breed should not be kept up in the Northern Provinces and the Northern States. It may also be kept up in Australia, which has a climate suited to our race, and has fortunately been

* Extracts from this remarkable letter are printed by Sir Edmund Head in his preface to Sir George Lewis's 'Historical Articles.' Longmans, 1864.

kept untainted by the curse of coloured slavery. There is nothing in Central American questions which ought to create any real embarrassment. They involve considerations of honour rather than of interest. Many people here think that there is a party in the United States who wish for a foreign war as a means of healing their internal differences. But, query, what would happen if, in a war provoked for this purpose, England were to invade the Southern States and to proclaim the emancipation of the slaves?

The session is now drawing to a close. The division on Moore's motion * showed that there is no wish to disturb this Government for the present. The only question of any importance which remains is the Bill on the appellate jurisdiction of the House of Lords, against which the feeling in the House of Commons is strong. This will be soon be settled one way or the other, and the session is likely to be over by the first days of August. I shall then go to Harpton, and pass the rest of the summer there. Bunbury's article in the 'Quarterly' on my book was a poor performance. It was, in fact, a mere expression of dissent, with scarcely any attempt at reasoning. His defence of Niebuhr was also qualified by such large admissions as destroyed a great part of its value, and left one in uncertainty what his meaning is. The truth is, that the arbitrary mode of dealing with historical evidence which he recommends can only be judged by an actual specimen—by a sample. Show us how you deal, for instance, with the war of Porsena, or the siege of Veii, and then we can

* A motion adverse to the Government, respecting the differences between England and the United States, was made by Mr. G. H. Moore, member for Mayo, and was supported by Sir F. Thesiger, Sir John Walsh, and other Conservative members. However, on a division, it was negatived by a majority of 191.

judge of your principles. My book is to be translated into German by a certain Dr. Liebrecht, who is a professor at Liége, but a native of Germany. He is a disciple of the Grimm school, and seems much stronger in mediæval than in classical antiquities. I have prepared some additions and corrections, which I am to send to him when I have time to write them out. The article in the 'Edinburgh' is by Grote.

Ever yours sincerely,

G. C. LEWIS.

Harpton: Nov. 5, 1856.

My dear Head,—Since I last wrote to you I have been passing a quiet life at Harpton, undisturbed by red boxes full of unpleasant despatches about foreign affairs; and my chief occupation has been to correspond with the Governor of the Bank about the state of affairs in the City during the late depression, and with divers authorities on the subject of the currency (including Lord Overstone) about the renewal of the Bank Act of 1844. The political state of the country is now tranquil to the point of stagnation. The only thing that keeps us at all alive is the disputes got up by the Foreign Office, which now holds the same place in our social economy as the Colonial Office used to hold—namely, in providing scrapes, and furnishing subject for parliamentary battles. If it were not for Naples, and Bolgrad, and the Isle of Serpents, the newspapers would scarcely have anything to write about. The protection cry has been unable to resist the influence of several consecutive years of high prices of agricultural produce, and the farmers-friends at the recent agricultural dinners have had scarcely anything but the very unpromising subject of agricultural statistics to talk about. I attended an agricultural dinner * at Hereford, for the first time since my election contest, a short time ago, and was sufficiently well received. The seat which I lost might now be recovered for the Liberal party, if there was a good candidate, but the difficulty is to find one.

* * * *

The chief occupation of the Conservative newspapers has been to quarrel with one another about the true principles of Conservatism, and to dispute as to the worthiness of their leaders. The 'Morning Herald' maintains that every true Conservative ought to agree with Spooner in disendowing Maynooth. The Press complains that this question is breaking up the party, and that the party ought to follow Disraeli and its other leaders without asking questions. The fact is, that Conservatism is now little more than a name. There is no cause, and no leaders whom the party care to follow. The result is, that they are divided into various sections, who show no disposition to act together when critical questions arise.

The United States seem to me to have come nearer to a separation of North and South than they ever were before. I take for granted that Buchanan will win. The Southern States are thoroughly in earnest. They are fighting for their property. The Northern States have only a principle at stake: they will be less united and less eager. At the same time, it is not at all clear that they can continue to form one State, or rather one political body; and they may reach a point when, like

* At this dinner he expressed a strong opinion that peace might and ought to be maintained with the Northern States. Other Members of the Cabinet had spoken in an opposite sense. He subsequently urged on his colleagues a peaceful policy towards America.

a married couple who cannot agree, they may part by common consent. Each may find his account in a separation. If I was a Southerner, and if I wished to preserve slavery at all risks, I should certainly be for a separation. Some extracts from Southern papers, which were lately copied in the 'Times,' expressed in plain and naked language the doctrine of the ancient politicians, that every community of free citizens must rest upon slavery, and that the working classes ought to be slaves without reference to the colour of the skin. I think they are imprudent in holding this language. The real strength of their case and the real practical difficulty lies in the physical and mental inferiority of the negro race, and in the unfitness of the whites for field labour under the tropics. If it was a simple slavery like that of the ancient Romans—a white slave class in a temperate climate—a practical solution might be found. The phrase 'Black Republican,' which I see used by the Southern speakers, is ingenious. It suggests the idea that the Republic is to consist mainly of negroes; and the word 'black' conveys a *nebenbegriff* of something ill-omened and inauspicious.

I read the revises of your interesting essay on 'Shall and Will,' which Murray sent me, and removed one or two errors of the press. I also altered one of your German examples, at the suggestion of Professor Liebrecht, a German, who is to translate my Roman book, and who was then staying with me.

* * * *

I am about to remove to London for Cabinets and other November occupations, but I hope to return to Harpton for Christmas. I send you a list of works upon the Hudson's Bay Company, copied from the catalogue in the Colonial Office. You will probably be able to select from it what you want.

Ever yours sincerely,
G. C. Lewis.

Harpton: December 24, 1856.

My dear Grote,—I have directed a copy of some letters from the Bank Directors, about the Act of '44, which have been printed privately for the Cabinet, to be sent to your house in town. They will, I think, interest you, though they do not contain anything remarkably new or striking. They all point in the same direction, viz. the renewal of the Act and the privileges of the Bank without any material alteration. The most plausible suggestion is to increase the amount of notes issued against securities from 14,000,000*l.* to 16,000,000*l.* Even Norman is in favour of this change. The Spoonerites would approve of the augmentation, because they believe that it would increase the quantity of paper in circulation. But I doubt whether the Bank would issue an additional note. They would simply keep two millions less of gold in their cellars. To all plans for giving the Government a direct legal control over the Bank, and a power of interfering on extraordinary occasions, I am decidedly hostile. In cases of extreme necessity, they can always interfere, by virtue of that authority which is lodged in all Governments to consult the 'salus populi,' but they ought to be themselves the judges of this necessity, and to be responsible for their judgment. You have, no doubt, seen Lord Overstone's letter in the 'Times.' It prepares the minds of the public for an enquiry; but I doubt whether, when the Committees are appointed, there will be much valuable evidence to be got. I had about two hours of Tooke one morning when I was in town. He is as hostile to the Bank Act as ever. One cannot help feeling a respect for Tooke, on account of his book on Prices, but he allowed a little of the laudator temporis acti to creep out, when he assured me that the Bank directors in 1812 understood their business better than those of the present day.

I was sorry to miss seeing you when I was in town, but you were unluckily at Burnham, and I was too much occupied to be able to offer to pay you a visit.

I have been reading the second volume of Schwegler's Roman History which has recently appeared. Substantially he follows Niebuhr, but differs from him in details. It is enormously learned and elaborate, 750 closely-printed pages for the history from the beginning of the Republic to the year *before* the Decemvirate, just sixty years; a great deal of it is in the style of a historical novel.

The smallest hint suffices as a foundation for a whole scaffolding of hypotheses, which serve as links to connect insulated notices. The problem with respect to the period from the commencement of the consular government to the landing of Pyrrhus is how far an annalistic form of narrative is to be taken as evidence of contemporary records, of itself, and without any proof that such records existed. The annual consuls, if they were regularly recorded, furnished an annalistic chronological notation, as the Olympic victors furnished a quinquennial chronological notation. But are we authorized in inferring that because the events are arranged by years under the successive consuls, therefore they were registered at or near the time, or at any rate while the memory of the particular year was fresh? This is Schwegler's doctrine, and it is distinctly laid down by him in the first page of his second volume. He deposes Niebuhr's 'annals' and 'annalists' but substitutes 'chroniken' in their place. I cannot see that we gain much by this beyond another word.

Gladstone is employing his ex-ministerial life in writing upon Homer. I have read an essay of his, which is to appear in the 'Quarterly.' It is esthetic and not historical; a comparison of Homer, Virgil, and Tasso. He writes me word, however, that he is treating the historical problem.

I hope that you are making progress with your philosophers. Do you adhere to your original plan—Plato and Aristotle—and then stop? I cannot help thinking that you might include Zeno and Epicurus. However, there is plenty to be said on the great academics.

I have been sorry to hear that Liddell, the Dean of Christ Church, is advised to go to Madeira on account of the state of his lungs. Arthur Stanley is to be interred in Ecclesiastical History. The appointment is, however, a good one.

My best regards to Mrs. Grote.

Ever yours sincerely,

G. C. Lewis.

Kent House: Jan. 27, 1857.

My dear Head,—I am ashamed to say that I have allowed a long time to elapse without thanking you for your last letters, and writing to you in return. I am just now returned to London to prepare for the session, having passed the whole recess at Harpton, with the exception of a few weeks in November, when I came up for cabinets. My chief occupation of a literary kind has been the revision of my work on Roman

History for the use of a certain Professor Liebrecht, a German who is attached to a sort of college at Liege. It has taken me more time and cost me more trouble than I anticipated. The number of new publications on Roman histories and antiquities is large, and they suggest new points; and when one begins altering anything which depends on a large number of passages the tangle becomes great. The history of the Republic down to the war of Pyrrhus still remains a puzzle to me. I do not think that there is anything else like it. The annalistic arrangement of the narrative under consuls, the apparent accuracy of the record of the consulates, and the close connection between the consuls and the events, form an enigma of which it is difficult to find a solution, when one remembers the late period at which historians began to exist. To tell the truth I was not much struck with Grote's article. His plan of assuming a great difference between the regal and consular periods, of treating the regal history as fabulous and making authentic history begin with the Republic, seems to me purely empirical and arbitrary.

The chief subjects of interest now to the public are foreign policy and finance. The disputes about the Bessarabian frontier are settled and we shall hear no more of Bolgrad. The Neapolitan affair has blown over for the present. The Neufchâtel business, which does not much affect us, is settled. There remains the Persian war, of which the actual state is, that our expedition has landed at Bushire, and that we hear uncertain reports of the submission of the Shah

Bowring and the consul at Canton have also got up a serious dispute with the Chinese, and another China war is impending. The country is not very fond of these disputes, but the pugnacious spirit of the people is strong when the Government has once got up the quarrel.

With respect to finance there has been a well-sustained agitation for reducing the Income Tax to the peace standard. There will be considerable difficulty with this year's Budget, on account of the large amount of army and navy estimates, which will much exceed those of any former year of peace. The country is prosperous, and all branches of industry are thriving. George Clive's opponent at Hereford has announced his retirement, and he will walk over the course when the vacancy about to be made by Sir Robert Price's retirement occurs.

* * * *

I have not yet seen Lowe since his return from America, but I shall shortly see him almost nightly, and I will then inquire his views about Canada. Our American affairs seem to be going on smoothly. My best regards to Lady Head.

Ever yours sincerely,

G. C. LEWIS.

Harpton: Sept. 3, 1857.

My dear Head,—There are not many things in the personal relations of official life from which I derive much satisfaction; but I had real pleasure in seeing you take your seat at the Council Board,* and in thinking that I had been to some extent useful to you in the matter. No honour was ever better deserved; and I trust that you may find this proper recognition of your services strengthen your position in your Government.

* Sir Edmund Head had just been made a Privy Councillor.

I have every reason to expect that we shall be at home between October 8 and 18, and I trust that you will be able to execute your intention of making us a visit, which is now easily accomplished from Ross.

I have been reading some letters from the wife of a Scotch officer in the native cavalry regiment which began the mutiny at Meerut. They confirm very strongly my belief, that, although there was much smouldering discontent, there was no preconcert, and that the outbreak was caused by mismanagement and want of judgment in the English commanders.

Ever yours sincerely,

G. C. LEWIS.

Downing Street: Oct. 2, 1857.

My dear Twisleton,—I enclose a number of 'Notes and Queries,' in which you will find an article* illustrative of your exposure of Niebuhr's wonderful delusion respecting the historical forgery of Soulavie.†

Yours very sincerely,

G. C. LEWIS.

Sir George Lewis enjoyed the friendship of Earl Stanhope long before his publication of the 'Life and Times of Pitt;' but their friendship was increased when

* *Notes and Queries*, vol. iv. p. 173. Sir George Lewis writes, 'That Niebuhr should deliberately put a production of the Abbé Soulavie at the head of French historical literature, and on a level with the greatest histories of classical antiquity, must be considered as an indication of the predominance of fancy uncontrolled by judgment and discretion.'

† Niebuhr, in a letter to Count Adam Moltke, pronounced the spurious *Memoirs of the Minority of Louis XV.*, published by the Abbé Soulavie as the work of Massillon, to be the 'best historical work in the French literature,' and worthy to be placed 'beside Thucydides and Sallust.'—*Notes and Queries*, vol. iii. p. 401.

Sir George became also the historian of the same period in a series of articles in the 'Edinburgh Review.' And an important common interest gave rise to a correspondence, a part of which Lord Stanhope has very obligingly placed in my hands.

The next letter is addressed to him.

Kent House: Jan. 20, 1858.

My dear Stanhope,—I inquired of the Treasury authorities if it was possible to make the arrangement respecting the grant for the Portrait Gallery which you suggested, and I regret to say that such a course seems never to be followed. I am afraid that the money must remain in the paymaster's hands until it is wanted.

The article in the recent number of the 'Edinburgh Review' to which you allude is mine, and I am much pleased at finding that you consider the narrative of facts correct. I made it with considerable care and with every desire to bring out the precise truth. With regard to Pitt's sudden change of intention after his resignation in 1801, it is possible that I have not allowed sufficient weight to his feeling about the King's madness. I knew that he was often placed in a most painful position on this account, and that he was often beset by the doctors and the sons and princesses, who implored him to do nothing to agitate the King. At the same time it was impossible for Pitt to act upon the principle of humouring the King in *all* his fancies and caprices; and Pitt could hardly treat the King's objection to the Catholics, and his scruple about the coronation oath, as a monomania. I can understand Pitt, who, ill as the King had used him, nevertheless entertained a strong feeling of personal allegiance to him, being much pained by the remark which was repeated to him. Still I cannot clearly understand his change of intention, and it is an awkward circumstance his concealing it from Lord Grenville, who was certainly the second man in his Cabinet. It is certain that Pitt (differing in this from Lord Grenville) acted afterwards upon the principle of yielding to the King's strong objections unless he considered the point vital, and of not attempting to coerce him by parliamentary means. In the 'Life of Wilberforce,' vol. iv. p. 32, is a remark which Wilberforce quotes from a conversation with a 'good authority.' Pitt had told Fox that he never would force the King. This communication must have been made at the time alluded to in the letter to Dundas published by you. If I remember rightly, Pitt says in this letter that he conveyed to Fox a message to the above effect.

I have heard an anecdote on good authority that when Pitt was pressing Mr. Fox on the King, the latter objected that 'Mr. Fox was the most unpopular man in his dominions.' 'If he is so,' said Mr. Pitt, 'it is I who have made him so, and I will restore him his popularity in six months.' It is possible, or probable, that something to this effect passed between Pitt and the King; but there is a tone in this repartee which does not sound to me worthy of Pitt. He was as far removed as possible from being a vainglorious man; and anything in the nature of a boast, even if it was true, does not suit his character.

I am much flattered by your suggestion as to collecting my articles and printing them as a series; but this could only be worth doing in the event of my being able to bring them down to the Peace. At present I am fully occupied with other things; but when I have more leisure I intend to write another article in continuation.

Is there any prospect of any of Mr. Pitt's papers being published? He died so unexpectedly, that all which he had preserved must have passed into the hands of his executors.

I hope that Lady Stanhope's arm, against which fortune seems to have a spite, is becoming better.

Believe me yours very truly,

G. C. Lewis.

Kent House: Feb. 5, 1858.

My dear Head,—I had the pleasure of receiving your letter written after your return to your proconsular dominions, and was glad to hear that you had so good a passage. Since you went we have passed through a commercial crisis, mainly caused by the over-trading of the Americans, and I had an anxious week in November, when the limit fixed on issues began to press on the Bank and to threaten a suspension of payments in their banking department. The interference of the Government removed the momentary pressure, and things have since righted themselves with wonderful rapidity. We are now beginning the real session, the week before Christmas having merely been præludia pugnæ. Some of the recent appointments have given dissatisfaction, and the Government does not stand so well as it did a month or two ago. The India Bill is to be launched next week, and upon this a concerted attempt will unquestionably be made to turn out the Government. The ground chosen will mainly be *time*; it will be declared to be premature, and it will be argued that there is danger in meddling with the Government of India while the country is still in an unsettled state. It is believed that Graham will lead the van in this attack. T. Baring is likewise playing a prominent part on the same side. At first I was disposed to think that there was a good deal of force in the argument of time, but on reflection, I doubt whether much can be made of it. It may be wrong for the Government to propose the abolition of the Company, but when they have once proposed it, Parliament must decide the question. They cannot merely postpone the decision, leaving the Company hanging between heaven and earth, condemned by the Government, and not directly and distinctly supported by Parliament. This would be the worst state of things for the public service imaginable, and would tend more than anything to weaken the Government of India. The attempt will be to avoid a vote upon the *merits* of our India Bill, and to turn out the Government upon some bye issue which will not commit the majority to any line of Indian policy. I doubt whether it will succeed, but the feeling of the House will soon be put to the test. There may be objections to legislating in the midst of a crisis, but we seldom legislate when things are prosperous. Parliament and the public are inert bodies not easily set in motion; and a body like the East India Company is not easily demolished by abstract reasoning. I am satisfied that the right course has been taken, and I have little doubt that sooner or later the policy which we have adopted will triumph. I see more difficulty about a Reform Bill; for however moderate it may be, the large majority of the House will be, openly or secretly, against it, and without more popular pressure than is likely to be applied to them, they will hardly be induced to pass it. Nevertheless they will not like to get rid of it by a directly adverse vote. There is still much to be done for suppressing the outstanding portions of the Indian revolt, particularly in Oude; but I look upon it that all serious struggle is at an end, and that the ultimate result has ceased to be doubtful. I bear the Indian mutiny a particular grudge, because it was the cause of my not seeing more of you during your visit last summer to England.

Lady Lewis has been passing the winter at Rome—she complains much of the cold. Lady Gordon and her daughters are also there.

Ever yours sincerely,
G. C. Lewis.

Downing Street: Feb. 16, 1858.

My dear Reeve,—I enclose a copy of Milman's letter, which will, I think, interest if it should not convince you. I showed it to Lord Lansdowne, who believes that Pitt *did* really resign upon the Catholic Question in 1801, and he says that Fox, having originally disbelieved it, afterwards changed his opinion. There is not much difference between us, except as to the strength of the epithets by which *the opposite of high-mindedness* in Addington's conduct is to be designated.

Ever yours truly,
G. C. Lewis.

Kent House: March 1, 1858.

My dear Reeve,—I am gratified by Brougham's approbation, for he knows the history of that time. I will send him Milman's letter and will try to extract some detailed opinions from him. I think I can prove by the dates, and by the comparison of Lord Malmesbury's diary and Lord Grenville's letters, that Pitt's communication with the King through Eldon was not an *intrigue*. Milman, however, is right in saying that *Eldon* played a shabby part, and turned to Pitt when he saw that Addington would not last.

Pitt was too proud a man to intrigue, and for him to attempt to intrigue with the King against Addington was absurd. It would have been like a husband intriguing with his wife against her lover.

Ever yours sincerely,
G. C. Lewis.

Kent House: March 4, 1858.

My dear Reeve,—I send you a letter from Brougham containing his views on Addington, which are worthy of attention. You will see what he says about the dissolution in 1804.

I have made some progress already with another article in continuation of that in the last number. I shall probably finish it in another week, so that it will be ready whenever you choose to have it.

Yours very truly,
G. C. Lewis.

The first reading of the India Bill was carried by a large majority, but on February 12 Lord Palmerston resigned in consequence of an adverse division, by which his government was censured for having left a despatch from Count Persigny unanswered. Lord Derby accepted office.

In the next letter to Mr. Reeve the change of government is alluded to; it also forms the subject of the succeeding letter to Sir Edmund Head.

Kent House: March 5, 1858.

My dear Reeve,—

* * * *

Every day brings new disclosures, and we shall soon be fully informed as to the intentions of these apostles of resistance to democratic aggression, and these organs of the great Conservative party. If they go on as they promise, we can do nothing better than support them. Their reckoning will be with the gentlemen at their backs.

I suppose that Malmesbury's despatch, which is to remove a difficulty which does not exist, and Walewski's answer, which is to explain what has been already explained and was never misunderstood, will shortly be made public. The whole affair is broad comedy, but I suppose that it will be treated as serious by the country, who see that they have made a mistake and will not acknowledge it.

* * * *

Yours very truly,
G. C. Lewis.

Kent House: May 3, 1858.

My dear Head,—

* * * *

The late change of government was quite a surprise to us; we none of us anticipated it when we went down to the House. * * * The present Ministry adopted our Indian policy reluctantly, but refused to adopt our Bill. In order to gain popularity, as they thought, they concocted a marvellous Bill of their own, which was received with a chorus of laughter and was speedily withdrawn. They have since brought in some modified resolutions which, with certain alterations, will pass and become the foundation of a Bill. Their Budget has no marked feature, and is in fact a mere stop-gap to get over present difficulties.

Gladstone has lately published a marvellous book on Homer, in three thick volumes. There is a volume on the mythology, in which he traces a large part of the Greek mythology to traditions from the patriarchs, to whom he moreover assumes that Christianity was in some way revealed by anticipation. Hence he finds the doctrine of the Trinity in Homer, and holds that Latona is compounded of Eve and the Virgin Mary. It seems to me a *réchauffée* of old Jacob Bryant.

* * * *

Ever yours sincerely,
G. C. Lewis.

I insert the following extract from a letter from Mr. Twisleton to Sir George Lewis, because the next letter from Sir George Lewis is a reply alluding to the same subject:—

From the Honourable Edward Twisleton to Sir George Lewis.

Rome: May 5, 1858.

My dear Lewis,—

* * * *

I have been here twelve weeks and do not expect to leave till the first week in June, so that I am likely to have a full experience of a Roman May. I heard of you from Dr. Pantaleone in reference to some inquiry which you had made concerning the existence of vultures in these parts. I presume your object was mere information, but that you would not lay much stress on their possible absence from Rome now as bearing on the auguries of Romulus and Remus. Herodotus, I think, mentions the existence of the lion in parts of Northern Greece, where no lion has been seen for centuries, except in a menagerie, possibly, under the Romans. What a strange form of superstition is the belief in auguries and auspices; and what a dreamy state it indicates in the popular mind, when it was first accepted. Subsequently men of intellect would acquiesce in what they had been taught them in childhood. You probably know Ammianus Marcellinus's defence of it in the 21st book of his History, chap. i. It is a mere begging the question, and asserts that 'Volatus avium dirigit Deus,' without giving a particle of proof of it.

*   *   *   *

I was very sorry that you individually ceased to be in the Cabinet.* It must be a great satisfaction, however, to have been Chancellor of the Exchequer for three years in difficult times with credit and honour.

*   *   *   *

Yours very truly,
EDWARD TWISLETON.

Sir G. C. L. to Mr. Twisleton.

Kent House: May 15, 1858.

My dear Twisleton,—On the receipt of your letter of the 5th, I sent the interesting paper† enclosed in it to the editor of 'Notes and Queries,' who will insert it without delay. I have requested that the proof may

* There had been a change of Government, and Mr. Disraeli had succeeded Sir George Lewis as Chancellor of the Exchequer.

† The paper contains explanations relative to the power of speech possessed by the Confessors of Tipasa, which has been regarded as miraculous. See *Notes and Queries*, second series, vol. v. p. 409.

be sent for my correction, and when it is published I will send you a copy by the post. Dr. Pantaleone was good enough to send me some information about Italian vultures, which are still found in the High Apennines. Brydone states that they likewise occur at Etna; whether this is true I doubt. The story of the augury of Romulus and Remus seems to me to imply a violation of natural phenomena, not because vultures are unknown in Italy, but because the vulture is a solitary bird which haunts the high grounds. It never flies in flocks on the plains and low grounds. Even when vultures are attracted to the low grounds by abundance of food (as after a battle), they do not come in flights though they may be numerous. The Alban tunnel is a highly curious work, and implies an amount of labour for which no adequate motive appears. The rock is stated not to be hard, and to have been entirely worked by the chisel. There is a similar tunnel from the Fucine Lake, the history of which is known. I have a heresy with regard to the Cloaca maxima, as to which I should like to know your opinion. My belief is that the arch was not introduced into Greek and Roman architecture until after the age of Alexander, and that its occurrence in any construction is a proof of a date later than that period. Hence I infer that the received chronology and stories as to the Cloaca maxima are fabulous, and that it is not in fact much anterior to the Via Appia.

The members of the late Government have been very quiet since their resignation, and have abstained from every attempt to bring on another Ministerial change. The present ministers might have had no difficulty in reaching the end of the session. They might have adopted our India Bill as well as our Indian policy, and thus have saved themselves from the marvellous scheme which covered them with ridicule, and would, if persisted in, have infallibly led to their defeat. They might have abstained from the attempt to gain popularity with the Bright and Gibson school, at the expense of Lord Canning and of the safety of India. Their weakness and incapacity would not alone have been sufficient to overcome the various motives which induced the Liberal party to remain passive. Their determination not to allow the Opposition to leave them alone has, however, brought upon them a vote of censure, which was moved yesterday by Cardwell and supported by Lord John Russell.* The division will probably take place on Monday, and it is expected that there will be a fair majority against the Government. They threaten a dissolution, but I know not whether their threat will be carried into effect. If you have any thought of looking for a seat in this event, pray let me know. I will attend to what you say about the Suez Canal, and will see if anything can be done.

Ever yours sincerely,

G. C. Lewis.

Kent House: August 1, 1858.

My dear Head,—

* * * *

The session of Parliament has now come to a close, and I have gone through the unpleasant and not very useful task of attending the debates on the India Bill. The party connected with the directors tried to defeat the measure by delay; but they were out-voted by the union of the parties of the present and late Government, which produced an overwhelming number. As

* The vote of censure was withdrawn on May 21.

soon as the Indian party saw that they could not defeat the measure, they tried to make the best terms they could with the Government, and the Government were willing to negotiate with them, in order to emancipate themselves from a dependence on the support of the late Government and their friends. A bargain was struck, and the Government carried clauses modified so as to suit the Directors, by the assistance of about fifty men on our side of the House, who, subtracted from the Opposition, and added to the Government, gave the latter a majority. The result is, that a Bill has been passed which is substantially an abolition of the Board of Control, and a substitution of the Secretary of State for the Chairman of the Court of Directors. However, the organization of the Company and its separate existence are destroyed, and the result is as good as could be expected to be produced when a Government takes up a measure of its predecessor which it had opposed immediately before coming into office. Lord Stanley showed a spirit of fairness and a perfectly even temper in managing the Bill; but the whole matter was arranged underhand with the Company. Bulwer * is said not to be a man of business, but he speaks well in the House, and he makes upon me the impression of understanding what he is about, and of having a comprehensive mind. His deafness is a disadvantage to him in debate. I should think that, for the present at least, he will leave things to the management of the Under Secretaries. The conduct of the Government on the Jew Bill has given a shock to the old-fashioned Tories, but the bulk of the party seem still disposed to support the Government for the sake of the men, without reference to their measures.

* Sir Edward Bulwer Lytton, the Colonial Secretary.

The promised Reform Bill is a difficulty for them ahead; some think that Disraeli and Lord Stanley will insist on a strongly democratic measure, and will go out if they do not prevail. In that case Gladstone would be incorporated. I doubt, however, as to Disraeli taking any line which would produce disruption of the Cabinet.

*   *   *   *

I believe the alarm about a war with France to be groundless; but Louis Napoleon has certainly lost prestige and stability since February, and is more likely to be driven to desperate measures.

Ellice is to visit Canada, and Senior is to meet him on your side the water, but, I believe, in the States. We go to Harpton to-morrow.

Ever yours sincerely,

G. C. Lewis.

Harpton: August 11, 1858.

My dear Reeve,—I have to-day returned my corrected proof to the printer, and you will soon receive a revise. I have expunged a good many notes, but have left those which contained interesting extracts from recent works. I have likewise omitted all the remarks on the Peninsular war, and have added an ending on home policy, which is better suited to the article.* Many years ago I had a conversation with Lord Grenville on the policy of this war. He retained his opinion as to its impolicy, on the ground that we had no right to expect that Bonaparte would deviate from his constant system of crushing one antagonist before he attacked another. I had likewise conversations with Brougham and Lord John this season on the

* *Edinburgh Review*, vol. cviii. p. 290.

question; and I stated to them my views. They both differed from me, and thought that the Whigs were wrong. I am still convinced—first, that the policy, though successful, was hazardous and unpromising; and, secondly, that our patriotic feelings, combined with Napoleon's interested misrepresentations, lead us to exaggerate the share which we had in producing the downfall of 1814. I should like much to know what Guizot or Lord Aberdeen would say on this point, or how much an unprejudiced German would attribute to the Spanish war. You will observe that the question of continuing the war against Napoleon is quite distinct from the question of continuing it *in Spain*. Nobody could be more belligerent in his feelings than Lord Grenville: he stood almost alone for a time in his disapprobation of the Peace of Amiens. Yet he was perhaps more hostile than anybody to the policy of fighting in Spain. The drain of men no doubt assisted; but it was the Russian expedition which ruined Napoleon, and that failure was not produced by want of men.

I am rejoiced to hear that Pemberton Leigh* is at last made a peer.

I am thinking of an article for the period from 1760 to 1780, as a review of Massey's History, but this would be for some time hence.

Yours ever truly,
G. C. Lewis.

Harpton: August 21, 1858.

My dear Reeve,—I have not the smallest objection to your showing the article to Brougham. His remarks, if he reads it, could not fail to be instructive and

* He was created Baron Kingsdown in 1858; died in 1867.

valuable. I had a long conversation with him on the period, and I made a few slight alterations and additions in consequence of what he told me.

* * * *

I have had a correspondence with a gentleman in the British Museum about the origin of Byron's verses, 'Weep, daughter of a royal line,'* &c. It is astonishing how many incorrect explanations of them have been given, including the note in Lockhart's edition. * * * I have been looking into some curious letters of Lady Charlotte Lindsay, relating to the Queen's trial. They are not fitted for publication; but they have suggested to me that the period from 1812 to 1830 might furnish the subject for another article. There is not much new for this period in the way of private letters. Something might be gleaned from books, such as Moore's and Raikes's Journals; but, on the other hand, more could be obtained from oral information. I feel satisfied, from looking over the 'Annual Register,' that the Ante-Reform Bill period is beginning to be forgotten. Those who lived under Eldon and Sidmouth, and Vansittart and Castlereagh, would have little idea that the main object of the Liberal party during an entire session would be to bring in a Conservative Government and to keep it in when this object had been effected. This circumstance shows how much

* Weep, daughter of a royal line,
  A sire's disgrace, a realm's decay;
Ah! happy if each tear of thine
  Could wash a father's fault away.

Weep—for thy tears are virtue's tears—
  Auspicious to these suffering isles;
And be each drop, in future years,
  Repaid thee by thy people's smiles.
Miscellaneous Poems.

the character of our Government has been altered since 1830.

Froude may answer the article in the 'Edinburgh Review,' but he will not easily refute it.

I am sorry that we have no chance of seeing you.

Ever yours truly,

G. C. LEWIS.

Harpton: Sept. 7, 1858.

My dear Reeve,—Lord Brougham's notes are extremely curious and interesting, and I am much obliged to you for sending them to me. I have not, however, thought it necessary to make any considerable changes in consequence of them. Page 300. I have expressed myself more doubtingly about the proposal to Lord Wellesley in 1807. I think it not impossible that he was seconded by some of the Cabinet, as being a zealous adherent of Pitt. I asked Lord Lansdowne if he had heard of this offer, but he had not; and he said that he was sure that *the King* (who had no taste for Lord Wellesley) was at least no party to it. Horner was not a man to record rumours without *some* foundation.

Page 300.* King's consent to Fox. Lord Brougham says that the King was now helpless, but his position during Pitt's life was different. My argument is, that if Pitt had stood by Lord Grenville, the King would have given way in 1804. His position in 1804 would then have been the same as his position in 1807. What

* The pages refer to vol. cviii. of the *Edinburgh Review*, containing Sir G. C. Lewis's article on the Grenville, Portland, and Perceval administrations. This and Sir G. C. Lewis's other historical essays, first published in the *Edinburgh Review*, have been republished by Messrs. Longmans in a separate volume.

made it different was the willingness of Pitt to form a Government *without* Fox.

Page 304. I have added a note containing a reference to the facts recorded by Lord Brougham. You can judge whether you think it material.

Page 306. I have inserted a reference to the dissolution. I omitted it only for brevity's sake. Lord Brougham repeats what he stated in his article in vol. lxvii. of the 'Edinburgh Review,' p. 28, that the King had formed the design of turning out the ministry in 1806, upon the report called the 'Delicate Investigation.' I have not mentioned this suspicion, because I have been unable to find the slightest confirmation of it either in Lord Holland's book, or in the Grenville letters, or in any other quarter. I will enquire of Lord Lansdowne what he thinks of it; but I have great doubts whether the King could have succeeded, even if he had made the attempt, and the attempt would have been a dangerous one for the Royal Family, as he must have appealed to the people virtually against his own son and the heir to the throne. The King was very wary and cunning in such matters, and never made an attempt to turn out a ministry which failed.

Page 311, *note*. I was aware of the passage in 'Peter Plymley;' it is at the end of the second letter, but it does not go to the length stated by Lord Brougham. The passages which I have quoted are decisive as to the tendency of a negotiation when the ministry was *in extremis*.

Page 321. Lord Brougham thinks that Canning wished to go into quarantine for a few months, and then to return to office. My firm belief is, that he wished to succeed the Duke of Portland as Prime

Minister, and that if he could have accomplished this object he would not have retired for a day. All his proceedings at this time show clearly that this was his object.

Page 326. I have added, on Lord Brougham's authority, a statement that Lord Castlereagh voted for Lord Porchester's motion, but I am unable to verify it, as the 'Annual Register' (which is my only means of reference) does not show what line he took on this question. Perhaps you would have the kindness to refer to Hansard, and to see whether it contains a division list for this debate. The date is February 23, 1810. I heard the story about Canning taking the King's hand at the levée, and placing it on his thigh to make him feel the mark of the wound made by Castlereagh's bullet, from Lord John Russell. He told me that the King resented it extremely as an extraordinary breach of decorum—at which I do not wonder. It is to be observed that at this time the King was nearly blind.—Page 330. I have no doubt that in January 1811, Lord Grenville and Lord Grey, if they had come into power, would have stopped the Peninsular war. It does not follow from this that they would have stopped it in July 1812.

Page 341. Lord Brougham's opinion, that the Whigs were wrong in breaking off about the household point in 1812, is important, and quite accords with the view which I have taken. I do not, however, agree with him that Lords Grenville and Grey were actuated by *vanity*; at least, I am sure that Lord Grenville had not a particle of vanity in his composition. They were, it is true, actuated to a great extent by *personal* motives.

It is difficult to state the case of leadership between Castlereagh and Canning fairly. Both Lord John and

Brougham himself assured me that Lord Castlereagh was preferred to Canning upon his *merit*, and not on grounds of favour. You will observe that Lord Castlereagh's mother was a Seymour, and that he was therefore closely connected with the Hertford family. Lady Hertford was at this time in great favour; and Lord Yarmouth held a place at Court, and was much with the Prince. I believe, however, that it was not this connection which led to his being preferred, but his courage, his frankness, and other *moral* qualities which gave him an ascendency in the House of Commons. His birth and family no doubt assisted; but, on the other hand, his Irish origin was a drawback. Lord Grenville had a prodigious contempt for Lord Castlereagh's knowledge and abilities; but it is certain that he maintained his ground well as a leader, and that Canning found it necessary to yield his pretensions, and first to take a subordinate office from him, and then serve under him in the Cabinet.

I am working now at the Liverpool period, and have made a narrative of the proceedings relative to the Princess of Wales, from her marriage, which will, I hope, be interesting. The period from 1812 to 1830 is too long for a single article, unless it is made a mere dry summary of events.

* * * *

I consider the Liberal party at present to be extinct as a *party*. There is in the House of Commons a majority composed of persons holding Liberal opinions which no dissolution will, I believe, convert into a minority; but the only organization which at present exists within it is for the purpose of keeping in the Government and preventing the formation of a Liberal ministry. I see no reason why this state of things should not continue for another session, beyond which I do not pretend to look.

I consider the conduct of the Government on the India Bill to have been mean and discreditable, and I do not think that the course which they took in striking a bargain with the Company is understood by the public. With regard to Church rates, I cannot but think that the course taken by the Dissenters, in insisting on their abolition and refusing all compromise, is unreasonable, but the question has been well agitated in the boroughs, and the pressure on Liberal members is great. The feeling on our side is extraordinarily strong. I will return Brougham's notes in a day or two.

Ever yours,

G. C. L.

Harpton: September 16, 1858.

My dear Reeve,—My views upon Gladstone's book and on Homeric criticism generally differ so much from Merivale's, that I am afraid that my opinion on his articles is of little value. In the first place, it seems to me that Merivale's remarks upon the devotion by a man of business of his spare hours to classical literature apply more to himself than to Gladstone. He is the working Under Secretary of the Colonial Office, bound to give the best part of every day to his official business. Gladstone has been out of office since February 1855. During the recess his time is at his entire command. During the session he has much spare time. I cannot, therefore, admit that Gladstone can justly plead want of time, provided he chooses to devote it to Homer. In the next place, the Homeric question, as he treats it, is not a question of extensive reading. The amount of positive testimony about the preservation of the Homeric poems lies within a small compass; and for the rest, according to his method, what is principally wanted is a careful study of the poems themselves. I cannot go the length of Merivale's scepticism with regard to the uncertainty of the Homeric text. I do not concur in Colonel Mure's view of their having been written by the original poet, but I am willing to allow much for faithful recitation and to think that (with the exception of a few interpolations) we have substantially the poems in the form in which they were originally composed. Merivale's statement as to each Greek town having a peculiar version of Homer is, I believe, an enormous exaggeration, and the testimonies about rhapsodists may, I think, be explained by supposing that the poems were often recited in fragments, and not continuously. I should be willing to meet Gladstone upon his own ground, of the substantial integrity of the traditional text (which certainly is identical with what was read by Herodotus and Thucydides), but to contend that his view of Homer, as an historian and an exponent of religion, &c., is fundamentally wrong. A critique of his book ought, I think, to give a summary of his principal opinions and results, stated succinctly and in connection, so that the reader should understand what he is called upon to believe, and these should be controverted by radical objections. Merivale's attempts to identify the places visited by Ulysses with places in real geography are less startling than Gladstone's, and more in accordance with the views received among the Greeks; but I believe them to be equally chimerical. If Homer had known anything of Sicily, it is not likely that he should have been ignorant of Ætna. My conviction is, that Thrinakia, Ogygia, Scylla, and Charybdis, the Isle of Æolus, &c., are as unreal as Lilliput, and Brobdignag, and the Isle of Laputa.

Merivale is a very able man, with much reading, and he cannot treat a subject of this kind without being forcible and instructive.

*　　*　　*　　*

I cannot say that I see very distinctly what Lord —— means by saying that the Whigs want *views* as well as *leaders*. What are the questions on which they want views? The late Government explained its views very clearly about India, and brought forward a measure to which the House substantially agreed. As the Radicals wish for an entire and organic change in our institutions, and not merely a development of them, it is very easy for them to put forward *views*.

*　　*　　*　　*

What a strange book Alison's History is! Heaps of balderdash, with occasional gleams of acuteness and good sense.

Ever yours sincerely,
G. C. Lewis.

Harpton: Sept. 21, 1858.

My dear Reeve,—

*　　*　　*　　*

I have been working steadily at Lord Liverpool's administration, which I find a most interesting theme.

The materials are so ample that I have difficulty in bringing the subject within review limits, but I think now that I see my way to two articles, the one up to Lord Castlereagh's death, in 1822; the second from 1822 to 1830. Lord Castlereagh was the real Prime Minister of Lord Liverpool's Government so long as he lived, viz. during the ten years from 1812 to 1822. From that time to 1827 Canning took his place. He Liberalized the Tory ministry; and if he had lived, there would have been an amalgamation with the Whigs, and we should have had a moderate Reform Bill, without the violent break which occurred in 1830. As it was, the Duke of Wellington came in, and restored the Government to the *præ-Canningite* state. This produced Lord Grey's ministry, the reaction of 1830, and the Reform Bill. Canning likewise could have conceded Catholic emancipation without the violent blow to the public morality which its concession by Peel produced. I hope you approve of this division.

I have written a long letter to Tocqueville, to explain to him that the present state of politics is dangerous to nothing except the *morality of public men.* I have shown him how this danger equally besets both sides of the House—how public morality is equally perverted by finding excuses for supporting men who abandon their principles, and for not supporting men who act upon their principles; the motive in both cases being purely personal.

Froude is a complete historical sophist. He has undertaken to prove an historical paradox; and if the evidence will not support it—*tant pis pour elle*—it must be so forced into the service.

Ever yours,

G. C. Lewis.

Harpton: Sept. 22, 1858.

My dear Head,—I have received your interesting letter relative to your ministerial crisis, together with the newspaper containing copies of the correspondence. Merivale has likewise sent me some other newspapers containing articles on the subject. It appears to me that the course you took was right and quite successful. You gave the Opposition every chance, with the exception of a dissolution, which I do not think that you were bound to give. Since the dates of the newspapers which Merivale sent, there appears, from what I read in the 'Times,' to have been a further stage in the drama, viz. a fictitious tenure of offices for one day, in order to bring the ministers within the provisions of an Act which saves them from vacating their seats and facing a new election. I am unable from the accounts which I have seen to understand the rights of this question, which looks like a political manœuvre to keep in office a set of ministers who were afraid to go back to their constituents. If you think that this transaction is likely to lead to a debate in the House of Commons, pray send me before February or March next an outline of your case, as I might have an opportunity of saying a word upon it. Bulwer, in point of capacity, seems to me superior to most of his colleagues, and he is very competent to defend your policy. Roebuck is a likely man to take up a Canadian question; but there is no party feeling now on our side of the House, except so far as there is a feeling *in favour* of ministers. Whatever they do now is supported by the whole of their own side of the House from party feelings, and by half of our side of the House from spite against the other half.

The completion of the Atlantic cable seems to have produced far more interest and excitement in America than in England; but I fear there is some fatal defect which cannot be got over. It has been proved that a line can be laid down *unbroken*; they must now try to lay down a continuous line which will transmit messages. Money is sure to be found for so important an object.

The news from China, as to the conclusion of a treaty, is most satisfactory. Elgin will be a great man when he comes back. I see that he is gone to try to open Japan; but, as we have had no Bowring there to pick a quarrel, and no squadron to throw shells into Nangasarchi, he is not likely to succeed, unless the Emperor of Japan is influenced by the example of his brother of China. There were great differences of opinion about Elgin when he went out; he seems, however, to have conducted himself with prudence, sagacity, and courage, in the midst of very difficult circumstances, and to have earned the success that he has obtained. I never took a desponding view of the Indian rebellion, and never, since the fall of Delhi, thought that our empire was in danger. Considering, however, that the mutiny only broke out in May or June last year, and that for some months the mutineers had everything their own way, the rapidity with which all open and organized resistance has been put down seems to be marvellous. Remember that nearly all reinforcements have gone round the Cape.

I have been writing an article on our history from 1806 to 1812, which will appear in the October number of the 'Edinburgh Review;' and I am now working on the period from 1812 to 1830 for the same purpose. I have likewise begun a treatise, of an abstract political kind, on 'Federal, National, Provincial, and Municipal Government;' but there is little encouragement for works of this sort. I am thinking likewise of writing an essay to prove that the recent German attempts to interpret the Engubine tables and other Italian inscriptions in unknown tongues are frivolous and vexatious. Gilbert is at Worcester. We intend to stay here till February.

Ever yours sincerely,

G. C. Lewis.

Mr. Hayward has been obliging enough to allow me to print several of the letters which follow, addressed to him by Sir George Lewis.

Harpton, Radnor: Oct. 28, 1858.

My dear Hayward,—If you are not engaged in any other way just at present, would you like to come here on Tuesday next, the 2nd? We should be most happy to see you; and I am desired to mention that the roads are not yet blocked up with snow. If you leave Paddington by the 9.30 train, you will arrive at our station (Kington, beyond Leominster) about four.

The political article in the new 'Quarterly' is evidently ——'s. His antipathy to Palmerston has become a sort of mania. It is quite ludicrous for the admirers of the Duke of Wellington and Lord Castlereagh to talk of Palmerston's ignorance of domestic questions. Palmerston understands foreign policy, military and naval affairs, and the militia, thoroughly well. He has also got up all the sanitary questions, and *believes* in them, which is something to say for anybody. I am afraid it is more than I can say for you.

Disraeli does not seem to have got his Reform-prospectus ready, or at least not ready for publication. Query—will the shares come out at a premium or a discount? I look upon it that his scheme of having an aristocratic Reform Bill, to increase the power of the country gentlemen, must end in smoke. It would not live as long as their India Bill.

Ever yours truly,
G. C. Lewis.

In his letter to Mr. Reeve, dated August 11, 1858, Sir George Lewis stated his wish to ascertain what share in the downfall of Napoleon, in 1814, 'Guizot, Lord Aberdeen, or an unprejudiced German' would attribute to the war which was carried on by the English in Spain.

I insert two curious and interesting letters on this subject, written by Lord Aberdeen to Sir George Lewis in the following autumn.

The Earl of Aberdeen to Sir G. C. Lewis.

Argyll House: Nov. 6, 1858.

My dear Lewis,—The Duke of Argyll has truly informed you that it would give me great pleasure to answer any enquiries in my power connected with your present object. Your candour, moderation, and love of truth renders this a duty as well as a pleasure.

As far as I understand the object of your letter, it relates to the precise amount of influence which England may be supposed to have possessed in the overthrow of Napoleon in 1814; and especially the effect of the Spanish war.

You will easily imagine that this must be a matter respecting which great difference of opinion may prevail; but I think that I may safely answer for the great importance attached to our exertions by the Continental powers. I arrived at Teplitz in the month of August 1813, and, I believe, brought the intelligence of the battle of Vittoria. At all events, I was commissioned to send to the Duke the Grand Cross of the Order of Maria Theresa, very rarely given to anyone, and only to those who had gained a decisive victory. Living on intimate terms with Prince Metternich, I had the means of seeing the great interest and anxiety with which all the operations of the Duke were regarded by the Austrian Government; and frequent conversations with the Emperor Alexander led me to the same conclusion.

It is perfectly true that the battle of Leipzig was the great turning-point of the war, and after this that the Allies might have crossed the Rhine, and ultimately made their way to Paris, as in fact they did, without receiving any great assistance from the British army. After the battle of Leipzig the states of Germany hastened to join the Alliance, and although Talleyrand said that the poor King of Saxony's watch was a quarter of an hour too slow, this did not affect his subjects.

The Allies advanced through a wasted country, in frightful weather, and with a very imperfect commissariat; and although I have occasionally heard surprise expressed at the slowness of the Duke's advance in the south, it was still known that he was obtaining successes, the extent of which were exaggerated, but which I cannot doubt materially influenced the progress of the war. The system of concealment pursued by Napoleon tended to increase the alarm, and aggravate reports of hostile successes.

The perseverance of England did much to encourage the Powers of the Continent, and perhaps our subsidies may have done more, but we are accustomed to exaggerate their value and importance. No doubt the sums were enormous for us to pay, but they were a very poor indemnity for the Powers to receive, (*sic*) and very little able to meet the expenses of such a war. I was authorized to promise a million sterling to Austria, but anyone, looking to a ruined country compelled hastily to raise an army of 400,000 men, and to employ them in active operations, may see what a small part of the actual expense it would cover.

I am aware that it was the habit of Bonaparte to attribute the great cause of his ruin to the Spanish war; and, according to the habitual falsehood and trickery of the man, I have no doubt your explanation is the true one. At the same time, the personal absence of Bonaparte from Spain was of immense importance, and was fully appreciated by the Duke of Wellington. I recollect, at Paris in 1814, hearing Prince Schwartzenberg ask the Duke if he had ever been opposed to Napoleon in the field. He replied that he had not; and that at any time he would rather have seen a reinforcement arrive against him of 40,000 men.

In the absence of specific questions I do not very well know to what to direct my remarks, but a conversation, should such be possible, would speedily exhaust the subject. Or, if there should be any doubtful point which you think I could assist in clearing up, I beg that you would state it without scruple; and be assured that I should have the greatest pleasure in making myself of any use.

Believe me, very truly yours,

ABERDEEN.

The Earl of Aberdeen to Sir G. C. Lewis.

Argyll House: Nov. 19, 1858.

My dear Lewis.—I ought to have written to you earlier, and indeed had fully intended to do so; but I found very little to add to my last letter, and scarcely any difference of views and statement to remark.

It is quite true that many of our popular writers, in consequence of England having taken a larger and more direct part in the overthrow of Bonaparte in 1815, have been led to regard our campaign in 1814 in a similar manner. This is clearly a great mistake. I would not on any account disparage the efforts of the Duke of Wellington. It is difficult to say to what extent the knowledge of his perseverance may have strengthened the confidence of the Allies; but it is manifest that he could not have materially influenced the great events of the war. Our communications with the Duke were rare and difficult, and we were often for weeks together without knowing anything of his movements.

The fact is, that until the battle of Leipsig, notwithstanding the junction of Austria and Prussia, Bonaparte carried on the war at least on a footing of equality; but when by a masterly combination he was compelled to fight at a disadvantage, all was lost. This was the real fight of giants, and decisive of the fate of Europe. The lesser German states lost no time in joining the Alliance, and made their treaties accordingly one after another.

I have heard Bonaparte greatly blamed for leaving numerous garrisons all over Europe, which were lost to him for any useful purpose; but his head had been turned by continual conquest; and he could not reconcile himself to the abandonment of any strategic point.

He made wonderful exertions with very reduced means in the beginning of 1814, and perhaps it may be considered in a military view the most brilliant period of his life. Some symptoms of discord began to pervade the Alliance which had not appeared at moments of distress. He took advantage of this by professing to desire peace, but was never in good faith. During the conferences at Chatillon he repeatedly changed his instructions to Caulaincourt, according to the events of the campaign.

Caulaincourt and others about him were sincerely desirous of peace. Lord Castlereagh was perfectly honest, although not especially desirous of peace. On one occasion we had brought the negotiation to a point at which Caulaincourt said he would be ready to sign. I asked Castlereagh what he wished; for that we might probably be ready in four-and-twenty hours. He replied, 'We shall be stoned when we return to England,' 'but if he should be ready, we must sign nevertheless.' He knew at that time that the Regent, as well as all England, were against any peace with Bonaparte.

You express surprise at the superior popularity of Castlereagh in the House of Commons, but this is not wonderful. His great courage, his mild and conciliatory manner, although without the brilliancy of Canning, were most attractive. The whole affair preceding the duel was so unjust towards him, that everyone took his part and sympathised with him. Although fully admitting the superior brilliancy of Canning, there was always a spice of intrigue about him.

Your extract from his speech at Lisbon, I must say, I think decidedly bad.

You refer to the intended marriage of the Princess Charlotte without being able to explain the rupture. I heard much about it at the time. No doubt the Princess of Wales was very active; and although the country was decidedly in favour of the marriage, I believe that some of the Opposition of the day were against it. I remember hearing that on one occasion the Prince of Orange was unfortunately exhibited before the Princess Charlotte in a state of intoxication, which greatly disgusted her. It was also said that the Duchess of Oldenburgh was very active, but I do not know what motive she could have had. The Prince of Orange subsequently married her sister, a Russian Grand-Duchess.

I have no belief in George IV.'s having any serious design of marrying again after he had got rid of his wife.

Ever most sincerely yours,

ABERDEEN.

The next letter is addressed by Sir George Lewis to his friend F. L. Bodenham, Esq., of Hereford, whose opinion of political affairs generally he held in high estimation. His views on voting by ballot will be read at this time (1869) with much interest.

Harpton: Nov. 17, 1858.

My dear Bodenham,—

* * * *

I am much obliged to you for your opinion on the subject of Reform. There can, I think, be no doubt that a 10*l.* franchise in the counties would be favourable to the Liberal interest. It is equally clear that a reduction of the borough franchise must have a democratic tendency. It would *certainly* in the large towns strengthen the Radical interest. In the towns of moderate size, and in boroughs such as Radnor, it would strengthen the Liberal interest generally. Where the small voters were venal, the politics of the purchaser would determine their votes, but I cannot think that *unpurchased* they would often be found on the Tory side. A new Reform Bill, lowering the borough franchise, followed by a general election, would probably give such an impulse to the question of the Ballot as to carry it in the House of Commons. The House of

Lords could not long resist. I cannot think, looking to the habits and feelings of this country on the subject of elections, that it would be possible to carry a Ballot Bill with a clause for fining or imprisoning a voter who exhibited his vote. The change would be so complete that one can hardly conceive such a provision acquiesced in. Now, if the concealment is *optional* and not *compulsory*, I am disposed to think that the Ballot would have little effect. There are in every constituency a large number of independent voters who care for nobody, who have political opinions, and who wish to proclaim them. All these would continue, if permitted, to vote openly. There are also a large number of persons, not so independent, and with little or no regard for politics, but who wish to please or serve somebody by their vote, and to place him under a sort of obligation. These of course consider it a great hardship to be debarred from voting openly. If these two classes are added together, I think you will in most constituencies leave only an inconsiderable minority. These persons might wish to find safety in concealment; but would concealment avail them? Would not those who had the means of intimidating or annoying them treat concealment as evidence of guilt, and proceed to extremities unless they were satisfied that the voter voted according to their wish? If this was the way in which the system worked, an optional Ballot would leave matters pretty much as they are. Pray turn this over in your mind. Nobody is more competent than yourself to judge how far such a system would produce the effects which *both* parties agree in anticipating from it.

A new Reform Bill would increase the cry for Ballot in two ways. In the first place, it would increase the number of borough members pledged to Radical measures. In the next place, it would strengthen the argument for the Ballot by adding to the number of poor and dependent voters.

St. Martin has played us a trick this year. Instead of summer, he has sent us cutting cold winds from the north-east. I hope your brother has not suffered from them.

Yours very truly,

G. C. L.

Harpton: Nov. 21, 1858.

My dear Reeve,—I congratulate you and Mrs. Reeve on your safe return from the perils of land and sea, and am glad to hear that you have had a pleasant journey.* I am much obliged to you for carrying my volumes† to Pantaleone. In vol. i. p. 390–407 I have shown that the occurrence of vultures in large flights in the plains of Italy is inconsistent with natural history. Even in the Alps and high grounds which the vulture alone frequents it is a solitary bird. I see that in p. 516 I have mentioned eagles, which I ought not to have included, but I believe that my statements about the vulture are correct. The vulture is stated to be still found in the mountains of southern Italy, and Brydone says that it is found in Ætna. My statement respecting the date-palm is taken from Rothman's curious tract on 'Ancient Climate,' which is quoted in the note to vol. i. p. 515. I afterwards found a similar statement in Tournon's book on Rome. I knew that there were one or two palms at Rome in warm situations, but had no idea that there were as many as you mention. There are (or were) two or three scrubby ones at Nice, but none at Pisa.

* They had been travelling in Italy.

† Sir G. C. Lewis's work on Roman history.

I forgot to answer your question about the antiquity of eruptions at Ætna. Lyell treats the subject at length in his 'Principles of Geology,' and states that the volcanic character of the mountain ascends to thousands of years anterior to any historical period. He arrives at this conclusion upon geological data.

* * * *

I have written two articles on the period from 1812 to 1830, and I should be glad if they could appear in your two next numbers,* as the second contains a history of the Reform question which would be read with interest while the question is pending. I am afraid, however, that I could not prepare the first article for January number without making a journey to London on purpose. I have had some very interesting correspondence with Lord Aberdeen upon the share of England in the first downfall of Napoleon. I find that my opinions agree very closely with his, which has given me much satisfaction, as he was in Germany at the time and knew what was going on.

* * * *

Ever yours sincerely,
G. C. LEWIS.

Harpton: Dec. 7, 1858.

My dear Reeve,—

* * * *

I think Charras hypercritical and unwilling to give Napoleon credit for what he accomplished. Charras † evidently wishes to throw the blame of defeat from the French army on their generals, and to deny the superiority of the English troops, which he never

* Of the *Edinburgh Review*.

† Charras (Lieutenant-Colonel), *Histoire de la Campagne de* 1815. 2 vols. Bruxelles, 1858.

admits. There is a passage from a letter of the Duke of Wellington to Lady Mornington, his mother, quoted in Scott's 'Visit to Paris in 1815.' The Duke said that 'Bonaparte did his duty—that he fought the battle with infinite skill, perseverance, and bravery: and this' (he added) 'I do not state from any motive of claiming merit to myself; for the victory is to be ascribed to the superior physical force and constancy of British soldiers.' I cannot help thinking that this is the true explanation —that the two generals were evenly matched, and that the English troops fought better than the French. Charras's theory is that the troops were equal, but that the English were better commanded than the French.

* * * *

Ever yours sincerely,

G. C. Lewis.

Harpton: Dec. 13, 1858.

My dear Reeve,—

* * * *

Could you ask any of your big wig friends whether the account which I have given of the parts played by the Counsel * in the Queen's trial is correct? I know that the account which I have given of Brougham agrees with Parke's opinion,† who was himself one of the Counsel for the Crown.

Napoleon lost the battle of Waterloo; and it is possible that some other management might have succeeded better. He may have made some errors; but would Ney, or Soult, or any other of his generals have made so few? I have often heard my father quote a remark

* See *Edinburgh Review*, vol. cix. p. 157.

† Lord Wensleydale.

of the Duke of Wellington, that if he had had his Peninsular regiments at Waterloo, the battle would not have lasted till two o'clock. I think he said this to my father, or in his presence. I confess it seems to me, on the whole, that Napoleon fought the Waterloo campaign with extraordinary skill. It was a desperate game, and he was forced to play his last card. France was, in truth, sick of him, and the Allies were determined to bring him down. Delay would only have made his position worse. As to the Peninsular war, it certainly operated to a certain extent as a diversion and a drain —but the question is to what extent? The view which I have taken accords very much with that entertained by Lord Aberdeen, whose letters I will show you, together with those of my other correspondents, if you like to read them.

The Duc d'Aumale's opinion is a good one, and I feel much respect for it. Tocqueville promised to send me his view, but he has not done so. I feel satisfied that it was what the Germans call the 'Befreiung's Krieg' which really brought down Napoleon in 1814. England contributed powerfully, but indirectly, to its successful result.

Ever yours sincerely,

G. C. Lewis.

Kent House: Jan. 20, 1859.

My dear Head,—We have just migrated to London, and on arriving there I found your letter of the 2nd and its enclosures. I am glad to hear so good an account of the position of your affairs. Unless there is a great struggle, and great dissidence of opinion in the colony, I do not expect that the question will be taken up seriously in Parliament. I shall, however, know more in about a week after the meeting of Parliament. By that time it will probably appear if there is any intention of raising the question. I have not yet received the 'Relations de Jésuites,'* but do not doubt it will reach me in due time. I am much obliged to you for sending me a copy. I will try to get Curtis's book, and to read it.

The two subjects which now engross attention here are the Reform Bill and the threats of a war in northern Italy. Bright's campaign has, on the whole, been a failure. His plan of *Americanising* our Government has met with no response from the country; and he has now put forward an extensive scheme of disfranchisement and enfranchisement—for abolishing all boroughs with a population under 8,000, and for reducing all boroughs with a population under 16,000 to one member. Under this plan, Radnor, Leominster, Ludlow, Tewkesbury, Brecon, and even larger places, go into Schedule A; and Durham, Winchester, Taunton, Stafford, Hereford, and other of the smaller class of county towns, go into Schedule B. The seats thus liberated are chiefly distributed among the large towns; six to Manchester and Liverpool, four to the Tower Hamlets and Marylebone, &c. I doubt whether the country desire anything of this sort. They are prepared to abolish nomination, and to give a reasonable weight to the manufacturing and mercantile classes, but I do not think they are prepared for such a large transfer of power as this change implies. However, the practical decision will be made upon the Government Bill, which will probably be introduced early in the session. If it is a tolerably fair measure, there will be a strong

* *Relations de Jésuites, contenant ce qui s'est passé de plus remarquable dans les missions des pères de la Compagnie de Jésus dans la nouvelle France.* 3 vols. Quebec: Augustin Coté, 1858.

disposition among many of the Liberal party to support it on the second reading, and vote against such parts of it as they object to in Committee. Nothing is known as to the details of the Government Bill, and I strongly suspect that they content themselves with general discussion, and settle no details until the last moment.

As to the Italian war, the experiment tried by Louis Napoleon has probably convinced him that the French are not so anxious for war as he supposed. The King of Sardinia is, however, very reckless, and the Emperor of Austria not reluctant; and if a cannon is once fired Louis Napoleon is almost sure to put into the pool.

Gladstone's mission to the Ionian Islands has been a singular business. It has ended in the recall of Young, and in his temporary appointment without salary. Whether he is to be a sort of legislative dictator, a Lycurgus or Solon, I know not; but it is understood that he will return to England before the end of March. I have not heard anybody named as likely to be his permanent successor.

I have been, while I was in the country, preparing an essay on the 'Characteristics of Federal, National, Provincial, and Municipal Government,' and I have attempted to treat the question of federal government as a security against war, with reference to the ideas circulated by the Peace Society. The more I consider the federal system the more I am impressed with its defects. If I were an American, I greatly doubt whether I should wish to perpetuate the existing union; and I do not see that the good of mankind would be promoted by attempts to introduce or extend the federal system in Europe. I asked Lowe to put on paper for me what he considered to be the principal motives which induced the Americans to uphold their federal system; and he gave me the following list.

1. They are afraid of each other. If separate, they must maintain armies.

2. They find in federation some slight counterpoise to democracy.

3. They have the advantage of a Zollverein.

4. They can gratify their aggressive spirit by remaining one country as regards foreign states.

5. The South, separate from the North, would be in danger of extermination by a servile war.

6. The North would lose a market for its manufactures.

7. The long rivers of America render separation difficult. The Mississippi runs through ten states.

Pray tell me at your leisure whether you assent to this statement of reasons, and whether there are any other motives of importance to be added.

The second volume of the German translation of my work on Roman history has recently appeared. The translator writes me word that its reception has been good. The sale of the translation has been larger than that of the original.

The article on Lord Liverpool's ministry in the January number of the 'Edinburgh Review' is by me.

* * * *

Ever yours sincerely,

G. C. LEWIS.

Kent House: March 2, 1859.

My dear Reeve,—I read yesterday the narrative of Sir Ralph Abercrombie's proceedings when he had the chief command in Ireland. It is an interesting account, and throws much light on the state of things immediately before the arrival of Lord Cornwallis. Abercrombie, like Lord Cornwallis, adopted a humane policy and attempted to restrain the cruelty of the ascendency party. But as he was not Lord-Lieutenant as well as Commander-in-Chief, and as Lord Camden, though a well-meaning was a weak man, he was unable to maintain his ground, and his principal order was disapproved by the Irish Government. Differences arose between him and the Castle—and in a short time he resigned.

The 'Castlereagh Correspondence,' vol. i. p. 164, contains the letter directing the military to act without the authority of the civil power of which Abercrombie so much complained. Assuming that the narrative is correct, and that the Government had nothing to urge in favour of their view—assuming likewise that Abercrombie was not more peremptory or obstinate than he ought to have been—it may be true that Lord Cornwallis erred in calling him 'wrong-headed.' The point can scarcely be determined without further information. Substantially, Abercrombie was no doubt in the right, and the course which he took was honourable to him. It showed his humanity and independence. All this would appear in a detailed narrative, but I hardly see how it could be treated in a short note referring to an incidental expression. Abercrombie had left Ireland before Lord Cornwallis went there.

Ever yours sincerely,

G. C. Lewis.

From Sir George Lewis to his brother, the Rev. Gilbert Lewis.

Kent House: March 22, 1859.

My dear Gilbert,—Nobody seems to know what will be the result of the Reform debates. It is generally expected that Lord John will carry his resolution, and by a large majority, but it is thought that the Government will make such concessions as will enable them to move the second reading and to persuade the House to agree to it. If this takes place, they will probably fix the Committee for after Easter, and trust to the chapter of accidents. Everything depends on the extent to which they are ready to yield. If they will treat the Reform Bill as they treated the India Bill of last session —that is to say, abandon their own scheme and allow a new Bill to be made and passed by their opponents— they may get through their difficulties, and reach the end of the session. This is not an impossible event, but many things must happen before it can be accomplished.

The prospects of peace are better. Cowley's mission to Vienna has smoothed the way; and if a congress is assembled to discuss the question of Central Italy, war will probably be averted. I do not expect a dissolution. The leaves in this garden are as much out as they usually are at the middle of April.

Ever yours,

G. C. L.

On April 1, 1859, Lord Derby's Government was beaten, on a division in the House of Commons, by a majority of 39; and in consequence, on April 23, the Parliament was dissolved. The elections took place immediately. Sir G. C. Lewis was again chosen for the Radnor Boroughs without opposition; and on May 31 the new Parliament assembled.

A vote of want of confidence in the Conservative Cabinet was soon afterwards moved by Lord Hartington; there was again a majority of 13 against the

Government, and on June 17 Lord Derby resigned. The Queen sent for Lord Granville, who failed to make a Government. Differences which had existed between Lord John Russell and Lord Palmerston were reconciled. Lord Palmerston became Prime Minister, and Lord John Russell went to the Foreign Office. Sir G. C. Lewis was again appointed Chancellor of the Exchequer. A doubt, however, whether Mr. Gladstone should be included in the Government having been decided in the affirmative, and it being known to Sir G. C. Lewis that Mr. Gladstone was anxious to be Chancellor of the Exchequer, he wrote at once to Lord Palmerston to put that office at his disposal, and to request that the offer of it which had been made to him might not be permitted in any way to interfere with the arrangements he wished to make. The result was, that Sir G. C. Lewis became Secretary of State for the Home Office and Mr. Gladstone Chancellor of the Exchequer.

Kent House: April 9, 1859.

My dear Head,—I was much obliged to you for the copy of your speech, and for the account of your proceedings. The question seems now to be put fairly before the Legislature; and it is clear that the public opinion of the Province has acquiesced in the course which you took at the change of Government. Not a word has been said on the subject in the House of Commons since its meeting, and as far as England is concerned the matter is concluded, unless it should be revived from your side the water.

The Government Reform Bill was formed on the principle of making a popular concession directly, and of taking it back as far as possible indirectly. The result of this was, that the Liberal party would not accept it. They were determined that the concession should be *pure et simple*, without qualifications, conditions, and mutual concessions. The debate was well kept up for seven nights; and the Bill was completely demolished. Even those who spoke for the Government gave up the Bill, and only defended it on the ground that it might be re-modelled in Committee. The majority was somewhat larger than our whips reckoned upon (39): rather more than thirty of our men voted with the Government. If they had voted with the Opposition we should have had a majority of 100. Had this been the case, the ministers would hardly have ventured to advise a dissolution. The dissolution is to take place either in Passion or Easter week. I do not anticipate any great change in the relative strength of parties. The probability of another dissolution at an early period deters candidates, and there is no strong feeling either for Reform or against it.

* * * *

The new Parliament will meet about the end of May; and if there is an united Liberal majority, it is likely to be followed speedily by some vote adverse to the Government. At the same time, our lead is in such a state as to render a combined movement of this sort difficult and uncertain.

I am afraid that the prospects of peace are gradually becoming darker and darker. Louis Napoleon has committed himself to such an extent with Cavour and the Sardinian Government that he can scarcely recede, and the French preparations for war on the south-east frontier are threatening in the extreme. I have gone on for a long time refusing to believe in war, but I fear that it is now imminent. There is no *necessity* for our taking any part in it, but it is impossible to be sanguine as to our remaining long mere spectators of an European war. It is to be hoped that the modern improvements in artillery may lead to a rapid decision, and to its speedy termination by the defeat of one or the other power.

Lord Radstock has not yet sent me the copy of Curtis.* I am much obliged to you for the gift, and shall read it with pleasure. The article on Lord Cornwallis in the forthcoming 'Edinburgh Review' is mine.

Ever yours sincerely,

G. C. L.

Kent House: July 17, 1859.

My dear Hayward,—I shall be highly flattered by your taking the trouble to review my pamphlet. If you do, pray explain clearly the proceedings about the Conspiracy Bill and Bernard's case, which are stated correctly in my pamphlet,† and which the public have never understood. The state of the law is highly unsatisfactory, but it has suited the purposes of numerous persons to represent it as satisfactory and adequate. Somebody has published at the same time a pamphlet on 'Unpunished Offences committed at Sea,' which bears on a branch of the same subject. I have not yet seen it. It might be worth your while to look at it.

I will read your two articles, but have not yet had time to do so. I see that both the reviews have articles on our defences.

Ever yours truly,

G. C. Lewis.

* 'History of the Constitution of the United States,' by George Ticknor Curtis. 2 vols. Harper, New York.

† A pamphlet on 'Foreign Jurisdiction and the Extradition of Prisoners,' by Sir George Cornewall Lewis. Parker, 1859.

Kent House: July 25, 1859.

My dear Hayward,—I am much obliged to you for your notice of my pamphlet in the 'Examiner,' which does more than justice to the author.

My answer to what you say about extradition is this. I believe the system is carried to a great extent among the German states, and to a considerable extent among other Continental states, which have comprehensive extradition treaties, with an obligation to surrender upon the inhibition of a simple *mandat d'arrêt*. The extent to which the system *may* be carried depends mainly upon the wording of the treaties. The expense of verifying the criminal and sending him home to be tried is small, and opposes no serious obstacle to the working of the system. But if you attempt to try your subjects at home for crimes committed abroad, you must not only have a police abroad to look after them, but you must bring over the witnesses for the trial. Now this you have, in the first place, no power to do; and in the next place, if you had, or if they were willing to come, the expenses would be a practical bar.

The foreign jurists who write on extradition give no facts from which the practical operation of the system can be judged.

Yours very truly,

G. C. Lewis.

Kent House: Aug. 1, 1859.

My dear Head,—I send you by this post a pamphlet* which I have recently published on the questions raised last year by the *attentat* on Louis Napoleon, and by the Conspiracy Bill and Bernard's case. The subject

* Pamphlet on the 'Extradition of Prisoners.'

branches into various directions, and it has never yet been treated as a whole. The collection of the materials cost me a good deal of trouble, as they were scattered in different books of reference, as well as parliamentary and official documents, and I was assisted by the advice of some good legal heads. I asked Dallas whether questions ever arose between the United States and England on the Canadian frontier, but he was not aware of their existence. It seems to me that wherever there is a land frontier there is always a tendency to the state of things of which the English and Scotch border affords so striking an example.

The change of Government was effected by a combined party move, but after the challenge offered before the dissolution, there was no difficulty in inducing Liberal members to vote. The chief difficulty lay in bringing about a reconciliation between the leaders; but that object having been effected, the construction of the new Government proceeded without any serious impediment. The arrangement which I should have preferred was that Lord Palmerston should, as Prime Minister, go into the House of Lords, and that Lord John should lead the House of Commons and that Clarendon should be Foreign Secretary. However, Lord Palmerston was unwilling to leave the House of Commons, and so this arrangement could not be effected. The office of Chancellor of the Exchequer was originally offered to me, but as Gladstone expressed a wish to have it I gave way to him. I have found the Home Office excessively troublesome, rather than laborious. My entire time has been occupied by an uninterrupted succession of petty business, each subject, however, having a certain importance, and requiring attention and accuracy, in order to avoid scrapes. The session will probably end about the fifteenth, and then I go to Harpton, where I am to give a bow meeting at the end of the month.

The Indian finances are in a deplorable state, and people are beginning to ask themselves what benefit they derive from the large territories which we have annexed in that part of the world. The 'Times' talks of shearing off the border provinces and re-establishing the native princes, which I take to be a very hopeless enterprise.

I received the copy of Curtis, which you were so good as to send me, and I have read a good deal of it. It is written in a perspicuous and agreeable style.

Yours very sincerely,

G. C. LEWIS.

Sir George Lewis to Henry Reeve, Esq.

Kent House: Dec. 4, 1859.

My dear Reeve,—

* * * *

Bright's plan (for taxation) is not properly understood; the 'Economist' comes the nearest, but the 'Daily News' praises it, and the article in the 'Times' was weak, and evidently written by a person who did not see through it. I will try to write an exposure of this and the scheme in the 'People's Blue Book' (on which it is, in fact, founded), to serve as a tail-piece to ——, in about two or three pages.* You can judge whether you think it worth adding. I should not wish to write anything which —— would consider as interfering with the effect of his article; but my conviction is, that Bright's finance would be more ruinous than his Reform,

* See the last few pages of the article on 'Taxation,' *Edinburgh Review*, January, 1860.

and that this admits of a simple exposure to all who understand the elements of Political Economy.

Yours very sincerely,

G. C. Lewis.

Home Office: Jan. 17, 1860.

My dear Reeve,—The account which you have received of the rapidity and mysteriousness of the Emperor's change of policy appears to me, so far as I have the means of judging, greatly exaggerated. While the negotiation of the treaty of Zurich was in progress, he was kept constantly in mind of his engagements at Villafranca, and of the understanding of Austria (not shared by him) that the Grand-Dukes were to be re-instated. This naturally turned his policy in a somewhat Austrian direction. There was then no good feeling between Austria and Russia. The approximation between France and Russia rested on quite different grounds. But the Emperor's personal feelings, consistently with the policy of the war, have always been pro-Italian; and Walewski tendered his resignation on this account some time in October, I think, but was pacified by an article in the 'Moniteur.' Since the summer, time has told in favour of the Italian states. The conduct of their provisional governments has been rational and moderate. It has become evident that their former rulers cannot be restored without force; and if France were to join in, or even permit, the use of force for this purpose, it would counteract the policy of its late campaign in northern Italy. The English Government has held the same language throughout, and the Emperor, finding that the course of events has rendered forcible intervention to restore the old rulers impossible, has turned in the direction of England, which has constantly maintained this principle. It seems to me that this is a simple and natural explanation of his conduct. I doubt the existence of those profound and far-sighted designs which people are so fond of attributing to Louis Napoleon. If his popularity were waning, if his throne were in danger, and if a bold stroke were required, he might attack the Rhine provinces of Prussia. But he knows that this would bring all Europe about his ears, and that England would probably before long be found in the ranks against him. My notion of him is that his views are changeable, and that he generally shapes his policy with a view to immediate objects.

This free trade scheme, which he has just entered upon, has, I suspect, been taken up hastily and without a full consideration of the consequences to which it may lead him. However, if he can carry it, he will be an enormous benefactor of his country. This, and his anti-papal manifesto, will give him much support in this country, from quarters where he has hitherto been regarded with suspicion and dislike; and his altered position will naturally produce a close approximation to our Government. That approximation, however, will not arise from any change in our policy of principles of government, and I apprehend that our course of foreign policy will be consistently pursued, with such adaptations to circumstances as the state of Europe may render necessary. The great question now to be solved is, whether the congress will meet. If it does not meet, an attempt must be made to solve the Italian difficulty by other means. I confess that my own impressions are in favour of an attempt to come to a solution through a congress; but many great authorities take a different view, and I admit that no good would be done by a congress meeting merely to record irreconcilable opinions and then to separate. Pray give me a line, if you have anything further of importance.

Yours very sincerely,
G. C. L.

Kent House: March 12, 1860.

My dear Head,—I am afraid that I have allowed a long time to elapse without writing to you, and without thanking you for your last letter. The interval has been lengthened by a troublesome attack of neuralgia in the head, from which I have suffered much since the beginning of February, and from which I am only just now recovered. My doctor thought it was produced by malaria, owing to the neglected state of the drainage at the Home Office. It was accompanied with great depression, and for a time I could do very little work.

The affairs of the Government have, on the whole, gone on prosperously since the opening of the session. The French Treaty originated in the visit of Cobden to Paris, and in the impression which he made upon the Emperor. It was not suggested by the Government. It is founded on a somewhat hazardous and experimental policy. The certain sacrifice of revenue which we make is large. The advantages to be obtained are problematical. My own belief is, that the reduction of the duties on wines and brandies will not lead to any great increase of the import of these articles. On the other hand, if the French faithfully perform their share of the contract, there ought to be a large increase in the sale of some of our manufactures in France. It must, I think, end in a considerable increase of the permanent rate of the Income Tax, which cripples our power of increasing taxation for an extraordinary or temporary purpose, and renders it necessary on any such occasion to have recourse at once to borrowing. The country, however, have been captivated by the benevolent character of the scheme, and all the questions hitherto have been carried in the House by large majorities. Even the annexation of Savoy, the prospect of which comes at an inopportune moment, does not seem to influence the result. After the consent of the Sardinian Government to put the question to the vote, it cannot scarcely be doubted that the cession of the province will take place. All that is required is the expressed consent of the inhabitants, and their vote must be given under the influence of fear. It is plain that the conditional consent of their own Government to the cession is obtained, and they will naturally be afraid by an independent vote to offend those who may so soon become their masters. The Reform Bill has, on the whole, been well received. The measure was carefully prepared, and it is studiously moderate with respect to disfranchisement and the distribution of the liberated seats. It makes a large addition to the existing constituency both in counties and boroughs. It is not expected that the Conservatives will make any fight on the second reading.

I have heard nothing up to the present time of any intention to make any change in your Government. If you wish it, I could speak to the Duke of Newcastle on the subject, and ascertain his views.

Believe me ever yours sincerely,

G. C. Lewis.

Sir George Lewis to W. R. Greg, Esq.

Kent House: March 24, 1860.

My dear Greg,—I have been for some days confined to my room by an obstinate attack of influenza, and have been prevented from thanking you for your letter relative to the Budget and the Reform Bill.

The Budget and the French Treaty have been founded upon liberal and philanthropic views, which proceed upon the assumption that everything is to march uninterruptedly to its pre-appointed end. If these anticipations are all verified, there will be an increase in our foreign trade, an extension of our manufactures, an improvement in our working classes, and a consequent increase in the productiveness of the remaining taxes. There will likewise be more pacific and settled relations between England and France, and a consequent reduction of armaments on both sides of the Channel. With a revenue thus increased and an expenditure thus diminished, the deficiency created by the Budget will disappear. All political calculations of this sort, dependent on the absence of disturbing causes during a considerable series of years, are necessarily uncertain. It is for each person to judge them according to his own views of probability.

With regard to the Reform Bill, I cannot but think that your fears are exaggerated. If they were really shared by any large number of persons, it is not likely that the second reading should have been debated two nights without an amendment either being moved or threatened; when the Bill reaches Committee, many amendments will doubtless be moved, and some may be carried. No material change is likely to be made in the county franchise, or in the transfer of seats. If it be true that many members on our side of the House wish for an 8*l.* rental franchise in the boroughs, it will probably be carried. From all I have heard, however, my impression is that a majority of the House would support the Bill as it stands.

Yours very truly,
G. C. LEWIS.

The next letter is written by Sir George Lewis to his cousin, Miss Duff Gordon.

Kent House: April 30, 1860.

My dear Georgiana,—The translation in the 'Times' of the 23rd is an extract of a literal version of Theocritus,* made and published by Mr. Banks, son of Mr. Banks of Kington. He has now taken the name of Davies, from his uncle, and lives at Moor Court. He is a good scholar, and is about to publish an English verse translation of some Greek fables† which I edited.

There are many points of resemblance between the fights of ancient and modern pugilists, but you will observe that the ancients did not fight with the naked fist. They covered it with thongs of bull hide, so that their blows were much more severe, and the contest was more sanguinary and dangerous. They likewise bound similar thongs round the arm; so as to avoid such an accident as befell Sayers in the last battle.

The covering for the fists was called by the Romans a *cestus*; and it appears, from the description in Virgil, to have been armed with lead and iron. This must

* Idyll 22 of Theocritus. Castor and Pollux, going in search of water, meet the gigantic Amycus. A quarrel ensues, and a fight takes place; the description of which is singularly like the contest for the championship between Heenan and Sayers, which, at the date at which Sir George Lewis was writing, had recently occurred.

† The Fables of Babrius.

have made it a most formidable weapon, similar to the steel knuckles of the Yankees.

Ever yours affectionately,

G. C. L.

Kent House: April 22, 1860.

My dear Twisleton,—I was much obliged to you for your note, which contains the skeleton of the whole subject. In Hale's 'Analysis of Chronology' vol. i., there is a collection of the different dates which have been assumed for the chief events in the early Biblical history. The dates for the creation fill three closely printed pages. The dates for the deluge vary from 3246 to 2104 B.C. Those for the exodus vary nearly 350 years. Even for the foundation of the Temple there is a discrepancy of 280 years.

Wiener begins his Biblical chronology with Saul, but attempts no consecutive tables for the previous period.

Is it possible, from internal evidence, to determine the commencement of contemporary history among the Jews? Can it be safely assumed that they had annalistic registration as early as the building of the Temple, about 1000 B.C.? If the two books of Kings are written by the same author, it is clear that he could not have been a contemporary of the earlier part of the period, more than 400 years.

Among the great officers of Solomon are named two scribes and a recorder. (1 Kings iv. 3.) In the same chapter, verses 32, 33, Solomon is stated to have spoken 3,000 proverbs, and to have made 1,005 songs: also to have spoken of trees, beasts, fowl, reptiles, and fishes. This latter statement seems to mean that he had written a work on the Naturai history of animals and plants. The very idea of such a work did not occur to the Greeks till centuries after the time of Solomon, who may be considered as about contemporary with Homer.

A book of the acts of Solomon fuller than the account given in the book of Kings is referred to in 1 Kings xi. 41.

Are you acquainted with the articles 'Abel,' 'Adam,' 'Cain,' 'Eve,' and 'Lamech,' in Bayle? They touch in part upon questions of chronology.

Ever yours sincerely,

G. C. Lewis.

Kent House: April 27, 1860.

My dear Twisleton,—Clinton, in the first volume of his 'Fasti,' has a dissertation on the Scripture chronology down to 561 B.C. It treats the whole series of dates up to Adam as equally certain, because it rests upon the evidence of witnesses both inspired and contemporary. What he can mean by saying that Moses was a contemporary witness for all the period before his lifetime, I do not understand. He professes to avoid all arbitrary alterations of texts, but he rejects the 480 years in 1 Kings vi. 1, as being irreconcilable with other statements and computations.

If you have not got Clinton's book, and should wish to read his dissertation, I shall be happy to lend you the volume. There is a work by Des Vignoles on the early Biblical chronology which is much quoted by the German writers. I believe the author was a French refugee Protestant, who went to Berlin after the revocation of the edict of Nantes.

Many thanks for your letter. There is nothing improbable in the supposition that the Jews used writing for historical purposes as early as David and Solomon. Ever yours sincerely,

G. C. LEWIS.

Kent House: May 5, 1860.

My dear Twisleton—The early part of Genesis contains frequent references to the *year* as a recognised measure of time. Bohlen says that the account of the deluge shows that the *solar* year is meant, and he thinks that the use of the solar year is inconsistent with an early date of composition. I question the force of this inference; but I have likewise a difficulty in extracting any distinct result as to the length of the year from the account of the deluge.

The deluge is represented as lasting a year, Gen. vii. 6—viii. 13.

From viii. 5–12, the following appears to be the interval of time:—9 months + 1 day + 40 days + flight of raven + flight of dove + 7 days + 1 day + 7 days.

The following is another computation, founded on vii. 11, 12, 17–24; viii. 3:—

1 month + 17 days + 40 days + 150 days + 150 days = 357 days.

But this period appears to include a portion of the time when the waters were running off, not included in the former calculation. Unless there is some other mode of reckoning up this sum which has not occurred to me, I do not see how Bohlen can maintain that the account of the deluge contains a clear reference to the *solar* year. At the same time, I have no doubt that every nation had from the earliest times a solar year more or less accurate.

Ever yours sincerely,

G. C. L.

Kent House: May 7, 1860.

My dear Twisleton,—I observe that Bohlen treats the interval between the 17th day of the second month and the 17th day of the seventh month as equal to 150 days, and therefore as implying a month of 30 days. The Greek year, even in the time of Aristotle, was usually considered as consisting of 12 months of 30 days each, and this is probably the assumption in the account of the deluge.

The deluge is described as lasting from the 17th of the second month of the 600th year of Noah's life to the 27th of the second month of the 601st year of his life. Gen. vii. 11—viii. 13. 14. I am unable to discover the motive for making the duration of the deluge ten days longer than a year. Bohlen's remarks are in vol. i. p. 222; vol. ii. p. 157, of the English translation.

There is a curious passage, viii. 21, 22, which contains a recognition of the permanence of the phenomena upon which the solar year is founded. Their permanence is conceived as a sort of concession made to man by God, in consequence of His repentance for the mischief which He had done by the deluge.

Ever yours sincerely,
G. C. Lewis.

July 23, 1860.

My dear Head,—

*　　*　　*　　*

This has been the most fatiguing session I remember since I have been in Parliament; but the work done has been by no means proportioned to the fatigue. I heard the other day a story of some county magistrates who insisted that the convicts on the treadmill in the county prison should be made to believe that they were grinding air, when they were, in fact, grinding corn. There is no necessity to practise any such delusion upon us: we are quite aware that we have been grinding air.

The Queen is to go to Balmoral on the 6th of next month, and to stay till September 14, when she intends to go to Germany for a short time. Parliament is not likely to be proregued until the last week of August.

There is an article of mine on 'George Rose's Memoirs' in the last number of the 'Edinburgh Review.'* His account of Pitt is curious, and may be relied on.

* * * *

Ever yours sincerely,
G. C. Lewis.

Kent House: May 7, 1860.

My dear Head,—

* * * *

Your conflagration† was a most unfortunate event: but I am glad to learn from your account that you have not sustained any material pecuniary loss. In a country where you are dependent on fires for very existence during so large a portion of the year, it seems extraordinary that more precautions against this danger should not be taken in building large houses.

* * * *

* *Edinburgh Review*, vol. cxii. p. 34.

† Sir Edmund Head, the Governor of Canada's, house at Spencer Wood, near Quebec. Dinner was served; the Bishop and heads of departments, &c., were the guests; but as soon as they had sat down an alarm of fire was given, and they gave assistance in carrying the furniture and goods out of the house into the snow. The house, being principally of wood, burnt very quickly.

I do not write at length, as I am uncertain whether this letter may find you in Canada. The Prince of Wales's visit will be a great event in the province, and it will also attract much attention in this country.

Ever yours sincerely,

G. C. Lewis.

Harpton: Oct. 2, 1860.

My dear Reeve,—I cannot at all see my way in Italian affairs. If the quarrel between Cavour and Garibaldi continues, the King of Naples may return. I am not at all a fanatic for Italian freedom, but I should much rejoice to see a nation with such fine intellectual endowments as the Italians withdrawn from the deadening pressure of the Church, and of such Governments as the Church encourages, and as encourage the Church. I do not see how this is to be done unless all Italy, *minus* Rome and Venetia, becomes one nation under one king and one parliament. It does not seem that this is at present practicable, and yet an attempt to govern the several provinces of Italy by viceroys nominated by Sardinia and by separate parliaments must *fail*. I know of no other alternative; a federation such as Louis Napoleon proposed is out of the question.

All my spare time lately has been given to an enquiry on a question of antiquity; and I have not thought of anything for your review. I have likewise written some additional remarks on foreign jurisdiction, for a French translation of my pamphlet on that subject which is to be published by a Belgian advocate at Brussels. They are in answer to Professor Mohl, of Heidelberg, who is very severe on England for not assisting in maintaining the 'Welt-Rechtsordnung' by a system of universal interference.

I have looked through Sir Robert Wilson's volume on the Russian campaign,* and I should be disposed to write an article upon it, if you think the subject would be interesting. Of course, I should not attempt to go into the military details.

I hope you may have a pleasant tour in Spain. Everybody says that the country is improving; but the improvement has been long in coming.

I agree with you in thinking that we shall not have war. Neither France nor Austria wishes it, and all the other powers will do what they can to prevent it. At the same time, it is impossible to answer for the future, when so many people are flinging about fire-brands.

Yours sincerely,

G. C. L.

Kent House: 1860.

Dear Mrs. Austin,—

*   *   *   *

Garibaldi would have been called a buccaneer, if he had failed. Having succeeded, he will be regarded as a hero. For myself, I shall rejoice in his success, if he should succeed in permanently deposing the present Government of Sicily, and in substituting a better form of rule. Revolutions against a Government so bad as that of Naples are merely a question of prudence. I always *presume* against a sanguinary revolution of any sort, because, in general, they fail of their intended object, and end in making things worse than before. But they do not *always* fail, and one hopes that this case may be an exception to the rule.

I am very sorry to hear what you say of yourself;

* 'Narrative of Events during the Invasion of Russia by Buonaparte,' by General Sir Robert Wilson. 1 vol. Murray, 1860.

but remember that Miss Berry was subject to violent palpitations of the heart, and she lived to be near ninety.

Ever yours sincerely,

G. C. L.

Kent House: Dec. 22, 1860.

My dear Stanhope,—It was very kind of you to send me a copy of the engraving of Mr. Pitt as a Cambridge student. I am much obliged to you for it. It is an interesting memorial, and I am glad to possess it. His face (as was natural) acquired a more forcible and manly expression as he grew older.

I have looked through the new collection of Lord Auckland's papers,* with the exception of the Spanish Journal, which I found wholly unreadable. There is not much about Lord Auckland himself in them, and the letters of his correspondents (as you truly remark) contain no new fact. Many of them, however, are interesting, and illustrate the feeling and state of opinion of the time, particularly those written during the French Revolution. Lord Loughborough's letters are worthy of notice. He was evidently a sagacious, contriving, active-minded man; and after reading his letters I understand better how he could have intrigued to oust Pitt and make himself Prime Minister in 1801, which appears to me clearly to have been his intention.

I cannot understand why the editor should begin with the Coalition and go on to 1788, and afterwards return to 1781 (see vol. i. p. 309). The result is, that one letter of Wedgwood's, about the French Treaty, appears in p. 133, and another in p. 427. No explanation is given why the collection should end with an

* 'Auckland (William Lord), Journal and Correspondence,' with a preface by the Right Rev. Lord Auckland, Bishop of Bath and Wells. 4 vols. London, 1860.

insignificant letter in 1793, which is needed, seeing that Lord Auckland held office (with the sole exception of M. Pitt's second ministry) until 1807, and lived till 1814. One should wish to have an authentic account of his proceedings in 1801.

The editor entirely mistakes the meaning and effect of Mr. Pitt's letter in vol. ii. p. 401. It contains no such overture as he states. I suspect that he confounded a meeting of the Cabinet with a meeting of the Council.

By the way, this letter shows that meetings of the Privy Council had not become the mere forms which they are at present. They are now attended only by members of the Cabinet, with the exception of the Prince, and not a word is ever said at them.

I hope that Lady Stanhope has been benefited by the sea-side. I shall be very glad to have the pleasure of meeting you again, an event which the session will at least bring about.

Ever yours sincerely,

G. C. Lewis.

The Grove, Watford: Dec. 26, 1860.

My dear Mrs. Austin,—I came here on Monday to pass a few days, and I thought that I had put Montalembert's letter in my box, but I find that I unluckily omitted to do so. I will return it in a day or two. In the meantime I thank you for sending it to me. I read it with interest, as showing his present views. I can perfectly understand why the leaders of the French constitutional party (among whom Montalembert wishes no doubt to be included) should have been indignant at the support given to the Emperor by the Government and people of this country.

How far the support or toleration of a new *de facto* Government should be carried is always a difficult point; but the feelings of the Orleanists, and of the other public men in France who sigh after a tribune, with respect to the conduct of England are natural and intelligible. These, however, are not the grounds of Montalembert's present denunciations of England. He denounces us, not for being the friend of Louis Napoleon, but for being the enemy of the Pope. Now, without being at all fanatical about Italian liberty and nationality, I confess I see with great satisfaction the demolition of the Austrian power beyond the Alps, the overthrow of the King of Naples, and the spoliation of the Pope. All this was done by Catholic powers. It is ludicrous to talk of 'fanatisme protestant.' The Pope has had his territory taken from him by good Catholics, by men who go to confession, and believe in the immaculate conception; and if it were not for the defence of the French army, the Romans themselves would pitch the Pope and his cardinals into the Tiber. I conceive that the ascendency of the Roman Church has been the curse of Italy, and anything which tends to weaken it I look upon with unmixed satisfaction. Such I believe to be the feeling of a considerable portion of the educated classes in France. They do not sympathize with the views of Montalembert and the Ultramontane party, and I am utterly indifferent to reproaches against England springing from this source. As to Thiers, he is no doubt thoroughly soured by his long exclusion from office, and he is about as fair a judge of political opponents as Fox was of Pitt in the year 1801 or 1802.

I am very sorry to hear what you say of Lucy.* Alexander,† whom I saw a short time ago, did not

* Lady Duff Gordon. † Sir Alexander Duff Gordon.

appear to think her in any danger. I trust he may prove right in his security.

Ever yours sincerely,
G. C. L.

Kent House: Jan. 21, 1861.

My dear Twisleton,—I read with much interest the articles in the New York papers which you had the kindness to send me. It is certain that this break up of the Union, for such it apparently is, has taken the world by surprise. When the Prince of Wales was at Washington in last October, nobody thought that Buchanan would be the last President of the old Union. The greatest events seem to be the least anticipated. Nobody in England expected that the great rebellion would end in the execution of the king; and when Charles II. was in exile, nobody expected that he would be restored. When Napoleon was at the height of his power, nobody expected that he would be deposed; and when he was at Elba, nobody expected that he would again be Emperor of France. The French Revolution itself was clearly a universal and complete surprise, both to France and the rest of Europe. Everybody thought that the old French monarchy rested on an immovable basis. Revolutions, as Aristotle has remarked, spring from small causes, but they are made on account of great interests. The immediate cause in this case is small. The importance of Lincoln's election was not great one way or the other. But it is clear that the feelings and interests about slavery have been gradually growing to the point of difference at which common discussion and decision by vote of a joint Assembly becomes impossible. The assault upon Sumner was not, if properly regarded, a proof of the brutal manners of the Southern gentlemen—it was the first blow in a civil war. It was an outward sign that the Hall of Congress was not a place where slavery and anti-slavery could settle their disputes. Olmsted's third volume, which I have been reading with great interest and profit, shows the width of the chasm between the North and the South on the subject of federal compacts, if it is resisted by the Slave-holding States. However, so far the practical problem is clear. There is no doubt that free labour is preferable to slave labour, if the option exists. But there is a point at which the heat is such that white labour in the open air becomes impossible. I want to know what the Northern States propose to do from that point. What is their slavery legislation south of the line, where none but niggers can work in the fields? Olmsted's book does not, so far as I see, contain a vestige of an attempt to answer this question, and yet, if the United States are to remain in their present extent, it must receive a practical answer. Buchanan's conduct has been weak and impolitic in the extreme—the natural result of a position of political dishonesty. One of the strongest objections to the present political state of the Union seems to me to be that every leading public man is almost of necessity driven to disgraceful compromises and to dishonest compliances and professions. If he had used coercion at first, before the other States of the South were committed, he might possibly have succeeded. I doubt, even so, whether he would have brought South Carolina back, but this was the only chance. Now, however, that six or seven States have virtually joined, coercion can lead to nothing but an armed struggle; and an armed struggle will not hold the Union together. The means are inconsistent with the end. It is the most singular action for restitution of conjugal rights which the world ever heard of. You may conquer an insurgent province, but you cannot conquer a seceding State. The Roman plebs used secession as a means of extorting concessions from the patricians, but they would not have returned until they had gained their end. In this case the seceders are to be brought back by force, the concession of the point at issue is to be refused, and the two contending [parties] are to live harmoniously and happily ever after in the tender embraces of federal union. Such an idea seems to me utterly absurd and extravagant.

The progress of events is so rapid that I confess I cannot see my way at all as to the probable form of the new system which is to emerge from the chaos. Head thinks it not impossible that the Western States will form a Union of their own.

* * * *

Ever yours sincerely,

G. C. Lewis.

Kent House: March 10, 1861.

My dear Head,—I was very glad to receive your letter giving an account of your arrival at New York, and of your having had on the whole a good voyage. I trust that your cold journey to Quebec will be equally prosperous. The *dénouement* of the Anderson affair has been fortunate. A release on technical grounds is not a bad solution of the difficulty. I should hope that the Federal Government, which has enough on its hands at present, will not renew their claim of this *fugitivus*.

I was much interested by your account of the state of feeling at New York. The refusal of Tennessee and Arkansas to join the new Confederacy may give some hopes of a compromise; but I cannot see how it can be expected that men who have committed themselves so far as the leaders of the secession movement can be expected to come back, except upon such terms as they themselves would dictate. They would not only lose their present position, but they would scarcely be safe from proscription, if they acquiesced in the re-establishment of the old Union, and thus to a certain extent put themselves in the power of a republican executive.

Nevertheless, I hear that the latest letters from the North still speak of peaceable re-union as a possible event.

If the seven States of the extreme South finally separate, the chances are that the separation will not be effected without their coming to blows. If it was a mere question of cutting off a Federal limb, I think the operation might be performed without hostilities; but they have common property to divide, and as this cannot be done by a decree of the Court of Chancery, and as the joint owners are not likely to agree about the partition, the arbitration of the sword will probably be called in.

Our own politics have been pretty stationary since your departure. The House of Commons has been seized with a mania of appointing Committees, and there have been some long debates on Italian affairs, and on the occupation of Syria. The Volunteer Reform Bills await their second reading, but nobody expects that they will pass the House of Commons. Pray give my best regards to Lady Head. I hope Miss Lefevre* has been amused by her adventure across the Atlantic.

Ever yours sincerely,

G. C. L.

* Miss Lefevre, daughter of Sir John Lefevre, who was paying a visit to Sir Edmund and Lady Head.

Kent House: April 9, (probably) 1861.

My dear Reeve,—

* * * *

There is a circumstance relating to the early expeditions in Flanders, which Lord Grenville told my father, and of which Lord Stanhope does not seem to be aware. The King insisted on appointing the general, and he would select the Duke of York, who used to dine during the campaign at four o'clock, and was never visible after that hour, as he drank all the evening. After one of his disasters, Pitt wrote to the King, insisting that the Duke should be brought before a court martial. The King's answer to this letter is given in Mahon's series. Pitt remained firm for a time, but at last consented to yield, on condition that the appointment of general, and all other arrangements of the foreign expeditions, should be made in future by the ministers, and not by the King. The King was forced to consent to this condition, in order to save his son from exposure; and accordingly the appointments for the Egyptian expeditions were made by Pitt himself and Lord Grenville, without the interference of the King.

You may rely on the substance of this story being quite authentic. I will introduce it into my article, if I write one.

I do not altogether defend Pitt's warlike policy during the Revolution, but (subject to the explanation which I have given) I do not go the length of Macaulay's censure. I think worse of his giving in to the reactionary spirit during our little Tory reign of terror, and sanctioning the war of prosecutions, together with suspension of Habeas Corpus, Coercion Acts, &c., which were then resorted to. I suspect that the number of persons in this country who really sympathized with the French Revolution after 1792–3 was very small and perfectly contemptible in a political point of view. In Ireland, I admit, the state of things was different; but in Ireland Pitt's policy was always mild and conciliatory, and almost ultra-Whiggish. Lord Grenville told me that Pitt never would have allowed any person to call him a Tory—but then he used Whig and Tory in the old sense.

* * * *

Ever yours sincerely,
G. C. L.

Kent House: May 13, 1861.

My dear Head,—I have been, I am afraid, remiss in thanking you for your interesting letters on the state of things in America. You will see, however, that I profited by your views of the probable course of events in the article which I wrote for the 'Edinburgh Review.' The Northern States has been drifted, or rather plunged, into war without having any intelligible aim or policy. The South fight for independence; but what do the North fight for, except to gratify passion or pride? Ticknor, in his curious letter, talks of averting anarchy; but if the North had remained quiet, they had nothing to fear from anarchy. If the North intended to resort to coercion, they should have lost no time in attacking the South, before they had made preparations for war. Having lost much precious time, their true policy was to negotiate with the South and recognise the secession, in which case the Border States would, for a time at least, have stuck to the North. By following their present course, they have lost Virginia, and the other Border States, if not against them, are at least not with them. We have been engaged during the last week in deciding on the line to be taken by this country with respect to the contending parties. We recognise the Southern States as a belligerent power, but not as an independent State; and we have settled a proclamation, founded on the Foreign Enlistment Act, which will shortly be issued.

* * * *

The new American Minister for France, who lately passed through this country, sent us a message through Dallas that his Government wished to purchase arms of our Government. We shall decline on the ground of neutrality.

The Budget is passing slowly through Parliament. People are very reluctant to part with the paper duty, and our majority of eighteen was obtained only by the reluctance to give a vote which might turn out or endanger the Government. The Opposition are pursuing a dilatory policy, in the hope that some news may arrive from America which will show the necessity of further expenditure. I trust that these disturbances may not in any way interfere with your plans of returning in the summer or autumn.

Ever yours sincerely,

G. C. Lewis.

Kent House: June 9, 1861.

My dear Mrs. Austin,—I received yesterday at the Office a copy of the Lectures,* from twelve to seventeen, in continuation of the published set; but I have *not* received the 'Middle Temple Lectures,' which you say you have sent through Alfred Austin. I will read

* 'Lectures on Jurisprudence,' by the late John Austin. Edited by Mrs. Austin.

these lectures, and return them in a few days. I sent you the MSS. of the published lectures by the railway. I hope they reached you safely.

* * * *

The Epicureans taught that the touch was the most important of the senses, but I doubt whether any such doctrine as that expressed in the enclosed note can be found in Lucretius, or was held by the Epicureans. They certainly did not hold that the sight was identical with the touch, though they held that all objects of the sense are corporeal. (See book iv. 299–305).

I am much obliged to you for your kind advice, and am very glad that anything that I have lately said in Parliament has given you satisfaction. I fear it has not been of much importance. My health has been better of late; but if I thought that it was materially affected by my present mode of life, I should not hesitate in giving it up; it would cost me nothing, as far as my own tastes and inclinations are concerned, but rather the reverse.

* * * *

Ever yours sincerely,
G. C. L.

Kent House: June 24, 1861.

My dear Head,—I return Ticknor's interesting letter, which you had the kindness to send me. Another letter, which you sent me previously, I am ashamed to say that I cannot at this moment find, but I will return it when I recover it.

We hear threatening accounts from Washington of the bad disposition of Seward towards this country, and of the possibility of their declaring war against us. It seems, however, incredible that any Government of ordinary prudence should at a moment of civil war gratuitously increase the number of its enemies, and, moreover, incur the hostility of so formidable a power as England. The first effect would be that we should raise the siege of the Southern ports and ourselves blockade the Northern ports. I cannot, however, believe that Seward will be so insane as to take such a step. Their speculation, I believe, is, that they will bring about a war between France and England; but how a quarrel with us is to effect this object, I do not see.

I am rather apprehensive as to the effect of our sending three regiments to Canada. It may be misconstrued, and produce irritation; and the danger of invasion from the United States cannot be considerable.

Our own session is dragging on. A great effort was made by the Opposition upon the Paper-duty question; but that attempt having failed, it is not likely that any other party motion of importance will be tried. The sudden death of Lord Campbell creates the necessity of appointing a new Chancellor, and, as Bethell will probably have the great seal, of appointing a new Law Officer. We are very ill off for lawyers in the House of Commons, and the move will weaken the Government. Lord Campbell was in perfect health on the day preceding his death. He seems to have died sleeping.

I have no private news to send you.

Ever yours sincerely,

G. C. Lewis.

Kent House: July 8, 1861.

My dear Twisleton,—It seems to me that the course of the Bonn Gymnasium very much represents the ideas of our public school reformers, except that I doubt whether they would be satisfied with the proportion of time allotted to the modern languages. The highest class gives as much time to Hebrew as to French. Two hours a week for several years ought, however, to enable a student to acquire enough of French to be able to *read* it. I observe that French is taught by Germans. If this could be done in our public schools, it would get over one of the chief obstacles to the teaching of the modern languages. The number of hours accounted for is six per diem, without allowing for holidays and half-holidays. I suppose that exercises are done—that they are practised, for instance, in writing Latin prose—and that this is done out of school hours.

Ever yours sincerely,

G. C. L.

Among the arrangements that had been made when Lord Palmerston returned to the Treasury in June 1859, was the appointment of Mr. Sidney Herbert to be Secretary for War. We believe that at that time there already existed in him the seeds of the fatal disease that soon deprived the country of one of its most accomplished and trustworthy statesmen. Gradually his health failed; and as the session of 1861 advanced, it became clear that he must relinquish his office. A difficulty arose in the nomination of his successor, from the fact of two, the Secretaries of State, Lord Russell the Foreign, and the Duke of Newcastle the Colonial Secretary, being in the House of Lords. Under these circumstances, it was very desirable that the new Secretary for War should have a seat in the House of Commons. After some consideration and the discussion of various alternatives, Lord Palmerston decided to ask Sir G. C. Lewis to leave the Home and accept the War Office. Sir G. C. Lewis had always asserted the principle that a member of a Government, sinking personal wishes, ought to undertake such office and business as his colleagues thought it desirable to assign him. His want of acquaintance with military business, and in a minor degree other causes, made him extremely unwilling to consent to the change. Many of his friends urged him to decline, but his own opinion was unchanged, namely, that he ought to do what was required of him; so he set aside alike his own wishes and his friends' advice. The following letter to the Editor expresses the aversion in which he personally held the change.

Home Office: July 9, 1861.

My dear Gilbert,—It seems that Sidney Herbert's state of health is such as to render it impossible for him to retain his office, and that another arrangement for filling it will speedily become necessary. Lord Palmerston's wish is, that I should change to the War Department. He thinks that it is necessary that there should be a commoner at the head of this office, and he is unable to prevail on any other person in the House of Commons to accept it. The proposal is in the highest degree distasteful to me, but I do not well see how I can refuse to acquiesce in the transfer. In the event of the change taking place, Sir George Grey would return to the Home Office.

I know scarcely anything of the details of military administration, and I should have to learn my business from the first elements.

Ever yours affectionately,

G. C. L.

Harpton: Sept. 8, 1861.

My dear Head,—After much deliberation your successor has been appointed, and will, I presume, be ready to assume the administration during the autumn, so as to enable you to return before the winter. Lord Monck was a Lord of the Treasury when I was Chancellor of the Exchequer, and therefore I had frequent official relations with him. He lost his English seat, and being an Irish peer cannot sit for an Irish seat, so that he has been thrown out of a political career. He is a man of good sense and judgment, and of fair abilities and application. He has never been tried in anything difficult, but I should not be surprised if he acquitted himself with propriety in his new office.

There is, however, a great difference between being first and being second. There is no saying more true than the Greek proverb:—*ἀρχὴ τὸν ἄνδρα δείξει.* It shows what he is in a variety of ways. It shows what is bad and it shows what is good in him.

I have not written to you since my change of office, which, as you may suppose, was not of my seeking. The reports which were current as to the very laborious nature of its duties, turn out, as I partly suspected, to be quite fabulous. What it may be during war, I know not; probably its duties are then harassing and anxious, but during peace its duties appear to be less than those of the Home Office, so far as mere correspondence is concerned, and during the session, the parliamentary attendance is much lighter. Poor Sidney Herbert died of the Bright disease. He was not sufficiently frightened about himself in time, and went on with his office when he should have devoted himself exclusively to his health. He is a great loss both in private and public. The poor Bishop of Durham likewise died about the same time, of an obscure but painful disease, which affected his biliary system. His death is a severe blow to his large family.

The Duke of Newcastle has probably written to enquire your opinion as to the policy of sending further reinforcements to Canada. The subject has been under the consideration of the Government, and a premature announcement of a decision on the subject has found its way into the newspapers. Notwithstanding the paragraph which you had the kindness to send me I cannot but think that the Washington Government is bent upon punishing the South, and will strain every nerve to accomplish this object, without allowing its attention to be diverted to other quarrels. This being the case, I believe that, however they may swagger, they will keep their eyes steadily pointed to the South without turning them for a moment in the direction of Canada. There is likewise a difficulty about finding barrack-room for additional troops. I should be glad to know your opinion on this point, as the question must be decided speedily. My best regards to Lady Head. It will be very pleasant to see you again in England. I fear your return will be too late for paying us a visit at Harpton.

Ever yours, &c.,
G. C. Lewis.

My dear Mrs. Austin,—I was very sorry to miss seeing you when you were in London. I hope that I may be in better luck when you make your next visit.

I enclose some copies of my inscription,* and will send copies to anybody in Paris whose direction you will give me. I am rather in hopes that some foreigner ignorant of English may take it for a genuine inscription. I have heard that when Champollion† was in Egypt, some of his scholars played him a trick by inventing a hieroglyphical inscription of their own upon plaster, and burying it in a place which he was excavating. He found the inscription, believed it to be genuine, included it in his collection, and published it with an interpretation. I should like to verify this story. Perhaps St. Hilaire might know something of it. If it is true it goes far to support Brownius, as it shows that the method of interpretation is lax enough to include everything.

Ever yours sincerely,
G. C. L.

Harpton: Sept. 30, 1861.

My dear Mrs. Austin,—I was very glad to receive your interesting letter, and particularly to find that you had been able to do so much in France. I am sure that the exertion of travelling and of seeing different people cannot fail to be beneficial to you after your

* *Inscriptio Antiqua in Agro Bruttio nuper Reperta*; edidit et interpretatus est Johannes Brownius:—

HEYDIDDLEDIDDLE
THECATANDTHEFIDDLE
THECOUIUMPEDOVERTHEMOON
THELITTLEDOGLAUGHED
TOSEESUCHFINESPORT
ANDTHEDISHRANAUAYUITHTHESPOON,

Is treated and interpreted after the manner of an ancient inscription.

† A few years ago the scribbling of a German boy was imported from America, and published by a librarian in Paris as an Aztec manuscript.—[Editor.]

long seclusion. There never was so accomplished a sphinx as Louis Napoleon: for while one man sees in him a poisonous serpent, another sees in him a gentle dove; and both profess to be equally well-informed, and to speak from indubitable authority. My conviction is that England is the last country he will attack. His wars will be made for territorial aggrandizement—for the Rhine province—for a slice of Switzerland or of Spain. He cannot annex England—and the utmost he can hope is to inflict some loss or disgrace upon us. He must, however, be perfectly aware that this is a game at which two can play; and that if he was to burn Portsmouth or Plymouth we should never rest until we had done him some similar mischief. Besides, after all, wars are generally made for some supposed interest and not out of mere passion. I was not aware of the remark of Tocqueville, to which you refer, but I do not think that he knew any Greek, and even as to Latin, he probably knew about as much as all Catholics learn, and no more. He had no acquaintance with ancient literature, and no fondness for it. His mind was entirely formed upon modern models. Pray present my best remembrances to your host, and propound to him, as a point of literary interest, when Dante first became known in French literature? As far as I can make out, he was comparatively unknown in England until the middle of the last century. Bayle's article on Dante shows that his 'Divine Comedy' was nearly unknown in France at that time. So far as I am aware, there is no trace of an imitation of Dante in Milton.

There is no political news. The statement in the newspaper about sending troops to Canada, is, to say the least, premature. The Washington Government has been a little more civil lately; their hands, moreover, are pretty full of their own quarrel with the South.

Sir Edmund Head is to return to England in November. I sincerely hope that Lucy's* voyage will answer, but I suppose it will be some time before you can hear of her arrival at the Cape.

Ever yours sincerely,
G. C. L.

War Office: Nov. 30, 1861.

My dear Twisleton,—I am much obliged to you for your interesting letter, and I quite agree with you as to the lessons which history teaches of the superiority of military organization over undisciplined forces. All experience, from that of Sparta downwards, bears witness to this truth. It is clear that whatever may be thought of the Volunteers, we are not now in a condition to reduce our regular army. This unfortunate affair of the 'Trent' renders it quite uncertain whether we may not, before Easter, be engaged in a war with the Northern States. I cannot help hoping that they may not refuse to make reparation. It is anything but clear that the Washington Government ordered the act which has been committed. I hear that the Lieutenant who boarded our ship stated distinctly that they were not acting under orders from their Government. This is quite consistent with the statement which is attributed to General Scott. Lincoln's cabinet have doubtless been desirous of catching the Southern envoys, and may have caused their wish to be known; but it does not follow that they gave the instructions to board the 'Trent.' It seems incredible that Seward can seriously

* Lady Duff Gordon, who had gone to the Cape for the sake of her health.

desire to provoke a war with England. If he wishes it, the banking and commercial interests, who will surely make themselves felt, cannot be so insane. There must surely be an interval after the receipt of our despatch, when the voice of reason and prudence has some chance of being heard.

December 3.—Since I wrote the above, the news from America shows that the Captain acted without orders from his Government, but the manner in which Slidell and Mason have been received, and the general tone of the New York press, leave little hope of a peaceable solution. The question will have been virtually settled before our despatch is received. Seward ought not to delude himself with the hope that we fear war or shall recede from our demand. I believe, moreover, that the notion of separating France from England, and inducing her to join the Northern States, is quite fallacious. Louis Napoleon wishes to break the blockade, and he will take no step in the opposite direction. —&c., &c.

Ever yours sincerely,

G. C. LEWIS.

War Office: Dec. 5, 1861.

My dear Twisleton,—I have no doubt that, as you say, the gravity of the recent event was not appreciated in America. However, as Cockburn said of Graham, we shall soon *iron the smile* out of their face. The case of Laurens is irrelevant, as he was captured in an enemy's ship, not in a neutral vessel. I do not know the particulars of the case of Lucien Bonaparte, but if the ship was in a port, either friendly to France or at war with France, we were justified in using belligerent rights against her.

It is quite certain that the French Government wish for war between England and America. The blockade of the South would be raised, and they would get the cotton which they want. I suspect, moreover, that Louis Napoleon would lose no time in recognizing the independence of the Southern States.

Ever yours sincerely,
G. C. LEWIS.

Kent House: Dec. 11, 1861.

My dear Twisleton,—It is, I think, certain that there is no decided case in our Admiralty courts which justifies the seizure of Slidell and Mason. I have not yet heard of any act of our cruisers which is parallel. The Lucien case, as you may have seen in the 'Times,' is wholly different. The only question is, whether our Government or law advisers have not formerly laid down general principles which would justify this act. Now, in a question of this sort, you must interpret the principles of a government by its practice. Few logicians are so cautious as not, *for their present purpose*, to assume major premises unnecessarily wide, and which they would be forced to abandon if applied to different minor premises.

The doctrine which we advanced in 1812 respecting the search made for seamen in neutral ships is one of which *individually* I do not approve; but nationally, I admit we are committed to it. It certainly approaches to the act which we now condemn, but it is not identical. The extract from the 'Annual Register,' reprinted in the papers which I sent you, does not represent our pretensions correctly; but you will find them well stated (and certainly without any disposition to recede from them) in the enclosed pamphlet by Croker, who, as

Secretary to the Admiralty, thoroughly understood the question.

You will likewise find our claims on the subject defined in the declaration of the Prince Regent, 'Annual Register' for 1813, State Papers, p. 330. All this is perfectly well known to the American Government, and I do not think that they would derive any information or support to their case from the papers which I sent you, if they were published to all the world. You will observe that if the principle contended for by the Americans were admitted, we could not object to a Confederate cruiser taking Adams out of one of Cunard's steamers, as we recognize the belligerent rights of both parties.

Ever yours sincerely,
G. C. LEWIS.

Kent House: Dec. 16, 1861.

My dear Reeve,—The Prince's death * is a terrible calamity; and it will be so regarded by the public, though they do not know the extent of their loss. It will entirely alter the Queen's existence: he cannot be replaced. I am quite unable to estimate the probable consequences of this most disastrous event.

Ever yours sincerely,
G. C. L.

Letter not having date of year, from G. C. L. to Mr. Twisleton.

Kent House: April 1, (probably) 1862.

My dear Twisleton,—I can add a good instance of the Hebrew *sh* becoming *s* in the Greek, viz. σίκλος or σίγλος from shekel; see Xen. 'Anab.' i. 5. 6; Hesychius in σίγλον, Photius in σίκλος.

* Prince Albert's lamented death took place on Dec. 14, 1861.

I can understand a hieroglyphic becoming an alphabetic system, but such is not the doctrine of Champollion. See the passage in my volume,* pp. 393 and 260. He supposes the hieroglyphic writing to have been phonetic from a remote period.

It appears to me that Renan is not an orthodox Egyptologist.

Ever yours sincerely,
G. C. L.

Kent House: April 2, 1862.

My dear Stanhope,—I enclose a few notes on the two last volumes of your interesting book.† I am afraid that they are of no great value, but such as they are I send them.

Ever yours sincerely,
G. C. Lewis.

Vol. III. ch. xxiii.—There was a celebrated quotation made by Mr. Pitt, in reply to Mr. Fox, on the occasion of the mutiny at the Nore,—'Si in tanto rerum omnium metu solus non timet,'‡ &c.—which might be worth notice.

Page 51.—I have not at this moment the means of referring to Wilberforce's Diary,§—but in general Lord Grenville was very tolerant in questions of religious dissent, though he had a strong religious belief, and I should have thought it very improbable that he would

* 'Astronomy of the Ancients,' by Sir George Lewis. Parker, 1862.

† 'Life of Pitt,' by Earl Stanhope. 4 vols. Murray, 1862.

‡ These words form part of a speech ascribed to Cato when replying to Cæsar in the Senate. See the 'Catilinarian War' of Sallust, chap. lii The sentence runs thus: Quare vanum equidem hoc consilium est, s periculum ex illis metuit: sin in tanto omnium metu solus non timet, e magis refert, me mihi atque vobis timere.

§ See vol. ii. p. 222 of 'Memoirs of Wilberforce,' by his Sons. 5 vols Murray, 1838.

have quarrelled with Pitt on such a subject. He was certainly very active in urging Pitt to the measure of 1801, on which his Government was broken up.

Page 86.- Mr. Frere told me that the first part of the 'Loves of the Triangles,'* together with the idea and plan of the poem, was his, and all the rest was Mr. Canning's.

Page 88.—I believe that you are quite right in supposing that none of the poetry, and I believe it may be added the prose, of the 'Anti-jacobin' was by Pitt. Some of the prose articles were contributed by Lord Grenville: I believe the financial ones.

Page 116.—Wearing the hair short, and without powder, was at this time considered a mark of French principles. Hair so worn was called 'a crop.' Hence Lord Melbourne's phrase † 'crop imitating wig.' This is the origin 'of croppies,' as applied to the Irish rebels of 1798.

Page 155.—In Howell's 'State Trials,' vol. xxvii., it is stated that Napper Tandy,‡ having been arraigned on his attainder, was acquitted by the jury. Query?—Was there any subsequent trial?

Page 176.—Lord Grenville told me that he mentioned his intention to Pitt, to use this quotation, § and

* 'Loves of the Triangles,' a mathematical and philosophical poem: 'Poetry of the Anti-jacobin,' p. 113.

† 'Poetry of the Anti-jacobin,' p. 49:—

I swear by all the youths that Malmesbury chose,
By Ell——'s sapient prominence of nose,
By Morpeth's gait, important, proud, and big,
By Leveson Gower's crop-imitating wig. &c.

‡ Napper Tandy, an Irishman who promoted a French descent on the coast of Donegal. 'He boasted that, land where he pleased, he would be joined by 30,000 men: but no signs of any junction appeared.' [I find no account of any subsequent trial.—EDITOR.]

§ Mr. Pitt was speaking in favour of the union of Ireland with Eng-

that Pitt was so pleased with it that 'he begged it of him.'

It was supposed that Pitt substituted *nova* for *mihi*, in order to avoid alluding to the imputation that he promoted the Irish rebellion from motives of personal ambition.

Page 181.—My belief is, that you might have denied still more strongly the prevalent imputation of bribery by secret means for carrying the Union. The small sums furnished from the secret service money appear to have been used for paying pamphleteers and writers in the press. All Lord Castlereagh's political bribery was avowed, and most of it was by Act of Parliament.

Appendix. p. xi.—I always suspected that George III. gave money for elections out of his civil list; but I never could find any proof. It is now furnished by the King's own letter, of January 23, 1798.*

Appendix. p. xvi.—There is a clear notice in the King's letter of June 11, 1798, that he will not consent to further relaxations of the laws against the Catholics. This is material with respect to Pitt's knowledge of the King's feelings on the subject. The King was likewise hostile to the payment of the Catholic Clergy, p. xviii. but he was highly favourable to the Union, pp. xvi. xvii.

Vol. IV. p. 212.—The origin of Martello Towers, I believe to have been that, when piracy was common in

land. See Lord Stanhope's 'Life of Pitt,' vol. iii. 175-6. 'Æneid,' xii. 197:

> Non ego, nec Teucris Italos parere jubebo,
> Nec *nova* regna peto: paribus se legibus ambæ
> Invictæ gentes æterna in fœdera mittant.

Pitt substituted *nova* for *mihi*.

* Lord Stanhope's 'Life of Pitt,' 3rd vol. Appendix, p. xi. The King's words are, 'As to the former, I have some debts, of which the sums borrowed for the late elections makes the most considerable part,' &c.

the Mediterranean, and pirates, like the Danes, made plundering descents upon the coasts, the Italians built towers near the sea, in order to keep a watch, and give warning if a pirate ship was seen to approach the land. This warning was given by striking on a bell with a hammer; and hence these towers were called 'torri da martello.' I cannot remember where I read this explanation, but I am sure that I found it in some credible book.

Page 398.—There is a full-length portrait of Pitt at Dropmore, in what was formerly Lord Grenville's sitting-room. My impression is, that it is a repetition of Hoppner's. There is likewise a full length portrait of Pitt at the Trinity House, in his uniform of Master. It is a good picture which I have seen. It may be remarked, that in the portrait at Windsor Castle, Pitt holds in his hand a copy of his Sinking Fund Bill. It seems from your statement that this must have been Lawrence's own view of Pitt's principal achievement.

Page 339.—It should be added that Lord Powis never went to Ireland, and never assumed the Lord Lieutenancy.

Page 416.—Lord Grenville told my father that Pitt had formed a plan for abolishing all customs duties, and that he would have carried it into effect if the war of the French Revolution had not broken out, which defeated all his financial and commercial plans. Lord Grenville said that the amount of the public expenditure at that time rendered such a plan quite feasible.

The Grove: April 26, 1862.

My dear Stanhope,—To say the truth, I did not buy 'Lord Auckland's Letters,' and it so happens that I have not yet fallen in with the two new volumes, so that I am ignorant of their contents. I will, however, take care to read them before long. I felt perfectly certain that Pitt and Lord Grenville were not parties to any plan for a partition of France in 1793–4, and I am not at all surprised to hear that the correspondence does not bear out the statement.

The lot of a Foreign Minister would indeed be a hard one, if he were responsible for every foolish plan which an over-zealous diplomatic agent may send him, and to which he is forced to give a civil answer.

I shall be curious to read Pitt's letter referring to Lord Auckland's intrigues in 1800. It is a dark passage in his history, but I am inclined to think that Lord Auckland was sincere in his fear of the Catholics, and that he was not, like Lord Loughborough, merely flattering the King's prejudices for personal objects. His connection with the Archbishop of Canterbury probably gave him facilities for communicating with the King on this subject. The sincerity of his opinion (for which I generously give him credit) did not, however, justify him, in his subordinate official position, clandestinely communicating with the King, on so delicate a question, against the policy of the Prime Minister, to whom he was under great personal obligations, and who regarded him as a private friend. I read your letter in to-day's 'Times' about Pitt's last words, with much interest. It is clear from other circumstances that he was conscious of approaching death, which frequently is not the case.

The article on your last volumes, in the 'Quarterly,' is, I conclude, by Lord Robert Cecil. It is a well written composition, but is in my opinion very unjust to Lord Grenville. Whether Pitt or Lord Grenville were right in the lines which they respectively took in 1801–5 is an arguable question, and candid judges may differ about it; but it is quite a mistake to say that Lord Grenville owed his political position exclusively to Pitt. Lord Grenville was brought into Parliament by his elder brother, without the smallest reference to Pitt, who had at that time no seats to give away. He made his parliamentary position by his own ability; and although Pitt no doubt took him into his cabinet, as much may be said of any other member of a cabinet who is not Prime Minister. Lord Grenville had much of that quality which his friends called firmness, and his enemies obstinacy; but to say that his obstinacy was 'unreasoning' is entirely to mistake his character. I will venture to say that Lord Grenville never took any important step in public life for which, whether right or wrong, he was not able to allege excellent reasons. Wraxall mentions that when Pitt was in want of a leader in the House of Lords, he sent Lord Grenville there, in order to get rid of a dangerous rival in the House of Commons. I do not believe that this was Pitt's motive: but the existence of the rumour shows what was the impression at the time with respect to their relative positions.

Ever yours sincerely,

G. C. Lewis.

Kent House: May 5, 1862.

My dear Stanhope,—I am glad that you approve of my suggestion of a catalogue of portraits. Pray bring it before the trustees in any way you think fit. I don't know whether my letter is worthy of being entered on the minutes.

I would propose to include the statues and busts, and to exclude miniatures. Engravings belong to a different category; an authentic list of them would be valuable, but might be made without the assistance of a public authority.

Pitt's letter to Lord Auckland shows that he believed the latter to have behaved towards him in an unfriendly manner. This can only allude to intrigues on the Catholic Question.

Pitt's opinion of Burke's writings on the French Revolution is curious—that they are rhapsodies in which there is much to admire and nothing to assent to.

My opinion of Burke's writings and speeches on the French Revolution, and on Hastings, is that there is much in them wild and rhapsodical, but that his view of both subjects is substantially right. Lord Grenville advised me to read the vindication of 'Civil Society' (written in imitation of Lord Bolingbroke), which he said was Burke's best writing in point of style. I always observed that his estimate of Burke was very different from that of the present generation.

Ever yours sincerely,

G. C. LEWIS.

Kent House: May 7, 1862.

My dear Stanhope,—You are quite welcome to publish the enclosed note, of the accuracy of which there is no doubt. I have often conversed on it with my father. Lord Grenville was himself a consistent free trader, and was always hostile to the corn laws, at a time when even free traders did not venture to utter a word against them. If Pitt had been minister in 1815, he would never have consented to increasing the rigour of prohibition after the war. There seems to have been much intimacy between Lord Grenville and Lord Auckland after Pitt's death—more than I was aware of.

I agree with you that the latter appears to have a peculiar obliquity of vision with respect to facts. His letter describing what took place in the House of Commons on the night on which he first appeared on the Treasury bench, after his change of politics, would be incredible, if it had not been published by his family.

Ever yours sincerely,
G. C. Lewis.

I enter (with his permission) one or two letters from E. A. Freeman, Esq. (the author of the valuable 'History of Federal Government,' and more recently of the 'History of the Norman Conquest of England'), because they serve to render complete a correspondence between him and Sir George Lewis on the subject of the former book, which Mr. Freeman has been kind enough to contribute.

Edward A. Freeman, Esq., to Sir George Lewis.

Somerleaze Wells: May 9, 1862.

My dear Sir,—I hope I am not taking a liberty in thanking you for putting out your book on 'Ancient Astronomy,' which I am reading with perfect delight. I cannot follow the astronomical part, but I cannot fancy a greater service to history than you have done, by upsetting all the Egyptian and Babylonian dreams which have filled people's heads for some years past. I only doubt about one thing. Is there not a fair presumption, if there be no evidence to the contrary, that modern Coptic represents old Egyptian in the same way that modern English represents old Teutonic, or the romance of the Klephts represents the Greek of Homer? At the same time I should doubt whether such a resemblance would enable anybody to make out the elder form of the language, if, as seems the case in Egypt, all intermediate forms and all cognate dialects had vanished.

Pray forgive my intrusion, and believe me yours truly,

EDWARD A. FREEMAN.

War Office: May 17, 1862.

My dear Stanhope,—I think that I have discovered, with the assistance of a friend, the origin of Windham's statement respecting Martello towers. An attack was made on the tower of Mortella * in Corsica, by the British forces, both by sea and land, in February 1794. The tower was taken after an obstinate defence; but the two attacking ships were beaten off. This circumstance is likely to have given rise to the confusion between Martello towers generally and this tower of *Mortella*. See James's 'Naval History of Great Britain' (Lond. 1822), vol. i. p. 286, where the event is described. Martello towers were intended for defences against a landing; and the successful defence of the tower of Mortella against two of our ships probably gave rise to the erroneous etymology in question.

Ever yours sincerely,

G. C. LEWIS.

* Sir G. C. Lewis's opinion of the origin of the name 'Martello' towers has been previously published by Earl Stanhope in his agreeable little volume of *Miscellanies*. Murray, 1863.

Kent House: May 19 (probably), 1862.

My dear Twisleton,—Many thanks. If I am not mistaken, there was an article on the Countess of Desmond in the 'Quarterly Review'* a year or two ago. There is likewise an account of old Parr by Hervey in Hervey's works, as well as in the 'Harleian Miscellany.'

I believe that it may be stated generally that no instance exists of any member of a royal or noble family, whose birth was registered when it occurred, having attained the age of a hundred years.

Ralegh appeals to the memory of all the noblemen and gentlemen of Munster; but one should like to know what it was exactly that they remembered.

The well known passage in the Psalms† shows what was the result of universal experience as to the duration of life at an early period of Hebrew History.

Ever yours sincerely,

G. C. L.

Note written on the above letter by Mr. Twisleton.

N.B. In the autumn of 1860, Sir G. C. Lewis told me at Harpton he did not think there was sufficient evidence to show that anyone had exceeded the age of

* *Quarterly Review* for March, 1853, vol. xcii. p. 355. The longevity of Old Parr and the Countess of Desmond,

'Who lived to the age of a hundred and ten,
And died of a fall from a cherry-tree then,'

is also the subject of various articles in *Notes and Queries.* She is sometimes stated to have died at the age of 140, sometimes of 162 years; while Old Parr has been said to have reached the age of 152 years and 9 months.

† Psalm xc. 10. 'The days of our years are three score years and ten, and if by reason of strength they be four score years, yet is their strength but labour and sorrow,' &c.

one hundred and nine years. I did not understand him to deny the possibility of the fact; but to speak only of evidence for the fact.

E. T.

Sir George Lewis to E. A. Freeman, Esq.

May 29, 1862.

My dear Sir,—

* * * *

I am greatly pleased to find that a judge so competent as yourself approves of my chapter on ancient Egyptian and Assyrian history. It seemed to me that the Egyptologists and the interpreters of cuneiform were taking undue liberties with the credulity of the public, and that it was high time for somebody to interfere. I wish that the task had been undertaken by some one who had more time to devote to the subject, and who had more knowledge of Oriental languages. But I have at least thrown down the gauntlet, and I am surprised that no one has hitherto taken it up, at least in print. I suppose they say that the arguments are so insignificant as not to deserve notice.

Believe me yours very truly,

G. C. Lewis.

Edward A. Freeman, Esq., to Sir George Lewis.

Somerleaze, Wells: May 30, 1862.

My dear Sir,—I do not see how anybody can answer the Egyptian part of your book, nor indeed the Assyrian either, though it is not quite so full. I want very much, if I can find a place, to treat of it along with Rawlinson's and the other side, but I am not sure that I shall be able to, as in the 'National Review' your book is to be written about by an astronomer, which I rather regret, as I look on it as much more historical than scientific, and mere scientific men are so fond of running down all ages which did not know so much as they do themselves. But I do not know who the astronomer is.

I hope about November to bring out the first volume of my History of Federal Government, bringing the subject down to the end of the Achaian League. I hope then to go on with Switzerland, Holland, and America. It has been actually begun since the disruption in America, but I have had the subject before my eyes for the last ten years. It seems to me that all English writers except Bishop Thirlwall have strangely neglected Grecian History since Alexander; so I hope I may be doing some good in that way.

Believe me very truly yours,

EDWARD A. FREEMAN.

Sir George Lewis to E. A. Freeman, Esq.

Kent House: June 7, 1862.

My dear Sir,—I am glad to hear that your first volume on Federal Governments,* is to appear in the course of the year; the subject is one which deserves historical treatment. M. Croix's volume is superficial and unsatisfactory.

Federal Government lies on the confines between International and National Law, and affords many interesting and instructive problems. It touches on the question of *Congresses*, on which much nonsense has been talked and written. The contrast between a federal system and a system of dependencies (like that

* *History of the Federal Government from the Foundation of the Achaian League to the Disruption of the United States*, by Edward A. Freeman. Macmillan. 1863.

of our Colonial Empire) is also instructive. The differences (as you doubtless see) are great and decisive. It is surprising that so able a man as Sir James Stephen should have supposed that our colonial system is *federal*. I agree with you as to the mistake of neglecting all Greek history after Alexander. I proposed to Mr. Grote, when he had completed his first history, to compose a second work, including the same subject as the history of Polybius; viz. an introductory sketch of Grecian History from Alexander, and a combined account of Greek and Roman History from the first Punic War to the taking of Corinth or Carthage. I am satisfied that this would form an excellent subject and might be satisfactorily treated, even with our present imperfect materials. It would take up Roman affairs nearly at the point when they begin to have a purely historical character.

I am afraid that I did not explain my meaning clearly about Coptic. I did not mean to assert that Coptic grew out of nothing. I have no doubt that it contains remnants of the ancient Egyptian language. What I meant to say is, that its form and substance have undergone such changes as to render the interpretation of the hieroglyphic language, by a reflex etymological process, 'periculosæ plenum opus aleæ.'

Ever yours truly,

G. C. LEWIS.

E. A. Freeman, Esq., to Sir George Lewis.

Somerleaze, Wells: June 10, 1862.

My dear Sir,—I have done my best to work out some of the points which you speak of in my introductory chapter. I have made the chief difference between a federation and a colonial system to be that though a colony may be as independent internally as a canton, yet neither it nor its citizens have any voice in deciding the general policy of the Empire, while a canton has as a canton or by the individual votes of its citizens. So I laid it down that though a purely municipal division, a city or province, might have as much internal independence as a canton, yet the rights of such city or province were merely concessions liable to be withdrawn by the central legislature, while the independence of a canton is inherent, and the Diet, or Congress, cannot touch it without its own consent. I hope this is right, but I do not profess to be a lawyer.

My first volume is mainly a constitutional history of the Achaian League. Till I began to write, I had no notion what a mass of materials there really is, incidental expressions of Polybius for instance, which I find, moreover, that German scholars continually fail to understand, simply from not being used to the goings on of a free country. But of course I only occupy a very small portion of the great subject; you trace it. I should doubt Mr. Grote being the man for it; his heart is so thoroughly with Athens that he cannot care for times when Athens has become contemptible. So he despises my Achaians, and hates my Macedonians.

Pray forgive this long letter, and believe me very truly yours,

EDWARD A. FREEMAN.

Harpton, Radnor: Oct. 4 (probably), 1862.

My dear Twisleton,—I have delayed too long thanking you for your letter, and for the little guide book containing an interesting account of the Scavi at Uriconium, of which I am ashamed to say I had not heard. The Romans seem to have understood the art of building durable brick walls; both their bricks and their cement were at least as good as ours. Chimneys are a comparatively modern invention; there is an article upon them in that excellent book, Beckmann's 'History of Inventions.' The Romans were unquestionably the most *practical* nation of antiquity, and in this respect they far excelled their teachers the Greeks. It is a curious circumstance that the Greeks, with all their scientific knowledge of astronomy, could not make a good calendar; and it was left to the Romans, who were comparatively ignorant of the subject, to establish a calendar which, with a trifling reform, is now used by all civilised nations.

Ever yours sincerely,

G. C. L.

Autumn of 1862.

My dear Mrs. Austin,—I have forwarded your letter to Head. His direction is 29 Chesham Street. I shall have much pleasure in seeing Barthélemy St. Hilaire if he remains in England until I return to town. He is an excellent writer, and I hear that his work on Buddha has already become so scarce that a copy sells for double the price of publication. I confess, however, that I am unable to set up any interest about Oriental philosophers and teachers. The only book in the whole circle of Oriental literature which seems to me worth reading is the 'Arabian Nights.'

* * * *

When you are at Oxford you will be some way on your road to this house. I wish that I could tempt you to come here and to bring B. St. Hilaire if he should be so disposed.

Ever yours sincerely,

G. C. L.

Harpton: Oct. 7 (probably), 1862.

My dear Mrs. Austin,—If I were in London I could easily find out the title of Feuerbach's book; and I might perhaps hit upon the passage in Leibnitz; but I have no means of reference in the country for these two writers. I have read Leibnitz's 'Théodicée,' but know little of his other works.

I cannot recall any passage in Bacon where he uses *viri civiles* for practical politicians, though I dare say such a passage exists. In 'Nov. Org.' i. 92, he applies *prudentia civilis* to the wisdom of practical politicians; and in the *De Augmentis*, e. g. lib. 8, he applies the term *doctrina* or *scientia civilis* to the doctrine of practical politics.

I am very sorry that we have no chance of a visit from you. My movements are now uncertain, for I shall be forced to come up to London on the 21st for public business.

* * * *

Ever yours sincerely,

G. C. L.

War Office: Dec. 16, 1862.

My dear Gilbert,

* * * *

Theresa has suffered a good deal of pain.*** There is no symptom to create alarm or even uneasiness, but she has not made much progress. B—— wrote me word that there was a report of Captain ——'s death.* Did you hear anything of it?

Yours affectionately,

G. C. L.

* The report of the death of Captain ——, which was generally believed in his neighbourhood, arose thus:—Two gamekeepers, brothers,

Jan. 1, 1863.

My dear Gilbert,—Your story about the two keepers is excellent, and deserves to be embalmed in the next edition of Joe Miller. It will make —— very angry if some indiscreet person tells it to him.

My pedigree * pamphlet remains in proof, and has not been printed off. I will not fail to send you copies as soon as I have any. * * * The Northerners have sustained a great reverse at Frederickburg; but the Southerners omitted or were unable to follow up their success, and although the moral effect has been considerable, the military position remains unchanged. The two armies are looking at one another across the Rappahannock, and neither is likely to cross it.

Ever yours affectionately,

G. C. L.

Kent House: Feb. 8, 1863.

My dear Hayward,—I read with much satisfaction your article on Lord Lansdowne. His most characteristic quality was in my opinion his excellent judgment. I have never in my life known a person whose judgment on things both public and private was more invariably sound than his. He wanted self-reliance, and he disliked steady hard work. These two latter

who were going their rounds on their respective masters' estates, which adjoined one another, met near the deer park of one of them Captain ——. Some of the deer had been in the habit of breaking through the fence of this park and wandering in the neighbouring woods, and one especially, an old buck, had given the keepers a great deal of trouble. At length some one killed the errant old buck: and in the course of conversation one keeper told the other—'Well, the old buck is dead at last.' By this, his less matter of fact and more metaphorical companion understood—not the deer—but the deer's proprietor; and informed the neighbourhood generally of Captain ——'s death.

* Pedigree of his own family.

qualities prevented him from accepting the office of Prime Minister, for which he was pre-eminently fitted, and caused persons who did not know him well to underrate his natural abilities, which were much greater than was generally believed. If he exerted himself, he was quite a match for any of his contemporaries in debate. He had lived in familiarity with nearly all the ablest men of his day, and his opinions were all enlightened.

I have read the first volume of Kinglake. * * * Kinglake's fault is that (as has been said of Sallust) he tries to write better than he can write. This constant strain and effort gives a stiff, pedantic character to his style, deprives it of flow and facility, and produces a sense of painful parturition which communicates itself to the reader. If he would consent to express himself in common English much of his book would be pleasant reading enough.* * * His attempt to throw all the credit or blame of the expedition to Sebastopol upon the Duke of Newcastle is a complete delusion. His story about the sleepy Cabinet may be partially true, but the plan of the expedition had been discussed by the Cabinet at repeated sittings, and the despatch in question only embodied a foregone conclusion. I do not agree with Kinglake that a careful discussion of the draft would have led to giving a wider discretion to Lord Raglan. The discretion which the despatch gave seems to me to have been unusually wide and scarcely justifiable. If it had been more discussed, the Cabinet would perhaps have thought that they were throwing on him undue responsibility.

There is no doubt that Lord Palmerston resigned on account of the Reform Bill.

Ever yours truly,

G. C. Lewis.

Kent House: Feb. 8, 1863.

My dear Mrs. Austin,—I am much obliged to you for kind letter of enquiry. I am happy to say that Lady Theresa bears this heavy blow * with fortitude, and that her health has not suffered from it, which I was afraid might be the case.

Poor Lord Lansdowne had almost anticipated death, though he kept up a good fight against his infirmities to the last. His place will remain vacant; there is no one to fill it up. Nobody ever administered a large fortune with greater consideration for others or with greater kindness to his numerous friends. His judgment was admirable; and his great natural abilities were only obscured by want of self-reliance and by excessive caution. It is much to be lamented that he never accepted the office of Prime Minister, for which he had pre-eminent qualifications.

I was very sorry at not being able to dine at Senior's, but I was unwell and confined to the house for nearly a fortnight.

Ever yours sincerely,

G. C. L.

Sir George Lewis to E. A. Freeman, Esq.

Kent House: Feb. 14, 1863.

My dear Sir,—I am much obliged to you for your kindness in sending me the first volume of your 'History of Federal Governments,' which I have read with much interest and advantage. The first part is very instructive and contains many new analogies.

* The calamity alluded to is the death of Lady Theresa Lewis's eldest daughter, Mrs. William Harcourt, for whom all her relations had the deepest affection.

It seems to me that the essential idea of a federal government as distinguished from a federation—of a Bundes staat as distinguished from a Staatenbund—is that the sovereignty is divided between a number of governments being one more than the number of states. If there are n states there must be $n+1$ governments. Each state must have a peculiar government, and the entire federation must have a common government. If you were to suppose a union of five monarchies, the formula would be equally true. Each state would have its monarch, and the five monarchs or their plenipotentiaries would form the federal government. Writers who call our colonial system a federal government overlook this important consideration, and forget that it wants the essential characteristic of federalism. If you suppose one of the state governments to exercise the powers of a federal government, the other state governments would speedily become mere municipalities. It seems, therefore, necessary that the federal government should be distinct from any of the state governments.

I agree for the most part with the analogies between ancient and modern institutions which you trace in the first part of your volume; but I rate less highly than you do, the effect of direct democracy upon the individual character. The Athenian Ecclesia met only once a month regularly, and probably the questions discussed at it were not numerous. The judicial functions of the Athenian citizen were probably quite as important as his functions of ecclesiast.

Page 250.—There is no English word which corresponds exactly with the word τύραννος. But the English word 'tyrant' implies a harsh, oppressive exercise of power, which the Greek word does not. A τύραννος was necessarily an usurper, or the descendant or successor of an usurper. Cromwell and Napoleon were both τύραννοι. If Lincoln happened to be an able man, with military talent, and were to make himself master of the Northern states, he would be a τύραννος.

Page 264.—It seems to me a mistake to refer the passages cited from Thucydides to the absolute rule of the demus of Athens at home. They apply exclusively to the ἀρχή, to the subject states. Over these the power of the demus, considered as an unit, was absolute.

Page 284.—It is here correctly stated that the English Cabinet has no legal existence. That is to say, the Cabinet has no corporate character; its decisions as such have no authority; it is merely a meeting of ministers to discuss important business. But the statement in p. 280, that the *Ministry* has no legal existence seems to me inaccurate. Every minister has legal power to do acts relating to his own department, and is legally responsible for them. The Cabinet may discuss a despatch to be written to a foreign government and may agree to it; but the Foreign Secretary has alone power to write the despatch, and he is alone responsible for it in a legal sense. A minister who signed a treaty might be impeachable for the contents of the treaty, but his colleagues could not be impeached, although they might have agreed to it in the Cabinet. It is true, as is stated in p. 313, that our law does not recognise a Prime Minister; but *somebody* is responsible for every ministerial act. The reasons why votes of censure or of want of confidence have taken the place of impeachment are not the defect of legal responsibility but the superior efficiency of the former remedy.

Page 296.—* I believe that an officer such as our

* Soon after this letter was written Sir George Lewis stated his opinions on this subject more fully. They are published in *Notes and*

Speaker was unknown to the ancients. Their deliberative assemblies had no president who maintained order, and put the question to the vote. The magistrates had generally the initiative, sometimes they had it exclusively; and they exercised a sort of control over the assembly. But a citizen who made a motion in the Roman comitia or senate, himself, as I conceive, put the motion. Rogare legem implied that the person who proposed the law, put the question to the vote. There is nothing in the passage of Polybius which implies that the magistrates put the question to the vote. (See Thucydides, i. 87, where the Ephor, after having spoken, puts the question.)

I take the liberty of sending you a copy* of a political dialogue, which I have lately published. You will find in it some of the questions about Federalism slightly touched upon. The best justification of a federal system is when the separate states are too weak to defend themselves separately against powerful enemies.

Believe me yours very truly,

G. C. Lewis.

War Office: Feb. 26, 1863.

My dear Head,—I am much obliged to you for the copy of your excellent translation, and also for the two volumes, which are useful books of reference at all times, but particularly at the present time. If you and Lady Head and Caroline should wish to see the procession of the Prince of Wales on the 7th, there will be places at this office at your disposition—or, if you care to go to Windsor to see the wedding, I can give

Queries, 3rd series, vol. iii. p. 281, where the article on the 'Presidency of Deliberative Assemblies' has his name attached to it.

* *Dialogue on the Best Form of Government*, G. C. Lewis, 1863.

you a ticket for the antechapel. You need not appear in full dress.

Seward's letter to the French government shows how utterly hopeless all attempts to move the Federal government must be until some strong necessity is applied to them.

Ever yours sincerely,

G. C. L.

War Office: April 4, 1863.

My dear Gilbert,—I enclose a copy of the bill for amending the Local Government Act.

I intend, if I am able, to go to Harpton on Monday with Theresa, and to stay there till the following Saturday. I am anxious to get some fresh air at Easter, and I think that a complete change may do Theresa good, after so many things to depress her.

I hear nothing new. The story of a congress for the affairs of Poland is, so far as I know, mere moonshine. Princess Alice is to be confined immediately. Lord Palmerston's speeches have been, on the whole, very good. His vigour is perfectly marvellous.

Ever yours affectionately,

G. C. L.

This was one of the last letters that Sir George Lewis wrote; *the last* that I ever received from him.

It will have been observed that on the 16th of the previous December he had mentioned the illness of Lady Theresa Lewis; he wrote 'that she had suffered pain,' that 'she had not made much progress.' Her illness had, in fact, been so serious as to give him constant anxiety during many weeks. To this anxiety succeeded deep grief for the death of Mrs. William Harcourt which occurred early in 1863; and for whom he entertained the love of a daughter. In March he himself was annoyed by an attack of a disorder which though of little consequence in itself served further to interfere with his habits and to depress his spirits. He was commonly disinclined to move from place to place, for railway journeys disagreed with him, but after the occurrence of these distressing circumstances he thought that country air and a change of scene would be beneficial both to Lady Theresa Lewis and himself. He consequently determined to spend the Easter holy days in Radnorshire. He left London on the 4th of April. It was his last journey. He had not passed more than a day at Harpton before he was seized with one of the bilious attacks from which throughout his life he had frequently suffered; congestion of lungs followed. The disorder, at the same time, of two organs which for many years had been weak and defective, was more than his constitution could withstand. In a few days he breathed his last.

INDEX.

LONDON: PRINTED BY
SPOTTISWOODE AND CO., NEW-STREET SQUARE
AND PARLIAMENT STREET

WORKS BY JOHN STUART MILL.

CHAPTERS and SPEECHES on the IRISH LAND QUESTION. Crown 8vo. price 2*s.* 6*d.*

ENGLAND and IRELAND. Fifth Edition. 8vo. 1*s.*

The SUBJECTION of WOMEN. The Third Edition. Post 8vo. price 5*s.*

PRINCIPLES of POLITICAL ECONOMY.
Library Edition (the Sixth), 2 vols. 8vo. 30*s.*
People's Edition, crown 8vo. 5*s.*

On REPRESENTATIVE GOVERNMENT.
Library Edition (the Third), 8vo. 9*s.*
People's Edition, crown 8vo. 2*s.*

On LIBERTY.
Library Edition (the Fourth), post 8vo. 7*s.* 6*d.*
People's Edition, crown 8vo. 1*s.* 4*d.*

SYSTEM of LOGIC. Seventh Edition. 2 vols. 8vo. 25*s.*

STEBBING'S ANALYSIS *of* MILL'S SYSTEM *of* LOGIC. Second Edition, revised, in 12mo. price 3*s.* 6*d.*

KILLICK'S STUDENT'S HANDBOOK *of* MILL'S SYSTEM *of* LOGIC, just published, in crown 8vo. price 3*s.* 6*d.*

DISSERTATIONS and DISCUSSIONS, POLITICAL, PHILOSOPHICAL, and HISTORICAL; reprinted from the Edinburgh and Westminster Reviews. Second Edition, revised. 2 vols. 8vo. 24*s.*

DISSERTATIONS and DISCUSSIONS, POLITICAL, PHILOSOPHICAL, and HISTORICAL; reprinted chiefly from the Edinburgh and Westminster Reviews. VOL. III. 8vo. price 12*s.*

UTILITARIANISM. Third Edition. 8vo. 5*s.*

An EXAMINATION of Sir WILLIAM HAMILTON'S PHILOSOPHY, and of the Principal Philosophical Questions discussed in his Writings. Third Edition, revised. 8vo. 16*s.*

PARLIAMENTARY REFORM. Second Edit. 8vo. 1*s.* 6*d.*

INAUGURAL ADDRESS at the UNIVERSITY of ST. ANDREWS. Second Edition, 8vo. 5*s.* People's Edition, crown 8vo. 1*s.*

ANALYSIS of the PHENOMENA of the HUMAN MIND. By JAMES MILL. A New Edition, with Notes Illustrative and Critical, by ALEXANDER BAIN, ANDREW FINDLATER, and GEORGE GROTE. Edited, with additional Notes, by JOHN STUART MILL. 2 vols. 8vo. price 28*s.*

London: LONGMANS, and CO. Paternoster Row.

39 Paternoster Row, E.C.
London: *January* 1870.

GENERAL LIST OF WORKS

PUBLISHED BY

Messrs. LONGMANS, GREEN, READER, and DYER.

History and Politics.

Lord Macaulay's Works. Complete and uniform Library Edition. Edited by his Sister, Lady Trevelyan. 8 vols. 8vo. with Portrait, price £5 5s. cloth, or £8 8s. bound in tree-calf by Rivière.

The History of England from the fall of Wolsey to the Defeat of the Spanish Armada. By James Anthony Froude, M.A. late Fellow of Exeter College, Oxford. 12 vols. 8vo. price £8 18s. cloth.

The History of England from the Accession of James II. By Lord Macaulay.

Library Edition, 5 vols. 8vo. £4.
Cabinet Edition, 8 vols. post 8vo. 48s.
People's Edition, 4 vols. crown 8vo. 16s.

An Essay on the History of the English Government and Constitution, from the Reign of Henry VII. to the Present Time. By John Earl Russell. Fourth Edition, revised. Crown 8vo. 6s.

Speeches of Earl Russell, 1817-1841. Also Despatches selected from Correspondence presented to Parliament 1859-1865. With Introductions to the Speeches and Despatches, by Earl Russell. 2 vols. 8vo. [*Nearly ready.*

Varieties of Vice-Regal Life. By Major-General Sir William Denison, K.C.B. 2 vols. 8vo. [*Nearly ready.*

On Parliamentary Government in England: its Origin, Development, and Practical Operation. By Alpheus Todd, Librarian of the Legislative Assembly of Canada. 2 vols. 8vo. price £1 17s.

The History of England during the Reign of George the Third. By the Right Hon. W. N. Massey. Cabinet Edition. 4 vols. post 8vo. 24s.

The Constitutional History of England since the Accession of George III. 1760—1860. By Sir Thomas Erskine May, K.C.B. Second Edit. 2 vols. 8vo. 33s.

History of the Reform Bills of 1866 and 1867. By Homersham Cox, M.A. Barrister-at-Law. 8vo. 7s. 6d.

Ancient Parliamentary Elections: a History shewing how Parliaments were Constituted, and Representatives of the People Elected in Ancient Times. By the same Author. 8vo. 8s. 6d.

Whig and Tory Administrations during the Last Thirteen Years. By the same Author. 8vo. 5s.

A

Historical Studies. I. On Precursors of the French Revolution; II. Studies from the History of the Seventeenth Century; III. Leisure Hours of a Tourist. By HERMAN MERIVALE, M.A. 8vo. 12s. 6d.

Revolutions in English History. By ROBERT VAUGHAN, D.D. 3 vols. 8vo. price 30s.

A History of Wales, derived from Authentic Sources. By JANE WILLIAMS, Ysgafell, Author of a Memoir of the Rev. Thomas Price, and Editor of his Literary Remains. 8vo. 14s.

Lectures on the History of England, from the Earliest Times to the Death of King Edward II. By WILLIAM LONGMAN. With Maps and Illustrations. 8vo. 15s.

The History of the Life and Times of Edward the Third. By WILLIAM LONGMAN. With 9 Maps, 8 Plates, and 16 Woodcuts. 2 vols. 8vo. 28s.

History of Civilization in England and France, Spain and Scotland. By HENRY THOMAS BUCKLE. New Edition of the entire work, with a complete INDEX. 3 vols. crown 8vo. 24s.

Realities of Irish Life. By W. STEUART TRENCH, Land Agent in Ireland to the Marquess of Lansdowne, the Marquess of Bath, and Lord Digby. With Illustrations from Drawings by the Author's Son, J. TOWNSEND TRENCH. Fourth Edition, with 30 Plates. 8vo. 21s.

An Illustrated History of Ireland, from the Earliest Period to the Year of Catholic Emancipation. By MARY F. CUSACK. Second Edition, revised and enlarged. 8vo. 18s. 6d.

The History of India, from the Earliest Period to the close of Lord Dalhousie's Administration. By JOHN CLARK MARSHMAN. 3 vols. crown 8vo. 22s. 6d.

Indian Polity: a View of the System of Administration in India. By Major GEORGE CHESNEY, Fellow of the University of Calcutta. 8vo. with Map, 21s.

Homo Politics: being a Consideration of the Causes of the Growth of Trade in relation to Labour, Pauperism, and Emigration. By DANIEL GRANT. 8vo.

[*Nearly ready.*

Democracy in America. By ALEXIS DE TOCQUEVILLE. Translated by HENRY REEVE. 2 vols. 8vo. 21s.

Waterloo Lectures: a Study of the Campaign of 1815. By Colonel CHARLES C. CHESNEY, R.E. late Professor of Military Art and History in the Staff College. Second Edition. 8vo. with map, 10s. 6d.

The Oxford Reformers—John Colet, Erasmus, and Thomas More; being a History of their Fellow-Work. By FREDERIC SEEBOHM. Second Edition. 8vo. 14s.

History of the Reformation in Europe in the Time of Calvin. By J. H. MERLE D'AUBIGNÉ, D.D. VOLS. I. and II. 8vo. 28s. VOL. III. 12s. VOL. IV. price 16s. and VOL. V. price 16s.

England and France in the 15th Century. The Contemporary French Tract intituled *The Debate between the Heralds of France and England*, presumed to have been written by CHARLES, DUKE OF ORLEANS: translated for the first time into English, with an Introduction, Notes, and an Inquiry into the Authorship, by HENRY PYNE. 8vo. 7s. 6d.

The History of France, from Clovis and Charlemagne to the Accession of Napoleon III. By EYRE EVANS CROWE. 5 vols. 8vo. £4 13s.

Chapters from French History; St. Louis, Joan of Arc, Henri IV. with Sketches of the Intermediate Periods. By J. H. GURNEY, M.A. late Rector of St. Mary's, Marylebone. New Edition. Fcp. 8vo. 6s. 6d.

The History of Greece. By C. THIRLWALL, D.D. Lord Bishop of St. David's. 8 vols. fcp. 28s.

The Tale of the Great Persian War, from the Histories of Herodotus. By GEORGE W. COX, M.A. late Scholar of Trin. Coll. Oxon. Fcp. 3s. 6d.

Greek History from Themistocles to Alexander, in a Series of Lives from Plutarch. Revised and arranged by A. H. CLOUGH. Fcp. with 44 Woodcuts, 6s.

Critical History of the Language and Literature of Ancient Greece. By WILLIAM MURE, of Caldwell. 5 vols. 8vo. £3 9s.

History of the Literature of Ancient Greece. By Professor K. L. MÜLLER. Translated by LEWIS and DONALDSON. 3 vols. 8vo. 21s.

Roman History. By WILHELM IHNE. Translated and revised by the Author. VOLS. I. and II. 8vo. The First and Second Volumes of this work will be published together early in 1870; and the whole work will be completed in Three or at most Four Volumes

History of the City of Rome from its Foundation to the Sixteenth Century of the Christian Era. By THOMAS H. DYER, LL.D. 8vo. with 2 Maps, 15*s.*

History of the Romans under the Empire. By Very Rev. C. MERIVALE, D.C.L. Dean of Ely. 8 vols. post 8vo. price 48*s.*

The Fall of the Roman Republic; a Short History of the Last Century of the Commonwealth. By the same Author. 12mo. 7*s.* 6*d.*

The Conversion of the Roman Empire; the Boyle Lectures for the year 1864, delivered at the Chapel Royal, Whitehall. By the same Author. Second Edition. 8vo. 8*s.* 6*d.*

The Conversion of the Northern Nations; the Boyle Lectures for 1865. By the same Author. 8vo. 8*s.* 6*d.*

History of the Norman Kings of England, from a New Collation of the Contemporary Chronicles. By THOMAS COBBE, Barrister, of the Inner Temple. 8vo. 16*s.*

History of European Morals from Augustus to Charlemagne. By W. E. H. LECKY, M.A. 2 vols. 8vo. price 28*s.*

History of the Rise and Influence of the Spirit of Rationalism in Europe. By the same Author. Cabinet Edition (the Fourth). 2 vols. crown 8vo. price 16*s.*

God in History; or, the Progress of Man's Faith in the Moral Order of the World. By the late Baron BUNSEN. Translated from the German by SUSANNA WINKWORTH; with a Preface by the Dean of Westminster. VOLS. I. and II. 8vo. 30*s.* VOL. III. nearly ready.

Socrates and the Socratic Schools. Translated from the German of Dr. E. ZELLER, with the Author's approval, by the Rev. OSWALD J. REICHEL, B.C.L. and M.A. Crown 8vo. 8*s.* 6*d.*

The Stoics, Epicureans, and Sceptics. Translated from the German of Dr. E. ZELLER, with the Author's approval, by OSWALD J. REICHEL, B.C.L. and M.A. Crown 8vo. [*Nearly ready.*

The History of Philosophy, from Thales to Comte. By GEORGE HENRY LEWES. Third Edition, rewritten and enlarged. 2 vols. 8vo. 30*s.*

The Mythology of the Aryan Nations. By GEORGE W. COX, M.A. late Scholar of Trinity College, Oxford, Joint-Editor, with the late Professor Brande, of the Fourth Edition of 'The Dictionary of Science, Literature, and Art,' Author of 'Tales of Ancient Greece,' &c. [*In the press.*

The English Reformation. By F. C. MASSINGBERD, M.A. Chancellor of Lincoln. 4th Edition, revised. Fcp. 7*s.* 6*d.*

Egypt's Place in Universal History: an Historical Investigation. By BARON BUNSEN, D.C.L. Translated by C. H. COTTRELL, M.A. with Additions by S. BIRCH, LL.D. 5 vols. 8vo. £8 14*s.* 6*d.*

Maunder's Historical Treasury; comprising a General Introductory Outline of Universal History, and a Series of Separate Histories. Fcp. 10*s.* 6*d.*

Critical and Historical Essays contributed to the *Edinburgh Review* by the Right Hon. Lord MACAULAY:—
CABINET EDITION, 4 vols. 24*s.*
LIBRARY EDITION, 3 vols. 8vo. 36*s.*
PEOPLE'S EDITION, 2 vols. crown 8vo. 8*s.*
STUDENT'S EDITION, crown 8vo. 6*s.*

History of the Early Church, from the First Preaching of the Gospel to the Council of Nicæa, A.D. 325. By the Author of 'Amy Herbert.' Fcp. 4*s.* 6*d.*

Sketch of the History of the Church of England to the Revolution of 1688. By the Right Rev. T. V. SHORT, D.D. Lord Bishop of St. Asaph. Seventh Edition. Crown 8vo. 10*s.* 6*d.*

History of the Christian Church, from the Ascension of Christ to the Conversion of Constantine. By E. BURTON, D.D. late Regius Prof. of Divinity in the University of Oxford. Fcp. 3*s.* 6*d.*

Biography and *Memoirs.*

The Life and Letters of Faraday. By Dr. BENCE JONES, Secretary of the Royal Institution. 2 vols. 8vo. with Portrait, 28*s.*

The Life of Oliver Cromwell, to the Death of Charles I. By J. R. ANDREWS, Barrister-at-Law. 8vo. 14*s.*

A Life of the Third Earl of Shaftesbury, compiled from Unpublished Documents; with a Review of the Philosophy of the Period. By the Rev. W. M. HATCH, M.A. Fellow of New College, Oxford. 8vo. [*In preparation.*

Dictionary of General Biography; containing Concise Memoirs and Notices of the most Eminent Persons of all Countries, from the Earliest Ages to the Present Time. Edited by WILLIAM L. R. CATES. 8vo. price 21s.

Memoirs of Baron Bunsen, drawn chiefly from Family Papers by his Widow, FRANCES Baroness BUNSEN. Second Edition, abridged; with 2 Portraits and 4 Woodcuts. 2 vols. post 8vo. 21s.

The Letters of the late Right Hon. Sir George Cornewall Lewis. Edited by his Brother, the Rev. Sir G. F. LEWIS, Bart. 8vo. [*Nearly ready.*

Life of the Duke of Wellington. By the Rev. G. R. GLEIG, M.A. Popular Edition, carefully revised; with copious Additions. Crown 8vo. with Portrait, 5s.

Father Mathew: a Biography. By JOHN FRANCIS MAGUIRE, M.P. Popular Edition, with Portrait. Crown 8vo. 3s. 6d.

History of my Religious Opinions. By J. H. NEWMAN, D.D. Being the Substance of Apologia pro Vitâ Suâ. Post 8vo. price 6s.

Letters and Life of Francis Bacon, including all his Occasional Works. Collected and edited, with a Commentary, by J. SPEDDING, Trin. Coll. Cantab. Vols. I. & II. 8vo. 24s. Vols. III. & IV. 24s.

Felix Mendelssohn's Letters from *Italy and Switzerland,* and *Letters* from 1833 to 1847, translated by Lady WALLACE. With Portrait. 2 vols. crown 8vo. 5s. each.

Captain Cook's Life, Voyages, and Discoveries. 18mo. Woodcuts. 2s. 6d.

Memoirs of Sir Henry Havelock, K.C.B. By JOHN CLARK MARSHMAN. Cabinet Edition, with Portrait. Crown 8vo. price 5s.

Essays in Ecclesiastical Biography. By the Right Hon. Sir J. STEPHEN, LL.D. Cabinet Edition. Crown 8vo. 7s. 6d.

The Earls of Granard: a Memoir of the Noble Family of Forbes. Written by Admiral the Hon. JOHN FORBES, and Edited by GEORGE ARTHUR HASTINGS, present Earl of Granard, K.P. 8vo. 10s.

Vicissitudes of Families. By Sir J. BERNARD BURKE, C.B. Ulster King of Arms. New Edition, remodelled and enlarged. 2 vols. crown 8vo. 21s.

Lives of the Tudor Princesses, including Lady Jane Grey and her Sisters. By AGNES STRICKLAND. Post 8vo. with Portrait, &c. 12s. 6d.

Lives of the Queens of England. By AGNES STRICKLAND. Library Edition, newly revised; with Portraits of every Queen, Autographs, and Vignettes. 8 vols. post 8vo. 7s. 6d. each.

Maunder's Biographical Treasury. Thirteenth Edition, reconstructed and partly re-written, with above 1,000 additional Memoirs, by W. L. R. CATES. Fcp. 10s. 6d.

Criticism, Philosophy, Polity, &c.

England and Ireland. By JOHN STUART MILL. Fifth Edition. 8vo. 1s.

The Subjection of Women. By JOHN STUART MILL. New Edition. Post 8vo. 5s.

On Representative Government. By JOHN STUART MILL. Third Edition, 8vo. 9s. crown 8vo. 2s.

On Liberty. By the same Author. Fourth Edition. Post 8vo. 7s. 6d. Crown 8vo. 1s. 4d.

Principles of Political Economy. By the same. Sixth Edition. 2 vols. 8vo. 30s. or in 1 vol. crown 8vo. 5s.

Utilitarianism. By the same. 3d Edit. 8vo. 5s.

Dissertations and Discussions. By the same Author. Second Edition. 3 vols. 8vo. 36s.

Examination of Sir W. Hamilton's Philosophy, and of the principal Philosophical Questions discussed in his Writings. By the same. Third Edition. 8vo. 16s.

A System of Logic, Ratiocinative and Inductive. By JOHN STUART MILL. Seventh Edition. 2 vols. 8vo. 25s.

Inaugural Address delivered to the University of St. Andrews. By JOHN STUART MILL. 8vo. 5s. Crown 8vo. 1s.

Analysis of the Phenomena of the Human Mind. By JAMES MILL. A New Edition, with Notes, Illustrative and Critical, by ALEXANDER BAIN, ANDREW FINDLATER, and GEORGE GROTE. Edited, with additional Notes, by JOHN STUART MILL. 2 vols. 8vo. price 28s.

The Elements of Political Economy. By HENRY DUNNING MACLEOD, M.A. Barrister-at-Law. 8vo. 16s.

A Dictionary of Political Economy; Biographical, Bibliographical, Historical, and Practical. By the same Author. Vol. I. royal 8vo. 30s.

Lord Bacon's Works, collected and edited by R. L. ELLIS, M.A. J. SPEDDING, M.A. and D. D. HEATH. VOLS. I. to V. *Philosophical Works*, 5 vols. 8vo. £4 6s. VOLS. VI. and VII. *Literary and Professional Works*, 2 vols. £1 16s.

Analysis of Mr. Mill's System of Logic. By W. STEBBING, M.A. New Edition. 12mo. 3s. 6d.

The Institutes of Justinian; with English Introduction, Translation, and Notes. By T. C. SANDARS, M.A. Barrister-at-Law. New Edition. 8vo. 15s.

The Ethics of Aristotle; with Essays and Notes. By Sir A. GRANT, Bart. M.A. LL.D. Second Edition, revised and completed. 2 vols. 8vo. price 28s.

The Nicomachean Ethics of Aris-totle. Newly translated into English. By R. WILLIAMS, B.A. Fellow and late Lecturer of Merton College, and sometime Student of Christ Church, Oxford. 8vo. 12s.

Bacon's Essays, with Annotations. By R. WHATELY, D.D. late Archbishop of Dublin. Sixth Edition. 8vo. 10s. 6d.

Elements of Logic. By R. WHATELY, D.D. late Archbishop of Dublin. New Edition. 8vo. 10s. 6d. crown 8vo. 4s. 6d.

Elements of Rhetoric. By the same Author. New Edition. 8vo. 10s. 6d. Crown 8vo. 4s. 6d.

English Synonymes. By E. JANE WHATELY. Edited by Archbishop WHATELY. 5th Edition. Fcp. 3s.

An Outline of the Necessary Laws of Thought: a Treatise on Pure and Applied Logic. By the Most Rev. W. THOMSON, D.D. Archbishop of York. Ninth Thousand. Crown 8vo. 5s. 6d.

The Election of Representatives, Parliamentary and Municipal; a Treatise. By THOMAS HARE, Barrister-at-Law. Third Edition, with Additions. Crown 8vo. 6s.

Speeches of the Right Hon. Lord MACAULAY, corrected by Himself. Library Edition, 8vo. 12s. People's Edition, crown 8vo. 3s. 6d.

Lord Macaulay's Speeches on Parliamentary Reform in 1831 and 1832. 16mo. price ONE SHILLING.

Walker's Pronouncing Diction-ary of the English Language. Thoroughly revised Editions, by B. H. SMART. 8vo. 12s. 16mo. 6s.

A Dictionary of the English Language. By R. G. LATHAM, M.A. M.D. F.R.S. Founded on the Dictionary of Dr. S. JOHNSON, as edited by the Rev. H. J. TODD with numerous Emendations and Additions. 4 vols. 4to. price £7.

Thesaurus of English Words and Phrases, classified and arranged so as to facilitate the expression of Ideas, and assist in Literary Composition. By P. M. ROGET, M.D. New Edition. Crown 8vo. 10s. 6d.

The Debater; a Series of Complete Debates, Outlines of Debates, and Questions for Discussion. By F. ROWTON. Fcp. 6s.

Lectures on the Science of Lan-guage, delivered at the Royal Institution. By MAX MÜLLER, M.A. Fellow of All Souls College, Oxford. 2 vols. 8vo. FIRST SERIES, Fifth Edition, 12s. SECOND SERIES, Second Edition, 18s.

Chapters on Language. By F. W. FARRAR, M.A. F.R.S. late Fellow of Trin. Coll. Cambridge. Crown 8vo. 8s. 6d.

A Book about Words. By G. F. GRAHAM. Fcp. 8vo. 3s. 6d.

Manual of English Literature, Historical and Critical: with a Chapter on English Metres. By THOMAS ARNOLD, M.A. Second Edition. Crown 8vo. 7s. 6d.

Southey's Doctor, complete in One Volume, edited by the Rev. J. W. WARTER, B.D. Square crown 8vo. 12s. 6d.

Historical and Critical Commen-tary on the Old Testament; with a New Translation. By M. M. KALISCH, Ph.D. Vol. I. *Genesis*, 8vo. 18s. or adapted for the General Reader, 12s. Vol. II. *Exodus*, 15s. or adapted for the General Reader, 12s. Vol III. *Leviticus*, Part I. 15s. or adapted for the General Reader, 8s.

A Hebrew Grammar, with Exercises. By the same. Part I. *Outlines with Exercises*, 8vo. 12s. 6d. KEY, 5s. Part II. *Exceptional Forms and Constructions*, 12s. 6d.

A Latin-English Dictionary. By J. T. WHITE, D.D. of Corpus Christi College, and J. E. RIDDLE, M.A. of St. Edmund Hall, Oxford. Third Edition, revised. 2 vols. 4to. pp. 2,128, price 42s.

White's College Latin-English Diction-ary (Intermediate Size), abridged from the Parent Work for the use of University Students. Medium 8vo. pp. 1,048, price 18s.

White's Junior Student's Complete Latin-English and English-Latin Dictionary. Revised Edition. Square 12mo. pp. 1,058, price 12s.

Separately { ENGLISH-LATIN, 5s. 6d.
LATIN-ENGLISH, 7s. 6d.

An English-Greek Lexicon, containing all the Greek Words used by Writers of good authority. By C. D. YONGE, B.A. New Edition. 4to. 21s.

Mr. Yonge's New Lexicon, English and Greek, abridged from his larger work (as above). Square 12mo. 8s. 6d.

A Greek-English Lexicon. Compiled by H. G. LIDDELL, D.D. Dean of Christ Church, and R. SCOTT, D.D. Master of Balliol. Fifth Edition. Crown 4to. 31s. 6d.

A Lexicon, Greek and English, abridged for Schools from LIDDELL and SCOTT'S *Greek-English Lexicon.* Twelfth Edition. Square 12mo. 7s. 6d.

A Practical Dictionary of the French and English Languages. By Professor LÉON CONTANSEAU, many years French Examiner for Military and Civil Appointments, &c. New Edition, carefully revised. Post 8vo. 10s. 6d.

Contanseau's Pocket Dictionary, French and English, abridged from the Practical Dictionary, by the Author. New Edition. 18mo. price 3s. 6d.

A Sanskrit-English Dictionary. The Sanskrit words printed both in the original Devanagari and in Roman letters; with References to the Best Editions of Sanskrit Authors, and with Etymologies and comparisons of Cognate Words chiefly in Greek, Latin, Gothic, and Anglo-Saxon. Compiled by T. BENFEY. 8vo. 52s. 6d.

New Practical Dictionary of the German Language; German-English, and English-German. By the Rev. W. L. BLACKLEY, M.A. and Dr. CARL MARTIN FRIEDLÄNDER. Post 8vo. 7s. 6d.

The Mastery of Languages; or, the Art of Speaking Foreign Tongues Idiomatically. By THOMAS PRENDERGAST, late of the Civil Service at Madras. Second Edition. 8vo. 6s.

Miscellaneous Works and Popular Metaphysics.

The Essays and Contributions of A. K. H. B. Author of 'The Recreations of a Country Parson.' Uniform Editions:—

Recreations of a Country Parson. FIRST and SECOND SERIES, 3s. 6d. each.

The Commonplace Philosopher in Town and Country. Crown 8vo. 3s. 6d.

Leisure Hours in Town; Essays Consolatory, Æsthetical, Moral, Social, and Domestic. Crown 8vo. 3s. 6d.

The Autumn Holidays of a Country Parson. Crown 8vo. 3s. 6d.

The Graver Thoughts of a Country Parson. FIRST and SECOND SERIES, crown 8vo. 3s. 6d. each.

Critical Essays of a Country Parson, selected from Essays contributed to *Fraser's Magazine.* Crown 8vo. 3s. 6d.

Sunday Afternoons at the Parish Church of a Scottish University City. Crown 8vo. 3s. 6d.

Lessons of Middle Age, with some Account of various Cities and Men. Crown 8vo. 3s. 6d.

Counsel and Comfort Spoken from a City Pulpit. Crown 8vo. 3s. 6d.

Changed Aspects of Unchanged Truths; Memorials of St. Andrews Sundays. Crown 8vo. 3s. 6d.

Short Studies on Great Subjects. By JAMES ANTHONY FROUDE, M.A. late Fellow of Exeter College, Oxford. Third Edition. 8vo. 12s.

Lord Macaulay's Miscellaneous Writings:—

LIBRARY EDITION, 2 vols. 8vo. Portrait, 21s.
PEOPLE'S EDITION, 1 vol. crown 8vo. 4s. 6d.

The Rev. Sydney Smith's Miscellaneous Works; including his Contributions to the *Edinburgh Review.* 1 vol. crown 8vo. 6s.

The Wit and Wisdom of the Rev. SYDNEY SMITH: a Selection of the most memorable Passages in his Writings and Conversation. 16mo. 3s. 6d.

The Silver Store. Collected from Mediæval Christian and Jewish Mines. By the Rev. S. BARING-GOULD, M.A. Crown 8vo. 3s. 6d.

Traces of History in the Names of Places; with a Vocabulary of the Roots out of which Names of Places in England and Wales are formed. By FLAVELL EDMUNDS. Crown 8vo. 7s. 6d.

Essays selected from Contributions to the *Edinburgh Review.* By HENRY ROGERS. Second Edition. 3 vols. fcp. 21s.

Reason and Faith, their Claims and Conflicts. By the same Author. New Edition, revised. Crown 8vo. price 6s. 6d.

The Eclipse of Faith; or, a Visit to a Religious Sceptic. By HENRY ROGERS. Eleventh Edition. Fcp. 5*s.*

Defence of the Eclipse of Faith, by its Author. Third Edition. Fcp. 3*s.* 6*d.*

Selections from the Correspondence of R. E. H. Greyson. By the same Author. Third Edition. Crown 8vo. 7*s.* 6*d.*

Families of Speech, Four Lectures delivered at the Royal Institution of Great Britain; with Tables and a Map. By the Rev. F. W. FARRAR, M.A. F.R.S. Post 8vo. [*Nearly ready.*

Chips from a German Workshop; being Essays on the Science of Religion, and on Mythology, Traditions, and Customs. By MAX MÜLLER, M.A. Fellow of All Souls College, Oxford. Second Edition, revised, with an INDEX. 2 vols. 8vo. 24*s.*

Word Gossip; a Series of Familiar Essays on Words and their Peculiarities. By the Rev. W. L. BLACKLEY, M.A. Fcp. 8vo. 5*s.*

Menes and Cheops identified in History under Different Names; with other Cosas. By CARL VON RIKART. 8vo. with 5 Illustrations, price 10*s.* 6*d.*

An Introduction to Mental Philosophy, on the Inductive Method. By J. D. MORELL, M.A. LL.D. 8vo. 12*s.*

Elements of Psychology, containing the Analysis of the Intellectual Powers. By the same Author. Post 8vo. 7*s.* 6*d.*

The Secret of Hegel: being the Hegelian System in Origin, Principle, Form, and Matter. By JAMES HUTCHISON STIRLING. 2 vols. 8vo. 28*s.*

The Senses and the Intellect. By ALEXANDER BAIN, LL.D. Prof. of Logic in the Univ. of Aberdeen. Third Edition. 8vo. 15*s.*

The Emotions and the Will, by the same Author. Second Edition. 8vo. 15*s.*

On the Study of Character, including an Estimate of Phrenology. By the same Author. 8vo. 9*s.*

Mental and Moral Science: a Compendium of Psychology and Ethics. By the same Author. Second Edition. Crown 8vo. 10*s.* 6*d.*

Strong and Free; or, First Steps towards Social Science. By the Author of 'My Life and What shall I do with it?' 8vo. 10*s.* 6*d.*

The Philosophy of Necessity; or, Natural Law as applicable to Mental, Moral, and Social Science. By CHARLES BRAY. Second Edition. 8vo. 9*s.*

The Education of the Feelings and Affections. By the same Author. Third Edition. 8vo. 3*s.* 6*d.*

On Force, its Mental and Moral Correlates. By the same Author. 8vo. 5*s.*

Mind and Manner, or Diversities of Life. By JAMES FLAMANK. Post 8vo. 7*s.* 6*d.*

Characteristics of Men, Manners, Opinions, Times. By ANTHONY, Third Earl of SHAFTESBURY. Published from the Edition of 1713, with Engravings designed by the Author; and Edited, with Marginal Analysis, Notes, and Illustrations, by the Rev. W. M. HATCH, M.A. Fellow of New College, Oxford. 3 vols. 8vo. VOL. I. price 14*s.*

A Treatise on Human Nature; being an Attempt to Introduce the Experimental Method of Reasoning into Moral Subjects. By DAVID HUME. Edited, with a Preliminary Dissertation and Notes, by T. H. GREEN, Fellow, and T. H. GROSE, late Scholar, of Balliol College, Oxford. [*In the press.*

Essays Moral, Political, and Literary. By DAVID HUME. By the same Editors. [*In the press.*

*** The above will form a new edition of DAVID HUME'S *Philosophical Works*, complete in Four Volumes, to be had in Two separate Sections as announced.

Astronomy, Meteorology, Popular Geography, &c.

Outlines of Astronomy. By Sir J. F. W. HERSCHEL, Bart. M.A. New Edition, revised; with Plates and Woodcuts. 8vo. 18*s.*

Saturn and its System. By RICHARD A. PROCTOR, B.A. late Scholar of St. John's Coll. Camb. and King's Coll. London. 8vo. with 14 Plates, 14*s.*

The Handbook of the Stars. By the same Author. Square fcp. 8vo. with 3 Maps, price 5*s.*

Celestial Objects for Common Telescopes. By T. W. WEBB, M.A. F.R.A.S. Second Edition, revised and enlarged, with Map of the Moon and Woodcuts. 16mo. price 7*s.* 6*d.*

Navigation and Nautical Astronomy (Practical, Theoretical, Scientific) for the use of Students and Practical Men. By J. MERRIFIELD, F.R.A.S. and H. EVERS. 8vo. 14*s.*

A General Dictionary of Geography, Descriptive, Physical, Statistical, and Historical; forming a complete Gazetteer of the World. By A. KEITH JOHNSTON, F.R.S.E. New Edition. 8vo. price 31s. 6d.

M'Culloch's Dictionary, Geographical, Statistical, and Historical, of the various Countries, Places, and principal Natural Objects in the World. Revised Edition, with the Statistical Information throughout brought up to the latest returns. By FREDERICK MARTIN. 4 vols. 8vo. with coloured Maps, £4 4s.

A Manual of Geography, Physical, Industrial, and Political. By W. HUGHES, F.R.G.S. Prof. of Geog. in King's Coll. and in Queen's Coll. Lond. With 6 Maps. Fcp. 7s. 6d.

The States of the River Plate: their Industries and Commerce, Sheep Farming, Sheep Breeding, Cattle Feeding, and Meat Preserving; the Employment of Capital, Land and Stock and their Values, Labour and its Remuneration. By WILFRID LATHAM, Buenos Ayres. Second Edition. 8vo. 12s.

Maunder's Treasury of Geography, Physical, Historical, Descriptive, and Political. Edited by W. HUGHES, F.R.G.S. With 7 Maps and 16 Plates. Fcp. 10s. 6d.

Physical Geography for Schools and General Readers. By M. F. MAURY, LL.D. Fcp. with 2 Charts, 2s. 6d.

Natural History and *Popular Science.*

Ganot's Elementary Treatise on Physics, Experimental and Applied, for the use of Colleges and Schools. Translated and Edited with the Author's sanction by E. ATKINSON, Ph.D. F.C.S. New Edition, revised and enlarged; with a Coloured Plate and 620 Woodcuts. Post 8vo. 15s.

The Elements of Physics or Natural Philosophy. By NEIL ARNOTT, M.D. F.R.S. Physician-Extraordinary to the Queen. Sixth Edition, re-written and completed. 2 Parts, 8vo. 21s.

Dove's Law of Storms, considered in connexion with the ordinary Movements of the Atmosphere. Translated by R. H. SCOTT, M.A. T.C.D. 8vo. 10s. 6d.

Sound: a Course of Eight Lectures delivered at the Royal Institution of Great Britain. By Professor JOHN TYNDALL, LL.D. F.R.S. Crown 8vo. with Portrait and Woodcuts, 9s.

Heat Considered as a Mode of Motion. By Professor JOHN TYNDALL, LL.D. F.R.S. Third Edition. Crown 8vo. with Woodcuts, 10s. 6d.

Light: its Influence on Life and Health. By FORBES WINSLOW, M.D. D.C.L. Oxon. (Hon.) Fcp. 8vo. 6s.

A Treatise on Electricity, in Theory and Practice. By A. DE LA RIVE, Prof. in the Academy of Geneva. Translated by C. V. WALKER, F.R.S. 3 vols. 8vo. with Woodcuts, £3 13s.

The Correlation of Physical Forces. By W. R. GROVE, Q.C. V.P.R.S. Fifth Edition, revised, and Augmented by a Discourse on Continuity. 8vo. 10s. 6d. The *Discourse on Continuity,* separately, price 2s. 6d.

Manual of Geology. By S. HAUGHTON, M.D. F.R.S. Fellow of Trin. Coll. and Prof. of Geol. in the Univ. of Dublin. Second Edition, with 66 Woodcuts. Fcp. 7s. 6d.

A Guide to Geology. By J. PHILLIPS, M.A. Prof. of Geol. in the Univ. of Oxford. Fifth Edition. Fcp. 4s.

The Scenery of England and Wales, its Character and Origin; being an Attempt to trace the Nature of the Geological Causes, especially Denudation, by which the Physical Features of the Country have been Produced. By D. MACKINTOSH, F.G.S. Post 8vo. with 89 Woodcuts, 12s.

The Student's Manual of Zoology and Comparative Physiology. By J. BURNEY YEO, M.B. Resident Medical Tutor and Lecturer on Animal Physiology in King's College, London. [*Nearly ready.*

Van Der Hoeven's Handbook of ZOOLOGY. Translated from the Second Dutch Edition by the Rev. W. CLARK, M.D. F.R.S. 2 vols. 8vo. with 24 Plates of Figures, 60s.

Professor Owen's Lectures on the Comparative Anatomy and Physiology of the Invertebrate Animals. Second Edition, with 235 Woodcuts. 8vo. 21s.

The Comparative Anatomy and Physiology of the Vertebrate Animals. By RICHARD OWEN, F.R.S. D.C.L. With 1,472 Woodcuts. 3 vols. 8vo. £3 13s. 6d.

The Primitive Inhabitants of Scandinavia. Containing a Description of the Implements, Dwellings, Tombs, and Mode of Living of the Savages in the North of Europe during the Stone Age. By SVEN NILSSON. With an Introduction by Sir JOHN LUBBOCK, 16 Plates of Figures and 3 Woodcuts. 8vo. 18s.

Homes without Hands: a Description of the Habitations of Animals, classed according to their Principle of Construction. By Rev. J. G. WOOD, M.A. F.L.S. With about 140 Vignettes on Wood (20 full size of page). New Edition. 8vo. 21s.

Bible Animals; being a Description of Every Living Creature mentioned in the Scriptures, from the Ape to the Coral. By the Rev. J. G. WOOD, M.A. F.L.S. With about 100 Vignettes on Wood (20 full size of page). 8vo. 21s.

The Harmonies of Nature and Unity of Creation. By Dr. G. HARTWIG. 8vo. with numerous Illustrations, 18s.

The Sea and its Living Wonders. By the same Author. Third Edition, enlarged. 8vo. with many Illustrations, 21s.

The Tropical World. By the same Author. With 8 Chromoxylographs and 172 Woodcuts. 8vo. 21s.

The Polar World: a Popular Description of Man and Nature in the Arctic and Antarctic Regions of the Globe. By the same Author. With 8 Chromoxylographs, 3 Maps, and 85 Woodcuts. 8vo. 21s.

A Familiar History of Birds. By E. STANLEY, D.D. late Lord Bishop of Norwich. Fcp. with Woodcuts, 3s. 6d.

Kirby and Spence's Introduction to Entomology, or Elements of the Natural History of Insects. Crown 8vo. 5s.

Maunder's Treasury of Natural History, or Popular Dictionary of Zoology. Revised and corrected by T. S. COBBOLD, M.D. Fcp. with 900 Woodcuts, 10s. 6d.

The Elements of Botany for Families and Schools. Tenth Edition, revised by THOMAS MOORE, F.L.S. Fcp. with 154 Woodcuts, 2s. 6d.

The Treasury of Botany, or Popular Dictionary of the Vegetable Kingdom; with which is incorporated a Glossary of Botanical Terms. Edited by J. LINDLEY, F.R.S. and T. MOORE, F.L.S. assisted by eminent Contributors. Pp. 1,274, with 274 Woodcuts and 20 Steel Plates. Two PARTS, fcp. 8vo. 20s.

The British Flora; comprising the Phænogamous or Flowering Plants and the Ferns. By Sir W. J. HOOKER, K.H. and G. A. WALKER-ARNOTT, LL.D. 12mo. with 12 Plates, 14s. or coloured, 21s.

The Rose Amateur's Guide. By THOMAS RIVERS. New Edition. Fcp. 4s.

Loudon's Encyclopædia of Plants; comprising the Specific Character, Description, Culture, History, &c. of all the Plants found in Great Britain. With upwards of 12,000 Woodcuts. 8vo. 42s.

Maunder's Scientific and Literary Treasury; a Popular Encyclopædia of Science, Literature, and Art. New Edition, thoroughly revised and in great part re-written, with above 1,000 new articles, by J. Y. JOHNSON, Corr. M.Z.S. Fcp. 10s. 6d.

A Dictionary of Science, Literature, and Art. Fourth Edition, re-edited by the late W. T. BRANDE (the Author) and GEORGE W. COX, M.A. 3 vols. medium 8vo. price 63s. cloth.

The Quarterly Journal of Science. Edited by JAMES SAMUELSON and WILLIAM CROOKES, F.R.S. Published quarterly in January, April, July, and October. 8vo. with Illustrations, price 5s. each Number.

Chemistry, Medicine, Surgery, and *the Allied Sciences.*

A Dictionary of Chemistry and the Allied Branches of other Sciences. By HENRY WATTS, F.C.S. assisted by eminent Scientific and Practical Chemists. 5 vols. medium 8vo. price £7 3s.

Handbook of Chemical Analysis, adapted to the *Unitary System* of Notation. By F. T. CONINGTON, M.A. F.C.S. Post 8vo. 7s. 6d.

Conington's Tables of Qualitative *Analysis*, to accompany the above, 2s. 6d.

Elements of Chemistry, Theoretical and Practical. By WILLIAM A. MILLER, M.D. LL.D. Professor of Chemistry, King's College, London. Fourth Edition. 3 vols. 8vo. £3.

PART I. CHEMICAL PHYSICS, 15s.
PART II. INORGANIC CHEMISTRY, 21s.
PART III. ORGANIC CHEMISTRY, 24s.

A Manual of Chemistry, Descriptive and Theoretical. By WILLIAM ODLING, M.B. F.R.S. PART I. 8vo. 9s. PART II. nearly ready.

A Course of Practical Chemistry, for the use of Medical Students. By W. Odling, M.B. F.R.S. New Edition, with 70 new Woodcuts. Crown 8vo. 7s. 6d.

Outlines of Chemistry; or, Brief Notes of Chemical Facts. By the same Author. Crown 8vo. 7s. 6d.

Lectures on Animal Chemistry Delivered at the Royal College of Physicians in 1865. By the same Author. Crown 8vo. 4s. 6d.

Lectures on the Chemical Changes of Carbon, delivered at the Royal Institution of Great Britain. By W. Odling, M.B. F.R.S. Reprinted from the *Chemical News*, with Notes, by W. Crookes, F.R.S. Crown 8vo. 4s. 6d.

Chemical Notes for the Lecture Room. By Thomas Wood, F.C.S. 2 vols. crown 8vo. I. on Heat, &c. price 3s. 6d. II. on the Metals, price 5s.

A Treatise on Medical Electricity, Theoretical and Practical; and its Use in the Treatment of Paralysis, Neuralgia, and other Diseases. By Julius Althaus, M.D. M.R.C.P. &c.; Senior Physician to the Infirmary for Epilepsy and Paralysis. Second Edition, revised and enlarged and for the most part re-written; with Plate and 62 Woodcuts. Post 8vo. price 12s. 6d.

The Diagnosis, Pathology, and Treatment of Diseases of Women; including the Diagnosis of Pregnancy. By Graily Hewitt, M.D. &c. President of the Obstetrical Society of London. Second Edition, enlarged; with 116 Woodcuts. 8vo. 24s.

Lectures on the Diseases of Infancy and Childhood. By Charles West, M.D. &c. Fifth Edition. 8vo. 16s.

On the Surgical Treatment of Children's Diseases. By T. Holmes, M.A. &c. late Surgeon to the Hospital for Sick Children. Second Edition, with 9 Plates and 112 Woodcuts. 8vo. 21s.

A System of Surgery, Theoretical and Practical, in Treatises by Various Authors. Edited by T. Holmes, M.A. &c. Surgeon and Lecturer on Surgery at St. George's Hospital, and Surgeon-in-Chief to the Metropolitan Police. Second Edition, thoroughly revised, with numerous Illustrations. 5 vols. 8vo. £5 5s.

Lectures on the Principles and Practice of Physic. By Sir Thomas Watson, Bart. M.D. Physician-Extraordinary to the Queen. New Edition in preparation.

Lectures on Surgical Pathology. By J. Paget, F.R.S. Surgeon-Extraordinary to the Queen. Edited by W. Turner, M.B. New Edition in preparation.

Cooper's Dictionary of Practical Surgery and Encyclopædia of Surgical Science. New Edition, brought down to the present time. By S. A. Lane, Surgeon to St. Mary's, and Consulting Surgeon to the Lock Hospitals; Lecturer on Surgery at St. Mary's Hospital; assisted by various Eminent Surgeons. Vol. II. 8vo. completing the work. [*Early in* 1870.

On Chronic Bronchitis, especially as connected with Gout, Emphysema, and Diseases of the Heart. By E. Headlam Greenhow, M.D. F.R.C.P. &c. 8vo. 7s. 6d.

The Climate of the South of France as Suited to Invalids; with Notices of Mediterranean and other Winter Stations. By C. T. Williams, M.A. M.D. Oxon. Assistant Physician to the Hospital for Consumption at Brompton. Second Edition, with Frontispiece and Map. Cr. 8vo. 6s.

Pulmonary Consumption; its Nature, Treatment, and Duration exemplified by an Analysis of One Thousand Cases selected from upwards of Twenty Thousand. By C. J. B. Williams, M.D. F.R.S. Consulting Physician to the Hospital for Consumption at Brompton; and C. T. Williams, M.A. M.D. Oxon. [*Nearly ready.*

A Treatise on the Continued Fevers of Great Britain. By C. Murchison, M.D. Physician and Lecturer on the Practice of Medicine, Middlesex Hospital. New Edition in preparation.

Clinical Lectures on Diseases of the Liver, Jaundice, and Abdominal Dropsy. By the same Author. Post 8vo. with 25 Woodcuts, 10s. 6d.

Anatomy, Descriptive and Surgical. By Henry Gray, F.R.S. With about 410 Woodcuts from Dissections. Fifth Edition, by T. Holmes, M.A. Cantab. With a New Introduction by the Editor. Royal 8vo. 28s.

Clinical Notes on Diseases of the Larynx, investigated and treated with the assistance of the Laryngoscope. By W. Marcet, M.D. F.R.S. Assistant-Physician to the Hospital for Consumption and Diseases of the Chest, Brompton. Crown 8vo. with 5 Lithographs, 6s.

The House I Live in; or, Popular Illustrations of the Structure and Functions of the Human Body. Edited by T. G. GIRTIN. New Edition, with 25 Woodcuts. 16mo. price 2*s.* 6*d.*

Outlines of Physiology, Human and Comparative. By JOHN MARSHALL, F.R.C.S. Professor of Surgery in University College, London, and Surgeon to the University College Hospital. 2 vols. crown 8vo. with 122 Woodcuts, 32*s.*

Physiological Anatomy and Physiology of Man. By the late R. B. TODD, M.D. F.R.S. and W. BOWMAN, F.R.S. of King's College. With numerous Illustrations. VOL. II. 8vo. 25*s.*

VOL. I. New Edition by Dr. LIONEL S. BEALE, F.R.S. in course of publication; PART I. with 8 Plates, 7*s.* 6*d.*

A Dictionary of Practical Medicine. By J. COPLAND, M.D. F.R.S. Abridged from the larger work by the Author, assisted by J. C. COPLAND, M.R.C.S. Pp. 1,560, in 8vo. price 36*s.*

The Theory of Ocular Defects and of Spectacles. Translated from the German of Dr. H. SCHEFFLER by R. B. CARTER, F.R.C.S. Post 8vo. 7*s.* 6*d.*

A Manual of Materia Medica and Therapeutics, abridged from Dr. PEREIRA'S *Elements* by F. J. FARRE, M.D. assisted by R. BENTLEY, M.R.C.S. and by R. WARINGTON, F.R.S. 1 vol. 8vo. with 90 Woodcuts, 21*s.*

Thomson's Conspectus of the British Pharmacopœia. Twenty-fifth Edition, corrected by E. LLOYD BIRKETT, M.D. 18mo. 6*s.*

Manual of the Domestic Practice of Medicine. By W. B. KESTEVEN, F.R.C.S.E. Third Edition, thoroughly revised, with Additions. Fcp. 5*s.*

Essays on Physiological Subjects. By GILBERT W. CHILD, M.A. F.L.S. F.C.S. Second Edition. Crown 8vo. with Woodcuts, 7*s.* 6*d.*

Gymnasts and Gymnastics. By JOHN H. HOWARD, late Professor of Gymnastics, Comm. Coll. Ripponden. Second Edition, with 135 Woodcuts. Crown 8vo. 10*s.* 6*d.*

The Fine Arts, and *Illustrated Editions.*

In Fairyland; Pictures from the Elf-World. By RICHARD DOYLE. With a Poem by W. ALLINGHAM. With Sixteen Plates, containing Thirty-six Designs printed in Colours. Folio, 31*s.* 6*d.*

Life of John Gibson, R.A. Sculptor. Edited by Lady EASTLAKE. 8vo. 10*s.* 6*d.*

Materials for a History of Oil Painting. By Sir CHARLES LOCKE EASTLAKE, sometime President of the Royal Academy. VOL. II. 8vo. 14*s.*

Albert Durer, his Life and Works; including Autobiographical Papers and Complete Catalogues. By WILLIAM B. SCOTT. With Six Etchings by the Author and other Illustrations. 8vo. 16*s.*

Half-Hour Lectures on the History and Practice of the Fine and Ornamental Arts. By. W. B. SCOTT. Second Edition. Crown 8vo. with 50 Woodcut Illustrations, 8*s.* 6*d.*

The Lord's Prayer Illustrated by F. R. PICKERSGILL, R.A. and HENRY ALFORD, D.D. Dean of Canterbury. Imp. 4to. 21*s.*

The Chorale Book for England; a complete Hymn-Book in accordance with the Services and Festivals of the Church of England: the Hymns Translated by Miss C. WINKWORTH; the Tunes arranged by Prof. W. S. BENNETT and OTTO GOLDSCHMIDT. Fcp. 4to. 12*s.* 6*d.*

Six Lectures on Harmony. Delivered at the Royal Institution of Great Britain. By G. A. MACFARREN. 8vo. 10*s.* 6*d.*

Lyra Germanica, the Christian Year. Translated by CATHERINE WINKWORTH; with 125 Illustrations on Wood drawn by J. LEIGHTON, F.S.A. Quarto, 21*s.*

Lyra Germanica, the Christian Life. Translated by CATHERINE WINKWORTH; with about 200 Woodcut Illustrations by J. LEIGHTON, F.S.A. and other Artists. Quarto, 21*s.*

The New Testament, illustrated with Wood Engravings after the Early Masters, chiefly of the Italian School. Crown 4to. 63*s.* cloth, gilt top; or £5 5*s.* morocco.

The Life of Man Symbolised by the Months of the Year in their Seasons and Phases. Text selected by RICHARD PIGOT. 25 Illustrations on Wood from Original Designs by JOHN LEIGHTON F.S.A. Quarto, 42*s.*

Cats' and Farlie's Moral Emblems; with Aphorisms, Adages, and Proverbs of all Nations: comprising 121 Illustrations on Wood by J. LEIGHTON, F.S.A. with an appropriate Text by R. PIGOT. Imperial 8vo. 31s. 6d.

Shakspeare's Midsummer Night's Dream, illustrated with 24 Silhouettes or Shadow Pictures by P. KONEWKA, engraved on Wood by A. VOGEL. Folio, 31s. 6d.

Shakspeare's Sentiments and Similes Printed in Black and Gold, and illuminated in the Missal style by HENRY NOEL HUMPHREYS. In massive covers, containing the Medallion and Cypher of Shakspeare. Square post 8vo. 21s.

Goldsmith's Poetical Works, Illustrated with Wood Engravings, from Designs by Members of the ETCHING CLUB. Imp. 16mo. 7s. 6d.

Sacred and Legendary Art. By Mrs. JAMESON. With numerous Etchings and Woodcut Illustrations. 6 vols. square crown 8vo. price £5 15s. 6d. cloth, or £12 12s. bound in morocco by Rivière. To be had also in cloth only, in FOUR SERIES, as follows:—

Legends of the Saints and Martyrs. Fifth Edition, with 19 Etchings and 187 Woodcuts. 2 vols. square crown 8vo. 31s. 6d.

Legends of the Monastic Orders. Third Edition, with 11 Etchings and 88 Woodcuts. 1 vol. square crown 8vo. 21s.

Legends of the Madonna. Third Edition. with 27 Etchings and 165 Woodcuts. 1 vol. square crown 8vo. 21s.

The History of Our Lord, as exemplified in Works of Art. Completed by Lady EASTLAKE. Revised Edition, with 13 Etchings and 281 Woodcuts. 2 vols. square crown 8vo. 42s.

The Useful Arts, Manufactures, &c.

Drawing from Nature. By GEORGE BARNARD, Professor of Drawing at Rugby School. With 18 Lithographic Plates and 108 Wood Engravings. Imp. 8vo. 25s. or in Three Parts, royal 8vo. 7s. 6d. each.

Gwilt's Encyclopædia of Architecture. Fifth Edition, with Alterations and considerable Additions, by WYATT PAPWORTH. Additionally illustrated with nearly 400 Wood Engravings by O. JEWITT, and upwards of 100 other new Woodcuts. 8vo. 52s. 6d.

Italian Sculptors: being a History of Sculpture in Northern, Southern, and Eastern Italy. By C. C. PERKINS. With 30 Etchings and 13 Wood Engravings. Imperial 8vo. 42s.

Tuscan Sculptors, their Lives, Works, and Times. By the same Author. With 45 Etchings and 28 Woodcuts from Original Drawings and Photographs. 2 vols. imperial 8vo. 63s.

Hints on Household Taste in Furniture, Upholstery, and other Details. By CHARLES L. EASTLAKE, Architect. Second Edition, with about 90 Illustrations. Square crown 8vo. 18s.

The Engineer's Handbook; explaining the principles which should guide the young Engineer in the Construction of Machinery. By C. S. LOWNDES. Post 8vo. 5s.

Lathes and Turning, Simple, Mechanical, and Ornamental. By W. HENRY NORTHCOTT. With about 240 Illustrations on Steel and Wood. 8vo. 18s.

Principles of Mechanism, designed for the use of Students in the Universities, and for Engineering Students generally. By R. WILLIS, M.A. F.R.S. &c. Jacksonian Professor of Natural and Experimental Philosophy in the University of Cambridge. A new and enlarged Edition. 8vo. [*Nearly ready.*

Handbook of Practical Telegraphy, published with the sanction of the Chairman and Directors of the Electric and International Telegraph Company, and adopted by the Department of Telegraphs for India. By R. S. CULLEY. Third Edition. 8vo. 12s. 6d.

Ure's Dictionary of Arts, Manufactures, and Mines. Sixth Edition, chiefly re-written and greatly enlarged by ROBERT HUNT, F.R.S. assisted by numerous Contributors eminent in Science and the Arts, and familiar with Manufactures. With 2,000 Woodcuts. 3 vols. medium 8vo. £4 14s. 6d.

Treatise on Mills and Millwork. By Sir W. FAIRBAIRN, F.R.S. With 18 Plates and 322 Woodcuts. 2 vols. 8vo. 32s.

Useful Information for Engineers. By the same Author. FIRST, SECOND, and THIRD SERIES, with many Plates and Woodcuts. 3 vols. crown 8vo. 10s. 6d. each.

The Application of Cast and Wrought Iron to Building Purposes. By the same Author. New Edition, preparing for publication.

Iron Ship Building, its History and Progress, as comprised in a Series of Experimental Researches on the Laws of Strain; the Strengths, Forms, and other conditions of the Material; and an Inquiry into the Present and Prospective State of the Navy, including the Experimental Results on the Resisting Powers of Armour Plates and Shot at High Velocities. By Sir W. FAIRBAIRN, F.R.S. With 4 Plates and 130 Woodcuts, 8vo. 18*s.*

Encyclopædia of Civil Engineering, Historical, Theoretical, and Practical. By E. CRESY, C.E. With above 3,000 Woodcuts. 8vo. 42*s.*

The Artisan Club's Treatise on the Steam Engine, in its various Applications to Mines, Mills, Steam Navigation, Railways, and Agriculture. By J. BOURNE, C.E. New Edition; with Portrait, 37 Plates, and 546 Woodcuts. 4to. 42*s.*

A Treatise on the Screw Propeller, Screw Vessels, and Screw Engines, as adapted for purposes of Peace and War: with notices of other Methods of Propulsion, Tables of the Dimensions and Performance of Screw Steamers, and Detailed Specifications of Ships and Engines. By JOHN BOURNE, C.E. Third Edition, with 54 Plates and 287 Woodcuts. Quarto, 63*s.*

Catechism of the Steam Engine, in its various Applications to Mines, Mills, Steam Navigation, Railways, and Agriculture. By JOHN BOURNE, C.E. New Edition, with 89 Woodcuts. Fcp. 6*s.*

Recent Improvements in the Steam-Engine in its various applications to Mines, Mills, Steam Navigation, Railways, and Agriculture. By JOHN BOURNE, C.E. being a SUPPLEMENT to his 'Catechism of the Steam-Engine.' New Edition, including many New Examples, among which are several of the most remarkable ENGINES exhibited in Paris in 1867; with 124 Woodcuts. Fcp. 8vo. 6*s.*

Bourne's Examples of Modern Steam, Air, and Gas Engines of the most Approved Types, as employed for Pumping, for Driving Machinery, for Locomotion, and for Agriculture, minutely and practically described. Illustrated by Working Drawings, and embodying a Critical Account of all Projects of Recent Improvement in Furnaces, Boilers, and Engines. In course of publication, to be completed in Twenty-four Parts, price 2*s.* 6*d.* each, forming One Volume, with about 50 Plates and 400 Woodcuts.

Handbook of the Steam Engine. By JOHN BOURNE, C.E. forming a KEY to the Author's Catechism of the Steam Engine. With 67 Woodcuts. Fcp. 9*s.*

A History of the Machine-Wrought Hosiery and Lace Manufactures. By WILLIAM FELKIN, F.L.S. F.S.S. With 3 Steel Plates, 10 Lithographic Plates of Machinery, and 10 Coloured Impressions of Patterns of Lace. Royal 8vo. 21*s.*

Mitchell's Manual of Practical Assaying. Third Edition, for the most part re-written, with all the recent Discoveries incorporated. By W. CROOKES, F.R.S. With 188 Woodcuts. 8vo. 28*s.*

Reimann's Handbook of Aniline and its Derivatives; a Treatise on the Manufacture of Aniline and Aniline Colours. Revised and edited by WILLIAM CROOKES, F.R.S. 8vo. with 5 Woodcuts, 10*s.* 6*d.*

Practical Treatise on Metallurgy, adapted from the last German Edition of Professor KERL'S *Metallurgy* by W. CROOKES, F.R.S. &c. and E. RÖHRIG, Ph.D. M.E. In Three Volumes, 8vo. with 625 Woodcuts. VOL. I. price 31*s.* 6*d.* VOL. II. price 36*s.* VOL. III. price 31*s.* 6*d.*

The Art of Perfumery; the History and Theory of Odours, and the Methods of Extracting the Aromas of Plants. By Dr. PIESSE, F.C.S. Third Edition, with 53 Woodcuts. Crown 8vo. 10*s.* 6*d.*

Chemical, Natural, and Physical Magic, for Juveniles during the Holidays. By the same Author. Third Edition, enlarged with 38 Woodcuts. Fcp. 6*s.*

Loudon's Encyclopædia of Agri-culture: comprising the Laying-out, Improvement, and Management of Landed Property, and the Cultivation and Economy of the Productions of Agriculture. With 1,100 Woodcuts. 8vo. 21*s.*

Loudon's Encyclopædia of Gardening: comprising the Theory and Practice of Horticulture, Floriculture, Arboriculture, and Landscape Gardening. With 1,000 Woodcuts. 8vo. 21*s.*

Bayldon's Art of Valuing Rents and Tillages, and Claims of Tenants upon Quitting Farms, both at Michaelmas and Lady-Day. Eighth Edition, revised by J. C. MORTON. 8vo. 10*s.* 6*d.*

Religious and Moral Works.

An Exposition of the 39 Articles, Historical and Doctrinal. By E. HAROLD BROWNE, D.D. Lord Bishop of Ely. Eighth Edition. 8vo. 16*s.*

Examination-Questions on Bishop Browne's Exposition of the Articles. By the Rev. J. GORLE, M.A. Fcp. 3*s.* 6*d.*

Archbishop Leighton's Sermons and Charges. With Additions and Corrections from MSS. and with Historical and other Illustrative Notes by WILLIAM WEST, Incumbent of S. Columba's, Nairn. 8vo. price 15*s.*

Bishop Cotton's Instructions in the Principles and Practice of Christianity, intended chiefly as an Introduction to Confirmation. Sixth Edition. 18mo. 2*s.* 6*d.*

The Acts of the Apostles; with a Commentary, and Practical and Devotional Suggestions for Readers and Students of the English Bible. By the Rev. F. C. COOK, M.A. Canon of Exeter, &c. New Edition, 8vo. 12*s.* 6*d.*

The Life and Epistles of St. Paul. By the Rev. W. J. CONYBEARE, M.A. and the Very Rev. J. S. HOWSON, D.D. Dean of Chester:—

LIBRARY EDITION, with all the Original Illustrations, Maps, Landscapes on Steel, Woodcuts, &c. 2 vols. 4to. 48*s.*

INTERMEDIATE EDITION, with a Selection of Maps, Plates, and Woodcuts. 2 vols. square crown 8vo. 31*s.* 6*d.*

PEOPLE'S EDITION, revised and condensed, with 46 Illustrations and Maps. 2 vols. crown 8vo. 12*s.*

The Voyage and Shipwreck of St. Paul; with Dissertations on the Ships and Navigation of the Ancients. By JAMES SMITH, F.R.S. Crown 8vo. Charts, 10*s.* 6*d.*

Evidence of the Truth of the Christian Religion derived from the Literal Fulfilment of Prophecy. By ALEXANDER KEITH, D.D. 37th Edition, with numerous Plates, in square 8vo. 12*s.* 6*d.*; also the 39th Edition, in post 8vo. with 5 Plates, 6*s.*

The History and Destiny of the World and of the Church, according to Scripture. By the same Author. Square 8vo. with 40 Illustrations, 10*s.*

Ewald's History of Israel to the Death of Moses. Translated from the German. Edited, with a Preface and an Appendix, by RUSSELL MARTINEAU, M.A. Professor of Hebrew in Manchester New College, London. Second Edition, continued to the Commencement of the Monarchy. 2 vols. 8vo. 24*s.*

Five Years in a Protestant Sis-terhood and Ten Years in a Catholic Convent; an Autobiography. Post 8vo. 7*s.* 6*d.*

The Life of Margaret Mary Hallahan, better known in the religious world by the name of Mother Margaret. By her RELIGIOUS CHILDREN. With a Preface by the Bishop of Birmingham. 8vo. with Portrait, 10*s.*

The See of Rome in the Middle Ages. By the Rev. OSWALD J. REICHEL, B.C.L. and M.A. Vice-Principal of Cuddesdon College. 8vo. [*Nearly ready.*

The Evidence for the Papacy as derived from the Holy Scriptures and from Primitive Antiquity; with an Introductory Epistle. By the Hon. COLIN LINDSAY. 8vo. [*Nearly ready.*

A Critical and Grammatical Com-mentary on St. Paul's Epistles. By C. J. ELLICOTT, D.D. Lord Bishop of Gloucester and Bristol. 8vo.

Galatians, Fourth Edition, 8*s.* 6*d.*
Ephesians, Fourth Edition, 8*s.* 6*d.*
Pastoral Epistles, Fourth Edition, 10*s.* 6*d.*
Philippians, Colossians, and **Philemon,** Third Edition, 10*s.* 6*d.*
Thessalonians, Third Edition, 7*s.* 6*d.*

Historical Lectures on the Life of Our Lord Jesus Christ: being the Hulsean Lectures for 1859. By C. J. ELLICOTT, D.D. Lord Bishop of Gloucester and Bristol. Fifth Edition. 8vo. 12*s.*

The Destiny of the Creature; and other Sermons preached before the University of Cambridge. By the same. Post 8vo. 5*s.*

An Introduction to the Study of the New Testament, Critical, Exegetical, and Theological. By the Rev. S. DAVIDSON, D.D. LL.D. 2 vols. 8vo. 30*s.*

The Greek Testament; with Notes, Grammatical and Exegetical. By the Rev. W. WEBSTER, M.A. and the Rev. W. F. WILKINSON, M.A. 2 vols. 8vo. £2 4*s.*

VOL. I. the Gospels and Acts, 20*s.*
VOL. II. the Epistles and Apocalypse, 24*s.*

Rev. T. H. Horne's Introduction to the Critical Study and Knowledge of the Holy Scriptures. Twelfth Edition, as last revised throughout. With 4 Maps and 22 Woodcuts and Facsimiles. 4 vols. 8vo. 42*s.*

Rev. T. H. Horne's Compendious Introduction to the Study of the Bible, being an Analysis of the larger work by the same Author. Re-edited by the Rev. JOHN AYRE, M.A. With Maps, &c. Post 8vo. 6*s.*

The Treasury of Bible Knowledge; being a Dictionary of the Books, Persons, Places, Events, and other Matters of which mention is made in Holy Scripture; Intended to establish its Authority and illustrate its Contents. By Rev. J. AYRE, M.A. With Maps, 15 Plates, and numerous Woodcuts. Fcp. 10*s.* 6*d.*

Every-day Scripture Difficulties explained and illustrated. By J. E. PRESCOTT, M.A. VOL. I. *Matthew* and *Mark*; VOL. II. *Luke* and *John*. 2 vols. 8vo. price 9*s.* each.

The Pentateuch and Book of Joshua Critically Examined. By the Right Rev. J. W. COLENSO, D.D. Lord Bishop of Natal. Crown 8vo. price 6*s.*

The Church and the World; Three Series of Essays on Questions of the Day, by various Writers. Edited by the Rev. ORBY SHIPLEY, M.A. 3 vols. 8vo. 15*s.* each.

The Formation of Christendom. By T. W. ALLIES. PARTS I. and II. 8vo. price 12*s.* each.

Christendom's Divisions; a Philosophical Sketch of the Divisions of the Christian Family in East and West. By EDMUND S. FFOULKES, formerly Fellow and Tutor of Jesus Coll. Oxford. Post 8vo. 7*s.* 6*d.*

Christendom's Divisions, PART II. *Greeks and Latins*, being a History of their Dissensions and Overtures for Peace down to the Reformation. By the same Author. Post 8vo. 15*s.*

The Hidden Wisdom of Christ and the Key of Knowledge; or, History of the Apocrypha. By ERNEST DE BUNSEN. 2 vols. 8vo. 28*s.*

The Keys of St. Peter; or, the House of Rechab, connected with the History of Symbolism and Idolatry. By the same Author. 8vo. 14*s.*

The Power of the Soul over the Body. By GEO. MOORE, M.D. M.R.C.P.L. &c. Sixth Edition. Crown 8vo. 8*s.* 6*d.*

The Types of Genesis briefly considered as Revealing the Development of Human Nature. By ANDREW JUKES. Second Edition. Crown 8vo. 7*s.* 6*d.*

The Second Death and the Restitution of All Things, with some Preliminary Remarks on the Nature and Inspiration of Holy Scripture. By the same Author. Second Edition. Crown 8vo. 3*s.* 6*d.*

Essays and Reviews. By the Rev. W. TEMPLE, D.D. the Rev. R. WILLIAMS, B.D. the Rev. B. POWELL, M.A. the Rev. H. B. WILSON, B.D. C. W. GOODWIN, M.A. the Rev. M. PATTISON, B.D. and the Rev. B. JOWETT, M.A. 12th Edition. Fcp. 5*s.*

Religious Republics; Six Essays on Congregationalism. By W. M. FAWCETT, T.M. HERBERT, M.A. E. G. HERBERT, LL.B. T. H. PATTISON, P. H. PYE-SMITH, M.D. B.A. and J. ANSTIE, B.A. 8vo. price 8*s.* 6*d.*

Passing Thoughts on Religion. By the Author of 'Amy Herbert.' New Edition. Fcp. 5*s.*

Self-examination before Confirmation. By the same Author. 32mo. 1*s.* 6*d.*

Readings for a Month Preparatory to Confirmation from Writers of the Early and English Church. By the same. Fcp. 4*s.*

Readings for Every Day in Lent, compiled from the Writings of Bishop JEREMY TAYLOR. By the same. Fcp. 5*s.*

Preparation for the Holy Communion; the Devotions chiefly from the works of JEREMY TAYLOR. By the same. 32mo. 3*s.*

Thoughts for the Holy Week, for Young Persons. By the same Author. New Edition. Fcp. 8vo. 2*s.*

Principles of Education drawn from Nature and Revelation, and Applied to Female Education in the Upper Classes. By the same Author. 2 vols. fcp. 12*s.* 6*d.*

Bishop Jeremy Taylor's Entire Works; with Life by BISHOP HEBER. Revised and corrected by the Rev. C. P. EDEN. 10 vols. £5 5*s.*

England and Christendom. By ARCHBISHOP MANNING, D.D. Post 8vo. price 10*s.* 6*d.*

The Wife's Manual; or, Prayers, Thoughts, and Songs on Several Occasions of a Matron's Life. By the Rev. W. CALVERT, M.A. Crown 8vo. 10*s.* 6*d.*

Singers and Songs of the Church: being Biographical Sketches of the Hymn-Writers in all the principal Collections; with Notes on their Psalms and Hymns. By JOSIAH MILLER, M.A. Second Edition, enlarged. Post 8vo. 10*s.* 6*d.*

'Spiritual Songs' for the Sundays and Holidays throughout the Year. By J. S. B. Monsell, LL.D. Vicar of Egham and Rural Dean. Fourth Edition, Sixth Thousand. Fcp. price 4s. 6d.

The Beatitudes: Abasement before God; Sorrow for Sin; Meekness of Spirit; Desire for Holiness; Gentleness; Purity of Heart; the Peace-makers; Sufferings for Christ. By the same Author. Third Edition, revised. Fcp. 3s. 6d.

His Presence not his Memory, 1855. By the same Author, in memory of his Son. Sixth Edition. 16mo. 1s.

Lyra Germanica; Two Selections of Household Hymns, translated from the German by Miss Catherine Winkworth. First Series, the *Christian Year*, Hymns for the Sundays and Chief Festivals of the Church; Second Series, the *Christian Life*. Fcp. 8vo. price 3s. 6d. each Series.

Lyra Eucharistica; Hymns and Verses on the Holy Communion, Ancient and Modern: with other Poems. Edited by the Rev. Orby Shipley, M.A. Second Edition. Fcp. 5s.

Shipley's Lyra Messianica. Fcp. 5s.

Shipley's Lyra Mystica. Fcp. 5s.

Endeavours after the Christian Life: Discourses. By James Martineau. Fourth and Cheaper Edition, carefully revised; the Two Series complete in One Volume. Post 8vo. 7s. 6d.

Invocation of Saints and Angels; for the use of Members of the English Church. Edited by the Rev. Orby Shipley, M.A. 24mo. 3s. 6d.

Introductory Lessons on the History of Religious Worship; being a Sequel to the same Author's 'Lessons on Christian Evidences.' By Richard Whately, D.D. New Edition. 18mo. 2s. 6d.

Travels, Voyages, &c.

England to Delhi; a Narrative of Indian Travel. By John Matheson, Glasgow. Imperial 8vo. with very numerous Illustrations.

Letters from Australia. By John Martineau. Post 8vo. price 7s. 6d.

Travels in the Central Caucasus and Bashan. including Visits to Ararat and Tabreez and Ascents of Kazbek and Elbruz. By Douglas W. Freshfield. With 3 Maps, 2 Panoramas of Summits, 4 full-page Wood Engravings, and 16 Woodcuts. Square crown 8vo. 18s.

Cadore or Titian's Country. By Josiah Gilbert, one of the Authors of the 'Dolomite Mountains.' With Map, Facsimile, and 40 Illustrations. Imp. 8vo. 31s. 6d.

The Dolomite Mountains. Excursions through Tyrol, Carinthia, Carniola, and Friuli. By J. Gilbert and G. C. Churchill, F.R.G.S. With numerous Illustrations. Square crown 8vo. 21s.

Pilgrimages in the Pyrenees and Landes: Their Sanctuaries and Shrines. By Dennys Shyne Lawlor. Post 8vo.

Pictures in Tyrol and Elsewhere. From a Family Sketch-Book. By the Author of 'A Voyage en Zigzag,' &c. Second Edition. 4to. with many Illustrations. 21s.

How we Spent the Summer; or, a Voyage en Zigzag in Switzerland and Tyrol with some Members of the Alpine Club. Third Edition, re-drawn. In oblong 4to. with about 300 Illustrations, 15s.

Beaten Tracks; or, Pen and Pencil Sketches in Italy. By the Authoress of 'A Voyage en Zigzag.' With 42 Plates, containing about 200 Sketches from Drawings made on the Spot. 8vo. 16s.

The Alpine Club Map of the Chain of Mont Blanc, from an actual Survey in 1863—1864. By A. Adams-Reilly, F.R.G.S. M.A.C. In Chromolithography on extra stout drawing paper 28in. x 17in. price 10s. or mounted on canvas in a folding case, 12s. 6d.

Pioneering in the Pampas; or, the First Four Years of a Settler's Experience in the La Plata Camps. By R. A. Seymour. Second Edition. Post 8vo. with Map, 6s.

The Paraguayan War: with Sketches of the History of Paraguay, and of the Manners and Customs of the People; and Notes on the Military Engineering of the War. By George Thompson, C.E. With 8 Maps and Plans and a Portrait of Lopez. Post 8vo. 12s. 6d.

Notes on Burgundy. By Charles Richard Weld. Edited by his Widow; with Portrait and Memoir. Post 8vo. price 8s. 6d.

History of Discovery in our Australasian Colonies, Australia, Tasmania, and New Zealand, from the Earliest Date to the Present Day. By WILLIAM HOWITT. With 3 Maps of the Recent Explorations from Official Sources. 2 vols. 8vo. 20*s.*

The Capital of the Tycoon; a Narrative of a 3 Years' Residence in Japan. By Sir RUTHERFORD ALCOCK, K.C.B. 2 vols. 8vo. with numerous Illustrations, 42*s.*

Guide to the Pyrenees, for the use of Mountaineers. By CHARLES PACKE. Second Edition, with Maps, &c. and Appendix. Crown 8vo. 7*s.* 6*d.*

The Alpine Guide. By JOHN BALL, M.R.I.A. late President of the Alpine Club. Post 8vo. with Maps and other Illustrations.

Guide to the Eastern Alps, price 10*s.* 6*d.*

Guide to the Western Alps, including Mont Blanc, Monte Rosa, Zermatt, &c. price 6*s.* 6*d.*

Guide to the Central Alps, including all the Oberland District, price 7*s.* 6*d.*

Introduction on Alpine Travelling in general, and on the Geology of the Alps, price 1*s.* Either of the Three Volumes or Parts of the *Alpine Guide* may be had with this INTRODUCTION prefixed, price 1*s.* extra.

Roma Sotterranea; or, an Account of the Roman Catacombs, especially of the Cemetery of San Callisto. Compiled from the Works of Commendatore G. B. DE ROSSI, by the Rev. J. S. NORTHCOTE, D.D. and the Rev. W. B. BROWNLOW. With Plans and numerous other Illustrations. 8vo. 31*s.* 6*d.*

Memorials of London and London Life in the 13th, 14th, and 15th Centuries; being a Series of Extracts, Local, Social, and Political, from the Archives of the City of London. A.D. 1276-1419. Selected, translated, and edited by H. T. RILEY, M.A. Royal 8vo. 21*s.*

Commentaries on the History, Constitution, and Chartered Franchises of the City of London. By GEORGE NORTON, formerly one of the Common Pleaders of the City of London. Third Edition. 8vo. 14*s.*

Curiosities of London; exhibiting the most Rare and Remarkable Objects o Interest in the Metropolis; with nearly Sixty Years' Personal Recollections. By JOHN TIMBS, F.S.A. New Edition, corrected and enlarged. 8vo. Portrait, 21*s.*

The Northern Heights of London; or, Historical Associations of Hampstead, Highgate, Muswell Hill, Hornsey, and Islington. By WILLIAM HOWITT. With about 40 Woodcuts. Square crown 8vo. 21*s.*

The Rural Life of England. By the same Author. With Woodcuts by Bewick and Williams. Medium, 8vo. 12*s.* 6*d.*

Visits to Remarkable Places: Old Halls, Battle-Fields, and Scenes illustrative of striking Passages in English History and Poetry. By the same Author. 2 vols. square crown 8vo. with Wood Engravings, 25*s.*

Narrative of the Euphrates Expedition carried on by Order of the British Government during the years 1835, 1836, and 1837. By General F. R. CHESNEY, F.R.S. With 2 Maps, 45 Plates, and 16 Woodcuts. 8vo. 24*s.*

The German Working Man; being an Account of the Daily Life, Amusements, and Unions for Culture and Material Progress of the Artisans of North and South Germany and Switzerland. By JAMES SAMUELSON. Crown 8vo. with Frontispiece, 3*s.* 6*d.*

Works of *Fiction.*

Vikram and the Vampire; or, Tales of Hindu Devilry. Adapted by RICHARD F. BURTON, F.R.G.S. &c. With Illustrations by Ernest Griset. Crown 8vo. 9*s.*

Mabeldean, or Christianity Reversed; being the History of a Noble Family: a Social, Political, and Theological Novel. By OWEN GOWER, of Gaybrook. 3 vols. post 8vo. 31*s.* 6*d.*

Through the Night; a Tale of the Times. To which is added ONWARD, or a SUMMER SKETCH. By WALTER SWEETMAN, B.A. 2 vols. post 8vo. 21*s.*

Stories and Tales by the Author of 'Amy Herbert,' uniform Edition, each Tale *or* Story a single volume:—

AMY HERBERT, 2*s.* 6*d.*
GERTRUDE, 2*s.* 6*d.*
EARL'S DAUGHTER, 2*s.* 6*d.*
EXPERIENCE OF LIFE, 2*s.* 6*d.*
CLEVE HALL, 3*s.* 6*d.*
IVORS, 3*s.* 6*d.*
KATHARINE ASHTON, 3*s.* 6*d.*
MARGARET PERCIVAL, 5*s.*
LANETON PARSONAGE, 4*s.* 6*d.*
URSULA, 4*s.* 6*d.*

A Glimpse of the World. Fcp. 7*s.* 6*d.*

Journal of a Home Life. Post 8vo. 9*s.* 6*d.*

After Life; a Sequel to the 'Journal of a Home Life.' Post 8vo. 10*s.* 6*d.*

The Warden; a Novel. By ANTHONY TROLLOPE. Crown 8vo. 1s. 6d.

Barchester Towers; a Sequel to 'The Warden.' Crown 8vo. 2s.

Uncle Peter's Fairy Tale for the XIXth Century. Edited by ELIZABETH M. SEWELL, Author of 'Amy Herbert,' &c. Fcp. 8vo. 7s. 6d.

Becker's Gallus; or, Roman Scenes of the Time of Augustus. Post 8vo. 7s. 6d.

Becker's Charicles: Illustrative of Private Life of the Ancient Greeks. Post 8vo. 7s. 6d.

Tales of Ancient Greece. By GEORGE W. COX, M.A. late Scholar of Trin. Coll. Oxford. Being a collective Edition of the Author's Classical Series and Tales, complete in One Volume. Crown 8vo. 6s. 6d.

A Manual of Mythology, in the form of Question and Answer. By the Rev. GEORGE W. COX, M.A. late Scholar of Trinity College, Oxford. Fcp. 3s.

Cabinet Edition of Novels and Tales by J. G. WHYTE MELVILLE:—

THE GLADIATORS, 5s. HOLMBY HOUSE, 5s.
DIGBY GRAND, 5s. GOOD FOR NOTHING, 6s.
KATE COVENTRY, 5s. QUEEN'S MARIES, 6s.
GENERAL BOUNCE, 5s. THE INTERPRETER, 5s.

Doctor Harold's Note-Book. By Mrs. GASCOIGNE, Author of 'The Next Door Neighbour.' Fcp. 8vo. 6s.

Our Children's Story. By One of their Gossips. By the Author of 'Voyage en Zigzag,' 'Pictures in Tyrol,' &c. Small 4to. with Sixty Illustrations by the Author, price 10s. 6d.

Poetry and *The Drama.*

Thomas Moore's Poetical Works, the only Editions containing the Author's last Copyright Additions:—

Shamrock Edition, price 3s. 6d.
Ruby Edition, with Portrait, 6s.
Cabinet Edition, 10 vols. fcp. 8vo. 35s.
People's Edition, Portrait, &c. 10s. 6d.
Library Edition, Portrait & Vignette, 14s.

Moore's Lalla Rookh, Tenniel's Edition, with 68 Wood Engravings from Original Drawings and other Illustrations. Fcp. 4to. 21s.

Moore's Irish Melodies, Maclise's Edition, with 161 Steel Plates from Original Drawings. Super-royal 8vo. 31s. 6d.

Miniature Edition of Moore's *Irish Melodies*, with Maclise's Illustrations (as above), reduced in Lithography. Imp. 16mo. 10s. 6d.

Southey's Poetical Works, with the Author's last Corrections and copyright Additions. Library Edition. Medium 8vo. with Portrait and Vignette, 14s.

Lays of Ancient Rome; with *Ivry* and the *Armada*. By the Right Hon. LORD MACAULAY. 16mo. 4s. 6d.

Lord Macaulay's Lays of Ancient Rome. With 90 Illustrations on Wood, Original and from the Antique, from Drawings by G. SCHARF. Fcp. 4to. 21s.

Miniature Edition of Lord Macaulay's Lays of Ancient Rome, with Scharf's Illustrations (as above) reduced in Lithography. Imp. 16mo. 10s. 6d.

Goldsmith's Poetical Works, Illustrated with Wood Engravings from Designs by Members of the ETCHING CLUB. Imp. 16mo. 7s. 6d.

Poems. By JEAN INGELOW. Fifteenth Edition. Fcp. 8vo. 5s.

Poems by Jean Ingelow. A New Edition, with nearly 100 Illustrations by Eminent Artists, engraved on Wood by the Brothers DALZIEL. Fcp. 4to. 21s.

Mopsa the Fairy. By JEAN INGELOW. With Eight Illustrations engraved on Wood. Fcp. 8vo. 6s.

A Story of Doom, and other Poems. By JEAN INGELOW. Third Edition. Fcp. 5s.

Poetical Works of Letitia Elizabeth Landon (L.E.L.) 2 vols. 16mo. 10s.

Bowdler's Family Shakspeare, cheaper Genuine Edition, complete in 1 vol. large type, with 36 Woodcut Illustrations, price 14s. or in 6 pocket vols. 3s. 6d. each.

Arundines Cami. Collegit atque edidit H. DRURY, M.A. Editio Sexta, curavit H. J. HODGSON, M.A. Crown 8vo. price 7s. 6d.

Horatii Opera, Pocket Edition, with carefully corrected Text, Marginal References and Introduction. Edited by the Rev. J. E. YONGE, M.A. Square 18mo. 4s. 6d.

Horatii Opera, Library Edition, with Copious English Notes, Marginal References and Various Readings. Edited by the Rev. J. E. YONGE, M.A. 8vo. 21s.

The Æneid of Virgil Translated into English Verse. By JOHN CONINGTON, M.A. Corpus Professor of Latin in the University of Oxford. Crown 8vo. 9s.

The Iliad of Homer in English Hexameter Verse. By J. HENRY DART, M.A. of Exeter College, Oxford. Square crown 8vo. 21s.

The Iliad of Homer Translated into Blank Verse. By ICHABOD CHARLES WRIGHT, M.A. 2 vols. crown 8vo. 21s.

Dante's Divine Comedy, translated in English Terza Rima by JOHN DAYMAN, M.A. With the Italian Text. 8vo. 21s.

Hunting Songs and Miscellaneous Verses. By R. E. EGERTON WARBURTON. Second Edition. Fcp. 8vo. 5s.

Rural Sports, &c.

Encyclopædia of Rural Sports; a Complete Account, Historical, Practical, and Descriptive, of Hunting, Shooting, Fishing, Racing, &c. By D. P. BLAINE. With above 600 Woodcuts (20 from Designs by JOHN LEECH). 8vo. 42s.

Col. Hawker's Instructions to Young Sportsmen in all that relates to Guns and Shooting. Revised by the Author's SON. Square crown 8vo. with Illustrations, 18s.

The Dead Shot, or Sportsman's Complete Guide; a Treatise on the Use of the Gun, Dog-breaking, Pigeon-shooting, &c. By MARKSMAN. Fcp. with Plates, 5s.

A Book on Angling: being a Complete Treatise on the Art of Angling in every branch, including full Illustrated Lists of Salmon Flies. By FRANCIS FRANCIS. Second Edition, with Portrait and 15 other Plates, plain and coloured. Post 8vo. 15s.

Wilcocks's Sea-Fisherman: comprising the Chief Methods of Hook and Line Fishing in the British and other Seas, a glance at Nets, and remarks on Boats and Boating. Second Edition, enlarged, with 80 Woodcuts. Post 8vo. 12s. 6d.

The Fly-Fisher's Entomology. By ALFRED RONALDS. With coloured Representations of the Natural and Artificial Insect. Sixth Edition, with 20 coloured Plates. 8vo. 14s.

Blaine's Veterinary Art: a Treatise on the Anatomy, Physiology, and Curative Treatment of the Diseases of the Horse, Neat Cattle, and Sheep. Seventh Edition, revised and enlarged by C. STEEL. 8vo. with Plates and Woodcuts, 18s.

Horses and Stables. By Colonel F. FITZWYGRAM, XV. the King's Hussars. Pp. 624; with 24 Plates of Illustrations, containing very numerous Figures engraved on Wood. 8vo. 15s.

Youatt on the Horse. Revised and enlarged by W. WATSON, M.R.C.V.S. 8vo. with numerous Woodcuts, 12s. 6d.

Youatt on the Dog. (By the same Author.) 8vo. with numerous Woodcuts, 6s.

The Horse's Foot, and how to keep it Sound. By W. MILES, Esq. Ninth Edition, with Illustrations. Imp. 8vo. 12s. 6d.

A Plain Treatise on Horse-shoeing. By the same Author. Sixth Edition, post 8vo. with Illustrations, 2s. 6d.

Stables and Stable Fittings. By the same. Imp. 8vo. with 13 Plates, 15s.

Remarks on Horses' Teeth, addressed to Purchasers. By the same. Post 8vo. 1s. 6d.

Robbins's Cavalry Catechism; or, Instructions on Cavalry Exercise and Field Movements, Brigade Movements, Out-post Duty, Cavalry supporting Artillery, Artillery attached to Cavalry. 12mo. 5s.

The Dog in Health and Disease. By STONEHENGE. With 70 Wood Engravings. New Edition. Square crown 8vo. 10s. 6d.

The Greyhound. By the same Author. Revised Edition, with 24 Portraits of Greyhounds. Square crown 8vo. 10s. 6d.

The Ox, his Diseases and their Treatment; with an Essay on Parturition in the Cow. By J. R. DOBSON, M.R.C.V.S. Crown 8vo. with Illustrations, 7s. 6d.

Commerce, Navigation, and *Mercantile Affairs.*

The Theory and Practice of Banking. By HENRY DUNNING MACLEOD, M.A. Barrister-at-Law. Second Edition, entirely remodelled. 2 vols. 8vo. 30s.

The Elements of Banking. By HENRY DUNNING MACLEOD, M.A. of Trinity College, Cambridge, and of the Inner Temple, Barrister-at-Law. Post 8vo.

[*Nearly ready.*

The Law of Nations Considered as Independent Political Communities. By Sir] TRAVERS TWISS, D.C.L. 2 vols. 8vo. 30s. or separately, PART I *Peace*, 12s. PART II. *War*, 18s.

Practical Guide for British Ship-masters to United States Ports. By PIERREPONT EDWARDS. Post 8vo. 8s. 6d.

M'Culloch's Dictionary, Prac-tical, Theoretical, and Historical, of Commerce and Commercial Navigation. New Edition, revised throughout and corrected to the Present Time; with a Biographical Notice of the Author. Edited by H. G. REID, Secretary to Mr. M'Culloch for many years. 8vo. price 63s. cloth.

Works of Utility and *General Information.*

Modern Cookery for Private Families, reduced to a System of Easy Practice in a Series of carefully-tested Receipts. By ELIZA ACTON. Newly revised and enlarged; with 8 Plates, Figures, and 150 Woodcuts. Fcp. 6s.

On Food, its Varieties, Chemical Composition, Nutritive Value, Comparative Digestibility, Physiological Functions and Uses, Preparation, Culinary Treatment, Preservation, Adulteration, &c. Being the Substance of Four Cantor Lectures delivered before the Society for the Encouragement of Arts, Manufactures, and Commerce. By H. LETHEBY, M.B. M.A. Ph.D. &c. Crown 8vo.

A Practical Treatise on Brewing; with Formulæ for Public Brewers, and Instructions for Private Families. By W. BLACK. Fifth Edition. 8vo. 10s. 6d.

Chess Openings. By F. W. LONGMAN, Balliol College, Oxford. Fcp. 8vo. 2s. 6d.

Whist, What to Lead. By CAM. Third Edition. 32mo. 1s.

The Cabinet Lawyer; a Popular Digest of the Laws of England, Civil, Criminal, and Constitutional. 25th Edition; with Supplements of the Acts of the Parliamentary Sessions of 1867, 1868, and 1869. Fcp. 10s. 6d.

The Philosophy of Health; or, an Exposition of the Physiological and Sanitary Conditions conducive to Human Longevity and Happiness. By SOUTHWOOD SMITH, M.D. Eleventh Edition, revised and enlarged; with 113 Woodcuts. 8vo. 7s. 6d.

A Handbook for Readers at the British Museum. By THOMAS NICHOLS. Post 8vo. 6s.

Maunder's Treasury of Know-ledge and Library of Reference: comprising an English Dictionary and Grammar, Universal Gazetteer, Classical Dictionary, Chronology, Law Dictionary, Synopsis of the Peerage, Useful Tables, &c. Fcp. 10s. 6d.

Hints to Mothers on the Manage-ment of their Health during the Period of Pregnancy and in the Lying-in Room. By T. BULL, M.D. Fcp. 5s.

The Maternal Management of Children in Health and Disease. By THOMAS BULL, M.D. Fcp. 5s.

How to Nurse Sick Children; containing Directions which may be found of service to all who have charge of the Young. By CHARLES WEST, M.D. Second Edition. Fcp. 8vo. 1s. 6d.

Notes on Hospitals. By FLORENCE NIGHTINGALE. Third Edition, enlarged; with 13 Plans. Post 4to. 18s.

Instructions in Household Mat-ters. Written by a LADY for the use of Girls intended for Service on leaving School. Seventh Edition. Fcp. 1s. 6d.

Mary's Every-Day Book of useful and Miscellaneous Knowledge; illustrated with Stories, and intended for the use of Children. By F. E. BURBURY. 18mo. 3s. 6d.

Tidd Pratt's Law relating to Benefit Building Societies; with Practical Observations on the Act and all the Cases decided thereon, also a Form of Rules and Forms of Mortgages. Fcp. 3s. 6d.

Collieries and Colliers: a Handbook of the Law and Leading Cases relating thereto. By J. C. FOWLER, of the Inner Temple, Barrister, Stipendiary Magistrate. Second Edition. Fcp. 8vo. 7s. 6d.

Willich's Popular Tables for Ascertaining the Value of Lifehold, Leasehold, and Church Property, Renewal Fines, &c.; the Public Funds; Annual Average Price and Interest on Consols from 1731 to 1867; Chemical, Geographical, Astronomical, Trigonometrical Tables, &c. Post 8vo. 10s.

Coulthart's Decimal Interest Tables at Twenty-four Different Rates not exceeding Five per Cent. Calculated for the use of Bankers. To which are added Commission Tables at One-eighth and One-fourth per Cent. 8vo. 15s.

INDEX.

SPOTTISWOODE AND CO., PRINTERS, NEW-STREET SQUARE AND PARLIAMENT STREET.

www.ingramcontent.com/pod-product-compliance
Lightning Source LLC
Chambersburg PA
CBHW021418300426
44114CB00010B/547

* 9 7 8 3 3 3 7 0 3 1 4 7 3 *